THE FUTURE
OF
THE JEWISH
COMMUNITY IN
AMERICA

Essays prepared

for a Task Force on

The Future of the Jewish Community in America

of The American Jewish Committee

THE AUTHORS

Walter I. Ackerman
Daniel J. Elazar
Seymour Fox
Sidney Goldstein
Ben Halpern
Wolfe Kelman
Charles S. Liebman
Mortimer Ostow
Nathan Rotenstreich
David Sidorsky
James A. Sleeper

Project Coordinator
Morris Fine

Project Assistant
Phyllis Sherman

Editorial Associate
Maier Deshell

THE FUTURE

PUBLISHED IN COLLABORATION WITH THE
Institute of Human Relations Press

OF THE JEWISH COMMUNITY IN AMERICA

EDITED BY

DAVID SIDORSKY

Basic Books, Inc., Publishers NEW YORK

THE PUBLICATION OF THIS VOLUME
WAS MADE POSSIBLE BY A GRANT
FROM THE LUCIUS N. LITTAUER FOUNDATION

Grateful acknowledgment is made for permission to reprint Walter Ackerman's chapter "The Jewish School System in the United States," and Sidney Goldstein's chapter "American Jewry: A Demographic Analysis" from the *American Jewish Year Book* published by The American Jewish Committee and The Jewish Publication Society of America.

TO THE MEMORY OF
LOUIS STERN
[1904–1973]

Chairman of the AJC Task Force
on The Future of the Jewish Community
in America

THE AUTHORS

WALTER I. ACKERMAN. Dean and Professor of Education, Hebrew Teachers College and College of Judaica, University of Judaism, Los Angeles, California

DANIEL J. ELAZAR. Director, Center for the Study of Federalism and Professor of Political Science, Temple University, Philadelphia, Pennsylvania

SEYMOUR FOX. Professor of Education and Director, School of Education, The Hebrew University of Jerusalem

SIDNEY GOLDSTEIN. Director of Population Studies and Training Center and Professor of Sociology, Brown University, Providence, Rhode Island

BEN HALPERN. Professor of Near Eastern Studies, Brandeis University, Waltham, Massachusetts; Research Associate, Harvard University Center for Middle East Studies

WOLFE KELMAN. Executive Vice President, Rabbinical Assembly of America; Member of Administrative Committee, Melton Research Center of the Jewish Theological Seminary of America, New York, New York

CHARLES S. LIEBMAN. Chairman and Professor, the Department of Political Studies, Bar-Ilan University, Israel

MORTIMER OSTOW, M.D. Edward T. Sandrow Visiting Professor of Pastoral Psychiatry, Jewish Theological Seminary of America, New York, New York

NATHAN ROTENSTREICH. Professor of Philosophy and former Rector, The Hebrew University of Jerusalem, Israel

DAVID SIDORSKY. Professor of Philosophy, Columbia University, New York, New York

JAMES A. SLEEPER. Community Youth Worker, Council on Parish Ministries, Wellesley, Massachusetts

vii

PREFACE

It is a striking characteristic of American society that it enabled so many immigrant groups of diverse religious, ethnic, and cultural origins to become an intrinsic part of American life while simultaneously permitting these groups to assert their unique characteristics within a pluralistic framework. Certainly for the American Jewish community this characteristic was of special significance, for from its earliest beginnings the American Jewish community sought to integrate into the larger American community while maintaining a distinctive Jewish identity.

When the American Jewish community was largely composed of first-generation immigrant Jews there was very little ambiguity between seeking integration and maintaining the trappings and substance of the Jewish religious and cultural heritage. However, as the American Jewish community changed from a society seeking to adjust to the American way into one composed primarily of third- and fourth-generation Jews actively involved in all aspects of American society, the tension between these two objectives grew more intense. Today the acculturation process has resulted in the almost complete acceptance of Jews into the mainstream of American life and has allowed for the enrichment of many Jewish cultural and religious institutions. It has also resulted in new questions regarding the continuity of Jewish identity and the quality of Jewish life.

In recent years these questions have motivated new self-examination on the part of many in the Jewish community. It was with the recognition of this mature readiness for self-examination and with a shared sense of concern about the character and direction of American Jewish life that The American Jewish Committee convened a Task Force on The Future of the Jewish Community in America. The chapters in this volume were prepared as position papers for the deliberations of the Task Force. They were commissioned because it is our belief that their authors represent the best informed Jewish thought on crucial areas of concern for the Jewish community.

The American Jewish Committee did not view the Task Force, however, solely as an instrument for generating research and study of the American Jewish community. These papers formed the basis for a series of conferences on their implications for a new agenda for the Jewish community for the next decade. The conferences were concluded with a report by the Task Force containing its proposals and recommendations. The report was prepared by Dr. David Sidorsky, who most ably served as Consultant to the Task Force. The Task Force Report is available from The American Jewish Committee upon request.

Throughout its work the Task Force was guided and led with superb sensitivity and insight by its Chairman, Louis Stern. Mr. Stern, a former President of the Council of Jewish Federations and Welfare Funds and of the National Jewish Welfare Board, as a founder of the reorganized Jewish Agency, and a member of the National Board of Governors of The American Jewish Committee, brought to his task a rare blend of practical judgment and rich knowledge. While he did not live to see the publication of this book, his creative contributions to it are a lasting testament to the valuable role he played in advancing Jewish communal life.

BERTRAM H. GOLD
Executive Vice-President
The American Jewish Committee

ACKNOWLEDGMENTS

The original planning for this book was a collaborative effort by a Steering Committee whose members included Philip Bernstein, Lucy Dawidowicz, Morris Fine, Bertram H. Gold, Yehuda Rosenman, Marshall Sklare, John Slawson, and Louis Stern. The chapters were edited for publication by Maier Deshell of *Commentary* magazine. I should like to express the degree to which this book is a product of this collaboration energized by Morris Fine and Phyllis Sherman.

D.S.

INTRODUCTION

By David Sidorsky

Each of the chapters in this volume was prepared as a part of a coherent study aimed at an increased understanding of the American Jewish community. The chapters reflect four major areas. The first area concerns the historical processes and ideological movements which have had a shaping influence upon the character of the American Jewish community. The second comprises the most important demographic trends and social patterns of the American Jewish society. The third includes the primary institutions of the community, in particular the synagogue and the school. The fourth involves issues which have become the focus of current debate and are considered significant for the future: the direction of Jewish education, the nature of the youth culture, and the process of ordering priorities and making decisions for communal action.

Each chapter was the subject of an extended discussion between its author and a panel of colleagues.* In this introduction I sketch briefly only some of the issues and problems that emerged in those sessions. The material in the present volume is, in a sense, an invitation to the reader to become a participant in an ongoing discussion.

A common point of departure for the three chapters grouped under the title "Perspectives" is the way in which the Emancipation and Enlightenment movements of Western Europe provide a frame of reference for interpreting the American Jewish community. As Nathan Rotenstreich indicates in his chapter "Emancipation and Its Aftermath," Emancipation meant the struggle for liberation from the ghetto. It was intended to secure for the individual Jew full civil rights and the opportunity to share in the heritage of Western, particularly Enlightenment, culture. The product of the Emancipation was to be an individual who participated with full equality in Western

---

* The summary and recommendations of those discussions have been printed in the pamphlet *The Future of the Jewish Community in America* (The American Jewish Committee, 1972). I have used parts of that text in this introduction.

society in the civil sphere. He would articulate both Western cultural patterns and Jewish religious values. The agenda of emancipation was carried out in Western Europe only to be brought to a catastrophic end with the Nazi domination. In Eastern Europe, the program of emancipation was partially redirected toward guaranteed rights of minorities and received a dramatic transformation with the coming of the Soviet revolution. The American Jewish society, which did not undergo a process of emancipation but which fused the successive waves of immigrants who came from Europe during the emancipation struggle, paradoxically has become the unique case of a reasonably successful paradigm of the ideal of the Emancipation.

In Professor Rotenstreich's view, the successful completion of a structure of an emancipated community has presented American Jewry with the unique and unprecedented challenge of postemancipation Judaism. In the past, the energies of the American Jewish community were absorbed in the construction of a framework for Jewish life under conditions of political and cultural freedom. This framework, according to Professor Rotenstreich, included the campaign for full civil rights for all minorities, the transplanting of primary Jewish institutions, and the guarding of the wall of separation between church and state so as to insulate the public domain—where Jews participated as citizens—from the private domains of the various institutional religions. It also included the development of those denominational patterns of Judaism—Neo-Orthodox, Conservative, and Reform—which for most Jews effectively replaced the separatist Orthodox patterns.

The widespread belief that American society is religiously divided among Protestant, Catholic, and Jew, coinciding with the growth of the suburban environment, has favored the continued expression of Judaism as a publicly sanctioned set of conventional behavioral responses by a minority religious group in America. Professor Rotenstreich's thesis then implies that for the postemancipation Jewish community, in the absence of any new source of religious or ideological direction, the programs which previously had proved viable will now be ineffective to stem an accelerating drift away from Jewish commitment.

This perspective, which views American Judaism as entering a new and more challenging period, is also present in the idea—advanced in my own chapter "Judaism and the Revolution of Modernity"—that American Judaism no longer defines its intellectual agenda as a response to the fundamental revolutions with which modernity has challenged the Jewish tradition. The American Jewish community has adjusted to the acceptance of a scientific and technological culture. The question posed by this acceptance is the degree to which the world view of modern science, which it was believed would erode traditional religion, has left open options for the practice and theory of Jewish religion in a secular and scientific society. One controversial phenomenon has been the accompaniment of a triumph of technology by a search for new forms of religious belief and by a quest for religious community, which often exploits or even perverts the traditional idioms of religious practice. This general phenomenon, as well as the surprising and self-conscious tenacity of the more recent wave of extremely Orthodox Jewish immigrants, has resulted in polarization within the religious spectrum of the American Jewish community.

The Emancipation movement also bequeathed to the Jewish community a thrust toward universal values as defined by rationalistic or liberal ideals. The dimming of the universalist vision, brought about by the resurgence within Western culture of irrationalist movements like Nazism or Communism, has had an inevitable impact upon Jewish optimism regarding adherence to philosophies which would ultimately abolish all ethnic or particularistic bonds. Hence, Jews concerned with the nature of Jewish ideology in this postemancipation age have begun to seek the reconstitution of the secular liberal faith of enlightenment thought in forms which are realistically cognizant of the bitter historical experience of the recent past and legitimately sensitive to Jewish ethnic or communal interests. It is a point of view which has close historical connections with Zionism.

It was an essential characteristic of Zionism, as Ben Halpern writes in the chapter "Zion in the Mind of American Jews," that it did not participate in the ideological consensus of European Jewry in favor of the Emancipation. Zionism shared, with the Emancipation, the intense desire for liberation from the ghetto, not only in order to eliminate violence and coercion but also to bring to an end the exclusion from Western social and cultural existence which the ghetto had imposed on European Jewry. Yet from the outset Zionism had greater skepticism about the ability of the European states to guarantee to Jews civic and cultural rights. Zionism had even greater reservations concerning the possible erosion of Jewish identity in the move from the ghetto. Fundamentally, as a nationalistic ideology, Zionism was insistent that emancipation required national self-determination, or, in the phrase of the period, "auto-emancipation." Historical events vindicated both the fears and reservations of Zionism. At the same time its own ideological program was realized. The destruction of European Jewry and the establishment of the State of Israel, Professor Halpern suggests, have resulted in a shift in Jewish attitudes affecting group relations and Jewish communal responsibility for Jewish interests in this country and abroad.

Professor Halpern also points out, however, that the Zionist movement has now become but one component of the American Jewish community's general support of the State of Israel. It is noteworthy that Zionist theory had no ideological framework with which to accommodate this kind of long-term Diaspora support for a Jewish state. Classical Zionist ideology advanced the view that the Jewish future in the Diaspora would evince a continuous and irreversible erosion of identity for the majority of the community and a pattern of emigration to the Land of Israel for the minority. An alternate Zionist ideology, that of Ahad Ha'am, advanced the view that a restored Jewish center in Israel would radiate transfusing energy to Jewish communities in the Diaspora. Neither of these theories, as it turned out, seems to reflect the realities of the contemporary situation. The pattern of relationships between Israel and the American Jewish community, as this pattern continues to evolve, will clearly be of crucial significance for the future of both societies.

It is a mark of the complexity of societal analysis, in general, and of the diversity of the Jewish community, in particular, that the assembling of fundamental demographic data (many of which have only recently become available) is widely recognized as the beginning of communal self-knowledge. Sidney Goldstein, in "American Jewry: A Demographic Analysis," summarizes and reviews the relevant data, providing an interpretation for projecting the future and for planning communal strategies. His facts and figures in effect constitute a demographic profile of the American Jewish community. Among its salient characteristics is the fact that American Jews now form a predominantly third-generation community, the members of which are largely and increasingly college-educated and undergoing a change from extended family units to nuclear units.

The profile Professor Goldstein draws indicates a range of urgent concerns for the well-being of the American Jewish community. Among these concerns is the shift of the Jewish population. This comprises regional movement from the Northeast United States to the

Southwest, and local movement from the inner city to the suburbs. The growing Jewish migration from the Northeast is identified as the single demographic trend most significant for Jewish continuity, because movement away from the heavily populated Jewish centers to areas of sparse Jewish settlement has led predictably to higher rates of intermarriage and to severe difficulty in developing the degree of agglomeration necessary for Jewish community life. Yet Professor Goldstein is also alert to the contrary possibility implicit in regional migration since it may be "crucial in creating the critical mass prerequisite to initiation and maintenance of the institutional facilities essential for continued Jewish identification."

The problems created by local population shifts from the cities to the suburbs are more familiar. One of the most acute aspects of this development is the problem posed by the remaining urban residents, including many elderly and poor Jews, who form a neglected constituency within the Jewish community. The demographic data here raise only the question of the adequacy of the strategies devised by the Jewish communal agencies to meet the urban crisis. They may suggest the need for an environmental, supportive approach to inner-city residents. The data do not, of course, decide policies. As Professor Goldstein argues, it is not within the power of the community to control the broad trends of demographic pattern set by immigration and birth rates. Practical response to these trends depends in large part upon the perception of what can be accomplished.

The size of the American Jewish community offers an interesting symbolic paradigm of the possibility for interpreting demographic facts to suggest contrary lines of policy. The Jewish population of 6 million is just under 3 percent of the general population of the United States. The slight decline in the percentage over the past two decades is the result of the end of large-scale Jewish immigration and the low Jewish birth rate. On the one hand, it can be argued that the significance of this statistic for the Jewish self-image has been marginal for a number of reasons. These include the recognition of Judaism as one of the country's three major faiths, the prominence of Jews in certain segments of American cultural life, and the concentration of the Jewish population in the Northeast section of the country. Yet there can be discerned a growing sense of insecurity stemming from an awareness of the proportional smallness of the Jewish minority. In the field of group relations, this sense of insecurity can be traced to the alleged introduction of quota systems in some areas of employment and to the de facto coerced exodus of Jews from residence, ownership, or entrepreneurship in urban neighborhoods. In the sphere of Jewish identity this insecurity is related to accounts of the specter of the "vanishing American Jew" because of the pressures of a low birth rate and a high rate of intermarriage.

On the other hand, the Jewish community in the United States is acutely aware of its relative size within the world Jewish population. American Jews count for nearly one-half of the total world Jewish population. This awareness contributes to American Jewry's sense of responsibility toward other Jewish communities, especially those in Israel and the Soviet Union, but also in Europe, North Africa, and Latin America. This sense of responsibility is a major factor in determining morale and self-image, and it has had a catalytic effect on the leadership and direction of the American Jewish community.

Paralleling the demographic profile is the effort of Charles S. Liebman, in "American Jewry: Identity and Affiliation," to adumbrate a sociological profile of the American Jewish community. Professor Liebman has sought to identify the significant tendencies that have shaped the behavior of the American Jew. In the course of his inquiry he discusses the patterns of American Jewish social adjustment, the modes of religious or ethnic self-definition, and the compatibility of Jewish religious development with American values.

Professor Liebman contends that the American social environment has been conducive to the maintenance of Jewish identity although it has been corrosive of many aspects of the traditional content of Judaism. Accordingly, in his view, the American Jewish pattern of adjustment has been marked by a continuous tension between integration with assimilative American society and assertion of Jewish behavioral modes which derive historically from a more segregated Jewish society. This tension functions amidst the widespread conviction held by most American Jews that Americanism and Judaism are compatible. Hence most American Jews, in Professor Liebman's account, express "pride" in their Jewishness, even when Judaism occupies, as it often does, a small part of their "life space." The completion of the initial phases of American Jewish adjustment suggests that the third-generation Jew is at home in America and hence is not very concerned with adapting inherited Jewish identity patterns to American social patterns.

Further, Professor Liebman concludes that American Jews have tended in the recent past to define Judaism in religious terms even when they are ambivalent about questions of religious faith. This religious self-definition takes place even though its institutional expression, the synagogue, often seems to serve as an ethnic shelter for Jews whose Jewish identity is demonstrated primarily in their Jewish association rather than their religious practice. To a significant degree, the content of the "religious" commitment becomes transposed to support for the State of Israel.

The religious self-definition of American Judaism, according to this view, may be construed as an effort to accommodate to the framework of the general American society which has supported religious pluralism more readily than cultural or ethnic pluralism. Jewish religious symbols and practices have been accepted as they fit into the framework of American social patterns and reinforce other American values. Accordingly, Professor Liebman argues, many "separatist" rituals or practices which stress the primacy of religious belief, or run counter to conventional American life styles, have been abandoned. On the other hand, those rituals which seem most compatible with American values, or which are supported by approved values like family integrity have fared well. Thus, the American social culture has had a selective impact in determining Jewish cultural and religious self-definition.

One question which emerges from this analysis is the degree to which American social culture has itself been changing with respect to the values of ethnicity and the legitimacy of particularistic cultural expression. The appearance of black nationalism, the revival of ethnicity, and the strength of the separatist Orthodox Jewish community, have all generated new evidence regarding the viability of pluralism in American culture and its apparent tolerance of nonconformist patterns. At an extreme, it has been argued that the current generation will rewrite the social contract implicit in the "melting-pot" ideology that previously obtained between American society and its immigrant masses in a way that will legitimize ethnic pluralism. On the other hand, the emergence of a postwar syndrome of "normalcy" may confirm the view that the nonconformist dissidence of the late 1960s, including the stress on ethnicity and the generational counter-culture, is an aberration within the dominant patterns of American society. Even if these phenomena are transitory, they do, to a degree, probe the possibilities open to American ethnic or religious communities to determine their own cultural patterns.

The legitimacy of more particularistic institutions and forms of religious expression has peculiar force on the controversial issue within the Jewish community of the interpretation of the doctrine of strict separation of church and state. Traditionally, Jews have given strong support to a conception of the American polity that regards religion as a matter of private concern free from official interference and with no government support. At the same time, Jews have welcomed those public aspects of American Jewish life, such as the military chaplaincy or the presidential invocation, which reinforce the concept of Judaism as one of the major religions of the country.

Alongside the historic American Jewish stress upon separation of church and state there has recently been some degree of flexibility in the application of the church-state separation doctrine. One element of the community, a clear majority of its major membership organizations, remains convinced that the only kind of American society that is viable for Jews and Judaism is a society which strictly adheres to the separation of church and state. Accordingly, it contends that any short-term advancement of Jewish interests which might come from the funding of Jewish parochial schools, for example, would be more than offset by the weakening of the political structure which provides the safeguards for Jewish religious and communal expression.

On the other hand, a significant segment of the Jewish community considers activity on behalf of a strict interpretation of the separation of church and state doctrine to be a species of "liberal reflex" to the illusory evil of an established church. This illusion, in their view, obscures the vital benefits which the Orthodox community and Jewish education would derive from public aid to religious schools and the harm which is generated by an adversary relationship to many in the Roman Catholic community. They would go further to argue that Jewish hostility to formulas that permit state aid to religious education is an illustration of the failure of some Jewish organizations to be aware of the needs of diverse Jewish constituencies and of the actual character of the threat to Jewish communal security.

The church-state issue has become symbolic of a cleavage in attitudes within the Jewish community. Yet on this issue there are shared perceptions and factual convergences from which a new consensus might emerge. One factor contributing to a solution is that of the new Jewish community-chest patterns of funding religious schools and cultural programs. Another factor would be a Supreme Court resolution of the issues raised by the new formulas of tax exemption for private- or religious-school education. In any event, this provides an interesting verification of Professor Liebman's interpretation of the symbiotic tendencies between the American social culture and Jewish ethnic and religious identification.

Two of the major Jewish institutions whose transformation has marked an adaptation to the American environment are the synagogue and the school. The synagogue has increasingly become the major institution of Jewish affiliation since World War II. Among the reasons given for its growth are the following: the transition from an urban Jewish community with informal patterns of natural association to a suburban community with greater need for formal affiliation; the accommodation of the synagogue to the societal framework of the triple melting pot; and the decline of the secularist Jewish movements whose membership was largely recruited from an immigrant generation. The result of these trends has been the consolidation of the "American synagogue" as a unique and distinctive institution which differs significantly from the synagogue as it has existed in previous periods of Jewish history.

As Wolfe Kelman shows in his chapter, "The Synagogue in America," there is no single archetype for the American synagogue. It fulfills many different functions within the American Jewish community. For some members the synagogue is a surrogate for the extended family; for many others in the community it is primarily a service center for Jewish rites of passage.

Since Rabbi Kelman's views include a self-conscious assertion of an optimistic projection of the future of the synagogue, it is noteworthy that this optimism generated divergence of opinion among his colleagues. Rabbi Kelman's critics contended that there has been a continuous erosion of religious practice in the Jewish community, placing the minority of religious observers in the community on the defensive position of guarding the relics of the faith. Rabbi Kelman holds that there has been a remarkable growth in synagogue constituency both in numbers and in quality of commitment. Analogously, it was argued that there is at present a severe generation gap between an affiliated and loyal older generation and an indifferent or hostile younger generation. Rabbi Kelman's view is that the present adult generation was in far greater revolt against the affiliation and content of their parents' Judaism than is true of today's younger generation.

Finally, many Jewish religious leaders assert that all religious institutions in America suffer from the general decline of religious belief. The counter-thesis suggested by Rabbi Kelman is that this derives from considering the Jewish situation as a mirror image of Christianity, which is undergoing a theological crisis. Even if this difference between the Jewish and the Christian situation derived from the permanence of Jewish ethnic and associational bonds, this would still be sufficient to defuse a crisis of religious faith since the expression or support of Jewish peoplehood has always been a part of traditional Jewish religious values.

There is an interesting, inconclusive pattern to the debate. Rabbi Kelman's colleagues relate impressionist evidence of their own experience of frustration with the institutions and rituals of organized Jewish religious life. The existence of this evidence is in turn cited as proof of the enormous concern for the quality of religious life, of the inevitably excessive expectations of its achievement, and of a characteristic and familiar anxiety which is itself functionally significant for reform and continuity.

In contrast to the range of disagreement about the synagogue, it is a commentary on the perception of Jewish education that there was a near unanimity about the desirability of reform of most Jewish schools in the United States. Walter I. Ackerman, in his chapter, "The Jewish School System in the United States," provides one of the most comprehensive and severe portraits of the situation. His analysis probes such problems as the teaching of a second language successfully to American children and the difficulties of providing professional status to the Jewish educator who is an employee of a part-time school—problems which remain unresolved items of the educational agenda.

One complementary angle of entry into the problem is provided by Seymour Fox in his examination of the goals of Jewish education, "Toward a General Theory of Jewish Education." There is a striking analogy between Professor Fox's comments and recent criticism of the public schools in the United States. The charge of the failure of the public school, it is now often claimed, stems from a lack of clarity about what schools can do and from a concomitant demand that they be held accountable to do too many things. The public school is charged with the task of compensating for disadvantaged family situations; with responsibility for the development of character, vocational training, and preparation for college admission; as well as with the responsibility to generate an integrated and trouble free social environment, which is often unattainable in the general society.

Professor Fox seeks to demonstrate, consistent with this characteristically generous American faith in the potentialities of education, that a similarly extraordinary weight has been placed upon Jewish education. It is charged with fostering a sense of Jewish identity, often in the absence of family initiative or reinforcement. It is required to train for institutional loyalties, often in an environment which may not be supportive of such attitudes. Further, it is expected to teach effectively great amounts of subject matter in several branches of curriculum. If this view is correct, or partially correct, then the clarification of goals or institutional reformation, as Professor Fox adumbrates, may be a prologue to an improved school performance.

Despite the commonly accepted role of religion and education in constantly evoking controversy, there is actually no single topic which elicits more passion among contemporaries than that of the youth culture. This is so although it is recognized that the segment of the youth population involved in any variant of the youth culture is a small proportion of the total youth population and hence an increasingly smaller proportion of the general population. The topic appears to function, however, as a touchstone for a cluster of other attitudes— political, social, and psychological.

For some, the existence of a youth culture demonstrates the alienation of the most sensitive and idealistic members of the future generation. Accordingly, even when youth culture is compromised by drug use or irrational excess, it is seen as a decisive symptom of the inability of the established institutions to legitimize their moral worth by generating the loyalty of the young to their institutions. In this view, the youth culture is often cited as evidence of the general moral decline or deterioration of the adult society; often it is argued that it provides the basis for programs of political reconstruction which listen, reach out, and respond to the moral sincerity of alienated youth.

For others, however, the youth culture is a demonstration of the breakdown of moral and intellectual standards, the consequence of permissive parents and the abdication of authority by those responsible for leadership in educational and cultural institutions. The phenomenon of the youth culture is to a great extent ascribed to the attention of the mass media in their need to select, highlight, and dramatize marginally differential phenomena within a complex, variegated society. It exists then as a phenomenon until interest is satiated, to be replaced by another selective dramatization of another aspect of American or world cultural experiences. These three disparate views do not begin to exhaust the causal or evaluative interpretations available.

To a degree these interpretations necessarily reflect the methodological predilection of the analyst of youth culture. Mortimer Ostow, on the basis of a psychoanalytic approach, has sought in the chapter, "Jewish Youth in Dissent: A Psychoanalytic Portrait," to examine some features of the involvement of Jewish youth in the counter-culture.

There is evidence that 10 to 15 percent of Jewish youth is involved in some way in the counter-culture. This percentage is sufficiently large to account for the marked visibility of Jewish youth within this culture. There are a variety of hypotheses that seek to explain this large percentage of involvement. Thus to some extent radical youth culture appears as a developmental reaction to liberal attitudes of the parent generation. This has particular significance for Jewish youth since the Jewish parent community is, on a comparative basis, overwhelmingly liberal. The sociopsychological factors usually correlated with New Left participation are relatively affluent economic status, protected family environment, and an extended adolescence which delays the need to assume mature responsibilities. All these factors are differentially present in American Jewish families.

According to Dr. Ostow, most of the Jewish youth participating in New Left or counter-culture activities are ambivalent about their Jewish loyalties and attitudes. Only a very small fringe is willing to be involved in ideological tendencies which advocate anti-Israel policies or support anti-Semitic activities. Further, he concludes that the repudiation of the Jewish community by the segment of youth in the radical counter-culture is "age-specific." In his view, these attitudes change with the assumption of familial responsibility and with the resolution of maturation problems. Even further, he suggests that the phenomenon of deferred obedience subsequent to revolt indicates the latent strength of generational continuity.

From Dr. Ostow's account, it would seem that the resolution of the issues posed by the youth culture depend in great measure upon various aspects of the American society. These would include the resolution of the social issues posed by extended adolescence, by economic affluence, and by confusion about the exercise of rational authority.

This view contrasts with that of James A. Sleeper who, in the chapter "A Radical View of Jewish Culture," contends that there is justification for the radical attitudes of the Jewish counter-culture derived from the inadequacy of established Jewish organizations. Further, Mr. Sleeper's view suggests that only radical reconstruction of various aspects of the community or the development of radical counter-institutions can resolve the alienation of youth or recruit them as participants in Jewish institutions. The evaluation of the critiques of major organized Jewish institutions, whether by radical representatives of the counter-culture, or perhaps even more frequently from those who urge the Jewish community to have a more "group-interested" or "inward" stance, presupposes an empirical understanding of that institutional structure and the character of its decision-making.

It is just such an understanding that is the goal of Daniel J. Elazar's chapter "Decision-Making in the American Jewish Community." Since the writings of de Tocqueville, the student of American politics has been aware of the distinctive significance of voluntary associations within the American polity. The proliferation of Jewish organizations in the United States thus reflects both the influence of American society and the tradition of communal organization within the Jewish society. The multiplicity of those organizations and their coordination, as reviewed by Professor Elazar, indicates the complexity and diversity of their principles of governance.

Decision-making within the Jewish community employs aspects of democratic procedure with a variety of electoral mechanisms in use. Yet the American Jewish community cannot be and ought not to be a one person—one vote, or even one organization—one vote, electoral body. Among the major Jewish community organizations, there are recognized areas of particular agency responsibility with developed interinstitutional lines of communication. Yet, the American Jewish community is not a voluntary federal system with a demarcation of autonomous regional or functional units.

The role of the professional staff, not only in executing policy but in initiating it, is of extreme importance. Yet the communal structure would not be correctly characterized as a functional bureaucracy. Fund-raising is a major factor in selection of leadership. Yet it would be a distortion to conclude that the decision-making process is dominated by a closed trusteeship of the wealthy. It is not insulated from membership attitudes and is even sensitive to criticism, particularly to avoid confrontation or sharp cleavage.

This review of some aspects of the Jewish communal polity, as sketched by Professor Elazar, indicates the variety of problems involved in evaluating the adequacy and quality of decision-making and the correctness of ordering priorities within the community. Two issues receive particular analysis by Professor Elazar.

First, the accountability of nonelected persons in exercising their office has been the source of much recent discussion. Since the leadership of the Jewish community depends upon volunteer participation, that leadership will necessarily be composed of a more affluent stratum of the community. This has not been a source of cleavage on issues where there is broad consensus, such as support for Israel or activity on behalf of Soviet Jewry. However, with regard to certain aspects of communal policy—affirmative action, public housing, governmental support for day schools, the urban crisis—critics of communal decision-making have argued that the leadership which makes the decisions is not in the position of experiencing the consequences of those decisions. This can adversely affect the responsibility with which the decision-making process takes place. This issue has already led to an increased concern for consultation with all segments of the community as well as with the development of sufficient expertise to deal with the new and complex issues on the agenda of the Jewish community.

Second, the disagreement over some of these policy questions, as well as the recent stress of the "new ethnicity" on strengthening internal Jewish values and identity, has again raised for Jewish organizations the need to balance their involvement in pursuit of general moral and political ideals, which the Jewish community shares with other citizens, with their special responsibility and concern for Jewish interests and Jewish group activities. At present, the attitudes of the Jewish leadership on these questions is open and changing. It is paradigmatic, perhaps, of the sense of the openness of the American Jewish future.

It is that sense of the openness of the future that informs the eleven chapters in this volume. They do not constitute eleven different and separate efforts to discover a future that is already implicit in the projectable present. Rather, they suggest some of the different ways or means in which a community might shape its future.

CONTENTS

Contents

I

Perspectives

1

Judaism and the Revolution of Modernity

DAVID SIDORSKY

The continuity of religious institutions in Western history and every-day observance of religious traditions in contemporary culture tend to obscure an awareness of the gap between the intellectual and social framework in which these institutions were developed and the environment in which they currently function. Recognition of this gap has served as a point of departure for both advocates and critics of religion in contemporary society. The critics view this gap as a confirmation of the anachronistic inappropriateness of continued belief and action which are premised upon a set of institutions and traditions with origins so remote from the conditions of modern life. The advocates point to the gap in confirmation of the vitality and viability of traditions which have successfully survived in social and intellectual milieus so alien and hostile to their original circumstances. Yet in either view, reflection upon the contrast between the culture in which religious institutions developed and the present society in which they are maintained can offer an important perspective on the significant adaptation and reconstruction which have taken place. Such a perspective would seem particularly appropriate since the acceleration of intellectual and social change in the recent past suggests an intensification of these demands for adjustment or adaptation in the foreseeable future. This perspective is especially relevant to an examination of American Judaism, which embodies one of the oldest continuous religious traditions of Western society and yet participates actively in one of the most dynamic social structures of Western history.

Among the major movements of modern culture which have

brought about a transformation of religious institutions and traditions, three seem most noteworthy by virtue of their pervasive influence and continuing significance.

The first is the development of modern science which has led to a dramatic shift in the locus of intellectual authority and cultural energy. This shift has been away from the authority of the revealed text or historical religious experience as explicated by exegesis or dialectic toward the investigation of natural or social phenomena by rational and empirical techniques.

The second movement comprises the growth of the secular ideologies of freedom and progress linked to movements of modern European Enlightenment. These ideologies have served as vehicles of moral expression and idealism, and have advanced criticism of religious or national traditions. Accordingly, they have not only provided programs for social or political reconstruction, but have served as secular faiths competing for ultimate allegiance with traditional religious views.

Third, there has been a psychological revolution, related to both the development of modern science and the emergence of secular ideology, which has replaced a commitment to transcendent or traditionalist values by a stress upon expression of individuality, pursuit of individual happiness, or satisfaction of individual interests and desires. This characteristically contemporary stress upon individuality relates to the current movements in search of transformation of traditional life styles. More generally, it involves issues of psychological self-identification, the viability of group loyalty, and the relevance of historical roots.

These three movements do not exhaust the major revolutions of modernity, nor can any single chapter in a book explore the significant ways in which even these three aspects of modernity have transformed religious institutions and traditions. The present chapter aims at a "tour of the horizon" which can highlight some of the theoretical concerns which seem most relevant for patterns of Jewish life in the next decade.

The Impact of Science

The confrontation between the historic religions of Western culture and a self-conscious and universally applicable scientific methodology is now more than three centuries old. As the recent vicissitudes of the Catholic *aggorniamento* and some of the cultural conflicts within Islamic countries suggest, among other similar evidence, the final phases of that confrontation have not yet been completed. Yet from an historical perspective, Western religions have successfully coexisted with a variety of social institutions and intellectual outlooks. Judaism, as a minority religion through much of its history, has perhaps been noteworthy in this respect. There is, for example, occasion for surprise in the reflection that the prevalent religion of Ur of the Chaldees, the city to which Judaism ascribes its origins, was worship of the moon. Traces of this have survived in personal names, in the adoption of the lunar calendar, and perhaps in the custom of the blessing of the new moon, down through an institutional framework within which there has recently been celebrated the safe human landings on the surface of the moon. The distance in knowledge and outlook is vast, but patterns of historical continuity, reinforced by directed reinterpretation and selective memory, stretch across the expanse. The conclusion emerges that the patterns of institutional adaptation are so flexible that the viability of Judaism as prescientific faith can be sustained even in the heartland of a technological or electronic society. From this perspective, it has been asserted that the adjustment of Western religions, such as Judaism, to the development of science has been completed, and that further scientific discovery or practice can no longer have any dramatic impact on religion.

In the contrasting view, which does not appear to have been decisively refuted, the achievements of modern science have been the fundamental intellectual basis for the erosion of religious faith. This process is extremely slow, cumulative, and, except for cataclysmic occurrences, historically irreversible. In the past, religious adjustment to the culture of science has involved more than reinterpretation of religious belief. Increasingly, for example, in Christianity, it has brought about a transformation of the religious impulse into movements for social change. In Judaism, the observance of religious culture becomes part of a search for ethnic community and expression. This process can only be accelerated, since we are only now entering into worldwide applications of technology. Also, the radical discontinuities which science will introduce have not yet been experienced, but they will reorient religious and cultural attitudes in the future.

The prediction that scientific development will bring about an accelerated discontinuity in contemporary institutions and inherited

5

traditions is difficult to confirm or refute for two reasons. First, the criteria for measuring rapid social change are vague and impressionistic. Second, scientific developments which have major social impact do so only as they become interrelated with other social and psychological patterns within a society. The automobile affected urban society, and the contraceptive pill influenced adolescent culture, because of other changes in social patterns which do not seem directly caused by science. Even in the light of these difficulties, it is possible to trace some of the significance of modern science for institutional transformation.

SCIENCE AND THE TRANSFER OF CULTURAL ENERGY

Some sense of the special significance of the development of science for the history of modern Judaism emerges in an important analysis of Jewish history by its major theoretician-interpreter, Yehezkel Kaufmann. Kaufmann has shown how Jewish communities, whenever they existed alongside a dynamic majority culture, were eager for and adept at cultural assimilation. The Jews of Alexandria knew Greek; the Jewish philosophers of Baghdad or Fez wrote in Arabic; the Jews of Toledo used contemporaneous Hispanic models for the architecture of their synagogues or their wine poetry. Jewish involvement in the linguistic, social, and aesthetic values of the majority culture is a constant of Jewish history. The sharp brake to this assimilative process was the refusal of the Jews to convert to the dominant religion or to participate in those many aspects of the culture which were articulated in religious terms, from schools or music to hospitals or painting. With the rise of modern science, however, or, more correctly, with the rise of secular culture of which science was a fundamental feature, there came into being a neutral area in which Jews could participate without religious conversion. The constant pattern of cultural assimilation then involves an enormous transfer of spiritual and intellectual energy and loyalty into the enterprise of science. From the point of view of the traditional framework of Jewish religious institutional life, this entry into scientific culture has a major impact upon the vitality of the religious tradition. It involves a redirection of the areas in which persons of high talent will seek self-expression, as well as acceptance of science as the seat of intellectual authority, a recognition tacitly conceded by religious leadership in this century. As a result, religion has been placed on the periphery of contemporary social life, and

6

sometimes even takes on aspects of a social club rather than a central assertion of personal identity or commitment.

There is evidence that this process has reached its zenith. The painful awareness that the gifts of science are always two-edged, that nuclear energy can destroy as well as liberate, that technological miracles create new problems as well as solve old ones, has already set in motion a frenetic search for new sources of moral authority. Symptomatic of this search is the resurgence of a significant number of religious movements which stress irrationality and which are anti-technological in their life style. These phenomena may reflect social malaise or the widespread impact of the drug culture, or they may be recognized as the minor recurrent awareness of some of the inevitable costs of technological progress. Yet even if a future generation should abandon faith in the beneficence of technological development and introduce a moratorium on its development, or denigrate scientific achievement as a paradigm for human expression and creativeness, there would still remain an enormous reliance on scientific methodology in framing a view of the facts of the human condition. This is so because it is the conception of science as the primary source of reliable knowledge that has placed religious attitudes and religious belief on the intellectual defensive throughout most of the modern period.

SCIENCE AND THE REINTERPRETATION OF RELIGIOUS BELIEFS

Within Jewish thought, there have been three distinctive efforts of reinterpretation which sought to adjust religious beliefs to the cognitive power of modern science. Perhaps the most dramatic took place at the very outset of modern scientific thought in the philosophy of Baruch Spinoza. Spinoza's vision of the potential achievement of modern science required that religion, to be credible, would have to be transformed into an appreciative understanding of the workings of nature. Religions would abandon entirely the inherited idiom and attitudes of supernaturalism. Thus, the first postscientific theology did not argue against concepts like God, the highest good, or human freedom, but aimed at systematic redefinition of these concepts in light of the new structures of nature and human nature which were to be discovered by science. As is well known, such a naturalistic reinterpretation of the tradition was rejected in the seventeenth century.

With the Enlightenment, a second major reinterpretive effort was advocated by Moses Mendelssohn. The most noteworthy aspect of that interpretation was the effort to separate sharply the particularistic or historical aspects of Jewish belief and practice from the allegedly demonstrable rational truth of ethical monotheism. Such a separation could lay the basis for development of competing liberal or conservative variants in beliefs or practices, while affirming the legitimacy and loyalty of each variant to the core doctrine of ethical monotheism.

Third, in the past five decades influential spokesmen for liberal religion have argued for the reconstruction of religious belief and ritual because of their self-conscious acceptance of scientific naturalism as a fundamentally truthful view of the facts of nature and history.

Assessment of the philosophical adequacy of any of these efforts toward a theology that would reconcile religion with the development of modern science is beyond the scope of this chapter. One relevant claim of these theologies in this context is the contention that such a reconciliation is, in some way, a necessary condition for the survival and continuation of Judaism. Failure to develop an appropriate reinterpretation of the religious tradition would place the Jewish community in the position of not having an interpretation which could be expected to generate loyalty from succeeding generations of Jews who would inevitably be active participants in a scientific civilization.

That thesis is essentially sociopsychological and has been countered by two observations. First, it has been suggested that persons committed to Jewish traditions or practices, as a matter of psychological fact, are prepared to tolerate the implicitly disparate intellectual assumptions embedded in the historical tradition. The parent who wishes his child to participate in a *Bar Mitzvah* rite is not concerned with the theological implications of the concept of *mitzvah* as religious commandment. The set of expectations with which a person approaches a cluster of traditional practices is not characterized by theological consistency.

The second, and related, claim is that a person whose psychological attitudes would cause him to abandon Jewish tradition because of its failure to reconstruct adequately its cognitive basis would abandon it in any event. The psychological grounds for commitment or involvement are less rationalistic than is assumed in the model of religious reconstruction.

Similar attitudes about the actual social or psychological motivations for Jewish involvement are undoubtedly reflected in the practice of the majority of Jewish religious leadership, which has moved slowly and with only tacit acknowledgment in the direction of reconciliation and restructuring of religious practices with the scientific sensibilities of contemporary culture.

There has been a significant change of mood, and possibly of the framework of the discussion, in the postwar period. This change has reflected the impact of two schools of contemporary thought upon theology and religious belief.

The emergence of existential philosophy has brought about a generalized challenge to the competence of scientific methodology in understanding the problems of man. Whatever the intellectual merits of the position, it has received strong psychological reinforcement from such phenomena as technological warfare, scientifically planned concentration camps, and totalitarian manipulation of the mass media. These phenomena seem to confirm that a postreligious secular society uses scientific techniques for inhuman purposes.

Existential philosophy has provided the intellectual rationale for a reinterpretation of religious texts in terms of their frankly mythopoeic character and a defense of religious traditions in terms of their symbolic or psychological adequacy. By doing so, the hierarchy of rationalistic values which have been adopted even by religionists in appraising the religious tradition has been reversed. A familiar example is the recent intellectual revival of Hasidism, a movement which had previously been evaluated negatively by most thinkers of the Jewish Enlightenment.

The second, and much more surprising, development stems from the new direction which analytical philosophy has taken in the recent past. In the clarification and justification of scientific methods, analytical and linguistic philosophers who championed science had sought to formulate the boundaries of human knowledge. In the idiom of that philosophy, these boundaries are limited only by the possibilities of sense experience. It is widely recognized that religious claims cannot be verified by experimental or sensory data in the manner of the empirical sciences. Accordingly, religious language was excluded from the realm of scientific discourse and confirmable knowledge. This conclusion, which had initially been construed as a rejection of religious truth, has become a point of departure for the reinterpretation of religious language as a species of noncognitive or emotive expression. While religious language, in this view, differs significantly from poetic or artistic uses of language, it resembles them in that its function is expressive and it is immune from canons of scientific verification. To cite a simple example: When T. S. Eliot tells us that "April is the cruelest month, . . . mixing/Memory and desire," he is not presenting a cognitive claim parallel to the view that April is the fourth month of the year or the rainiest month of the year. By analogy, the function of religious statements is ceremonial, celebratory, purgative, performative, but not quasi-scientific. Religious language then abandons any cognitive competition with scientific method and is tested by the appropriate fulfillment of its symbolic function and by its expressive adequacy.

It is too early to tell whether such an attitude is simply an intellectual curiosity or marks a redrawing of the conceptual boundaries between scientific and religious language. It is worth noting that this attitude has significant support in American Judaism, deriving from the extent to which the religious life of American Jews has been indifferent to the cognitive claims of religion, and primarily concerned with religious community as an ethnic shelter and a source of historical identification and self-expression.

SCIENCE AND THE STUDY OF RELIGION

Another major consequence of the confrontation of religion and science in the West has been the emergence of the scientific study of religion. This study, although continuous with the many medieval rational and historical studies of religious texts, involves a comparative approach to the phenomena of religion and an anthropological and psychological analysis of religious practices which has been profoundly threatening to religious faith and institutions. It would seem that the results of scientific method in fields as disparate as physics or biology can be exploited to provide materials for religious speculation or reinterpretation, but that scientific analysis of the social character of religious institutions and of the psychological function of religious belief inevitably involves a secular critique of the grounds of religious belief.

Three attitudes toward the scientific study of Judaism can be distinguished. The first views any critical analysis of the fundamental concepts or episodes of the religious experience, Revelation at Sinai, or the Covenant with Abraham, or the character of Biblical prophecy, as subversive. Such investigations may be welcomed when they confirm the historicity of a Biblical account and tolerated in exploring the background of these events, but they are construed as an alien endeavor which interferes with the normative understanding of the chain of tradition binding the generations.

The second attitude, which characterized the founding fathers of what was called the "Science of Judaism" in Western Europe in the nineteenth century, was that the scientific study of Judaism could document the triumphs of the national or religious spirit in overcoming the vicissitudes caused by paganism, intolerance, and cruelty. The point of view of that "science" could perhaps be labeled fairly as evolutionist and rationalist since it often sought to show how the rational traits of Judaism had successfully evolved from the more primitive. Fundamentally, it involved a commitment to scholarly objectivity in the confidence that such objectivity would confirm the character of a heroic religious and national culture which had overcome tragic circumstances to survive into an Age of Enlightenment. In part, the task of that enlightenment was to erect an appropriately scholarly epitaph for that history.

In the past few decades there has developed an attitude which places greater stress on the comparative analysis of Jewish religious culture in its appropriate historic context. To a marked degree, this study has been freed from apologetics even in such sensitive areas as Biblical archaeology. While the tradition has feared such an approach as subversive of religious faith, two unexpected results have occurred.

First, even when partisanship and scholarship are sharply separated, the act of the study of a culture generates its own special kind of interest or commitment. The defensive attitude toward the scientific study of the tradition fails to recognize the positive implications for the continuity of Judaism of a large body of informed investigators of that tradition.

Second, the scientific study of Judaism has opened up various traditions of the usable past which have been repressed or neglected within the normative or regnant interpretation. These traditions include such diverse phenomena as the communal doctrines of the Dead Sea sectarians, the aesthetic interests of various generations of synagogue artists, and the political aspirations of medieval messianism. This intellectual endeavor, conjoined with the search for historical roots encouraged by the founding of the State of Israel, suggests new attitudes toward the significance of science for the study of religion.

SCIENCE AND SECULARISM

Finally, the development of science has been a fundamental background factor in the rise of modern secularism. In helping to enlarge the areas of society which were considered to be religiously neutral, it was indirectly involved in the formulation of the political doctrine of separation of church and state which distinguished the neutrality of the public areas of the civil society from the private area of religious voluntarism. The development of modern science was a point of departure for the cluster of social values related to tolerance, intellectual freedom, and progress which became transposed in the ideologies of the Emancipation and Enlightenment. Of course, these movements developed their autonomous rationale and program independent of science. In turn, they gave rise to those Jewish secular activities and Jewish secular ideologies which have distinguished modern Judaism so sharply from the Jewish culture and society which preceded it.

Emancipation and Enlightenment

The most appropriate general characterization of American Judaism within the historical framework of modern Jewish history is that it is a postemancipation and postenlightenment community. This is so even though the Jewish community in the United States did not directly undergo either the emancipation process common to European countries or the self-conscious enlightenment movement of Western or Eastern Europe. Its historical processes are better described as the fusing of successive "waves" of immigrant tradition. Yet the community on the whole shared throughout the successive "waves" the ideology of the primacy of civil rights and of equality of opportunity first generated in Jewish life by the struggle for emancipation. It is deeply committed to a faith in liberal progress, which was the residue of the Enlightenment. These values and attitudes are not only of political significance, but also affect the character of Jewish culture in the United States.

Since the Emancipation, there has been a widespread tendency to assume that Jewish self-interest is identical with the furtherance of values of universal civil rights, religious toleration, and separation of church and state. In fact, the adoption of the doctrines of toleration, universalism, and separation represents a significant transformation in traditional Jewish religious attitudes. With the possible exceptions of the doctrinal status of "chosenness" within American Jewish religious thought and the function of women within institutional religious life, the compatibility of Judaism with "democratic liberalism" has been demonstrated. Yet the adjustment of what was partially a patriarchal family structure and partially an authoritarian religious value framework with that of the liberal ethos raises issues of cultural continuity.

Thus, the standard view of the critic of emancipation is that the fruit of freedom for the individual Jew is the deterioration of status of Jewish community. It is interesting, for purposes of contrast, that in the Eastern tradition, religious freedom meant freedom for the community to maintain its institutional life without state interference, but not the individual's freedom to abandon his religious community. We have long accepted the risks and benefits of individualism for the traditional religious and ethnic communities of this country. What may be recurring, however, is the striving for a type of communal expression as a significant manifestation of the quest for fraternity, until recently a neglected part of the liberal triad of liberty, equality, and fraternity.

The inevitable process of Jewish confrontation and adjustment with the majority culture took on special form in Jewish communities as a result of the Emancipation and the Enlightenment. The result has been the development of patterns of Jewish religious adjustment which significantly broke from the tradition of self-segregation. The career and thought of Moses Mendelssohn, which included translating the Bible into German, the development of a rational defense of Jewish beliefs and morals, and the demonstration of fruitful participation in the cultural life of the West is paradigmatic for later Jewish culture. Mendelssohn's thought formulated what many Jewish generations have wanted to believe in their process of adjustment with Christian culture. His doctrine was that the inner kernel of theism is morally and metaphysically valid, shared by "Judaeo-Christian" culture, while its various external wrappings are open to changes of taste, preference, tradition, or custom. It offered the formula for a partial revision and partial conservation of selected features of the tradition while maintaining loyalty to those doctrines which can be the religion of all enlightened men. In some measure, German Neo-Orthodoxy, and certainly Conservative and Reform Judaism, embraced parts of the doctrine. Similarity of environmental challenge as well as historical influences account for the fact that the three German Jewish denominations —Neo-Orthodox, Conservative, and Reform—have become part of the institutional fabric of American Jewish society. The reconciliation of Judaism with liberal ideology has become supportive of the aspects of suburban synagogue structure and has given to major Jewish institutions a reputation of moral conformism to liberal values on major political and social issues.

It is a commonplace that long before the 1970s the doctrinal distinctiveness of both Conservatism and Reform had eroded. Differences of generational piety, nostalgia for tradition among congregants or rabbis, or degrees of social status within local Jewish communities seemed to determine the patterns of Reform or Conservative Judaism. The theological basis which had motivated Reform and the historicist rationale that had characterized Conservatism were no longer central. Both Reform and Conservative intellectual leadership probed Hasidism, existentialism, and naturalism without finding unifying convergence. Both stressed the connection with Israel as a new motivating force for Jewish life.

The rapid growth of congregations in the past two decades has been conditioned by a Jewish community predisposed toward a religious movement that embodied liberal Judaism with a pattern of practices compatible with the American consensus and middle-class family ties. This raises sharply the problem of the stance and self-conscious values of the religious movements vis-à-vis the next generation.

The most forceful analogy against postemancipation Judaism, favored by partisans of Orthodoxy (and critically elaborated in Professor Isaiah Berlin's essay on the Emancipation), likens Judaism to an iceberg congealed in a harsh environment. The warm rays of freedom will melt the more accessible portions of the icy mountain, which then join the universal ocean while the remnant remains. In this view, patterns of flexible adjustment to democratic culture are inevitable way stations of Jewish assimilation. The historic grain of truth in the argument is that the bulk of leadership of Conservative, Reform, and secular Jewish community life are usually born and bred in traditionalist milieus. The challenge of self-renewal or replication in American Judaism is to be faced on a large scale only in the next decade.

The great secular movements of Jewish life, which developed in Eastern Europe and were successfully transplanted to America, advocated a particular reinterpretation of Jewish cultural history. The most prominent of these was the Yiddishist cultural movement, with its schools, theaters, and newspapers. The movements also represented significantly differing programs for effecting Jewish emancipation. The socialist argument was essentially that liberal bourgeois culture could never provide conditions for Jewish cultural freedom. Hence, the values of the Yiddish cultural renascence required the achievement of democratic socialism. Some of the Hebraic secular national movements also looked beyond the liberal consensus toward ethnic and cultural pluralism as the viable pattern for Jewish emancipation in America.

These movements have all but died out in the past few decades. They were displaced by the success of the prevailing religious patterns of Jewish adjustment and did not survive effectively beyond the immigrant generation. The actual pattern of adjustment has been the religious and congregationalist pattern of Jewish affiliation, as the primary locus of Jewish cultural expression and identity. It remains to be seen whether the dynamic energies of these movements have been transposed, or are simply lost to American Judaism.

Acceptance of the premises and of the promise of the Emancipation and the Enlightenment was the shared starting point of the major movements that today characterize American Judaism as well as the matrix of much contemporary assimilation. Rejection of emancipation-enlightenment has also brought about significant consequences for Judaism. Three kinds of rejection can be distinguished.

The first is represented by the self-segregationist segment of Jewish Orthodoxy, which seeks minimal contact with major social or cultural phenomena of Western society. It is interesting that those aspects of the current youth culture which reject American democracy have sought to set up some rapport with at least the superficial qualities of Orthodox culture. The major significance for other Jewish groups of this extreme Orthodox phenomenon is that it tests certain assumptions about the melting-pot, or integrative, aspects of American society. It also provides a laboratory for development of a parochial school system or other traditional, fairly self-contained Jewish communal endeavors.

Zionism provides a second pattern of ideological rejection of emancipation-enlightenment assumptions. There is a series of Zionist classics, starting with Leon Pinsker's *Auto-Emancipation*, which argued for a Jewish state as the sole condition to Jewish emancipation. Ahad Ha'am argued that emancipation in Western Europe is purchased only by denial of authenticity. Theodor Herzl contended in *The Jewish State* that Western Europe would itself default on the promise of emancipation and betray its ideals in wreaking catastrophe upon European Jewry. The destruction of European Jewry and the founding of the State of Israel have both confirmed and revised the ideology of

Zionism. The extent to which the future of Israel is tied up with the continuity of democratic institutions in the United States, and the extent to which American Jewish and Israeli institutions can intersect, are recent developments that go beyond the classic Zionist ideology.

The third and most provocative rejection of Emancipation has been provided by the Marxists. Karl Marx wrote that the true emancipation of the Jews was to be their emancipation from Judaism, presumably to citizenship in a truly free, secular, socialist, universalist society. This doctrine stressed rejection of the promise of the Enlightenment as a façade masking bourgeois exploitation, regardless of any apparent improvement in Jewish civic status or in the expression of cultural and religious freedom. Yet the subsequent Marxist attack upon civil rights and religious freedom shows a deep alienation from Jewish interests among the Jewish Marxists. For five decades the closest expression to the ideal society of socialism was one in which Jewish religious or cultural expression was either rigidly proscribed or systematically persecuted. Throughout this period, however, Marxism became the major secular religion. Its adherents comprise a sizable fraction of the intelligentsia in Europe, Russia, and America, including a significant minority of creative Jewish talent.

During the late 1950s and early 1960s, the Marxist episode seemed relegated to historical interest. The development of the New Left, however, has raised the question of the depth of the psychological connection between Jewish alienation and radical universalist utopianism. This question is particularly disturbing if the "Arab Liberation Movement," or anti-Semitic underclass movements, can be perceived as legitimate vehicles of revolutionary messianism.

The consensus which has been dominant in American society grew out of a set of values characteristic of democratic liberalism and representing in some way the success of both the Emancipation and the Enlightenment. These values have provided the basis for a public agenda of Jewish communal life. The diverse practices of religion, the linguistic or cultural differences among Jews, and, later, the educational school network, became the "private" domain of plural Jewish membership groups, movements, or religious congregations. The common agenda was defined in terms of shared commitments to nondiscrimination, civil rights, equality of opportunity, and so on. Widespread support for the political and social programs of the major Jewish communal agencies, including the American Jewish Committee, the American Jewish Congress, and the Anti-Defamation League of B'nai B'rith, was based on this consensus.

Recently, however, there have been major tensions in two contrary directions concerning the nature of the liberal consensus. First, "conservatives" within the Jewish community have argued that the liberal programs of the 1960s moved away from the shared values of traditional democratic liberalism. The new values have involved support of preferential discrimination, community control, or even of the ideology of national liberation movements, particularly those of black militants. Accordingly, they contend that Jewish support of these tendencies violates the liberal consensus, and the communal agencies, in pursuing such causes, become partisan ideological movements, not civil servants of the community. One possible defense to this charge is that the new programs represent fulfillment under changing circumstances of the values inherent in the liberal consensus. Even if this reply is correct, the fact that it is itself controversial may reflect the breakdown of the consensus.

In a contrary direction, it is argued that the drawing of the line between the public or communal agenda and the private or congregational movement agenda was too restrictive. It failed to take into account the more widely shared public agenda comprising concern with Jewish continuity, Jewish identity, and Jewish education and culture. In consequence, it seemed that Jews agreed communally on support of hospitals for the sick, or support of civil rights for Jews at home and abroad, but not on support of Jewish cultural life. Especially in the postwar period, the consensus on Israel, which had been an issue of political cleavage before 1947, has suggested the possibilities of a much broader public agenda for Jewish communal action.

The Psychological Issues

The transformations of modernity have not only been expressed in fundamental changes in Jewish religious beliefs and social attitudes. They have also brought to the fore the problem of the nature of Jewish self-identification and identity. It is demonstrable that what is considered Jewish in one generation may not be so considered in another. Thus, the patriarchal family structure which characterized Jewish identification formation in one generation has seemingly been

17

replaced by a permissive parental structure. The nature of Jewish distinctiveness which had been anchored in minority exclusion, or in a sense of religious people-covenanthood, becomes transposed to other dimensions. Consider, as a point of departure, the following statement of Freud's, made in Vienna in 1926, which Erik Erikson tells us is the only occasion on which Freud used the term *identity* in more than a casual way:

What bound me to Jewry was (I am ashamed to admit) neither faith nor national pride, for I have always been an unbeliever and was brought up without any religion though not without a respect for what are called the "ethical" standards of human civilization. Whenever I felt an inclination to national enthusiasm I strove to suppress it as being harmful and wrong, alarmed by the warning examples of the peoples among whom we Jews live. But plenty of other things remained over to make the attraction of Jewry and Jews irresistible—many obscure emotional forces, which were the more powerful the less they could be expressed in words, as well as a clear consciousness of inner identity, the safe privacy of a common mental construction. And beyond this there was a perception that it was to my Jewish nature alone that I owed two characteristics that had become indispensable to me in the course of my difficult life. Because I was a Jew I found myself free from many prejudices which restricted others in the use of their intellect; and as a Jew, I was prepared to join the opposition, and to do without agreement with the "compact majority."

Without pretending to any detailed understanding of how "the safe privacy of a common mental construction" is formed, it seems evident that early experience in the family must be extremely significant. Both Freud's autobiographical writings and those of his biographers trace his Jewish identification within the framework of the large Viennese Jewish *Haskalah* (enlightenment) family, one generation away from roots in rural Hasidic Orthodoxy.

Second, independent of considerations of impact of early family experience on the child's construction of this self, the pattern of family life is crucial for any institutionalized Judaism, concerned as it is with rites of passage. The stability or change in patterns of family life in this country, then, are going to influence dramatically Jewish continuity. Here we must turn to relevant empirical materials. One significant datum is that the extended family is still more prevalent among Jews than among other groups, although it is being replaced by the nuclear family. Another datum is that, with the lengthened adolescence of technological and affluent society, marriage decisions take place at a development period when identity role is being restructured. This is especially so in a culture which values hedonistic or individual expressiveness above loyalty to collective or historic ideals.

A familiar feature of Jewish life has been the residual emotional strength of certain religious, cultural, or ethnic patterns even among those who have broken with the Jewish way of life, and the apparently irrational discrepancy between support of certain aspects of Jewish life and neglect of others. Indeed, there have been many demonstrations of the "obscure emotional forces" to which Freud referred. Perhaps the moment of fear within the American Jewish community in 1967, just before the Six Day War, revealed repressed guilt for inactivity during the Nazi destruction of European Jewry. This fear and the elation that immediately followed it have had an enormous effect on American Jewry's identification with Israel.

There are also many examples of the psychic costs exacted by Jewish self-hatred or Jewish alienation. Surprisingly, it was Jean-Paul Sartre who argued, in the immediate aftermath of World War II, that every assimilated Jew became an "inauthentic" person since he was unable self-consciously to assert his primary being. Against this background, some psychologists have claimed that self-understanding would lead to a more consistent Jewish commitment.

On the other hand, the ability to find one's self only through commitment *against* an established tradition and the multiplicity of roles available as vehicles for authentic self-expression in a rapidly changing society, suggest the difficulties of any conclusion that the patterns of Jewish continuity uniquely satisfy psychological needs for authenticity. In this context, it is noteworthy that a sense of identity does not seem closely connected to the need for religious belief that had long been prevalent in human history. The needs that have motivated religious belief were summarized by Freud in *The Future of an Illusion* as the need to erect a framework in which to accept the processes of nature, the need to come to terms with death and the need to reconcile oneself to human hostility. In his view, these needs accounted for various aspects of religious functioning, including, for example, atonement processes which allow one to accept one's own or one's fellowman's cruelty, or burial rites as a means of coming to terms with death. The existence of these needs as a part of the human condition, or the inadequacy of alternative ways of satisfying them, might account for some of the well-known discrepancies in Jewish behavior and argue for the guaranteed continuation of the Jewish religion. Yet if the needs are in fact omnipresent, the remarkable phenomenon of the recent Jewish past has been the effort to find a secular faith, like Marxism or humanism, which would meet them while allowing for an escape from religious Judaism.

It may be that the world view implicit in secular society successfully responds to these three particular needs which have been among the major psychological roots of religious faith. The phenomena of religious resurgence and even of secular messianism suggest, however, that it is the need for community in a fragmented or technological society which is the main motive for contemporary religious affirmation. This search for community seems the shared theme in efforts at new patterns of religious institutions and in the significant revival of ethnicity in formulations of American self-identification.

For the Jewish community, four recent events of major magnitude presumably affect the sense of community concerning the formation of Jewish identity. The first is the Holocaust, and although it may be claimed that memory has dimmed its impact, it may also be true that only now is the realization of the event, which traumatized awareness by its overwhelming enormity, becoming absorbed into consciousness. Awareness of the nearly total destruction of European Jewry involves a latent recognition of Jewish guilt and communal responsibility, as well as a challenge to liberal optimism and good faith. Its subliminal impact on Jewish identification may transform the constant balance between assimilation and identity among American Jews for the coming generation.

The second major event is the founding of the State of Israel, which took place almost immediately after this destruction. Accordingly, concern with the survival and development of Israel is not only generated by the dynamism or attractiveness of the State of Israel or by the Zionist ideology, but becomes naturally intermingled with the Jewish sense of self-respect. It becomes part of a responsible and affirmative response, both physically concretized and historically symbolic, to the Nazi destruction.

Third, although more difficult to evaluate in terms of identity formation, there is the impact on American Jews of the persistence of Soviet-Jewish identity and commitment fifty years after a revolution which was to transform or erode all national and religious sentiment, and twenty-five years after the Stalinist program of repression and cultural genocide. This example has generated admiration and loyalty and serves as a reinforcement for American Jewish identity patterns.

Fourth, it has been suggested that the terms of the "social contract" within the American society have been rewritten. The implicit contract of an immigrant generation was the erosion of ethnicity in order to facilitate entry into the mainstream of American society. The current understanding permits and encourages ethnic expressiveness as a permanent factor of American identity. If this hypothesis is true, the institutional implications for ethnic education and organization become significant, suggesting a strengthening of the Jewish identity aspects within the American Jewish life style.

Reflections upon the Jewish adjustment to the revolution of modernity inevitably take place against a background which must acknowledge the resilience Judaism has exhibited throughout the history of the Diaspora. Some of that resilience may derive from the "failure" of Judaism to become a universalist religion, in the sense that the religion did not break its bond to Jewish peoplehood. It was perhaps this "failure" which denied wide acceptance to a proselytizing Judaism in the Roman Empire, and subsequently condemned it to the status of a minority religion suffering a seemingly unbroken chain of vicissitudes. Yet that connection of religious belief with peoplehood becomes a valuable resource in a period when creedal aspects of religion are discounted and the search for forms of communal participation and patterns of individual authenticity has become intense.

2

Zion in the Mind of American Jews

BEN HALPERN

The Traditional Idea

The peculiar relationship of Jews to Zion, the home of their ancestors, is familiar enough, but it never ceases to exert an extraordinary fascination. No other homeland, in spite of all the mythmaking and sentimentality common to patriots everywhere, has been so intricately, profoundly, and sublimely involved in the whole cultural tradition of a people. The union in the idea of Zion of ethnic history and universal religious eschatology raises the concept to a higher power than any ordinary patriotic sentiment, however ardent.

Yet if one seeks to delineate the features of this elemental Jewish idea, they remain elusive. Zion and Diaspora, Exile and Redemption were paired concepts in Jewish tradition, joining history and eschatology in one of the world's most influential cultural constructions. But while there was as much history as there was religion in the notion of exile, the idea of Zion redeemed was purely that of an eschatological utopia. It had very little to do with the experience of history.

The meaning of exile was specified for Jews in their daily lives and in the centuries of oppression which they recorded in chronicles, litanies, and continually renewed ceremonials of commemoration. A rich imagery exhibited the meaning of redemption too, but it was the product of imagination, not experience. If it reflected details of reality at all, it was only as an opposed image, not as a direct imprint. Thus, in the millennium Gentiles would pray in the Temple in Jerusalem instead of destroying it; the Jews would be restored and ingathered in Zion instead of expelled and dispersed; and of course the lion would lie down with the lamb and swords be beaten into plowshares. All this detail and specificity in no way reflected direct experience with the homeland; Maimonides was correct—in fact as well as in principle— when he concluded that one could not seriously discuss the course and character of the Redemption in Zion. So, too, Jews may have continued over the centuries to study the procedures of sacrifice in the Temple or the laws of agriculture in Israel, but this became increasingly an act of detached piety, not an engagement with practical projects for action.

This, by and large, was the situation for centuries, but not without exception. The Messianic implications of the idea of Zion often broke the bonds of passive piety and emerged in active chiliastic form. The *Yishuv* (as the Jewish community in Palestine was called before the establishment of the State of Israel), which survived or reappeared through every vicissitude of the Holy Land's violent history, included many varieties of religious enthusiast. Among sectarians particularly, the actual *Yishuv* was felt potentially to have Messianic significance, and visions of political restoration, sovereignty, and a reconstituted Jewish nation in the homeland were promoted with varying serious and immediate intent. A kind of religious proto-Zionism can be shown to have existed sporadically from the destruction and dispersion of Judea to the rise of modern, secular, political Zionism. Only in modern times, however, did these activist versions of the utopia of Zion become permanently embedded in social, economic, and political institutions.

Until the creation of the State of Israel—or, at least, until the first achievements of Zionist resettlement—the *Yishuv* as it existed could not arouse Messianic associations among Jews, since it was clearly perceived as a phase of exile, not of redemption. It was, nevertheless, an actual community in Zion and had a necessary impact on the idea of Zion among Jews. It attached a concrete, substantial, existing Land of Israel to the utopian image of Zion, and however remote the two perceptions were from each other, their necessary association invited cross references which could enrich and complicate the idea Jews had of each. Let us note here that whatever alters the idea of Zion may also alter the idea of exile, which is the most general idea encompassing, for Jews, their whole history in the Diaspora.

The old, pre-Zionist *Yishuv*—certainly in conception and very largely also in fact—functioned most significantly in the sphere of religion. Living in the Land of Israel was, of course, a religious commandment in itself, and Jewish tradition also holds that the soil of Zion sanctifies as well as enlightens, and that in Jerusalem prayers mount more directly to the divine throne. Given these assumptions, it is natural that an extraordinary proportion of the *Yishuv* devoted itself to prayer and study, and that Diaspora Jews everywhere tied themselves into the sanctity of the *Yishuv* by their pious contributions to *Haluka*, the organized collection and dispensation of funds for the *Yishuv*'s support.

The general institutional relationship of Diaspora and *Yishuv*, whereby the Diaspora organized to support the *Yishuv* and the *Yishuv* sanctified the Exile, assumed an even more specific form in the case of Ashkenazic sectarians. Various sects, both Hasidic and their opponents, the Misnagdic followers of the Gaon of Vilna, as well as certain groups from the Hungarian and Dutch-German communities, initially settled in Palestine with a vague view of strengthening their particular sects by association with the aura of the Holy Land so as to secure an advantage in the religious struggle within Jewry. Their fellow sectarians in the Diaspora, out of similar motives, gave these efforts active support and even kept a close eye on the sectarian infrapolitics of the *Yishuv*, as a strategically vital part of their general intracommunal holy wars.

However specialized for religious functions, the *Yishuv* was nevertheless a whole society, or "subcommunity," with all the normal social, economic, cultural, and political concerns. The larger part of the *Yishuv* until well into the nineteenth century was made up of Sephardic Jews, the majority of them native to Palestine or other parts of the Ottoman Empire. Pious donations supported the scholars, widows, and orphans of this community, but most Sephardim were an integral part of Palestine's economy, social and political structure, and cultural landscape.

In the nineteenth century the *Yishuv* was increasingly dominated by the growing Ashkenazi population. As the Ashkenazi community was in principle totally supported by *Haluka* donations, its rapid growth presented the changing *Yishuv* with a problem both to itself and to the Diaspora. Not only did sheer maintenance of the *Yishuv* become problematic, but the character of a community universally entitled to charity was increasingly questioned. Younger members of the *Yishuv* began to seek methods of reforming its structure and reestablishing the community upon normal secular foundations.

Ideas and projects of this kind were strongly encouraged by a new type of Diaspora support for the *Yishuv* and by other changing trends of the time. The nineteenth century brought with it, among other decisive innovations in the character of Jewish culture and identity, the growing involvement of a Western European type of emancipated Jew in the affairs of the *Yishuv*. Unlike the traditionalists who supported the *Haluka* effort, the men in Western countries who now adopted the *Yishuv* as their responsibility were "enlightened" modernists with leading positions in the whole Jewish establishment of their own emancipated communities. Even a pious Jew like Moses Montefiore, let alone Adolphe Crémieux or Carl Netter, was bound to analyze the *Yishuv* as a problem to be solved by secular methods of reeducation, relocation, and vocational change, as well as political means. Their essential approach to the *Yishuv* was the same as to the Jewish problem everywhere: the methods of enlightenment and emancipation which were solving the "Jewish question" in Western countries should be applied to all backward areas where these principles had not yet penetrated.

The rational, secular, and liberal interest of such Jews who, even if they were personally pious, approached the *Yishuv* as a problem of emancipation and reform, was spurred considerably by a growing intervention of Western Gentiles in the Bible lands, including the affairs of the Jewish community. Not only professional missionaries but consular representatives of the European powers were ready to take the *Yishuv* under their wing and provide education, political protection, and economic assistance, including the offer of colonization. More than one philanthropic effort of Jews in these spheres, both in Palestine and elsewhere—including, for example, certain activities of Mordecai Manuel Noah in America—was undertaken in order to forestall or counteract such missionary efforts. In other cases, Jews bestirred themselves in order to cooperate with philo-Semitic endeavors suggested or initiated by Christian proto-Zionists, like Colonel George Gawler or Laurence Oliphant.

Christian proto-Zionism, which flourished from the 1840s in the West, particularly in England, introduced a marked political element into the discussion of the *Yishuv*. Men like Shaftesbury may have thought in Christian eschatological terms, but they argued for Jewish resettlement and restoration in terms of the diplomacy of the Eastern

Question. Their projects aiming at political advantages for their own country's imperial interests also contemplated the rebirth of Judea as a sovereign nation. This was a factor which complicated the situation both for Jewish proto-Zionists who shared such dreams and for Western Jewish philanthropists who were interested in the *Yishuv* in the spirit of enlightenment and emancipation.

Zion for Modern Man

The emancipation of Western Jews, at first an unanticipated blessing and later a cause taken up with enthusiasm, involved significant reconsiderations in the Jewish ideas of the Diaspora as exile and Zion as redemption. The most direct impact was on the notion of exile, which informs all Jewish historical experience in the Diaspora.

As exiles, Jews for the most part did not consider themselves fully a part of the history or politics of the countries where they lived. Every country was a provisional domicile where Jews awaited the age of the Messiah, when they would return home to Zion. The Jew's appropriate attitude in exile was one of detachment from his country's politics, except, of course, in defense of the Jewish community. All this changed radically when the nations of the West offered, or seemed inclined to offer, equal rights to Jews.

The collective conversion of Western Jews to liberal principles which then followed had a critical impact on certain traditional attitudes. Jews claimed a place in both the national history and national politics of their respective countries, now declared to be their homes. No one was more chauvinistic than the Briton, American, or Frenchman of Jewish faith. Patriotism prompted Jews to proclaim that the American or French Revolution was the redemption and that Paris, London, or Baltimore was Zion-on-earth.

It followed that Jews expected no restoration in the real Zion and that, so far as they retained any Messianic beliefs, these were construed in a symbolic sense emphatically detached from history. Western Jews who held fast to their traditions did not, like the Reform sect, eliminate Zion from their prayers, but they were no less decided in their attachment to their respective countries as their true homes, in their patriotism and national acculturation, and in explaining away both exile and redemption in a strikingly nontraditional way as purely religious conceptions with no imaginable relation to historically possible, secular realities.

Notwithstanding this shift in attitude, Western Neo-Orthodox Jews, and also more liberal believers who took a lead in the communal establishment, retained old sentiments toward the Holy Land and took a special interest in the *Yishuv*. Old, suppressed elements of Jewish myth rose to the surface among rare Western Jews who adopted the logically available option of a nationalistic, and not merely individual, emancipation of the modern Jews. Moses Hess, with the bold pathos of one of the fathers of the Communist Manifesto, proclaimed the Jews as the bearers of the final social revolution and forecast the emergence of the universal socialist utopia in a Zion restored to the sovereignty of the Jewish nation. He was, of course, exceptional and was considered eccentric. But involvement with the affairs of the *Yishuv* made the attachment of more representative Jewish leaders amount to something more than bare sentiment, too.

This was particularly true of the Western Neo-Orthodox Jews, and above all of those whose acceptance of emancipation and acculturation was mixed with fears of their effect upon Jewish traditional loyalties. Such Western Jews found their own ways—for example, by separation from the more liberal, general Jewish community—to combine Western culture and national patriotism with a staunchly conservative loyalty to Jewish rituals and Hebraic learning. But they also looked to the East for their models of the authentic, untouched tradition, and saw the *Yishuv* in Zion as a bastion of Judaism unadulterated by modernity. The Dutch-German and Hungarian pilgrims who joined the *Yishuv* were more open to general culture than the ultra-traditionalist Lithuanian and Polish Jews, but they were also, on the whole, more hostile to innovations and reforms than the younger, rebellious Eastern Europeans in the *Yishuv*.

This conservative view expressed itself on several occasions when the need to find homes for emigrants and refugees from Russia and Poland arose in the latter half of the nineteenth century. Eastern Europe traditionalists and Western Neo-Orthodox Jews shared the qualms of other religious conservatives about sending their flocks to the obvious haven, America. Not only was Zion the natural symbolic destination for a Jew who had to leave his country in search of a home, but Jews who would go there might be expected to remain truer to tradition than those who entrusted their future to the American melting pot.

27

Together with this half-religious, half-secular consideration, the middle years of the nineteenth century saw the rise of a kind of religious nationalism among the Neo-Orthodox Jews who concerned themselves actively with the *Yishuv* and with Jewish immigration to Palestine. In conception, such men as Rabbi Alcalay, for instance, anticipated some of the most detailed schemes of secular Zionism, while resting their primary argument on traditional religious grounds. But, until the rise of true secular Zionism, this did not prevent Jews of a different type, such as those associated with the Alliance Israélite Universelle, who were committed to liberal emancipation as the solution of the Jewish problem, from cooperating in schemes to improve the condition of the *Yishuv* and to aid the resettlement of Jews there.

The Zionist Upheaval

The rise of historic Zionism, both in its first phase in the 1880s and in the Herzlian phase in 1897, as well as in the successive political emergencies in which Jews were involved through Zionism, had a twofold effect. First, it provoked a sharp ideological clash in the Jewish community, rendering more difficult the former sentimental interest of liberal Jews in Zion. In addition, it raised the question of Zion to a position of such central importance that it could no longer be the special interest of peripheral groups or occupy the attention of leading Jews peripherally, but concerned the whole community and demanded major efforts by Jewish leaders, whether sympathetic or opposed to Zionism.

Zionism, like other new Jewish ideologies, polarized the community initially, but in different ways in Eastern and Western Europe. Those aspects of Zionism which provoked anti-Zionist opposition in Eastern Europe made possible cooperation with non-Zionists in Western Europe; those aspects which caused opposed ideologies to sharpen their definition in Western Europe made possible a common Jewish consensus with Eastern European antagonists.

Zionism, and other forms of Jewish nationalism, arose and took hold in Eastern Europe in the 1880s. Awareness that emancipation would not solve the Jewish problem there was hammered home by the equivocal or anti-Jewish position taken by Gentile revolutionaries toward the pogroms of that period. This perception, basic to Zionism but widely shared by other Eastern European Jews as well, led to the general conclusion that a collective ethnic status, as well as individual civil emancipation, was needed to solve the Jewish problem. What provoked opposition in Eastern Europe was the Zionist tenet that the required ethnic status must be achieved by a national restoration in Zion. Opponents who believed in colonizing some other territory decried Zionism as chimerical. Others who believed the revolution would bring Jews minority rights or cultural autonomy called Zionism defeatist, a cowardly retreat from the barricades. But whoever opposed Zionism as illiberal ethnicism remained outside the ethnically committed Eastern European Jewish consensus.

Precisely the opposite situation prevailed in Western Europe. Zionist denial of civil emancipation as the solution to the Jewish problem— that is, the renewed awareness that Diaspora Jews remained subjugated and homeless in exile so long as their ethnic survival was not secure—repudiated a central belief which had enjoyed a consensus among Western European Jews. The rise of Zionism, challenging that consensus and splitting the community, caused opponents to formulate their anti-Zionism in sharp outlines, focusing their hostility upon the dangerous doctrine that the Jews were an ethnic entity and thus constituted a national problem. On the other hand, the interest of Zionists in building a modern *Yishuv* in Palestine brought them into an area where the Western Jewish establishment was already active. Once the political significance Zionists saw in this work was played down, owing to Turkish and Arab opposition that frustrated such aims, Western non-Zionists were able to cooperate with Zionist practical work in Palestine. But whenever events brought Zionist ethnic ideas and political nationalist objectives back into focus, many Western non-Zionists reverted to their former anti-Zionism.

American Jews had a communal establishment largely institutionalized and long dominated by German and other Western Jews, and their basic situation under American constitutional liberalism was of the Western type. However, beginning with the immigration of the 1880s, the population base of American Jewry was supplied increasingly by Eastern Europe. With the emergency of World War I, the Eastern European majority successfully challenged the German Jewish domination of the community. The sudden prominence of Zionism in the military and political plans of both sides, but particularly the Allies, was in part a result as well as a contributing cause of this development.

The American Jewish community that emerged from World War I (stabilized by severe restrictions imposed on further Jewish immigration in 1922 and 1924) was radically reorganized from the nineteenth century pattern, and many changes, both obvious and less apparent, reflected the impact of the Zionist issue. The prewar hegemony of the American Jewish Committee, successfully challenged by the Zionist-sponsored American Jewish Congress, never regained its unrivaled dominance, even though the Congress ultimately survived as only a shadow of itself. German Jewish dominance in massive overseas relief operations conducted by American Jewry continually provoked disputes with Zionists who wanted resettlement in Palestine, rather than rehabilitation in the Crimea, to be the main thrust of the American Jewish effort. The German Jews may have had the power of purse and position, but Zionists had the political advantage; events showed that the growing *Yishuv*, however hampered and lagging in its development, offered the best prospects for solving acute world Jewish problems. With the rise of Hitler, this realization became urgent and overwhelming. The rallying around the Jewish National Home of all American Jews, initiated with the accession of non-Zionists to the Jewish Agency in 1929 and growing through the union of Jewish appeals for overseas aid funds, became a firm and almost universal commitment in the crisis brought on by World War II.

These were the obvious, external developments which still form the basis of the coordinated establishment of major national Jewish agencies and organizations. They were backed up by a pervasive merging of Western and Eastern European personnel, ideas, and attitudes which gave a new, "common denominator" shape to American Jewry. The increasingly favorable attitude toward Zionism, which, as Eastern European elements prevailed, became the dominant community view, was one of the landmark indicators of a massive, gradual change in the significance of Zion for all segments of American Jewry.

This change can be traced most clearly in Reform Judaism, which in America developed its most distinctive and influential variant. The first stirrings of Zionism after the pogroms of the 1880s, faintly echoed by Emma Lazarus, evoked the rigorous ideological anti-Zionism enunciated in the 1885 Pittsburgh platform of American Reform Judaism. To be a Zionist was declared incompatible with Judaism, and attempts to voice Zionist sentiments in the Hebrew Union College, the Reform movement's rabbinical seminary, were put down unceremoniously.

But in the course of years Reform was infiltrated and then flooded by upwardly mobile Jews of Eastern European origin or descent. Zionist Reform rabbis, at first represented by a few mavericks like Gustav Gottheil, James Heller, Stephen Wise, and Judah Magnes, became a growing majority among the seminarians and younger rabbis. The congregations swarmed with new members recently emerged from the immigrant ghettos or areas of second settlement, for many of whom the ideological anti-Zionism of classical Reform was antipathetic. The ban on Zionism was lifted officially by the Central Conference of American Rabbis in 1935. In 1943 the participation of Reform Judaism in the pro-Zionist consensus of the American Jewish Conference signalized the sweeping change that had occurred. These developments aroused sharp opposition in the group that formed the American Council for Judaism. Rather than provoke open secession, the Reform Jewish bodies refrained from adopting an explicit Zionist position, but the dominant sentiment was unmistakable.

An evolution similar to that of Reform Judaism was experienced by the fraternal order of B'nai B'rith. Founded by German Jews in 1843, the organization remained strongly German and was concentrated in the Middle West, far from the mass of Eastern European immigrants through the nineteenth century. Thereafter its ranks were greatly extended by middle-class Eastern Europeans, creating a groundswell of Zionist sympathies. In the critical years of World War II, the Zionist leaning was even more strongly affirmed and, under Henry Monsky, B'nai B'rith took the lead in uniting American Jewry around a pro-Zionist position.

As for the Orthodox and Conservative Jewish movements, from the outset they represented both opposition to the antitraditional Reform attitudes, including the latter's explicit rejection of the hope to be restored in Zion, and the social preferences of an increasingly Eastern European immigrant mass. All the attitudes toward Zionism common among pious Eastern European Jews, whether traditional or modern, sympathetic or opposed, were to be found among Orthodox and Conservative Jews. The Conservative movement from its inception was distinguished by a rather partisan attachment to Zionism, in sharp contrast to its early German Jewish philanthropic sponsors (like Louis Marshall and Jacob Schiff) as well as to its Reform contemporaries. For a time before World War I, the Federation of American Zionists was officially led by members of the emerging Conservative movement. In later years, the leaders of Conservative Judaism were less directly identified with official Zionism, but the pro-Zionist complexion of the movement as a whole was strongly evident.

The Eastern Europeans brought to America not only their Zionist sympathies but also their distinctive type of ideological anti-Zionism. The immigrants were largely employed as factory workers in the needle trades, cigarmaking, and other Jewish metropolitan specialties. Radical socialist and anarchist leaders gained a powerful influence over this mass, who were also influenced by the anti-ethnicism of their American milieu (echoed by Abraham Cahan in his well-known pronouncement that there was no Jewish question in America, only the problem of keeping such questions from being introduced). As secular radicals, they could not be interested in maintaining Judaism as a religion; they were also subject to the influence of the Bund, which affirmed, to a degree, the validity of ethnic Jewishness while attacking the nationalist return to Zion as chimerical and defeatist.

Conversion of Jewish radicals to a pro-Zionist position was gradual, in response to successive crises in Jewish history. Disillusionment with the alternative solution projected by Communist Russia played its part, and a decisive factor was the repeatedly demonstrated need of Jewish refugees for a national homeland when all other havens of refuge were denied them. For any American Jew who cared to remain within the consensus, the Hitler era made impossible any stand other than support for the Jewish national home.

While pro-Zionism became virtually a matter of consensus among American Jews, the kind of consensus which resulted involved a good deal of ideological compromise. One might add that such dulling of acute ideological issues is characteristic of Zionism itself in all Western countries. Herzl may have wanted to project the Jewish question as a national problem, to be publicly discussed and politically solved by a surgical operation, and accordingly he tended to be sharp in his ideological formulations. Other Zionists in Central Europe, like Max Bodenheimer, were concerned about the compatibility of Zionism with their German patriotism. Like American Zionists they found a solution in a vicarious commitment to Zionist ideology; the return to Zion solved the Jewish problem primarily by removing Eastern European Jews from countries where emancipation was hopeless. Western Zionists had a different, essentially cultural, Jewish problem, for which the creation of the Jewish national homeland would produce a palliative, if not a solution.

The forms of Diaspora nationalism developed by such American Zionists as Horace Kallen or Mordecai Kaplan also had blunted ideological edges. Kallen's notion of cultural pluralism sounded bold when first advanced but has shown itself innocuous enough to become a general American, not merely American Jewish, piety. Similarly, Kaplan's idea of an organic community challenged anti-Zionists in their own bailiwick, for it proposed to reconstruct the organized frameworks of American Jewish communal life. But the organic community concept was far from being as politically relevant in its ethnicism as even the mildest form of Eastern European cultural autonomism. (Black nationalists, incidentally, and not Jews, have picked up this strand of the Eastern European tradition.) When American Jews favored the principle of national minorities' rights, it was exclusively on behalf of Eastern European Jews and strictly in relation to the latter's situation. This attitude was shared by American Zionists; if support of national minorities' rights became a consensus item for American Jewry at the Paris Peace Conference, it was in a form that represented an ideological compromise for Zionists no less than anti-Zionists. The current style of consensus Zionism is similarly innocuous, as we shall see.

The Rise of Israel

The rise of the State of Israel should, in principle, have rendered obsolete the major ideological disputes which raged prior to the state's establishment. But as few things in history ever became totally or immediately obsolete, some of these issues have survived even in their obsolescence.

The characteristic objections of Eastern European anti-Zionism faded away, and not merely because it was incongruous to argue that the idea of a Jewish state was chimerical or defeatist once it had been achieved. An even more pertinent factor in the decline of this sort of anti-Zionist criticism was the near total destruction of Eastern European Jewry in the Holocaust. Western-style anti-Zionism, which would deny Jews a sovereign state, is no less obsolete in principle than the rejection of Zion as the base of Jewish ethnicity. But Western anti-Zionists were not exterminated by Hitler, and while the establishment of Israel made some of their old formulas clearly obsolescent, they sought new ways to pursue the old ideas.

The slightest adjustments were made by the most extreme opponents of Zion. The American Council for Judaism, which had opposed the very idea of a Jewish state before it came into being, could no longer openly reject a state recognized by the United States government. It concentrated its hostility, therefore, on the alleged political identity imposed on American Jews by Israeli law and by Zionist plotting ("duplicity" was the word often used) in derogation of their duties and rights as Americans. This theme is veiled in prolixity because underlying it is the familiar canard about Jewish disloyalty ("dual loyalties" is the recent code term), which is too blatantly anti-Semitic for a Jewish body, even one beyond the tolerance limit of the Jewish consensus like the American Council for Judaism.

Similar preoccupations concerned a body firmly within the consensus—the American Jewish Committee—in the period immediately after the establishment of Israel. The Committee conducted negotiations with Israel to secure explicit statements that the Jewish state neither represented nor spoke for any but its own citizens, whatever its legitimate concern with the safety and welfare of the Jewish people everywhere. This was an assurance that Premier Ben-Gurion was glad to give, since he was equally anxious to stress the converse principle— that only Israeli citizens, and not Jews elsewhere, whatever the latter's natural concern with the safety, welfare, and character of the Jewish state, had a legitimate voice in determining Israel's foreign and domestic policies.

The main effect of the coming into being of the State of Israel was not to unite Jews in a common new identity, confusing their political allegiance, but to introduce a new division among Jews, unsettling their old ethnoreligious identity. The idea of Zion, and of course the concept of exile, underwent serious changes with the establishment of a sovereign state exemplifying Israel restored.

The most immediate impact, though not the most important, occurred among those most intimately involved in the creation of Israel —the Diaspora Zionists. With the doors of Israel open to all Jews who would not or could not live in exile, the solution to his personal Jewish problem was open to any Jew. Every Jew had the option of going to live in the national homeland, and Zionists, at least so the Israelis felt, were obligated by their beliefs to do so. This implied a rapid sifting of Zionists by which some, who migrated to Israel, would realize their ideal and others, who chose to remain behind, were challenged formally to abandon it.

Diaspora Zionists, especially in America, strongly disputed this interpretation of the nature and obligations of Zionism, and developed interpretations of their own. But even in their interpretation, and on some issues against their bitter opposition, the distinction between the realization of Zionism possible in Israel and the practice of Zionism in the Diaspora became a clear division. The centrifuge of migration to Israel, which separated Jew from Jew, operated in the fierce light of party debate within the Zionist movement.

Apart from the question of principle—how could one be a Zionist if he did not join the new Jewish State?—the centrifuge operated immediately, in the division of functions between Israel and its Diaspora supporters, to the detriment of the Zionist movement, which lost important organizational functions. The first and major function lost was that of political activity, of acting as the acknowledged representative of the Jewish people seeking creation of the Jewish state. To be sure, even for some time after Israel was founded, its cause continued to be defended in the United Nations by the Jewish Agency, the body authorized in the Palestine Mandate to represent Jews throughout the world in regard to the Jewish national home. (While in principle constituted of non-Zionists as well, and in practice enjoying their virtually universal support, the Jewish Agency was in fact composed of the same body of men as the World Zionist Organization.) But the time-sanctioned Zionist responsibility for conducting the international political drive for Jewish national liberation did not survive the creation of Israel for very long. The state took over the conduct of its own diplomacy, and the loss of a main function was an abrupt shock to many Zionists. The loss of status involved in relinquishing official responsibility for the destiny of the national home not only dimmed the Zionist movement's glamour and reduced its appeal to outsiders, but introduced a mood of oppression and, for a time, bitterness among the veterans.

It soon became clear that, like every other state, especially young and small ones, Israel could not dispense with the support of friends outside; it needed reliable political allies, both official and unofficial, Gentile and Jewish, non-Zionist and Zionist. The Zionist organization was no longer in a position to act with central responsibility and freedom of decision in this sphere, but it was the most reliable and least inhibited friend Israel had. A sense of duty, constantly revived by Israel's crises, sustained the morale of the old Zionists and, in the most recent crisis of 1967, brought into play a new stream of vigorous young recruits. Their main impulse to Zionist activity arises from the critical situation now facing Israel; this same cause has aroused many non-Zionist organizations to the need for action in Israel's defense, especially since, as we shall see, attacks on Israel and Zionism are a current vehicle for the propagation of more general anti-Semitic activity.

In another sphere, financial support of the Jewish national home, Zionist responsibilities had been fully shared since the 1930s by American non-Zionists. This had been a foundation on which was built the structure of general American Jewish consensus support of the creation of Israel, and which had ripened during the war years into united backing for the political conditions essential to Israel's rise. The subsequent enormous problems of absorption of immigrants, development, and defense that faced the Jewish state brought about quantum leaps in Jewish philanthropic contributions not only in the cause of Israel but to all associated Jewish causes. In this effort, which now included a bond-selling campaign organized by the State of Israel directly rather than by the Jewish Agency, the distinction between Zionists and non-Zionists all but vanished.

The distinction persisted, however, in regard to the employment in Israel's interest of funds contributed by American Jews. The Jewish Agency, which continued to control the great bulk of such funds, sought a legal restatement of its special relationship to the building of Israel as the representative of Jewish people the world over. This was especially important in view of the interest shown by other Jewish agencies, and encouraged by Israel, in undertaking independent projects of their own in the Jewish state. The Jewish Agency was not recognized by Israel as the authorized representative of the Jewish people, but its past achievements and present paramount role in Jewish voluntary assistance in immigrant absorption and welfare in Israel were acknowledged by statute and by a formal convention, enabling the Agency further to coordinate, in cooperation with the government, efforts in this vital field.

Thus Zionists continued to play a leading role as administrators of major funds raised in cooperation with the whole Diaspora Jewish community, Zionist and non-Zionist. In America especially, owing to legal considerations as well as to the intimate mutual involvement of the partners, leading non-Zionist "big givers" and fund raisers were enabled to share most significantly in the budgeting and control of these expenditures. Recently this has matured into the reconstitution of the Jewish Agency on the earlier basis of full Zionist and non-

Zionist partnership which was sustained during the 1930s. This will surely bring about an increasingly intimate relationship between the developing domestic concerns of Israel and a major part of the American Jewish establishment, encompassing not merely the fund raisers but the executives and lay leadership of the entire "philanthropic" community: the Council of Jewish Federations and Welfare Funds, community councils, professional organizations of Jewish social workers, and so on.

Far from being in opposition to Zionists (apart from minor transient frictions such as always arise in organizational readjustments), the increased, more direct non-Zionist responsibility for Israel's welfare has been negotiated no less upon Zionist initiative than in response to non-Zionist proposals. At the same time the Zionists have been opening up and broadening, while also tightening, their own structure by creating a new American Zionist Federation. While the reconstituted Jewish Agency formalizes the greater responsibilities shared by non-Zionists in projects within Israel, the Federation opens up easier access to those responsibilities, especially in the Diaspora, which are still considered exclusively Zionist.

The general acceptability of the new relationship with Zion, for all American Jews, is highlighted when one considers how little opposition there is in the Jewish establishment to what is still regarded as the special province of Diaspora Zionists. Two major doctrines remained to distinguish Zionist from non-Zionist ideologies for Diaspora Jews unable to acknowledge an obligation to live in Israel. The first, the unity of the Jewish people, rejected the implication, sometimes attached to the definition of Jews as a religion, that Jews were tied ethnically only to their fellow citizens, not to their coreligionists in other countries. The second, the centrality of Israel, opposed the idea that Jewish values were defined with equal validity by life in Diaspora countries as by the restored Jewish national culture in Israel. While both views could provoke ideological opposition when formulated in the Diaspora, opponents did not really question the basic mood that motivated these Zionist positions, nor the conclusions drawn from them.

What lay behind the Zionist doctrine of the unity of the Jewish people was the pervasive sense of the interdependence of all Jews everywhere. A threat to Jews anywhere evoking the memory of the Holocaust must necessarily be taken as a threat to Jews everywhere. These perceptions were shared equally by anti-Zionists who considered themselves members of a religion, not a people. Notwithstanding this distinction, few who held this view formally questioned the need for Jews to be alert, like an embattled people rather than a persecuted church, for ready defense, rescue, and reconstruction in united efforts across any boundaries that might separate Jews. Those few who rejected such solidarity, particularly in the case of threats to Israel, were treated like renegades by both Zionist and non-Zionist Jews.

The Zionist doctrine of the centrality of Israel evoked specific challenges from ideologists who defended the autonomy or even superior qualifications of the major Diaspora Jewish communities in creating Jewish values. But this too was a fairly academic dispute. Nobody could deny that in Israel the basic resources of Jewish culture, especially the Hebrew language and literature and the age-old Jewish tradition, were assured of survival, something that was far from true in the Diaspora. Diaspora Zionists did not usually draw the logical conclusion from this that the Diaspora could really share in Israeli culture only by training itself to the same mastery of these basic sources of culture as the *Yishuv* in Israel. Anti-Zionist ideologists, asserting the autonomous cultural validity of Diaspora Judaism, did not, on the other hand, reject such borrowings from Israeli folkways as American Jewry was capable of absorbing. Of course, these were of the most superficial quality, consisting for the most part of a few words, some songs and dances, and dress styles. Most American Jews, because of their illiteracy in the Hebrew language, were poorly equipped to assimilate a more serious form of Israeli culture.

The Religious Issue

The rapidly developing institutional involvement with Israel touched a major part of the Jewish establishment and individual American Jews, including, notably, the organized religious sector.

The major institutional problem that the rise of Israel posed for the American synagogue stemmed from the status granted to Orthodox Judaism by Israeli law. Under the Mandate all members of the Jewish community, consisting of persons over eighteen years of age who voluntarily registered as such, were subject in matters of personal status, primarily marriage and divorce, to rabbinic law and jurisdiction. The voluntary character and other limitations of this status, in comparison with the universal jurisdiction of the *Shari'a* courts over all Muslims in Palestine, not only seemed discriminatory but led to legal difficulties and complications. The Israeli legislature granted Jews equality with Muslims in their own national home by making rabbinical jurisdiction universal for all Jewish Israelis, but it thereby gave Orthodox Judaism a monopolistic position which discriminated against the Conservative and Reform denominations.

This had manifold effects, some immediate, others more indirect and far-reaching. The monopoly of Orthodox rabbis, even in the limited area of marriage and divorce, caused multiple difficulties for those not recognized as Jews, or as validly married or divorced, or subject to other strictures as to their personal status in the eyes of the Orthodox rabbinate in Israel. Attempts to extend this monopoly into all other legislation referring to Jews, often by quite different, secular definitions, were a fertile source of political squabbles among Israelis. These domestic issues impinged upon Reform and Conservative Jews, mainly American, who became residents of Israel. Their number was sufficient to produce a few controversial cases, but not to form a local political force that could count seriously in Israeli politics.

Apart from the inconvenience and outrage caused by particular cases, nonrecognition of the Conservative and Reform denominations raised issues concerning the validity of certain historic institutions thought to be well-established in the Jewish consensus, and cast doubt on their future. Ever since Jewish communities began to bow to the jurisdiction of civil courts in matters of personal status, a process that began in the absolutist monarchies and progressed swiftly in the course of emancipation, the traditional control of Jewish marriage and divorce became symbolic rather than effective. In the nineteenth and twentieth centuries, the dubiousness of personal status was increased when the uniformity of Jewish religious organizations was broken by the rise of denominations—a process particularly characteristic of America, where it was most fully developed. These developments, however repugnant to traditionalist Jews, were not seriously opposed; to put it differently, in the absence of a clear and firm rejection they were tacitly accepted. Now, with the legal authority granted to Orthodox rabbis in Israel, the valid existence of Jewish denominations acknowledged by Jewish history and the Jewish consensus was being implicitly, and sometimes explicitly, denied.

If logic were carried to its ultimate conclusion, Orthodox pressure might well be applied to carry out what has so far been only a threat by which further concessions to Orthodoxy have been extracted from the Israeli government: the lists of existing Jews, especially those classed as Reform, Conservative, or without synagogue affiliation, might be checked in order to eliminate from the Jewish community persons unqualified for Jewish marriage under Orthodox criteria.

While there has been no serious attempt at such a sifting in regard to American Jews—though some Indian Jews (the Bene Israel), Karaites, Falashas, and others have been less fortunate—repeated Orthodox threats have raised the issue (and been rewarded with concessions on certain Israeli domestic matters). In recent legislation, arising from litigation on the question of who is a Jew, specific, involved, and probably not conclusive decisions have been reached. The Orthodox definition of Jewishness, which undermines the recognition of Jews by purely ethnic identification as well as Reform or Conservative affiliation, was extended from the rabbinic jurisdiction to matters controlled by the Ministry of the Interior. Despite the inconsistency, the privileges of admission and citizenship granted to Jewish immigrants are also granted to their "non-Jewish" kin and dependents—a safeguard for Polish, Russian, and other Eastern European immigrants; immigrants who become Jewish by conversion abroad (that is, by non-Orthodox as well as Orthodox rabbis) are recognized as Jews—a concession to American Reform and Conservative Jews.

These legal issues only make more salient a quandary in which the Reform and Conservative denominations of Judaism, particularly in America, are cast by the rise of Israel. Whether or not one accepts Zionist views of the unity of the Jewish people and the centrality of Israel, the rise of the Jewish state creates a standard against which all values which claim to be Jewish must necessarily be tested. A religious denomination, however liberal its recognition of other denominations, is an implicit claim to the embodiment of universal truths; a version of Judaism which considered itself no more than an expression of the religious truth of American Jewry could hardly convince anyone that it was religiously valid. Any version of Judaism inherently claims the belief of all who are Jews, and following the rise of Israel, it is an inescapable challenge to any Jewish denomination not only to be recognized but to be represented there. If history serves as a tribunal of truth—a view which no Jew can truly deny, any more than he can fully and uncritically accept it—then anything claiming to be a valid version of Judaism faces the test of acceptance in Israel. Not particular grievances but fundamental historic considerations compel Conservative and Reform Jews to fight this issue—with tact and flexibility, to be sure, but to the end.

Postreligious Issues

The most widely disturbing and least openly discussed aspect of the rise of Israel is the fundamental challenge it poses to the whole sacred myth, shared in opposed versions by Jews and Christians alike, which defined the place of the Jews in world history. The Jews were to remain in exile, it was universally accepted, until the Messianic era— or, in the Christian version, the Second Advent—and only then be restored to Zion. During the long millennia of Exile they were to live dispersed, driven from place to place, in "subjugation to the [Gentile] powers," and only when all the world was redeemed would they be restored to sovereign freedom in their own homeland. This conception, underlying the whole range of specific attitudes of Gentiles to Jews and of Jews to themselves, is sometimes reflected in institutional positions such as those which have made the Vatican an inveterate opponent of Zionism far beyond what considerations of *Realpolitik* would require. The rise of Israel posed especially severe problems to the Vatican. But this is a relatively minor expression of the massive earth tremor in basic attitudes toward Jews produced by the Zionist upheaval. The major expressions occur at deep levels of a consensus so broadly shared that no particular institution (other than certain missions to the Jews) need be peculiarly related to it.

It is worth noting that secularism among both Jews and Christians had already, at least in principle, abandoned the main institutional expressions of the idea of Jewish Exile. After emancipation, the notion of Jewish "subjugation to the powers" lost its most concrete applications and became rhetoric, even more clearly than the more eschatological notions of exile and redemption. If Jews continued "subjugated" it was no longer clear that the "powers" who had lifted their legal disabilities were doing the subjugation.

But Jews and Judaism continued to be tolerated rather than fully liberated. They remained a dispersed minority and their deviant beliefs, challenging the consensus of every country they inhabited, were not the groundwork of the consensus in any country of their own. Though preachers of a new, liberal, Reform Judaism might implicitly deny the notion of exile, preferring to call dispersion a Mission, and might look to no restoration in a Zion redeemed, they recognized that the Jews in their time represented a people chosen for dissent, and awaited a millennium in which Judaism would no longer need to be tolerated because the world, converted to Jewish values, would be redeemed.

Even the Christian and Jewish unbelievers who had gone beyond religion acknowledged in the form of their iconoclasm, rejecting the sacred myth of their fathers, the traditional categories for describing the relation of Jews and Judaism to Judaism and Christianity. The outstanding example was the theological iconoclast and Biblical critic Bruno Bauer. Looking forward to a redeemed society freed from all positive religions, he nevertheless argued against the emancipation of Jews on the ground that, in the existing stage of the historical dialectic, Germany was and ought to be a Christian state. The argument assumed that Christianity was a higher stage than Judaism in the history of human belief. Accordingly, in order eventually to become humanists, Jews must first be converted to Christianity, and, failing conversion, be denied equality.

Few agnostics cared to be this explicit, but the basic assumption and conclusions are generally in effect in the whole secularized society that claims to be post-Christian as well as post-Jewish. The Jewish enlightenment and emancipation theorists not only held that a liberal, humanist Gentile society made religion irrelevant in all relations between Jews and Christians beyond the church. This was from the outset a utopian illusion, and in order to believe in it one required the subsidiary belief that the growth of reason in modern civilization was producing a common post-Christian and post-Jewish religion. But in adjusting to this futurist world faith to which a secular Messiah would bring redemption, it was tacitly accepted that Jews as the minority would discard their superstitions and outworn peculiar habits, while those of the Christians would survive as symbolisms emptied of their supernaturalist meanings, common to all in the post-Christian era.

In this spirit, believing as well as unbelieving Jews accepted Christmas trees, Easter eggs, Christian names, Sunday rest, and much else. Heinrich Heine accepted conversion to Christianity in a spirit of cynicism, not only to gain entry by whatever means necessary to Gentile society, but perhaps because he regarded this symbolic Christianity as innocuous. Other liberal and enlightened Jews would not go so far, but did something which, because it evaded consciousness, was in some ways worse. They accepted the whole anti-Jewish animus which pervades Christian culture and survives in by no means innocuous symbols of post-Christianity.

Experiences during World War II totally undermined the premise upon which such attitudes rested. Jews can no longer rely on Gentiles to absorb as well as to tolerate them, or even in critical times to tolerate them. They now know that in such times only fellow Jews will rally to help them, as they themselves will respond with a surging impulse of Jewish solidarity.

The passive, accommodating spirit in which Jews stood open to the Gentile world, accepting it unquestioningly and relying on its reason and goodness in the hope of a secularist utopia, now seems not merely foolish but shameful. To react with anything less than frank and bold activism to anti-Jewish threats is the great sin which our generation has learned to read in the records of the Holocaust. Even when pursuing the humanist utopia, our post-Hitler generation has bitterly learned to be bold; we demand that Christianity publicly renounce doctrines of the Jewish guilt of deicide and God's rejection of the Jews, and radically revise its liturgy and rites in order to extirpate the roots of anti-Semitism. Traditional Jews, knowing that they were in exile precisely in their inhibition against converting Gentiles (by which means exile could conceivably be ended), and being unable to conceive how one could remain a Christian or Muslim if Judaism were not stigmatized and decried, made no such demands and do not fight for them today.

The outstanding example of Jewish activism for our time is Israel. Many special features of Zionism, even before Israel was created, have become common in our generation. The old silent approach to anti-Semites together with the open expressions of Jewish self-hatred, which were continually assailed by Zionists in their polemics against assimilationism, are now viewed with contempt and aversion by post-Hitler Jews. Israel stands as a symbol of determination not to be dishonored and not to be trapped in a posture of passivity in the face of ultimate threats inherent in the Jewish situation.

This is another consensus item in the consciousness of present-day Jewry, whether or not it is openly articulated. Whatever their predecessors may have imagined, liberal, secularist, postreligious Jews today know that their beliefs and style of life grant them no exemption from the common fate of Jews, and they are always aware of the ultimate potentialities of this fate. To be tolerated, as we still are, means not to be fully trusted. There are occasions enough in which the general trustfulness and credibility of one part of society toward another is destroyed, exposing the Jews, the most generally available scapegoats of Christian and Muslim societies, to the extremes of intolerance, whose horrible possibilities we all know. In the face of these possibilities Jews today will react, normatively, not with self-denial but with self-respect; while American Jews live in a wary assurance that a victorious upsurge of political anti-Semitism is not *likely* to happen here, we are all aware that it is *possible* anywhere—and we know how we have to act in the face of it.

Whatever the confidence inspired by American conditions—and it has been shaken recently—we also know, whether or not we like to face it, that anti-Semitism, particularly political anti-Semitism, has never been dead. It has been discredited and rendered so unrespectable that certain American bigots cannot avow it in its old forms and have, therefore, found disguises for it. The most prominent of these is the cloaking of anti-Semitism in the guise of anti-Zionism, and mounting attacks on Israel, not on Jews.

Despite thin avowals of a distinction between Israel and Jews generally, the people involved, the symbols and arguments employed, and the whole venomous operating procedure leave no one in doubt that Arabs, Russians, and all their assorted friends, from Black Panthers and New Leftists to the Argentine Tacuara or the American Nazi Party, mean Jews when they say the Zionist-imperialist (or Communist) cosmopolitan world conspiracy. A cosmopolitan Central Intelligence Agency (CIA) agent drawn in the exact image of Julius Streicher's Jew caricatures evokes, and is intended to evoke, the same wellsprings of demonological anti-Semitism which produced *autos-da-fé* and massacres of the innocent through generations of Jew-haters. Streicher, one should recall, was no more a Christian than Brezhnev or Gomulka or Nasser.

These facts, at the backs of all our minds, move us all. They make Israel the prime target of political anti-Semitism today, a development that calls on the powerful impulse of Jewish identification shared by all. Our awareness forces us to hold in constant readiness responses which under ordinary conditions are palpably neurotic, but which our circumstances could well make realistic. Israel today constantly reminds us just how realistic the circumstances are—even more than the plight of Soviet or Communist-bloc Jewry or the remaining Jews in

Arab countries and other unsettled areas. Israel does not allow us to escape the haunting consciousness of our Jewish situation.

Some of us like to feel that our home in America may be reducing the Jewish problem to a minor peril far outweighed by a major opportunity. This calculation can be made both by those who see America as a permanent (capitalistic) revolution and those who look forward to the death and transfiguration of "Amerika" in a New Left revolution. But no Jew in our time can honestly suppress the visceral awareness that he remains a Jew; that to be a Jew means to be tolerated, and to be an object of anti-Semitism; that anti-Semitism politicized and detached from tolerance can mean genocide; and that in the face of all this he must be active and self-respecting as a Jew. Israel today not only reminds us of this, it stands as the exemplary demonstration of how a Jew should face the world. Awareness of Israel's symbolic power is fundamental in the consciousness of American Jews in our time.

3

Emancipation and Its Aftermath

NATHAN ROTENSTREICH

I

We might begin our exploration of the ideological issues facing American Jewry as seen against the background of the Emancipation by asking: What precisely does "emancipation" in this instance connote? The term derives from the root *e-man-cipatio*—which means to release the son from the authority of the father in order that the latter may assume the status of *homo sui juris* (a man in his own right). Over the course of time, however, emancipation came to apply to members of a collective group as well as to individuals. In the case of the Jews, this meant first that Jews were released from the condition of being strangers in lands where they had resided for centuries, but where their residence, prior to emancipation, was only of a *de facto*, never *de jure*, nature. Also, following their emancipation, Jews were no longer regarded merely as members of a religious or confessional group (to be viewed with hostility and at best tolerated), but as full-fledged citizens and human beings who may enjoy all rights enjoyed by others.

From the perspective of the state, emancipation implies a shift from the view that human beings are intrinsically defined by historical, traditional, or religious affiliations, to the view that all men share in a common humanity even though they may belong to various religious or ethnic subgroups. Thus, one of the major expressions of emancipation is the concept of separation between religion and state. This implies that a human being is perceived not through his inner convictions, beliefs, or modes of prayer, but rather as being to some extent an "external" or public person. The public aspect of personality is defined through the legal system, which places emphasis on behavior and not on motivations. It calls for conformity to a legal pattern and does not require agreement on values, nor does it stress the individual's historical antecedence.

This particular view of man and society found a ready response among Jews. Emancipation, when it arrived at last in Western and Central Europe in the late-eighteenth and early-nineteenth centuries, found Jews willing to abstract themselves from their own religious, historical, or eschatological confinement, and to conceive of themselves as human beings in the universal sense of the term. One of the major issues of the Jewish thrust for emancipation is strongly related to this point and can be phrased in a question, as follows: Does the universal option which the Jew is offered demand the total extinction of any remnants of particularity, or can the separation between the universal and the particular find its approximate reformulation in the Jewish sphere? The answer that evolved was that the Jew qua human being will be a citizen of his land, but as a Jew he will maintain and cultivate his traditional ties, even though his civil status has been recast. This realization had profound significance for the future direction of Jewish life. The fact that Jews could now step out from their full immersion in Jewishness, so to speak, and consider themselves as human beings in the universal sense implied awareness of a meeting ground between the Jews and mankind at large. It implied the involvement of the Jews in the rhythm of human history, and connoted a new Jewish interest in the character of the state and in the allowances made for considerations of human beings as such. Thus, for instance, the separation between church and state became not only a matter of Jewish self-interest, but a concern for the stage reached by political history in general.

Even for what might be called modern Orthodox Jews, as represented by Samson Raphael Hirsch, the distinction between *Torah* and *derech eretz*—*Torah* as Jewish Law and *derech eretz* as general normative moral guidance—connotes not only a compromise, but also an acknowledgement that there exists, outside the Jewish boundaries, a binding and meaningful realm of human behavior (*derech eretz*). The release from the particularist position of the Jews vis-à-vis the surrounding world thus lies in a convergence: the surrounding world abstracts from historical particularities, and the Jews, too, abstract from their own given and inherited particularities. The problem the Jews face is to what extent this abstraction becomes total or exclusive. From both sides there is a change delineated by the shift from tradition to humanity.

Empirically considered, emancipation can be defined as the aspiration to achieve equal rights, either through a deliberate struggle or derived from the structure of the state or its constitution. There is, in this context, an interesting line of demarcation. In Europe, the Jewish communities achieved emancipation only after a protracted struggle. In the United States, however, emancipation was conferred upon the Jews as a matter of course, thanks to the prevailing tenets of American political philosophy. European Jewry had to undergo deep internal ideological and philosophical changes, in effect to change its very nature, in order to gain emancipation (which in Eastern Europe was never even achieved), while American Jews found a ready-made emancipation in the existing political environment. Thus, European Jewry found itself caught between the change of its own heart and mind and the direction toward emancipation. For American Jewry, the change in heart and mind is an outcome of emancipation and, by and large, not the sum of the preparatory steps toward emancipation.

The difference in the respective situations of the two Jewries has had its effect. American Jewry was spared the tortures and frustrations of unfulfilled or only partially achieved aspirations. Since America granted emancipation to the Jews out of an inner logic of its own, the Jews could only conclude that the ideology underlying emancipation and the practical consequences which derive from this ideology are inherent in America, and not part of the historical process which at a certain stage provided Jews with a new locus. Moreover, Jews saw in the objective American condition a kind of Messianic situation in which a major hope of human progress had already been achieved. For the emigrant from Czarist oppression there was the joy of release and the exhilarating encounter with a free society.

Because Jews did not have to struggle for emancipation in America, their subsequent concerns centered around what may be called the extension of emancipation, that is, beyond the achievement of legal and political liberties to the securing of equal opportunities. The efforts of American Jews were also directed to the safeguarding of Jewish continuity in all its aspects. In this regard, American Jews became strong supporters of church-state separation, since this division embodied the abstract and universal character of statehood, and also provided sufficient leeway for the maintenance and cultivation of religious and ethnic ties.

Summing up our discussion so far, we may say that emancipation, from the Jewish point of view, implies the opting of the Jews to join the main currents—legal and political—of world history. As emancipated citizens of their respective countries, Jews began to see the world as opening new vistas for them and providing them with new status. Although emancipation afforded many new opportunities of advantage for the Jews, it would be one-sided to view emancipation only from this instrumental point of view. Emancipation was a new tool that also marked a new stand in Jewish thinking, with ramifications everywhere. For example, emancipation is rarely linked with Zionism, but from a broader point of view, Zionism and the State of Israel are part of the same process of emancipation. Zionism is also an attempt to place the Jews in the current of world history, to apply concepts and notions like peoplehood and statehood to the situation of the Jews. Zionism is, to some extent, perhaps skeptical about the distinction between the abstract human being and the Jews, but it does not shy away from participation in all the basic human processes as may occur in reality here and now.

II

The abstract character of emancipation results in a particular social outlook. Emancipation tends to place the center of gravity of collective human life in statehood, in legal institutions or constitutional settings, thus giving priority to the state over society. (By society, we mean the broader totality of modes of behavior, mores, associations, traditions, and so on.) It was a clash between society and statehood that brought about the fundamental Zionist disappointment in emancipation, as witness Theodor Herzl who sensed, during the Dreyfus Trial, the gap between juridical acceptance or equality and social rejection or hostility. Against this, partisans of emancipation adhered to the belief that the structure of statehood would eventually shape the structure of the society, that the mores and traditions would eventually be shaped on the model of universality implied in statehood. Such notions reveal a kind of naiveté which sometimes takes the form of an unalterable faith in reason—to wit, that reason will prevail, that the legal system ultimately will create its own mores, and that, generally speaking, the life of the people will move from statehood to society, and not the other way around.

Thus, waves of irrationalism, as exemplified in Nazi Germany and (to a lesser extent) by outbreaks of anti-Semitism elsewhere, are regarded as undermining the ideological presupposition of emancipation as a regression to irrationality or, in the most benign interpretation, as a still existing gap between what ought to be and what is. Yet, the adherence to emancipation creates a Jewish syndrome of legalism, of a stress on charters, documents, and treaties. After World War I, European Jews became excessively concerned with obtaining Minorities Treaties, somehow assuming that a legal document in itself would assure human rights and become an anchor for existence.

As already noted, emphasis on the separation between church and state is one of the major presuppositions and manifestations of emancipation. Here, too, Jews tend to be oblivious of the fact that the everyday life of a society does not permit a clear-cut separation between religion and life, that certain religious convictions, let alone religious symbols, are inherent in the life of human beings, individually and collectively. The clearest example of this is the position which Christmas occupies in society. There are many who do not believe in the religious aspects of Christmas, yet, because of the sheer weight of tradition, observe all the features of the holiday. Since emancipated Jews sought to maintain the aura of universality, they would not admit that the life of a real human being proceeds simultaneously on different levels, and that there might be clashes between universal documents, like a constitution, and traditional ties. This is another expression of the legalism which is inherent in emancipation and which sometimes renders the Jews more "Protestant"—more insistent on regarding religion as an internal affair of the soul—than the Protestants themselves. (Incidentally, only in a Protestant country, where the inner light of reason replaces the inner light of the soul, could the universalistic aspect of emancipation become prominent.)

In this context, more explicit mention should be made of the typological and not only historical affinity that exists between emancipation and what is called assimilation. Emancipation defines the position of the Jews as citizens or as human beings insofar as that position becomes manifest in citizenship. Assimilation defines the social and cultural adjustment of the Jews to the surrounding world. Nominally, this distinction can be maintained, but, as we have already noted, emancipation, as such, connotes the change in the Jewish world outlook; that is, emancipation is accompanied by a thrust toward universality and abstractness. Hence, assimilation is an additional facet of Jewish existence. Consider, for example, the dropping of the Jewish vernacular (Hebrew, Ladino, or Yiddish) and adoption of the language of the general society. This is not an expression of universality, as might be assumed, for every language is particularistic; rather it is an expression of cultural adjustment to the surrounding society. In short, it is assimilation.

Changes in religious outlook do not necessarily follow from the ideology of emancipation. Identifying the modern state based on the rule of law with the prophetic concept of justice which presupposes a divine judge, for example, might be congenial to the climate of opinion of the emancipation, but it does not follow from the belief in emancipation. The change in religious outlook is an attempt to enable Jews to strike deeper roots in the surrounding society. It means recognizing that it is not enough that both Gentiles and Jews share in the universalistic and abstract ideas of humanity. In order to safeguard this common heritage, Jews must adjust culturally to the world in which they live. One of the ways this adjustment may be achieved is to show that the universalistic rule is essentially a transformation of the Jewish prophetic tradition. Assimilation is thus a device for the enhancement of the harmony between the world and the Jews, not relying on the universalistic ideology, but supplementing this ideology with an additional step which might be called harmonization (as distinct from universalization). The device used by this trend of assimilation is paradoxical: Those who propagate assimilation understand, as it were, that the legal system is not a sufficient safeguard for the position of the Jews and that, realistically, the Jews have to take cognizance of the culture of the society, not only of the constitution of the state. Assimilation, to the extent that it is related to emancipation, is, from this vantage point, more realistic than emancipation proper.[1]

---

[1] To surrender the Jewish collective existence has been a demand of those to whom the Jewish request for emancipation was addressed, for instance, in France and in Germany. Some of those in the non-Jewish world who responded to the Jewish request expressed their demand in the well-known statement: For the Jews as individuals everything, for the Jews as a people nothing. But the demand for internal Jewish change in terms of Jewish religion as well as Jewish concrete collective existence has also been raised. The Jews were asked to become universalistic in their religious outlook, thus to be in tune with the changing outlook of the surrounding world. On this issue a significant controversy in nine-

This calls for one modification: nineteenth-century Jewish philosophy in Germany, so clearly related to the aspiration for emancipation
and to the impact of German classical philosophy, and to some extent
even to the Reform movement, tends not to identify Jewish religion
with Christianity. On the contrary, some of the most prominent philosophers of Judaism in the nineteenth century (and this applies to
Hermann Cohen and Franz Rosenzweig in the twentieth century as
well) insisted strongly on the difference between Judaism and Christianity. Some argued that Christianity is only a popular version of
Judaism, a kind of Jewish mission to the Gentiles. Others maintained
that precisely because Judaism is based on the distinction between
man and God, while Christianity is based on the identity between
man and God, Judaism prevents pantheism, while Christianity might
easily give birth to pantheism, or be akin to it. Only in the United
States did the notion of a Judaeo-Christian civilization take hold, even
becoming a household word in certain circles. This notion has to be
seen in the broad context of emancipation: not only is the public
sphere of human activity regarded as universal because of its grounding in reason and humanity, but the religious tradition is thus regarded as well, at least as far as Western religion is concerned, so that
fundamentally there are no differences between Christianity and
Judaism. This is a device—and here we must be frank—to convince
the non-Jewish world that they share with Jews a common tradition,
in terms of both subsequent historical changes and the hard core of
ideas and articles of belief. It is also a device to convince the Jews that
they share with the world not only the universal secular culture, but
also the universal Christian "cultian" culture, at least to the extent that
there exists a common Judaeo-Christian civilization. There seems to be
a kind of suspicion, vis-à-vis the Jews, that they have to be convinced
of the identity between themselves and the surrounding world, lest
they cultivate their own distinctiveness.

Thus we find, ultimately, a combination of motives: the distinction
between universality and particularity, and the identification between
particularity and universality, either in the sense that Jewish ideas
became universal, or that Jewish ideas are part of the common Judaeo-

---

teenth-century Germany involved some of the leading Jewish thinkers, among
them Samuel Hirsch, who then left Germany and became an outspoken representative of the Jewish Reform movement in America. On this controversy consult
Nathan Rotenstreich, "For and Against Emancipation: The Bruno Bauer Controversy," *Leo Baeck Institute Yearbook* 4 (1959): 3ff.

Christian climate of opinion, or else that the culture of the surrounding world, though not universal from a philosophical point of view,
has to be given preference from practical considerations, or because it
is broader or more contemporary than the authentic historical Jewish
culture. No wonder that in every historical phenomenon, be it ideological or social, there is a kind of disparity between motives, or even a
clash between them. Theoretically, they are distinct and sometimes
even antithetical, but the human psyche somehow absorbs them all
and finds its way among different orientations, directions, and tempta-
tions.

III

The next stage of our discussion is concerned with the status of the
Jews in the postemancipation period. First, a few words about the
term "postemancipation." It clearly is meant to conform to the fashion
of such current terms as "post-industrial era" and "post-technological
era," which are intended to suggest that the preceding industrial and
technological periods have not become obsolete and been superseded
by new eras, in the sense that mercantilism replaced feudalism. The
suggestion is of only partial disenchantment with ideas or systems that
did not altogether accommodate the problems they were meant to
solve. Thus, when technology engenders pollution, no one suggests a
return to horses as a means of transportation; there are attempts to
work "within the system," and to develop devices to overcome the
problems which arise out of it. Similarly, insofar as the Jews are
concerned, there is no suggestion to turn the clock back to the Middle
Ages, when Jewish status was regulated by special decrees or privileges. Emancipation, whereby the status of the Jews is regulated by
the statutes of the society at large, is not obsolete. What is problematic is the solution of the problems of the Jews within the limits of
emancipation.

Emancipation as a Jewish aspiration was never conceived as an
attempt to destroy the collective Jewish entity. It implied, in many
cases, a reinterpretation of the nature of Jewish collectivity—for instance, a shift from an ethnic to a religious orientation. It may be that
in some cases there was no thought about the consequences of emancipation, but lack of concern does not coincide with the deliberate

extinction of characteristic features pertaining exclusively to Jews. Moreover, assimilation is not annihilation; it is an adjustment, an acculturation, a *modus vivendi* with the surrounding world. No matter what the form of assimilation, some residue of reinterpreted Jewish existence remains, whatever its historical or practical validity.

After these preliminary observations, we may proceed to an investigation of the fundamental issue. Let us begin with a comment on the historical or ideological conjunction between the abstractness of universalism and liberalism as a social and political ideology. Perhaps in this context even the political aspect of liberalism as a "minimum of government" is most significant. From the outset, the decision not to separate the goal of freedom to participate in the life of society from the goal of equality, and to treat them both equally, did not imply that the Jews became active participants in the life of states conceived as political systems and ruled by governing bodies. Interestingly enough, achievement of political status became a tool in the process of participation in the economic lives of the societies. This applies to Western Jewry in general, and especially to American Jews. Participation in the economic life, understood as equality of opportunity, is clearly related to the economic and industrial development of the United States, as well as to the aspirations of the Jews who interpreted their release from oppression and poverty as taking advantage of opportunities which removed them from economic and social misery. To be sure, economic participation did not mean social emancipation (in the sense that Jews mixed socially with non-Jews after business hours), but it did mean participation in a major area of the life of a society.

We now live in a postliberal era as well—the period of minimum government is over. Governments have become major social instrumentalities, regulators of educational opportunities, providers of welfare services, planners, and implementers. In the United States the black community looks to the government—federal, state and local—to create opportunities for social and economic redress. The Jews, like many American liberals, believed that once the legal barriers barring blacks from full participation in the society were removed, the blacks would follow the patterns set by other minorities and move into the spaces opened up for them. This did not happen because the movement for full black emancipation—if we may use this term—has taken place in a postliberal era, with expectations of maximum government imposition or control. Thus, the black freedom movement does not seek merely to cultivate opportunities created by the conditions of a more tolerant society, but rather it demands that opportunities be made part of the system by law, in the same way that Jews, during the period of emancipation, sought to incorporate legal rights into the system.

Part of the uneasiness or disappointment felt by American Jews vis-à-vis the black community is rooted in this adherence to the liberal interpretation of universalism, or, to put it differently, to the projection onto the present-day situation of their own experience and the benefits derived from the conjunction between universalism and liberalism. Nathan Glazer, in a recent article, considers liberalism (and the Jewish attachment to it) as desirable and not to be regarded as a false idol.[2] It is not clear whether his reference is to liberalism as an atmosphere or as a political system, but one may wonder whether it is necessary to think of liberalism as either a false idol or a worthwhile aspiration.

The present-day position, objectively speaking, seems to demand that the state and society at large create equal opportunities and move people toward these opportunities, and not rely on opportunities that might be created by individuals with initiative, drive, strong aspirations, and educational background. The notion of equality has to be reinterpreted and the notion of a society's social responsibility reformulated. It is understandable that American Jews still cling to the liberal version of universalism and find themselves somewhat out of tune with the real social situation, especially since the real social situation pertains not to them, but to other minorities. Emancipation has made Jews, to some extent, part of the majority, and Jews are still haunted by the vision of achievement of the status of majority. This stems from the Jewish historical experience, but the particular vision often lacks validity when applied to individuals and groups whose background differs from that of the Jews.

We now touch on a paradox of Jewish emancipation which immediately places the Jews in a postemancipation period. It is related to the very notion of emancipation. As I have noted in the first part of this analysis, one concrete manifestation of the new notion of universality and of the new structure of the state is the separation between state and religion. This would mean that in order for the Jews to maintain their religious distinctiveness they must be genuinely religious, that is,

---

[2] "The Crisis in American Jewry," *Midstream* 16, no. 9 (November 1970): 3ff.

moved by convictions of a religious character, by a world outlook which gives prominence to the relations between man and the transcendent God, or to put it negatively, by a reservation vis-à-vis the overriding secular character of modern culture. Once religion is the nonuniversalistic aspect in one's life—since universalism is understood not as the universe at large but as humanity at large—religion has to assume its authentic meaning as man's awareness of the universe.

The paradox of emancipation lies precisely here. Emancipation takes place against a nonreligious or postreligious climate of opinion. Assimilation is an adjustment to the prevailing culture. Emancipation emerges out of an urge to keep pace with the current streams and enhances this urge. It is not congenial to religious renaissance. But— and here again is a paradox—to be a Jew in the era of emancipation calls on the Jew to be even more religious in the philosophical sense of the term than were his forefathers. The latter, who had ready-made patterns of behavior, prescriptions for what to do and what not to do, combined the religious and the historical separation of the Jews with visible, tangible features of their personal and public behavior. But a Jew in the period of emancipation is called on to become an internalized Jew, and thus to replace paraphernalia with credos, modes of organization with adherence to doctrines, social behavior with a philosophical outlook, and practice with an acquaintance with the treasures of religious thought.

There is no need to belabor this point; the internalized Jew did not appear. The renaissance of Jewish religion did not take place. The emancipated Jew clings, in the best of cases, to the congregational organization; to use an American Jewish idiom, he clings to the *shul* and not to the school. This is by no means a minor point since it eventually amounts to a separation between the synagogue and one's personal life, which parallels the separation between state and church. The Jew is a Jew when he is with other Jews. He may be deeply emotional about what is called "Jewish identity." He may be sincerely moved by feelings of Jewish solidarity, but, by and large, as an individual, he lacks the religious dimension which supposedly was his distinctive feature vis-à-vis society at large.

A telling example of this development is the fate of the ethnic aspect within the structure of Jewish religious convictions and organizations. One prominent feature of the Reform movement, in its German and American versions, was the attempt to distinguish between Jewish faith and the ethnic character of Jewish religion. This was a difficult undertaking because Jewish peoplehood occupies a special position within the scope of Jewish faith, not only because of the idea of the election of Israel, but also because along with that idea went the notion that the Jews are under a special yoke of duties and obligations. Just the same, the attempt was made, and the most plausible rendering of it has been Abraham Geiger's scheme of periods of Jewish history. According to Geiger, Jewish history alternates between periods where Jews maintain the message of their faith for themselves and subsequent periods when they become open to the world at large.

But what happened eventually? The historical conjunction between Jewish peoplehood and Jewish faith in the strict sense of the term did not cease to exist. Only Jews are Jews. This is not a necessary truth, but it is factual. Thus, any separation, even one motivated by religious convictions (for the sake of argument let us grant that this motivation carries weight), brings Jews back to the Jewish fold. The ethnic aspect, supposedly discarded, returns through the backdoor of the factual situation. But this is not the full story. Since the religious conviction, in the philosophical or doctrinaire sense of the term, is either missing or tenuous, the strongest motivation for the Jews to maintain their religious credo and identity is their desire to maintain their ethnic collectivity. Jewish religion becomes an instrument for this maintenance. The real cause of the crisis of Jewish secularism in secularist societies is that secular Jews wanted to maintain Jewish collective existence and discovered, eventually, that the Jewish religious congregational affiliation was the only acceptable (or available) mode of collective organization. The paradigm of religious organizations sets the dominant pattern. The reason for the proliferation of Jewish organizations in the United States is not because Jews are "organization men," but because Jewish existence has shifted from the personal to the public domain. Organizations and institutions, of course, are the embodiment of the public realm.

Thus, since Jewish religious separation could not live up to its own ideology or expectations, it sought out other sources of nourishment, the most available source being the Jewish ethnic factor, however disguised. This creates the paradox of the emancipation for the post-emancipation Jew, which might be called the paradox of "other-orientedness," of relying on sources and resources which lie outside the delineated orbit of the Jew's existence gauged according to his own ideological standards.

Since this reliance on Jewish ethnic sources becomes so prominent, the fate of the Jewish collective existence looms large for the post-emancipation Jew. First, he is nourished by the folk elements, represented by the masses of immigrants from Eastern Europe, deeply steeped in Jewish law and folk mores. What German Jews tried to achieve at the beginning of the century by translating the Yiddish literature into German, the American Jews achieved en masse through the East European immigrants who replenished and regenerated the unconscious strata of Jewish feelings. Later, the fate of Jews outside the United States became an important factor for American Jewish solidarity and identity. This development started with the American Jewish response to the situation of the Jews under the Czars, reached a culmination during the horror of the Nazi era, and remains in effect because of continuing concern for the security of Israel. The "other-orientedness" of American Jews, as related to the paradox of emancipation, is now not only an ideological feature, but an historical habit. (There is, however, a natural limitation to "other-orientedness." Even Israel, the most prominent symbolic factor in forging a sense of cohesion among American Jews, does not create a life style for the Jews; that is, Israel does not create a personal province of Jewish existence in the way that traditional Jewish religion does.)

In this connection, I might briefly note the role to be played by Jewish education in the United States. Education is fundamentally an attempt to develop the potentialities of the individual through and beyond traditional cultures. Jewish education in America, being concomitant with the "other-orientedness" of Jewish existence in general, does not face the question of the potentialities of the individual in relation to tradition. It is, in fact, largely behavioristically minded, and behaviorism, in the loose sense of the term, is but another version of "other-orientedness."

An additional observation might be apposite at this juncture. The internalization of Jewish religion, which perforce had to follow from the separation of state and religion, had eventually to bring about a version of Jewish Protestantism—the notion that redemption resides in faith. But this was not possible, not only because of the dialectic of the overriding climate of opinion, which does not promote a religious renaissance, but also because of the stumbling block presented by the Jewish religion, which is a code of behavior, not merely a philosophical world outlook, and hence calls for tangible expressions of faith. Thus, the Jew in the postemancipation period finds himself caught between the spirit of the times and the intrinsic limitations imposed upon him by the residuum of Jewish religion.

The outcome of this process is that the Jews share in the liberal philosophy of human rights. They are convinced of the value of tolerance and of the significance of tolerance for their own survival. But they now apply the notions of liberty and tolerance not to their personal existence, but to their semipublic existence, that is, as a collective entity with an emphasis on ethnic character. The rise in ethnic self-awareness of other minorities in the United States may have accelerated this process of Jewish self-awareness, but it would be an exaggeration to assume that it engendered the process, since this flows from the inherent dilemma of the Jewish situation. The Jews of the period of emancipation sought to be regarded by the outside world as individuals, sharing in the common humanity. Yet they remained a distinct minority group, fighting for their rights, just like the Jews in Poland or Romania or Latvia during the period following World War I.

As long as there are minorities, there are also majorities, no matter how these are defined. Since the concept of minorities relates so much in our day to the blacks, Jews hesitate to develop an outspoken self-awareness of themselves as a minority. Not only a matter of hesitancy or inhibition, this is also related to the demarcation between the majority and the minority. If the color of one's skin becomes the pivotal point for distinction between minority and majority, Jews find themselves in an in-between situation. It seems to me, as an outside observer of the American scene, that this is an undercurrent in the present-day situation of American Jews.

The dichotomy between the public and the personal becomes even more accentuated by the postliberal notion that what really counts is personal sincerity and feelings, and not one's behavior, let alone such imposed modes of behavior as dietary laws or synagogue attendance. Once one's experience is seen as more important than any symbols, no argument referring to symbols as factors of social cohesion can be effective. The only way open for those who are aware that withdrawal from public existence endangers the Jewish collectivity—because a collectivity is by definition transpersonal—is to deal in terms of culture or philosophy with the relation between the personal and the transpersonal. The ideologies and attitudes of emancipation and post-emancipation are subject to this particular dilemma—they transfer the transpersonal to the broad framework of universalism or statehood, and either adopt or help to create the dichotomy between the public (qua open, qua human) and the private (qua separated, qua Jewish).

Only a restatement of the position of the transpersonal as having many facets (i.e., both universal and historical, traditional and ethnic, and so on) and the restatement of the personal as not being identical only with an outflow of emotions can bring about at least a fruitful discussion or controversy within the Jewish fold. The Jew of the Emancipation attempted to live a tranquil life while maintaining a kind of continuity among the different facets of his existence. He was, for the most part, harmonistically minded. The Jew in the period of postemancipation somehow retains the phraseology inherited from his predecessors, though he is not unaware that the situation is filled with contradictions. There is a need for the courage to be controversial vis-à-vis the society, the patterns of Jewish existence, the direction of Jewish education, and the factor of "other-orientedness," even insofar as it relates to Israel.

The psychological dilemma can be stated as follows: Can "other-orientedness" generate a controversial attitude? It seems that the courage to be controversial can emanate only from an attitude of moral and intellectual courage. But who will generate the generator?

Courage is contradictory, to some extent, to an apologetic attitude, and Jews are prone to take up the apologetic stance. Jewish inclinations in this regard are obviously related to the longstanding position of being in the minority and forced to be defensive. (After all, apology is a kind of defense.) Aristotle says that the mark of a brave man is to face things as they are. He also remarked that while brave men are excited in the moment of action, they are calm beforehand. Jews escape in some measure from things as they are and this seems, at least to the present observer, related to the situation of emancipation. It is not that emancipation has failed. On the contrary, its significant achievements are the bread and butter of contemporary Jewish existence. Yet, on a basic issue, emancipation did fail.

Emancipation was an attempt by Jews to gain both a position in the non-Jewish world and a new version of Jewish existence. But can one achieve the best of two worlds? It turned out to be impossible to have both, pulling as they do in opposite directions. The achievements of emancipation are the result of advantage being taken of the openings provided by new political situations and new societies. But Jewish existence per se is thus not safeguarded. To maintain Jewish existence within emancipation calls for a parallel principle related to the Jews themselves, to their self-reflection, and to the problems engendered by emancipation. To take one principle and apply it in two diametrically opposed directions engenders the attitude of apology. Vis-à-vis the world, Jews still maintain the principle of emancipation. They continue to advocate rule of law, civic rights, tolerance, and so on. But there are factors of political or social framework which are important when we aspire to achieve them which cannot provide guides to action when they have become realized and even taken for granted. To continue to speak in the language of emancipation while facing problems which emancipation did not resolve, or possibly even created, is an attitude of apology.

We do that because our Jewish world became translucent. There is no wall to hide behind, not even a special vernacular, as there used to be when Yiddish was a flourishing Jewish medium of expression. Today, Jews live in glass houses and are afraid of losing their achievements by betraying the principle of emancipation, by acknowledging its lack of exclusive validity. This makes Jews apologetic and amounts to a lack of self-esteem. What is needed now is a new Jewish consciousness that is aware of the problem of emancipation while acknowledging its piecemeal victory. We must see things as they are. Here both the obligation for truthfulness and the virtue of courage coincide.

II

Profiles

4

American Jewry: A Demographic Analysis

SIDNEY GOLDSTEIN

Basic to an evaluation of the current status and future prospects of the Jewish community in the United States is an analysis of the group's demographic structure: its size, distribution, and composition, and factors affecting its future growth and character. The demographic structure of the American Jewish population, like that of the United States population as a whole, has been undergoing steady change under the impact of industrialization and urbanization. An evaluation of the Jewish community therefore requires an assessment of changes which are a function of the total American experience, as well as those which may be unique to the Jews. At the same time, the changing demographic structure also calls for continuous further adjustment in the behavior of individual members of the Jewish community and in the structure of the community as a whole. Thus, the sociodemographic structure is both a product and a cause of change in Jewish life in the United States.

In the most recent definitive work on the world's Jewish population, Professor U. O. Schmelz of the Hebrew University points out that "the task of drawing even a rough outline of the present demographic situation of world Jewry is greatly complicated by vast lacunae in our knowledge."[1] This is especially true in the United States. Because of the high premium placed on separation of church and state, a question on religion has never appeared in a decennial U. S. census; with

---

[1] U. O. Schmelz and P. Glickson, *Jewish Population Studies, 1961–1968* (Jerusalem: Hebrew University, Institute of Contemporary Jewry, 1970), p. 13.

the exception of the marriage records of two states, neither does it appear in any vital registration records.[2] In the general absence of official and comprehensive information on religion, social scientists concerned with research in which religious differentials are a key focus have had to rely largely on specialized sample surveys to obtain their data. But in most instances, because these surveys focus on the total population, the sample seldom includes more than several hundred Jews, and often considerably less, thereby making comprehensive analyses of the Jewish subgroup difficult, if not impossible. For needed information, Jewish groups have had to collect their own data on the size, distribution, composition, and vital processes of the Jewish population.

Since 1955, more than 20 Jewish communities have undertaken surveys. Yet, because most of the communities have been of moderate size, legitimate questions have been raised about their typicality in relation to the Jewish population of the United States as a whole, particularly about whether they are representative of Jewish communities in such large metropolitan centers as New York, Chicago, and Philadelphia. Both to satisfy the need for national data and to insure coverage of large communities, the National Jewish Population Survey (NJPS) is currently in the process of collecting data that will permit the first comprehensive assessment of the Jewish demographic situation in the United States. Until the results of this study are complete, insights must rely heavily on information provided by the individual community surveys and the limited number of national surveys focusing on demographic characteristics by religion.

For an understanding of the dynamics of change characterizing the Jews in the United States, a brief outline of the demographic and sociohistorical setting is essential.[3] Two interrelated factors set into motion the social forces which have determined the pattern of Jewish life in the United States. First, from 1880 to the mid-1920s, the size of the Jewish population increased rapidly, from less than a quarter of a million to an estimated 4.2 million. This phenomenal growth con-

---

[2] Conrad Taeuber, "The Census and a Question on Religion" (Paper presented at a conference sponsored by the National Jewish Community Relations Advisory Council, the Synagogue Council of America, and the Council of Jewish Federations and Welfare Funds, New York, October 23, 1967).

[3] For a fuller discussion of the sociohistorical setting of contemporary American Jewry, see Sidney Goldstein and Calvin Goldscheider, *Jewish Americans: Three Generations in a Jewish Community* (Englewood Cliffs, N.J.; Prentice-Hall, Inc., 1968); C. Bezalel Sherman, *The Jew within American Society* (Detroit: Wayne State University Press, 1965).

verted the Jewish population in America from an insignificant minority, too small to establish anything more complex than localized Jewish communal life, to a substantial and vibrant national American
subsociety. At the beginning of the 1970s the American Jewish community, numbering about 6 million, constitutes the largest concentration of Jews in the world, more than two and one-half times the
number of Jews in Israel, and accounts for nearly half of world Jewry.
Yet, although Jews are considered one of the three major religious
groups in the United States, they are less than 3 percent of the total
population, and, in fact, are undergoing a continuous decline in proportion as the total population grows at a faster rate than do the
Jews.

The second major factor transforming the American Jewish community is the source of its population growth. The tremendous increase in number was not the result of natural growth—the excess of
births over deaths—nor was the growth evenly spread over the nine
decades. Rather, the increase was primarily the consequence of the
heavy immigration of East European Jews between 1870 and 1924.
Before 1870, the American Jewish community was composed largely
of first and second generation German Jews who had immigrated in
the fifty preceding years. Of the remaining number, some were of
Sephardic origin, descendants of the original Spanish-Portuguese set-
tlers of the Colonial period; others were from Central Europe, descendants of a pre-nineteenth century migration. By the 1920s German
and Sephardic Jews no longer constituted the dominant Jewish subcommunity in America, but were submerged in the overwhelming
numbers of East European immigrants, 2.5 million of whom arrived
between 1870 and 1924. The immigration quota laws of the 1920s
ended the mass influx of East European Jews, and since then the
growth of the American Jewish population has been remarkably slow.
As a result, conditions defining the character of the American Jewish
community at the beginning of the 1970s evolved out of the Jewish
immigration at the turn of the century. Increasingly, however, the
character of the American Jewish community is the result of internal
changes among native-born American Jews. The growing dominance
of this segment of the population has set the stage for the significant
social and cultural changes within the Jewish population which will
take place in the closing decades of the twentieth century. The transition from a foreign-born, ethnic immigrant subsociety to an Americanized second and third generation community has had, and increas-

ingly will have, major consequences for the structure of the Jewish community and for the lives of American Jews.

Sources and Limitations of Data

As indicated, there is no single authoritative source of information on the demography of American Jews; a variety of sources must be used, each varying in comprehensiveness, representativeness, and quality of data. For national coverage, the best single source of information probably is the set of data collected by the Bureau of the Census in its March 1957 Current Population Survey,[4] which included a question on religion. Unlike the decennial census, this survey of some 35,000 households was voluntary. The data gained remain one of the best bases for determining the religious composition of the American population and the social and economic characteristics of individuals in various religious groups.

Until recently, the only source of statistics from the 1957 survey was the Current Population Report of February 2, 1958, "Religion Reported by the Civilian Population of the United States: March, 1957." When the report was released, it was generally assumed that others would follow; but various pressures on the Bureau of the Census prevented this from happening, and a wealth of data on the social and economic characteristics of Protestants, Catholics, and Jews was repressed. In 1967, however, the Freedom of Information Act was passed by Congress and, in accordance with its provisions, the Bureau of the Census made available upon request unpublished tabulations from the 1957 survey, covering a considerable amount of information on the demography of religious groups in the United States.[5] Although the survey was made a number of years ago, the data nevertheless provide an important base against which future changes in composition can be measured. In the absence of other national statistics, they constitute

---

[4] U. S. Bureau of the Census, "Religion Reported by the Civilian Population of the United States, March, 1957," *Current Population Reports*, Series P-20, No. 79 (Washington, D. C.: U. S. Government Printing Office, 1958). All other references in this chapter to the 1957 census sample survey refer to this publication or to the unpublished data emanating from the same survey, "Tabulations of Data on the Social and Economic Characteristics of Major Religious Groups, March, 1957."

[5] Sidney Goldstein, "Socioeconomic Differentials among Religious Groups in the United States," *American Journal of Sociology*, May 1969, pp. 612–631.

one of the few comprehensive sets of information on characteristics by religion of the American population.

Other nationwide statistics on religious composition are available from various surveys undertaken by public-opinion polls and other organizations. Use of such data has been made by Donald Bogue and by Bernard Lazerwitz.[6] From 1906 to 1936 limited data were available from the Census of Religious Bodies, periodically taken by the U. S. Bureau of the Census through a questionnaire mailed to the pastors and clerics of parishes or congregations. It enumerated the membership of the various religious groups, but provided no information on their social and economic characteristics.

Finally, insights into the characteristics of Jews and the differences between the Jewish population and the total population are available from a number of community population surveys, usually sponsored by the local Jewish federation.[7] These studies differ considerably in quality, depending in particular on the manner of selecting the sample population, but also on the quality of the interviewers and the analysis. Some of these surveys relied exclusively on lists of families available to the local federation. The representativeness of these lists varies considerably and often is strongly biased in favor of individuals and families who identify themselves as Jewish. In other communities, a concerted effort was made to insure coverage of both affiliated and nonaffiliated families. The success of such attempts obviously varies both with the community's size and with the ease of identifying nonaffiliated units. In the limited instances in which these efforts are successful, the master lists provide a good basis for selecting a representative sample of the entire population. In communities where there is serious doubt about the comprehensiveness of the coverage, use of master lists for sampling purposes must be supplemented by efforts to identify those segments of the population not included in the file. Most frequently this is done through area samples in which all households in the area, both Jewish and non-Jewish, are surveyed in order to identify the Jewish households for further interviewing. Such screening is essential, since any conclusions concerning such matters as the nature of Jewish identification, membership in Jewish organiza-

[6] Donald J. Bogue, *The Population of the United States* (New York: The Free Press, 1959), pp. 688–709; Bernard Lazerwitz, "A Comparison of Major United States Religious Groups," *Journal of the American Statistical Association,* September 1961, pp. 568–579.

[7] For a selected bibliography of community surveys, see the *American Jewish Year Book,* 1971, vol. 72, pp. 87–88.

tions, and intermarriage would be seriously biased if individuals and families who are most assimilated and therefore least likely to be included in a master list are omitted from the survey. Yet community surveys frequently fail in this respect. For this reason in particular, their findings must be interpreted with great care; the patterns noted may apply only to the affiliated segments of the population.

An additional problem is the extent to which any particular community, or group of communities, adequately represents the Jewish population of the United States as a whole, or even of a particular region. Most surveys have been conducted in moderate-sized communities, with Jewish populations of 25,000 or less; Boston, Los Angeles, Washington, Detroit, and San Francisco are the exceptions. Conspicuously absent from any such list are New York City, accounting for approximately 40 percent of the American Jewish population, Philadelphia, with approximately 330,000 Jews, and Chicago, with an estimated 270,000 Jews. Until data become available from these large communities, the extent to which the findings of the smaller communities are typical of the total American Jewish population must remain questionable. Yet the findings of the individual community surveys display impressively similar patterns for the characteristics of the Jewish populations they analyze.[8] Variations can generally be accounted for by the nature of the community itself, that is, whether it is an older community or a newer suburban area, and whether it is in the East or the West. Taking these variations into account, the relatively high degree of homogeneity suggests that the demographic profile of American Jewry as a whole does not deviate significantly from that depicted by already existing sources, incomplete as they are.

The following discussion of what is known about the sociodemographic structure of the American Jewish community, and the implications of this structure for the future, will rely heavily on the sources of data just reviewed. Data from one of the surveys for which this author was personally responsible—Providence, Rhode Island—will be cited frequently because, as part of the analysis plan for this survey, special emphasis was placed on using cross-sectional data to gain insights into the nature of past and future changes in the demographic

---

[8] A general review of community surveys was made by Ronald M. Goldstein, "The Nature, Character and Trends of Post World War II American Jewry as Reflected in Communal Surveys" (Master's thesis, Hebrew Union College–Jewish Institute of Religion, 1969). For an extensive summary of the thesis see Ronald M. Goldstein, "American Jewish Population Studies Since World War II," *American Jewish Archives*, April 1970, pp. 14–46.

structure. No claim is made that this is a typical American Jewish community. Nonetheless, to the extent that the patterns noted in this community correspond closely with those observed elsewhere, there is no reason to believe that it is atypical of what may be true of the American scene in general.

Population Growth

From a small community of only several thousand persons at the time of the American Revolution, the Jewish population of the United States increased to about 6 million persons in 1970.[9] This growth has been very uneven. In the mid-nineteenth century, the Jewish population still numbered only 50,000 persons; by 1880, the year before the major immigration from Eastern Europe set in, Jews in America were estimated to number only 230,000. Out of a total United States population of 50 million, Jews represented less than one-half of 1 percent. Within the next 10 years the Jewish population almost doubled, and by 1900 it numbered just over 1,000,000 persons. Thus, in a twenty year period, when the total United States population increased by only 50 percent, the Jewish population increased fourfold. As a result, at the turn of the century Jews constituted 1.4 percent of the American population. Rapid growth continued through the first years of the twentieth century, interrupted only by World War I. By the mid-1920s, when national origins quota laws restricted further large-scale immigration from both Southern and Eastern Europe, Jews in the United States numbered 4,250,000 persons, or 3.7 percent of the total population.

Since then, except for a slight increase in immigration after the rise of Hitler, when laws were relaxed to permit entrance of refugees, immigration has not been a major factor in the growth of the American Jewish community. Between 1964 and 1968, for example, an estimated total of only 39,000 Jews, or 2.3 percent of all immigrants,[10]

---

[9] Estimates for 1818–1899 are based on "Jewish Statistics," *American Jewish Year Book*, 1899–1900, vol. 1, p. 283. Estimates for 1790 and 1907–1937 are from Nathan Goldberg, "The Jewish Population in the United States," in *The Jewish People, Past and Present* (New York: Jewish Encyclopedic Handbooks, Central Yiddish Culture Organization, 1948) vol. 2, p. 25. The 1950–1968 estimates are from *American Jewish Year Book*, 1969, vol. 70, p. 260.

[10] Jack J. Diamond, "Jewish Immigration to the United States," *American Jewish Year Book*, 1969, vol. 70, pp. 289–294.

entered the United States as permanent residents. Jewish population increase now depends largely on an excess of births over deaths, and since the Jewish birth rate is below that of the general population, the rate of increase of Jews has been below that of the total American population. Thus, whereas the United States population has increased by almost two-thirds between 1930 and 1970, the Jewish population has grown by only 40 percent. According to the latest estimate prepared by the *American Jewish Year Book*, the Jewish population in 1968 was 5,869,000, or 2.94 percent of the total American population.[11] If the rate of growth characterizing the 1950s and 1960s has persisted, the Jewish population should have reached 6,000,000 by 1970. Because of the differential rates of growth of the Jewish and the total population, the proportion of Jews in the total, after peaking at about 3.7 percent in the 1920s, has declined to below 3 percent. It is likely to continue to decline as long as the Jewish birth rate remains below that of the rest of the nation.

This decline in relative numbers may not be very significant, since Jews have never constituted a numerically large segment of the population. If anything, it is noteworthy that, despite their small numbers, they are generally afforded the social position of the third major religious group in the country. There seems little reason to expect that this situation will change even though their percentage in the total population declines further, particularly since Jews, both as a group and individually, will undoubtedly continue to play significant roles in such spheres of American life as cultural activities, education, and urban politics. From the demographic point of view, more important factors may be influencing the position of the Jewish community within the total American community, among them changes in the geographical concentration of Jews in certain parts of the nation as well as their disproportional representation in selected socioeconomic strata. But before turning to these considerations, some attention must be given to the operation of the vital processes in the growth of the Jewish population, since this is a key to understanding the total pattern of Jewish growth in the future.

[11] Alvin Chenkin, "Jewish Population in the United States," *American Jewish Year Book*, 1970, vol. 71, pp. 344–347.

Mortality

As part of his classic studies of the social and religious history of the Jews, Salo W. Baron observed that, as early as the mid-seventeenth century, it had already become noticeable that the "great destructive forces, contagious diseases and wars, seem to have claimed fewer victims among the Jews than among their Gentile neighbors."[12] The explanation for such differentials favoring greater longevity among Jews has varied, including the effect of religious life on health conditions through prescriptions requiring continual washing, restricted food selection, and a weekly day of rest. Some, including Baron, have suggested that the Jews' relatively longer experience of living in a "civilized environment" and in an urban setting may have affected them genetically to the extent that they are more immune to certain contagious diseases. Others have suggested that the higher than average socioeconomic status of the Jews permits them to obtain more and better medical attention and to live in a better environment.

Whether the health and mortality differentials noted by Baron for the mid-seventeenth century Jewish population in Europe also characterize the American Jewish community has been the subject of only limited research. Again, the limitations of available data restrict the opportunities for exploring the question. Religion is not recorded on death certificates in the United States, and only by resorting to information available through funeral directors and cemetery records has some insight been gained into the mortality patterns of American Jews. At varying times, such studies using different approaches have been conducted for New York City, St. Louis, Providence, Detroit, and Milwaukee.[13]

Although specific findings differ somewhat, the data permit the gen-

12 Salo W. Baron, A Social and Religious History of the Jews (New York: Columbia University Press, 1937), vol. II, p. 169.

13 H. Seidman, L. Garfinkel, and L. Craig, "Death Rates in New York City by Socio-Economic Class and Religious Group and by Country of Birth, 1949–1951," Jewish Journal of Sociology, December 1962, pp. 254–272; K. Gorwitz, "Jewish Mortality in St. Louis and St. Louis County, 1955–1957," Jewish Social Studies, October 1962, pp. 248–254; Sidney Goldstein, "Jewish Mortality and Survival Patterns: Providence, Rhode Island, 1962–1964," Eugenics Quarterly, 1966, no. 13, pp. 48–61; S. Joseph Fauman and Albert J. Mayer, "Jewish Mortality in the U. S.," Human Biology, September 1969, pp. 416–426.

eral conclusion that differences exist between the age-specific death rates, life expectancy, and survival patterns of Jews and of the total white population, generally more so for males than for females. Jewish age-specific rates are below those of the white population at younger ages, and higher at older ages. The differences for males tend to be sharper than for females at all ages. The lower death rates of Jews at younger ages may result from a combination of the conditions already outlined. There has been some speculation that proportionately more Jews with physically impaired lives may survive until later years, when the effects of chronic disease may take higher tolls, thereby raising the age-specific death rates of older Jews above those of the general population. For example, the data by cause of death for Providence lend support to such a contention; for Jews aged 65 and over, the death rates from all major chronic diseases were higher than for the total white population.

Comparison of life tables for Jews and total whites suggests that average life expectancy at birth favors Jewish males, but shows little difference for females. The advantage of Jewish males declines with advancing age, and actually becomes less than that of all whites beyond age 65. For females, the life expectancy of Jews remains below that of total whites throughout the life cycle, and the differential tends to become increasingly higher from middle age onward. Because the proportion of individuals surviving to a particular age reflects the effects of mortality only up to that age, the lower Jewish mortality in childhood, as well as in the early and middle adult stages of the life cycle, accounts for higher proportions of Jews surviving into middle age and, in the case of males, even into the lower range of old age.

Fertility

Whatever the source of information, fertility research in the United States has consistently found a lower birth rate for Jews than for members of other religious groups. As early as the late nineteenth century, a study of over 10,000 Jewish families in the United States revealed that the Jewish birth rate was lower than the non-Jewish.[14] In the Rhode Island census of 1905, the only state census that ob-

[14] John S. Billings, "Vital Statistics of the Jews in the United States," *Census Bulletin*, no. 19, December 30, 1889, pp. 4–9.

tained information on religion and related it to family size, the average family size of native-born Jewish women was 2.3, compared to an
average of 3.2 for native-born Catholics and 2.5 for native-born Protestants.[15] Similarly, the birth rates of Jews in the 1930s were shown to
be lower than those of economically comparable Protestant groups;
Jews also were found to have a higher proportion using contracep-
tives, planning pregnancies, and relying on more efficient methods to
achieve that goal.[16] The Indianapolis fertility study conducted in
1941 included Jews only in the screening phase of the investigation,
which was designed to focus exclusively on Protestant couples; even
here the fertility rates, standardized for age, were about 18 percent
higher for Catholics than for Protestants and about 25 percent lower for
Jews than for Protestants.[17]

Beginning in the 1950s, a series of important surveys were undertaken to investigate the fertility behavior of the American population.
Among these were the Growth of American Families Studies (GAF),
the Princeton Fertility Studies, and investigations based on the Detroit
Area Studies.[18] In each of these, Jews constituted only a small proportion of the total sample, thereby precluding detailed investigation of
Jewish fertility. Yet the data on Jews yielded by these studies were
clear-cut in pointing to lower Jewish fertility. The results of the GAF
study indicate, for example, that in 1955 the average family size of
Catholic and Protestant couples was 2.1, compared to an average of
only 1.7 for Jewish couples.[19] Overall, the GAF study found that Jews
had the smallest families, married later, expected and desired to have
the smallest families, had the most favorable attitudes toward the use

[15] *Rhode Island Census of 1905*, Tables VII and VIII, pp. 550–553.

[16] R. K. Stix and Frank Notestein, *Controlled Fertility* (Baltimore: The William
and Wilkins Co., 1940), p. 29; Raymond Pearl, *The Natural History of Population* (New York: Oxford University Press, 1939), pp. 241–242.

[17] Pascal K. Whelpton and Clyde V. Kiser, "Differential Fertility Among Native
White Couples in Indianapolis," *Social and Psychological Factors Affecting Fertility*, I, *Milbank Memorial Fund Quarterly*, July 1943, pp. 226–271.

[18] Ronald Freedman, Pascal K. Whelpton, and Arthur A. Campbell, *Family
Planning, Sterility and Population Growth* (New York: McGraw-Hill Book Com-
pany, 1959); Pascal K. Whelpton, Arthur A. Campbell, and John E. Patterson,
Fertility and Family Planning in the United States (Princeton: Princeton Uni-
versity Press, 1966); Charles F. Westoff, Robert G. Potter, Jr., Philip C. Sagi, and
Eliot G. Mishler, *Family Growth in Metropolitan America* (Princeton: Prince-
ton University Press, 1961); Charles F. Westoff, Robert G. Potter, Jr., and Philip
C. Sagi, *The Third Child* (Princeton: Princeton University Press, 1963); David
Goldberg and Harry Sharp, "Some Characteristics of Detroit Area Jews and
Non-Jewish Adults," in *The Jews: Social Patterns of an American Group*, ed.
Marshall Sklare (New York: The Free Press, 1958), pp. 108–110.

[19] Freedman, Whelpton, and Campbell, *Family Planning*, pp. 608–610.

of contraception, were more likely to have used contraception, were most successful in planning the number and the spacing of all their children, and were most likely to use the most effective methods of birth control. The 1960 GAF study recorded similar patterns.[20] Although the findings of the 1965 National Fertility Study suggest some narrowing of differentials, the overall patterns generally remained the same.[21] Although focusing on a somewhat different population, and using a follow-up approach to their original sample rather than an independent cross section of the population in successive rounds of interviews, the Princeton Fertility Studies of 1960 and 1967 reached the same conclusions as those reported by GAF.[22]

In its 1957 sample population survey, the United States Bureau of the Census collected information on the number of children ever born. With this information, it is possible to calculate fertility rates expressed as the number of children ever born to women within specific age groups. Here, too, the results confirmed the lower fertility of Jews. The cumulative fertility rate of Jewish women 45 years of age and over was 2.2, compared to 3.1 for Catholic women and 2.8 for Protestant women. Lower fertility also characterized Jewish women at younger ages. Moreover, controlling for area of residence, the fertility rate for Jewish women in urban areas was 14 percent below that of urban women of all religions combined. Finally, the evidence available from over a dozen Jewish community studies points to similar lower Jewish fertility. In Providence, for example, there were 450 Jewish children under five years of age for every 1,000 women aged 20 to 44. This was significantly lower than the fertility ratio of the total population in the metropolitan area (620) or the total white urban American population (635). A similar differential characterized Springfield.

Low Jewish fertility is significant for Jewish population growth because the average number of children born is so close to the minimum number needed for replacement. Replacement level is generally cited as 2.1, taking into account that a small proportion of adults will never marry and a small percentage of those who do will not produce children. The importance of fertility is accentuated as the rate of inter-

[20] Whelpton, Campbell, and Patterson, *Fertility and Family Planning*, pp. 71–72, 247–252.
[21] Norman B. Ryder and Charles F. Westoff, *Reproduction in the United States—1965* (Princeton: Princeton University Press, 1971), p. 68.
[22] Westoff, Potter, and Sagi, *The Third Child*, p. 89.

marriage increases, contributing to possible losses in the population through both conversion of the Jewish partner away from Judaism and socialization of children of mixed marriages either in non-Jewish religions or in an entirely nonreligious environment.

Within the Jewish group itself, research, particularly on the Providence community, has shown considerable variations in birth levels among groups differing in religious identification (Orthodox, Conservative, Reform), social class, and generation status. The Providence data emphasized the importance of generation changes in the relation of social class to fertility. The data clearly indicate the trend toward convergence and greater homogeneity in the fertility patterns of socioeconomic groupings within the Jewish population with distance from the first generation. This contraction of socioeconomic differentials may be regarded as the result of the widespread rationality with which the majority of contemporary Jews plan their families, the absence of rapid upward mobility characteristic of earlier generations, and the greater homogeneity of the contemporary Jewish social structure.

Third generation American Jews are largely concentrated in the college-educated group and in high white collar occupations. The lack of wide social class distinctions may account for the absence of striking fertility differences within this segment of the Jewish population. It may thus be fortunate from the point of view of Jewish population growth that such a large proportion of the younger generation are concentrated in the higher education and higher socioeconomic groups. Reflecting a reversal in the older pattern of high fertility among the lower socioeconomic segments of the population, the fertility data from the Springfield survey show that it is the higher educated among the younger groups within the Jewish population who have the highest fertility levels.[23] Had the lower fertility characterizing the more educated segments of the Jewish population of earlier generations persisted and become dominant in the younger generations, the problem of demographic survival facing the Jewish community today would be accentuated. For the immediate future, all available evidence continues to point to inadequate birth levels among Jews, insuring little more than token growth. This being so, the total

23 Sidney Goldstein, "Completed and Expected Fertility in an American Jewish Community," *Jewish Social Studies*, vol. 33, nos. 2–3 (April–July 1971), pp. 212–227. Published by the Conference on Jewish Social Studies, New York.

Jewish population is not likely to increase rapidly beyond its present 6 million level.[24]

Marriage and the Family

The family, as one of the primary institutions of society, not only functions to reproduce and maintain the species, but acts as one of the major agents of socialization in the transmission of values, attitudes, goals, and aspirations. Any investigation concerned with the future of American Jewry must give some consideration to the composition, structure, and nature of the American Jewish family, particularly at a time when broader changes in society as a whole have had an important effect on family and marriage patterns.

The Jewish family is generally characterized as having strong ties, tightly knit kinship relations, and great stability. Yet, despite the importance Jews have traditionally attached to the family, few community surveys have given much consideration to it. Attention has generally been restricted to the percentage of individuals in the Jewish population who are married, widowed, or divorced. Only recently have surveys also focused on the type and size of the family unit, age of marriage, and frequency of marriage. Two sets of data are available for examination of demographic aspects of the Jewish family in America. The 1957 census survey contains a limited amount of information on marital patterns by religion. Additional insights into family and marriage patterns can be gained from selected community surveys, particularly that of Providence.

The 1957 census survey data confirm that Jews, compared to the general population, are more apt to marry at some point in their life cycle, to marry at a somewhat later age, and to have more stable marriages. These statistics show that 70 percent of the men 14 years and over in the total population were married, compared to 73 percent of the Jewish males. Concomitantly, lower proportions of Jewish men were widowed and divorced. The gross data, however, reflect the differential age structure of the Jewish and total male populations. Examination by specific age group is more revealing.

---

[24] For a fuller review of patterns and trends in Jewish fertility see Calvin Goldscheider, "Fertility of the Jews," *Demography*, 1967, no. 4, pp. 196–209; Calvin Goldscheider, "Trends in Jewish Fertility," *Sociology and Social Research*, 1966, pp. 173–186.

Among males aged 25 to 34, for example, only 17.9 percent of those in the total population were still single, as contrasted with 29.8 percent of the Jewish males, attesting to the later marriage age of Jewish men. By age 35 to 44, this differential disappeared and, in fact, was to some degree reversed. Among men aged 65 and over, 7 percent in the total population were still single, compared to only 4.8 percent of the Jewish men. Although these data are cross-sectional, they do indicate that by the end of the life cycle a somewhat higher proportion of Jewish men than of males in the general population were married, although in both cases the proportions reached over 90 percent.

The value of the census data is limited because it determines only marital status. Also important for an evaluation of the Jewish family are questions of stability of marriage, as judged by number of times persons have been married, changes in age at first marriage, and changes in household types.

The one fact emerging from the various community studies which collected information on marital status is the high proportion of the Jewish population that is married, usually three-fourths or more. Also, judging by those studies which present the percent married and ever-married by age group, almost all Jews (95 percent or more) marry at least once. Three other observations emerge from the data: (1) In the Jewish population, as in the general population, the proportion of widows is considerably higher than the proportion of widowers, reflecting the higher mortality rates of men. (2) The average Jewish male marries later in life than does the Jewish female. (3) The rate of remarriage is higher for widowers than for widows.[25]

The data collected in the Providence survey lend weight to the assumption that the high value placed by Jewish tradition on marriage and the family leads to both a high marriage rate for Jews and a greater stability of Jewish marriages.[26] In Greater Providence, among both males and females, a higher percentage of the Jewish population was married, while the percentages of separated and divorced persons were below those in the general population. The differential pattern generally persists even when age is controlled. Differences in the proportion divorced in the total and Jewish populations are affected by the extent of remarriage, as well as by the different age structures of the two populations. Attesting to the higher stability of Jewish mar-

---

[25] R. Goldstein, "American Jewish Population Studies Since World War II," p. 14.

[26] Goldstein and Goldscheider, *Jewish Americans*, pp. 103–104.

riages is the fact that the proportion of persons married more than once in the Jewish population was one-third lower than in the general population.

Several national studies have found that Jews marry at later ages than do either Protestants or Catholics.[27] The 1957 census survey found the median age at first marriage of Jewish women to be 21.3, compared to 19.9 for Protestants and 20.8 for Catholics. The Providence data also revealed such differentials. The average age of Jewish males at first marriage was 26, compared to 23 for the total population; Jewish women, on the average, were married at age 23, compared to age 20 for the total female population. Moreover, grouping women according to the date of their first marriage suggests that later age of marriage has characterized Jewish women since at least 1920. Age at first marriage has been declining since World War II, after having risen between the 1910 and the 1935–1939 marriage cohorts from 19 to 23. The decline in the average marriage age of Jewish women parallels a development in the general population, but the change has been greater for Jewish women, resulting in a narrowing of the differences in the average marriage age between women in the Jewish and the total populations. The pursuit of higher education has often been cited as a reason for delayed marriage among Jews. Although this is undoubtedly a factor, it may not be the only explanation, since the decline in the average age at marriage has taken place at a time when the proportion pursuing higher education has been reaching new peaks. Changes in general social and economic environment and the greater reliance of Jews on birth control, and its more efficient practice, may be factors in explaining the more rapid decline in the marriage age of Jews.

A related dimension of family structure is household composition, that is, whether the Jewish household contains only the immediate family of husband, wife, and children, or includes other relatives, such as grandparents. In Providence, the average size of Jewish households was 3.25 persons, similar to the average found in a number of recent Jewish community studies, most varying between 3.1 and 3.3. This reflects both the low level of fertility characterizing Jewish families and the great tendency for Jewish households to be organized as

[27] Ronald Freedman, Pascal K. Whelpton, and John W. Smit, "Socio-Economic Factors in Religious Differentials in Fertility," *American Sociological Review*, August 1961, p. 610; Whelpton, Campbell, and Patterson, *Fertility and Family Planning*, p. 321.

nuclear rather than extended household units. In Greater Providence, 85 percent of all households consisted only of the immediate family of husband, wife, and children. Only 8 percent included other relatives. An equal proportion were one person units, but almost all of these were concentrated in the older age groups. That the trend is clearly in the direction of nuclear households is evidenced by the generational differences in the percentage of nuclear household units, which rose from 85 percent of households headed by a first generation person, to 97 percent headed by a third generation individual. Part of the difference stems from the different age composition of the generations, but even when age is held constant, the increase in nuclear households among third generation Jews remains.

In organizing their families in nuclear units, Jews are conforming to the pattern characterizing families in the United States as a whole. Such a development is consistent with the trend toward greater geographical separation of childrens' from parents' residences. This has significant implications for the strength of Jewish identification as it is reinforced through the extended family unit. It also has a number of immediate and practical implications for the burdens that the community may be asked to assume as nuclear families break up through the death of a spouse, leaving single individuals who will not be absorbed into the household units of children or other relatives. Coupled with the trend toward an aging population, the predominance of the nuclear family among Jews takes on added significance.

Intermarriage

Increasing concern with the demographic growth and survival of the Jewish population in the United States is based not only on the low fertility of the Jews; low growth rates or actual decline can also result from excessive losses to the majority group through assimilation. A constant threat, not only to the maintenance of Jewish identification but also to the demographic maintenance of the Jewish population, is interfaith marriage. If marital assimilation takes place at a high rate, the Jewish group faces demographic losses through the assimilation of the Jewish partner to the marriage and the loss of children born to such a marriage. In recent years, concern with the "vanishing American Jew" has reached considerable proportions as a variety of evidence has suggested an increasing rate of intermarriage. In the face of earlier evidence that the Jewish group had been remarkably successful, compared to other groups, in maintaining religious endogamy, the disquiet caused by this new evidence is understandable.[28] It has generated considerable research in Jewish community surveys on the extent of intermarriage, both as an indication of the possible impact of intermarriage on Jewish demographic survival and as an index of the extent of group conformity, loyalty, and cohesiveness among Jews.

No definite assessment of the level and character of Jewish intermarriage and of changes over time can be made without a considerably better body of data than is currently available. Although statistics on rates of intermarriage are available from a number of community surveys, the quality of the data varies; their use must be preceded by careful attention to the type of community studied, the comprehensiveness of the study's population coverage, and the way intermarriage was measured. The rate of intermarriage tends to be considerably higher in areas where Jews constitute a smaller percentage of the population. The rate of intermarriage is also higher if the data are based on a study in which both Jewish and non-Jewish households in the community are surveyed, since such surveys are most apt to find families on the fringes of the Jewish community. Finally, care must be given to the manner in which intermarriage itself is measured. Studies relying exclusively on the current religious identification of marriage partners run the risk of undercounting intermarriages, since those partners to a mixed marriage who changed their religion in conjunction with the marriage would not be identified as having intermarried.

There is general agreement that the rate of Jewish intermarriage has increased, but because of the lack of data by which to measure trends, as well as serious questions about the quality of available statistics, the extent of the increase has not been clearly determined. A study of intermarriage in New Haven, Connecticut, for example, showed that Jewish intermarriages increased from zero in 1870 to 5.1 percent in 1950,[29] but New Haven is one of the very few communities where statistics are available over such a long period of time. Most other statements concerning increased rates of intermarriage are

[28] Milton M. Gordon, *Assimilation in American Life* (New York: Oxford University Press, Inc., 1964), pp. 181–182.

[29] Ruby Jo Reeves Kennedy, "What Has Social Science to Say About Intermarriage?" in *Intermarriage and Jewish Life*, ed. Werner J. Cahnman (New York: Herzl Press, 1963), p. 29.

based on general comparisons of the current levels of intermarriage in various communities with those in a different set of communities at an earlier time.

For example, in a series of communities cited by Nathan Goldberg, where surveys were taken during the 1930s, the rates of intermarriage generally ranged between 5 and 9 percent.[30] These included such communities as Stamford and New London, Connecticut; and Dallas and San Francisco. But during the same period, Duluth, Minnesota, showed an intermarriage rate of 17.7 percent. A number of communities surveyed in the late 1950s and 1960s also showed levels of intermarriage between 5 and 10 percent: Camden, New Jersey; Rochester, New York; Los Angeles, California; Jacksonville, Florida; Long Beach, California; and San Francisco, California. Judging by the similarity between these levels and those noted for a number of communities in the 1930s, one could conclude that there has been no significant rise in the level of intermarriage. Also, in the March 1957 nationwide sample survey, the United States Census found that 3.8 percent of married persons reporting themselves as Jews were married to non-Jews, and that 7.2 percent of all marriages in which at least one partner was Jewish were intermarriages; both of these figures are probably somewhat low, since no information was collected on the earlier religion of the marriage partners. Couples with one converted spouse were therefore not enumerated as mixed marriages. However, in the late 1950s and the 1960s, other estimates of the rate of Jewish intermarriages based on local studies ranged as high as from 18.4 percent for New York City to 37 percent for Marin, California and 53.6 percent for Iowa.[31] Judging from these latter studies, recent intermarriage rates were higher, but the typicality of these high rates remains questionable.

Other data used to document the rising trend in intermarriage are those comparing differentials among either the various age segments or the various generation levels of the population in a given community. An analysis of this kind by Erich Rosenthal for the Jewish popu-

[30] Nathan Goldberg, "The Jewish Population in the United States," in *The Jewish People, Past and Present* (New York: Jewish Encyclopedic Handbooks, Central Yiddish Culture Organization, 1948) vol. 2, p. 29.

[31] New York data are taken from Jerold S. Heiss, "Premarital Characteristics of the Religiously Intermarried in an Urban Area," *American Sociological Review*, 1960, pp. 47–55. Iowa data were analyzed by Erich Rosenthal, "Studies of Jewish Intermarriage in the United States," *American Jewish Year Book*, 1963, vol. 64, pp. 34–51.

lation of Washington, D. C., in 1956 found that rate of intermarriage was directly related to distance from the immigrant generation.[32] Whereas the mixed marriage rate was 11.3 percent for the total Jewish population, it increased from 1.4 percent among foreign-born husbands to 10.2 percent among native-born husbands of foreign parentage, up to 17.9 percent of native-born husbands of native parentage. Questions have been raised, however, about the typicality of the Jewish community of Washington, and whether findings based on it can be generalized to more stable communities.

Rosenthal's more recent research on Indiana, using marriage records and covering the years 1960 to 1963, cites an extraordinarily high rate of intermarriage, 48.8 percent of all marriages occurring in that period.[33] The data indicate that intermarriage increases as the size of the Jewish community decreases. In Marion County, containing Indianapolis, the intermarriage rate was 34.5 percent; in counties with very small Jewish populations it rose to 54 percent. Rosenthal suggests that "the larger the Jewish community, the easier it is to organize communal activities, to effect the voluntary concentration of Jewish families in specific residential neighborhoods, and to maintain an organized marriage market.[34] The key variable is the number of potential marital partners. Although the Indiana situation cannot be considered typical of United States Jewry, the high rates in themselves are alarming. They do confirm the much greater probability that intermarriage will occur in those regions and communities where the Jewish population is of inadequate size to encourage and permit high levels of in-marriage.

In assessing our current knowledge of intermarriage, it must be recognized that several important areas of research concerning marriages between Jews and non-Jews have been largely neglected. Not all cases of intermarriage necessarily lead to loss of the Jewish partner. Conversion of the non-Jew to Judaism may actually add to the Jewish population, and also increase the likelihood that the children of such a marriage will be raised as Jews.[35] In order to ascertain the extent to which this happens, surveys focusing on intermarriage must obtain information on the extent of conversion, as well as on the religion in

---

[32] Rosenthal, "Studies of Jewish Intermarriage."

[33] Erich Rosenthal, "Jewish Intermarriage in Indiana," *American Jewish Year Book*, 1967, vol. 68, p. 263.

[34] Ibid., pp. 263–264.

[35] Marshall Sklare, "Intermarriage and Jewish Survival," *Commentary*, March 1970, pp. 51–58.

which the children of mixed marriages are raised. Both the Providence and Springfield surveys collected such information. Although these are limited by their reliance on master lists, steps were taken to insure maximum opportunity for inclusion of all Jewish households. While no claim is made that the resulting statistics have identified all intermarriages, the findings probably do not depart excessively from the real level of intermarriage. This probability, coupled with the opportunity provided by these data for examining both extent of conversion and extent to which children of mixed marriages are raised as Jews, argues in favor of their brief examination here.

The Providence survey identified 4.5 percent of all marriages as intermarriages, that is, a marriage in which one of the spouses was not Jewish by birth. In the vast majority of these cases, the husband was Jewish and the wife non-Jewish by birth. Only 0.1 percent represented the Jewish wife whose husband was born non-Jewish. This pattern of sex differentials, in which more Jewish men than women marry non-Jewish partners, is typical of almost all communities for which data were collected. Compared to the statistics cited for Washington, San Francisco, and Indiana, the intermarriage level in Providence was quite low. Yet it was not atypical, being comparable to levels of intermarriage noted for Rochester, Camden, Springfield, Los Angeles, and New Haven. Since these communities do vary in both size and location, no obvious common denominator helps explain their similar levels of intermarriage.

Of all the intermarried couples, 42 percent had experienced the conversion of one partner to Judaism, thereby creating religious homogeneity within the family unit. The survey could not fully ascertain the number of Jewish partners to a mixed marriage who converted away from Judaism. But the survey data do suggest that, in a considerable proportion of intermarriages, conversion to Judaism does occur, thereby enhancing the chances that the family unit will remain identified as Jewish, and that the children will be raised as members of the Jewish community.

For Providence, as for Washington, insights into the trend in level of intermarriage can be gained only by cross-sectional comparison of the intermarriage patterns of different age and generation groups within the population. With the exception of the 30 to 39 year age group, the Providence data pointed to an increase in the rate of intermarriage among the younger segments of the population; the highest percent intermarried (9 percent) characterized the youngest group.

On the other hand, the proportion of persons who converted to Judaism consistently increased with decreasing age, from none of the non-Jewish spouses in the 60 and over age group, to 4 out of 10 among those aged 40 to 59, to 7 out of 10 among those under age 40. This clear-cut pattern is consistent with a conclusion reached by Gerhard Lenski, based on a Detroit study, that the probability of mixed marriages leading to a conversion is considerably greater among younger persons.[36]

Like the Washington studies, the Providence data indicate that generation status affects the rate of intermarriage; however, they also show that it affects the extent of conversion. Among the foreign born, only 1.2 percent were reported intermarried. Among third generation Americans, this proportion was almost 6 percent. Moreover, the pattern of differentials by generation status operated within the respective age groups. Only one-fourth of the mixed marriages of the foreign born resulted in a conversion of the non-Jewish spouse, compared to over half of the intermarriages involving third generation males. This pattern of generational differences remains even when age is held constant. While confirming that the rate of intermarriage has risen among third generation, compared to first generation, Jews, the Providence levels are well below those observed for Washington, D. C. The Providence data also show a higher rate of conversion of the non-Jewish spouse to Judaism among the third, compared to the first, generation.

Comparisons of levels of intermarriage among the children of the heads of households surveyed in the Providence study support the higher rates for younger segments of the population. Whereas the intermarriage rate of Jews in the survey was 4.5 percent, that among the children of these households was 5.9 percent. Since the children enumerated here included those living outside Greater Providence, the higher rate may reflect not only their younger age but also a tendency for persons who intermarry to move away from their family's community. Although this may partially represent an attempt at anonymity, it is more likely related to the fact that the children were already living away from home and from parental control, thus enhancing the possibility of courting and marrying non-Jews. Most likely presenting a more correct image of the sex differential in levels of

---

[36] Gerhard Lenski, *The Religious Factor* (Garden City, New York: Doubleday & Company, Inc., 1963), pp. 54–55.

intermarriage, the data for the children of the survey units indicate that almost 8 percent of the male children intermarried, compared to only 4 percent of the females.

The Providence data were also used in an attempt to assess the effect of intermarriage on fertility levels.[37] Comparison of the fertility of the intermarried with that of the nonintermarried shows that both for women 45 years old and older, who had completed their fertility, and for those under 45 years of age, who may still have additional children, intermarried couples had lower fertility than the nonintermarried. Intermarried couples had a lower average number of children ever born, a much higher percentage of childlessness, and a lower percentage of families with four or more children. Intermarriage clearly resulted in lowered fertility, but the differences were not as great among the younger women in the population as among the older, suggesting that whatever factor served earlier to restrict the fertility of intermarried couples operated to a lesser degree for the younger couples.

Finally, the Providence survey ascertained the religious identification of all children in households of intermarried couples. Of the 280 children in this category, 136 were children of couples in which the non-Jewish spouse had converted to Judaism and were therefore being raised as Jews. Of the 144 children belonging to families in which the non-Jewish spouse had not converted, 84 children were being raised as Jews and 60 as non-Jews. The fact that only 22 percent of the 280 children of intermarriages were being raised as non-Jews is in strong contrast to the findings of the Washington survey that 70 percent of the children of mixed marriages were being raised as non-Jews. Too few studies have explored this relationship, and more research is essential to obtain meaningful data on a national level.

The Springfield survey collected data comparable to that of Providence, and its findings, including an overall intermarriage rate of 4.4 percent, are so similar that presentation of the detailed results would be repetitious. Finally, mention must be made of the Boston survey of 1965 because of its comprehensive coverage of the population and because it represents a Jewish community of about 200,000 persons. This survey found that 7 percent of the marriages represented intermarriages. Although higher than the level noted for Providence and Springfield, this percentage is still markedly below the high levels

---

[37] Goldstein and Goldscheider, *Jewish Americans*, pp. 166–169.

noted in some other communities. However, the Boston data do suggest a sharp rise in level of intermarriage among the very youngest segment of the population. Intermarriage characterized only 3 percent of the couples in which the age of the husband was 51 and over, and only 7 percent of those with the husband between ages 31 and 50; but 20 percent of the couples in which the husband was 30 years old or younger were intermarried. Regretfully, the Boston study did not report how many of the intermarried persons had converted, or in what religion the children of such marriages were being raised.

Another recent investigation of intermarriage, by Fred Sherrow, based its findings on data collected from 1964 follow-up interviews of a national sample survey of 1961 college graduates.[38] The study thus refers to a young population. By 1964, 57 percent of the Jewish respondents had married. Of these, between 10 and 12 percent married non-Jews by birth. The data further show conversion by the non-Jewish spouse to Judaism at a rate of less than 20 percent. This rate is considerably below that found in a number of Jewish community studies, but in the absence of comparable data for older cohorts of college graduates, it is not possible to determine whether conversion is increasing among the young. Sherrow suggests that the low rate of conversion he identified may reflect a weakening of the proscription against intermarriage. In addition, the data reveal that 55 percent of the Jews who intermarried retained their Jewish identification. Combining this retention rate with the gains from conversion to Judaism indicates an estimated overall net loss of 30 percent of the population involved in intermarriages. This information seemed to justify the conclusion that the rates are not yet high enough to signal the imminent dissolution of the American Jewish community through intermarriage.

What is the overall picture that emerges? No simple answer seems possible. A heterogeneous pattern characterizes the United States, depending on the size, location, age, and social cohesiveness of the particular community. Yet within these variations in level of intermarriage, analysis of the data in terms of age and generation status does suggest that the intermarriage rate is increasing among young, native-born Americans. Eventually, intermarriage rates in the United States may reach a plateau around which the experience of individual com-

[38] Reported in Arnold Schwartz, "Intermarriage in the United States," *American Jewish Year Book*, 1970, vol. 71, pp. 101–121.

munities will fluctuate. But for the immediate future, the overall rate of intermarriage is likely to rise further, as an increasing proportion of the population becomes third generation Americans and moves away from older areas of dense Jewish population to newly developed, more integrated areas within both the cities and suburbs, and to more distant communities with fewer Jews and less organized Jewish life. At the same time, the data for several communities suggest that although the rate of intermarriage may be increasing among the third generation, a high proportion of these intermarriages result in conversion of the non-Jewish spouse to Judaism; the rate of conversions is higher among the groups having a higher intermarriage rate. Moreover, a significant proportion of children in such marriages are being raised as Jews. Finally, the fertility rates of the younger intermarried and nonintermarried couples more closely resemble each other than they do in the older age groups. These changes suggest that the net effects of intermarriage on the overall size of the Jewish population may not yet be as serious demographically as suggested by several Jewish community studies. What their effect is on Jewish identification and religiosity is beyond the scope of this evaluation. There can be little doubt that the problem of intermarriage warrants considerable concern on both policy and research levels, but, from a demographic point of view, there is also much need to focus on questions of Jewish fertility and Jewish population redistribution.

Population Distribution

In considering the future of the American Jewish population, attention must be given to its geographical distribution among the various regions of the United States, as well as within the large metropolitan areas where so many of the country's Jews live. That New York City and the Northeastern region contain the greater part of the Jewish population of the United States is well known. Yet this concentration has not always been as great as in recent decades, nor is it likely to remain so.

The 1900 *American Jewish Year Book* estimates indicate that, at that time, 57 percent of American Jewry lived in the Northeast, in contrast to only 28 percent of the total American population;[39] virtu-

---

[39] "Jewish Statistics," *American Jewish Year Book*, 1899–1900, vol. 1, p. 283.

ally all these Jews were in New York, Pennsylvania, and New Jersey, with New York alone accounting for about 40 percent of the national total. The North Central region accounted for the next largest number of Jews—about one-fourth—with most concentrated in Illinois, Ohio, Indiana, Wisconsin, and Michigan. By contrast, one-third of the total United States population lived in this region in 1900. Compared to the general population, Jews were also underrepresented in the South, where 14 percent were located, largely in Maryland. Florida at that time had only 3,000 Jews. The proportion of Jews in the West in 1900 was identical to that of the general population, just over 5 percent.

The decades following 1900 saw continued mass immigration from Eastern Europe, resulting in a fourfold increase of Jewish population between 1900 and 1930. Reflecting the tendency of the immigrants to concentrate in the large cities of the Northeast, especially New York, considerable change occurred in the regional distribution of the American Jewish population. The *American Jewish Year Book* estimates for 1927 place over two-thirds of the Jewish population in the Northeastern region, with 60 percent in New York, New Jersey, and Pennsylvania;[40] New York State alone accounted for 45 percent of the Jews in the United States. This considerable increase in the number of Jews in the Northeast, from 57 percent in 1900 to 68 percent in 1927, contrasts with the stability of the American population as a whole; both the 1900 and 1930 censuses found 28 percent of all Americans living in the Northeast. The percentage of Jews living in each of the other regions declined. In 1927 only one in five lived in the North Central region, only 8 percent in the South, and just under 5 percent in the West. As a result, the overall differential between the distribution patterns of the Jewish and the total population increased. The sharpest changes were in the South and West. The South's share of the total Jewish population declined from 14 to 8 percent, while it continued to account for about 30 percent of the total population. The West increased its share of the total population from 5 to 10 percent in these 30 years, but its Jewish population declined from 5.5 to 4.6 percent of the national total.

For the United States population as a whole, the period between 1930 and the present showed a continuous westward shift. The pro-

---

[40] H. S. Linfield, "Statistics of Jews," *American Jewish Year Book*, 1931–1932, vol. 33, p. 276.

portion of Americans living in the Western region had increased to 17 percent by 1968, and both the Northeastern and North Central regions accounted for smaller proportions of the total American population than they did in 1930. The South's share increased a little, but this was attributable to the greater population concentration in the South Atlantic states, particularly Florida.

With the cutoff in large-scale immigration, changes in distribution of the Jewish population of the United States in the period between 1930 and 1968 became largely a function of their geographic mobility. These changes were considerable; in fact, Jewish redistribution represented to a somewhat accentuated degree the general redistribution of the population as a whole. For example, between 1930 and 1968, the proportion of all American Jews living in the Western region increased from under 5 to 13 percent. Similarly, the proportion of Jews living in the South increased from under 8 percent of the total to 10 percent. By contrast, the proportion living in the North Central region declined from one out of five in 1927 to only 12 percent in 1968. By 1968 the Northeastern region, including both New England and the Middle Atlantic states, although containing almost two-thirds of all American Jews, had a smaller proportion of the total American Jewish population than it did in 1930.

This decline in the proportion living in the Northeast may be indicative of developments that will become more accentuated in the future: (1) as Jews increasingly enter occupations whose nature requires mobility because of the limited opportunities available in particular areas; (2) as family ties become less important for third generation Jews than they had been for the first and second generation; (3) as more Jews no longer feel it necessary to live in areas of high Jewish concentration. In short, the available data suggest the beginning of a trend toward the wider dispersal of Jews throughout the United States.

Assuming that such a pattern develops, the Jewish population in the future will not only be an increasingly smaller proportion of the total American population, but it will also be increasingly less concentrated in the Northeastern part of the United States. In an ecological sense, therefore, the population will become more truly an American population, with all this implies regarding opportunities for greater assimilation and less numerical visibility. Although this may be a trend of the future, it must be emphasized that the Northeast, and New York in particular, will remain a large and dynamic center of American Jewry. At the same time, its population will probably grow increasingly older as more and more of the younger Jews leave this section of the country to become part of the mainstream of American life through the process of geographic mobility.

Urban-Rural Residence

Closely related to the concentration of Jews in the Northeast is their distribution between urban and rural places of residence. Jews in the United States are unique in their exceptionally high concentration in urban places, particularly in very large ones. The best source of information for this, the 1957 Bureau of the Census survey, found that 96 percent of the Jewish population 14 years old and over lived in urban places, compared to only 64 percent of the total American population. Moreover, 87 percent of all Jews in the United States 14 years old and over lived in large urbanized areas of 250,000 or greater population, in contrast to only one out of every three persons in the general population. The high concentration of Jews in New York City is, of course, a major factor in this differential.

The census data also show that under 4 percent of American Jewry live in rural places, and almost all of these in nonfarm residences. The reasons for the heavy concentration in large urban places are well known and require no discussion here. However, it is noteworthy that, though Jews constituted only 3 percent of the total American population, they comprised almost 8 percent of the total urban population; in all other types of residence Jews accounted for 1 percent or less of the total. In this respect, the experience of the Jews may foreshadow that of the total population, for one of the major demographic and ecological developments in the United States over the last several decades has been the increasing concentration of the American population in metropolitan areas. As this trend continues, the proportion of Jews in the metropolitan population will decline as more of the total American population comes to live in such areas. Since the American Jewish population is so highly concentrated in major metropolitan areas, a key focus must be on what is happening to the population within such areas.

Suburbanization

There is a considerable sociological literature on the Jewish ghetto in the United States.[41] Yet, from a demographic point of view, there are few reliable statistics for documenting either the character of the ghettos into which the immigrant populations moved or for measuring the speed with which such ghettos broke down. For only a limited number of cities have there been demographic studies of the Jews of either adequate historical depth or sufficient comparability over time to permit such documentation. In very few communities has more than one population survey of the Jewish community been undertaken, so that opportunities of measuring trends in residential patterns are quite limited. Yet, given the high concentration of Jews in urban areas and the fact that they tended to live in a segregated fashion, an analysis of the distribution of the Jewish population must take note of this situation and attempt to suggest the future pattern of development.

The pattern of Jewish settlement in large cities by no means remains stable. Radical shifts in distribution are clearly evident, for example, from estimates of the Jewish population in New York City in 1930 and 1957, and a projection for 1975.[42] Although the New York data are only crude estimates, they do point to the pattern of development in the single largest American Jewish community, and therefore have social significance.

By 1930 the large area of Jewish population density on the lower East Side had already passed its peak; only 16 percent of New York City's Jews lived in all of Manhattan. By contrast, one-third lived in the Bronx and almost one-half in Brooklyn; less than 5 percent of the total Jewish population of New York City lived in Queens. Within one generation, a sharp redistribution occurred. In 1957 only one in four Jews in the city lived in the Bronx, whereas Queens now accounted for one in five. Manhattan continued as the residence of 16 percent of

[41] See, for example, Louis Wirth, *The Ghetto* (Chicago: University of Chicago Press, 1928); Peter I. Rose, ed., *The Ghetto and Beyond* (New York: Random House, Inc., 1969).

[42] C. Morris Horowitz and Lawrence J. Kaplan, *The Jewish Population of the New York Area, 1900–1975* (New York: Federation of Jewish Philanthropies of New York, 1959).

New York City's Jews, but the proportion living in Brooklyn had decreased. While the projections for 1975 must be taken as very tentative, they indicate a continuation of the trends already observed for the 1930–1957 period: relatively fewer Jews living in the Bronx and Brooklyn, and more in Queens.

What these data do not show is the considerable development of Jewish communities in the suburban sectors of the New York metropolitan area. Although data for the larger area are restricted, both in the area covered and in the method of estimates, they do, in a crude way, point to the nature of developments. According to the statistics, the total Jewish population in 1957 in the New York area, including both the city and adjoining Nassau, Suffolk, and Westchester Counties, numbered 2,580,000 persons, of whom 81.9 percent lived in the city proper.[43] While the number of Jews in the city between 1957 and 1975 is estimated to remain relatively stable at 2.1 million persons, it is expected to grow for the total area from 2.58 million to 2.72 million. Thus, the proportion of Jews living in the suburbs will increase from 18.1 percent in 1957 to 21.5 percent in 1975. The New Jersey and Connecticut segments of New York's suburbs are not included here; if they were, much sharper changes would doubtless be noted.

Even more dramatic changes occurred in the distribution of the Jewish population of Chicago. In 1931, 47.6 percent of Chicago's Jews were concentrated on the West Side. According to 1958 estimates, only 5.5 percent remained in that area of the city, a decline from an estimated 131,000 to 12,000 persons. By contrast, the North Side of Chicago had increased its Jewish population from 56,000 persons in 1931 to 127,000 in 1958, or from 20 to 57.7 percent of the total. In 1958 an estimated 62,000 of the Chicago area's 282,000 Jews were living in the suburbs.

A somewhat similar picture emerges from a comparison of the 1949 and 1959 residential patterns in Detroit. In 1949 Dexter, the largest single area of residence, accounted for almost half of the Detroit area's total Jewish population; the second largest was the North West, accounting for one-fourth. In 1949 no Jews lived in the suburban Oak Park and Huntington Woods sections. By 1959, 18 percent of the Detroit area's total Jewish population had moved to the suburbs. The old center of Dexter was virtually abandoned as an area of Jewish settlement, with only 10 percent of all Detroit Jews remaining. It was

[43] Ibid.

replaced as a leading center of residence by the North West, with 50 percent of the total. In fact, by that time research had identified a new residential area, the New Suburbs, which extended beyond the older suburban areas; 3 percent of the Jewish population already lived there, and future growth was expected. Overall, the Detroit area data point to a pattern common to many of the metropolitan areas with Jewish communities. The total geographic area in which Jews live has become much larger. Their dispersion within that larger area has increased considerably, yet distinct areas of Jewish concentration remain identifiable; even as the older areas disappear, newer concentrations are emerging. The resultant strain on Jewish institutions represents a major adjustment problem which many Jewish communities must face as they undergo significant population redistribution.

In a recent investigation, Serge Carlos analyzed the influence of the urban and suburban milieus on religious practices.[44] Although his study focuses on Catholics, it may have some significance for religious behavior in general. Carlos found that the level of church attendance increases as people move from the central area of the city to the periphery. He interprets this pattern as an effect of the need for community identification and integration, both largely missing in suburban communities. At the same time he notes that the higher rates of suburban church attendance represent mainly nominal religious participation, with the result that the proportion of churchgoers who engage in devotional religious practices is lower in the suburban areas.

As a reflection of the older age structure of the Jewish population living within central cities, as well as the higher proportion of Orthodox and Conservative, one would expect a higher degree of devotional religious practice in urban than in suburban places of residence. Indeed, research on Greater Providence, where an attempt was made to measure residential differences in religious assimilation, suggests a pattern of greater assimilation for suburban residents.[45] They have higher intermarriage rates, lower scores on indices of ritual observance, higher rates of nonaffiliation, and higher proportions with no Jewish education. These appear even after controlling for generation status, suggesting both that migration to the suburbs may be selective of those not eager to maintain as strong a Jewish identity as those in

---

[44] Serge Carlos, "Religious Participation and the Urban-Suburban Continuum," *American Journal of Sociology,* March 1970, pp. 742–759.

[45] Goldstein and Goldscheider, *Jewish Americans,* pp. 161–163, 181–183, 190–191, 208–210, 241–242.

the cities, and that the greater residential dispersion of Jews within the suburbs removes the reinforcement of traditional patterns formerly provided by the older, more densely populated urban areas. Despite this weakening, a high percentage of suburban Jews continue to identify as Jews and to follow selected religious practices. In short, residential differences exist, but they are not so sharp as to lead to the conclusion that suburbanization itself will cause high rates of assimilation. Similar changes in identification and practice are also occurring in the older urban areas as the generation composition of their population changes.

Jewish communities in the United States vary considerably in their patterns of residential distribution. We have inadequate information on why, despite redistribution, some communities in both suburbs and central cities continue to maintain areas of considerably higher Jewish concentration. Little is known about the extent to which, or way in which, high density of settlement substitutes, as it seems to do in the New York area, for high levels of organizational affiliation and participation as the mechanism for Jewish identification. Research in depth, like that undertaken by Carlos, is needed to ascertain how the communal orientation of Jews living in the cities and in suburbs of differing Jewish density varies, and what meaning the various activities have for the individuals, particularly as they relate to the larger question of Jewish identification and survival.

Migration

Among the demographic concerns which have received the least attention in research on the American Jewish population is the extent and character of Jewish migration within the United States. National data are essential for such an analysis, but to my knowledge, no such data exist. Even the March 1957 census survey provided no information on migration patterns. On a national level, therefore, only indirect insights into the migration of Jews can be obtained, through examination of available statistics on the changing distribution of the Jewish population among various regions of the country. These were examined earlier. More direct insights on the role of migration in Jewish population redistribution come from local Jewish community surveys. Questions on date of movement into the state, city, and house of residence at the time of the survey, and place of residence before the last move, permit determination of the redistribution of population in the area under investigation and of the role of in-migration in the growth of the total area's Jewish population. Losses through out-migration are more difficult to identify, since most local surveys restrict themselves to current residents. However, limited insights into out-migration can be obtained from questions on residence of children of heads of household in the survey sample. Insights into possible future movement are possible through questions on plans to move within the next one to five years and the anticipated destination.

The importance of migration in the future development and growth of the American Jewish community has been seriously underrated. Data on both the national regional distribution of population and the increasing suburbanization of the Jews suggest that population mobility is a major development in the United States, and may have significant impact on the vitality of the local Jewish community. As indicated before, more widespread distribution within the metropolitan area will have an impact on rates of intermarriage, the degree of integration of Jews into the local community, the ease with which Jewish identity can be maintained, and the strength of Jewish institutions themselves, as the population they serve becomes more dispersed. The national scene may also be seeing a higher rate of redistribution as Jews, in increasing numbers, enter the salaried professional and executive world and transfer to branch firms located in places where large Jewish communities do not exist. Moreover, the repeated movement associated with such occupations may well be a new phenomenon on the American Jewish scene that may lead to less stable family and communal ties.

What does the evidence available from local Jewish community surveys indicate? The 1963 Detroit study, which ascertained the place of birth of the resident population, found that only one-third of the total Jewish population of Detroit was born in that city; another 28 percent were foreign-born; 36 percent had come to Detroit from other places in the United States, a little over half of these from other cities or towns in Michigan, and the rest from other states. A somewhat similar picture emerges from comparable statistics on Camden, New Jersey, where one-third of the residents were born in the Camden area, and almost 60 percent had moved there from other places in the United States; a small percentage were foreign-born. Using the state as a unit, the Providence study found that 60 percent of all Jews living in Greater Providence were born in Rhode Island. Of the 40 percent born elsewhere, 16 percent were foreign-born and the remaining 24 percent were equally divided between natives of New England and of other states. Virtually identical patterns emerged for Springfield, Massachusetts. Comparison of the mobility of Jews with that of the general population is best achieved by examining the proportion of the native born who were living in their state of birth. For Greater Providence, 76 percent of the general population, compared to 72 percent of the American-born Jews, were born in Rhode Island. Judged by state of birth, therefore, the Jewish population closely resembles the total population in its migration level. It also resembles the general pattern, in that most of the movement of native-born Jews to the state is from nearby areas.

Mobility can also be judged by length of residence in the area. The Milwaukee study, for example, found that 60 percent of the city's Jews had been living at their current address for less than 10 years, and 40 percent for less than 5 years. These data suggest a higher degree of residential mobility among Jews, although they do not specify whether it took the form of intra-urban mobility or migration across larger distances. The recent Boston study also suggests a high degree of mobility. Half the population had lived at their present address for under 10 years, and 31 percent for 5 years or less. These percentages varied considerably by age. Among those 21 to 29 years of age, 70 percent were at their present addresses for less than 5 years; by contrast, at the other end of the age hierarchy, only 10 percent of those 60 to 69 years old were living in their present homes under 5 years. Further reflecting the higher mobility of Boston's Jews is the finding that 34 percent intended to move within the next two years. Thus a high turnover is indicated both by the recency of the in-move and by the high percentage intending to move in the near future. A large proportion of the intended mobility is within the Boston metropolitan area itself, and the projected patterns indicate a heavy movement to the newer suburban areas. At the same time, the decline of the older areas in Boston is underscored by the low percentage of persons moving into them, and the high percentage of those still living there who indicated an intention to move out. For example, less than 25 percent of those living in Central Boston came in the last five years, but 42 percent planned to move out during the next two years. In contrast, of the population living in the south suburbs, 32 percent moved in within the last five years, and only 12 percent indicated an intention to move out within the next two.

Migration and population redistribution are important for the development of an area. They affect not only its size, but also the characteristics of its residents if they are selective of age, education, occupation, and income groups. At the same time, migration may have an important effect on the migrant himself, particularly on the degree of his integration into the community. A large turnover of population may also have a significant impact on community institutions. To the extent that community ties within the Jewish population are expressed through membership in temples, enrollment of children in educational programs, participation in local organizations, and philanthropic activities, a high degree of population movement may either disrupt such patterns of participation or weaken the loyalties they generate. More seriously, they may result in the failure of families and individuals to identify with organized life in the local community. Sociological research has suggested, for example, that recent migrants to a community are much less active in its formal structure than are longtime residents.[46] Although their participation eventually increases, the adjustment has been shown to take at least five years, and sometimes migrants never reach the same level of participation as persons who grew up in the community. Obviously, if a significant proportion of in-migrants know in advance that their residence in the community is not likely to be permanent, tendencies toward lower rates of participation and affiliation may be even stronger.

We have minimum historical evidence to document whether the level of mobility of the Jewish population is increasing. Available data, both on mobility and on changes in the educational level of Jews and the types of occupations they are entering, suggest that one of the major changes taking place in the American Jewish community is an increasing rate of population movement. For example, some recent statistics from Toledo, Ohio, indicate that one-fifth of the city's Jews move each year. The study reports that national chain operations have brought to Toledo a surprisingly large number of Jewish men in managerial positions, and that the university had a substantial increase in the number of Jewish faculty. At the same time, the study reported

[46] Basil Zimmer, "Participation of Migrants in Urban Structures," *American Sociological Review*, April 1955, pp. 218–224.

that 45 to 60 percent of young Jews raised in Toledo find permanent residence in distant cities after graduation from college. This pattern is likely to be more typical of the general American scene, resulting not only in the increasing migration of Jews within the United States, but also in an increasingly higher rate of repeated movement by the same persons. We know from general migration studies that higher than average mobility rates have always characterized professionals and highly educated individuals because of the more limited demands for their talents in particular localities. Also, as Toledo shows, in recent years many national firms have adopted a company policy of repeated relocation of their executives and professionals to their different branches. As the proportion of Jews holding such positions increases, the rate of Jewish population mobility is likely to increase.

As Glazer and Moynihan observed: "The son wants the business to be bigger and better and perhaps he would rather be a cog in a great corporation than the manager of a small one. He may not enjoy the tight Jewish community with its limited horizons and its special satisfactions—he is not that much of a Jew any more."[47] In short, they suggest that status may be the drawing force of third generation Americans, as financial success was the major consideration of second generation Americans. Finally, as discriminatory practices diminish and executive positions formerly closed to Jews open up, this too will be conducive to the greater geographic dispersal of Jews willing to develop occupational careers outside the communities where they grew up.

From all we know, it would seem that the American Jewish community is becoming increasingly mobile; such mobility must be taken into account in any evaluation of Jewish life in the United States. Mobility is not a new facet of Jewish life. But whereas at a number of points in Jewish history it may have served to strengthen the Jewish community and insure its very survival, there is serious question whether this is generally true of increased internal migration. Such mobility may still serve a positive function in a given situation. Small Jewish communities may benefit considerably from the influx of other Jews who are attracted by nearby universities or modern, technological industries. Such in-migration may be crucial in creating the critical mass prerequisite to initiation and maintenance of the institu-

---

[47] Nathan Glazer and Daniel P. Moynihan, *Beyond the Melting Pot* (Cambridge, Mass.: The M.I.T. Press, 1963), p. 150.

tional facilities essential for continued Jewish identification. Migration may thus constitute the "blood transfusion" which greatly enhances the chances of the community's survival.

More often, however, especially in the case of repeated movement, mobility may weaken the individual's ties to Judaism and to the Jewish community, which in turn weakens the community, as it becomes more difficult to call upon the individual's loyalty to local institutions. For all too long the local Jewish community has assumed that most Jews remain within it for a lifetime, and are therefore willing and obligated to support it. This may no longer be true for many Jews. An increasing number may be reluctant to affiliate with the local community, not so much because they do not identify with Judaism, but because they do not anticipate remaining in the local area long enough to justify the financial investment required. All this suggests the need for greater concern with the role of migration than of intermarriage in the future of American Judaism. The latter may largely be only a by-product, along with other undesirable consequences, of increased mobility.

Generational Change

Of all demographic characteristics of the Jewish community, perhaps the one with the greatest relevance for its future character is the changing generation status of the Jews—how many are foreign-born, how many are children of foreign-born, and how many are at least third generation Americans. In the past, a major factor in the continued vitality of the American Jewish community has been the continuous "blood transfusions" it received through the massive immigration of Jews from ghettos of Eastern Europe. Now, for the first time in the community's history, a third generation Jewish population faces the American scene without large-scale reinforcement at the same time that it enjoys much greater freedom than ever before. The Jewish community in the United States is increasingly an American Jewish community in every sense of the word.

Information on the generation status of American Jews must be gleaned from local community studies. These show beyond any doubt that the vast majority of America's Jews today are native-born. Of all community studies presenting information on the nativity of the Jewish population, Dade County, Florida, reported the highest percentage of foreign-born, 33 percent in 1961, and Camden, New Jersey, the lowest, 9 percent in 1964. These extremes largely reflect the differential age composition of the population of the two areas. For most communities the percentage of foreign-born ranges between 20 and 25. Yet even this range is somewhat high because the surveys in many of the communities were conducted in the 1950s. If one considers only those communities where surveys were taken in the 1960s, the proportion of foreign-born was generally under 20 percent. In several communities comparable data were collected at two different points in time, indicating the pattern of change. For example, the 1953 Los Angeles survey reported 32 percent foreign-born; by 1959, the proportion had fallen to 25 percent. The Trenton, New Jersey, survey of 1949 reported 24 percent of the population as foreign-born; by 1961 the percentage was only 15. In 1937 the foreign-born in Des Moines comprised 35 percent of the Jewish population; in 1956, only 22 percent were foreign-born. An even sharper decline in the foreign-born characterized Pittsburgh in the 25-year period between 1938 and 1963, from 38 to 12 percent.

Evidence of the growing Americanization of the Jewish community is also provided by comparative data on the percentage of foreign-born in different age segments of the population. Here, the Greater Providence statistics provide a useful example. They have the added advantage of not only distinguishing between the foreign-born and native-born segments of the population, but of subdividing the latter into second and higher generations. Of the total 1963 Jewish population of Greater Providence, only 17 percent were foreign-born. The remaining 83 percent were almost equally divided between second generation Americans (with either one or both parents foreign-born) and third or fourth generation Americans (both parents born in the United States). The statistics on generation status by age indicate that not only was the percentage of foreign-born in the population declining, but that of second generation Jews as well; at the same time, the proportion of third and fourth generation persons was increasing.

The percentage of foreign-born Jews also declined according to age, from 73 percent of those 65 years old and over, to less than 2 percent of those under 15 years of age. Furthermore, among those under age 15, only 13 percent were either foreign-born or the children of foreign-born parents; a vast majority (87 percent) were American-born children of American-born parents. In the absence of any large-scale immigration, the Jewish population of Greater Providence, and that of the United States as a whole, should be well over 90 percent native-born within several decades; an increasing proportion of this number should be third or fourth generation Americans.

The majority of the foreign-born have spent the greatest proportion of their lives in the United States. Over one-third have been in this country for over half a century, and another one-third for at least 25 years. The fact that 84 percent of all foreign-born were over 45 years old, and that most of these came to the United States as children and have lived here for three decades or more, lends further weight to the conclusion suggested by the overall analysis of the changing generation status of the Jewish population—that it is an increasingly American-bred and -raised population.

The New York community represents a unique situation. Stemming from the city's role as a port of entry, it still has a disproportionately large foreign-born population, estimated at 37 percent of its 1963–1964 adult population. This contrasts with about 20 to 25 percent of all adults in most other communities. Attesting to its attraction for new immigrants, 11 percent of all New York Jews between ages 20 and 34 were foreign-born, compared to only 1 percent in other places. As a result, changes in the generation composition of New York's Jewish population will lag behind that of the balance of the United States.[48]

Because of the importance of generational change for the structure of the Jewish community, Dr. Goldscheider and I based our analysis of Jewish Americans on a comparison of the demographic, social, economic, and religious characteristics of three generations in the Jewish community.[49] That study emphasizes that the future of the American Jewish community depends to a great degree on how its members (largely third generation) are reacting to the freedom to work toward integration into the American social structure as an acculturated subsociety, or toward complete assimilation and loss of Jewish identification. Whether they are reversing or accelerating certain trends toward assimilation, initiated by their second generation parents or by the smaller number of older third generation Jews, provides the insights for the detection and projection of the patterns of generation change.

The physical dispersal and deconcentration of the Jewish popula-

[48] American Jewish Year Book, 1968, vol. 69, p. 273.
[49] Goldstein and Goldscheider, Jewish Americans.

tion were rapid, marking for many not only a physical break from the foreign-born, but symbolizing the more dramatic dissociation of American-born Jews from the ethnic ties and experiences that had served as unifying forces in the earlier generation. The degree of identification with Judaism of the third generation Jews who participate in this dispersal has become a key issue. At the same time, sharp rises have taken place in secular education as distance from the immigrant generation has increased. This provided the key to Jewish participation in the professions and, more recently, in high executive positions.

Dispersal of the Jewish population and its greater exposure to public education increased the interaction between Jews and non-Jews and, as earlier analysis documented, has resulted in higher intermarriage rates with increasing distance from the immigrant generation. These generational changes in residential location, social class structure, and marriage patterns have been accompanied by redirection of the religious system. Striking first to third generation shifts in identification and membership, from Orthodox to Conservative and Reform, were observed, as well as declines in regular synagogue attendance, observance of *kashrut*, Jewish organization affiliation, and use of Yiddish as a spoken language. Yet these trends were counteracted by a clear tendency toward increased Jewish education for the young, as well as increases in selected religious observances. Overall, some aspects of religiosity appeared strengthened, others declined, and some remained stable over the generations. Religious change among three generations of Jews is a complex process involving abandonment of traditional forms and development of new forms of identity and expression more congruent with the broader American way of life. Our generational analysis suggests that, evolving out of the process of generational adjustment, the freedom to choose the degree of assimilation was exercised in the direction of Jewish identification.

Age Composition

Among all demographic variables, age is regarded as the most basic because so much of the sociodemographic structure of the population, as well as the processes of birth, death, and migration, are affected by age composition. The significant impact of age on the generation status of the Jewish population has already been noted. At present, the only source of information on the national age composition of Jews is the 1957 census survey. Changes have undoubtedly occurred since then; Jewish community studies indicate that differences observed by the census have been accentuated.

The 1957 census data clearly indicated that the Jewish population was, on the average, older than the general white population of the United States. The median age of the Jewish group was 36.7 years, compared to 30.6 years for the total white population. The sharpest differentials in distribution characterized the youngest age group, under 14 years of age, and the 45-to-64 age category. The youngest group constituted 23 percent of the total Jewish population, compared to 28 percent of the total white population. By contrast, while only 21 percent of the white population of the United States was between 45 and 64 years of age in 1957, this was true of 28 percent of the Jewish group. The Jewish and the total white populations had similar proportions in the 65 and over age category, 10 and 9 percent, respectively, of the total population! The significant differential in the proportion of young persons reflects the lower fertility of the Jewish group, which leads to fewer children and, in turn, results in an older population. The same phenomenon helps account for the lower proportions of Jews in each of the age groups between 14 and 34.

Ben Seligman has examined the age composition of 13 Jewish communities which were surveyed between 1947 and 1950.[50] He found the median age in these communities to range between 28 and 40, compared to an estimated median age of 31 for the total white population of the United States in 1950. Comparison of more recent community surveys with earlier ones suggests an increasing proportion of individuals in the older age groups. The upsurge in the birth rate after World War II, in which Jews participated, increased somewhat the proportion of Jews in the younger age groups, but differentials persisted between the Jewish and general population. In 1963, 10.5 percent of the total United States white population was under 5 years of age. But in the Jewish communities of Camden, Detroit, and Providence the percentage of children under 5 varied between 6.2 and 8.5 percent, the highest being in Camden, which in many respects is a suburban community and therefore has a disproportional number of

[50] Ben B. Seligman, "Some Aspects of Jewish Demography," in Sklare, *The Jews*, p. 54.

mothers of child-bearing age. The type of community also affects the proportion of aged persons. In 1963, just under 10 percent of the United States white population was 65 years and over. In Providence, the comparable proportion for the Jewish community was 10.1 percent and in Detroit it was 8.0 percent; in Camden it was only 5.7 percent.

The age structure of the American Jewish community is clear: on the whole, the Jewish population is older than the total United States white population, and over time, both because of lower fertility and because it has in most places such a large proportion of individuals in the 45-to-64 age group, the Jewish population can be expected to become increasingly older. In American society the problems associated with an aged population are many. During the next few decades such problems may become even more serious for the Jewish community than for the population as a whole. This can be illustrated by projections of the age composition of the Jewish population of Greater Providence for 1978, fifteen years after the survey. It must be emphasized that these projections assume that fertility and mortality will continue at the 1960 levels and that the total metropolitan area's population will not be affected by migration. The results point to an aging of the population: a rise from 10 to 17 percent in the proportion of persons 65 years of age and older. In actual numbers, there will be a 70 percent increase in the number of aged. At the same time, the percentage under 15 years of age will decline from 25 percent in 1963 to 19 percent in 1978. Reflecting both the low fertility rates of 1960 and the fewer women of child-bearing age, the absolute number of children under 15 will be 20 percent lower in 1978 than in 1963, affecting the community's task in educating and providing leisure activities for youngsters.

Changes will also occur in the middle segment of the age hierarchy, as the reduced number of persons resulting from the especially low Jewish birth rate during the Depression move into the 45 to 54 age range. The percentage of this group is projected to decline from 16 percent of the total in 1963 to only 10 percent in 1978. In actual numbers, there will be a decline of almost one-third. This may create some serious problems for the community, as the pool of persons to whom it can turn for leadership and financial contributions is greatly reduced. Given the possibility of these developments, Jewish communities may want to reevaluate and reorganize their services, deciding which to retain for the Jewish community because of their Jewish component, and which to relegate to the larger community because of their secular character.

Overall, therefore, the dynamic character of the Jewish age structure requires continuous monitoring, not only for the demographic impact it will have on births, deaths, migration, and socioeconomic structure, but also because of its broader social implications.[51] While recognizing the general trend toward an aging population, with its associated problems of housing for the aged, financial crises resulting from retirement, and more persons in poor health, one must also be aware that changes are taking place at other points in the age hierarchy, and that the need for schools, playgrounds, camps, and teenage programs also vary as the age profile changes. Too often the Jewish community has been guilty of planning its future without taking account of the basic considerations of the probable size, distribution, and age composition of the population.

Education

For a large majority of the Jews who immigrated to America in the late 1800s and early 1900s, the major incentive was the supposed equal opportunities permitting significant social and economic mobility. But lacking secular education, adequate facility in English, and technical training, many found that rapid advancement proved an unrealistic goal. For others, both educational and occupational achievement were made difficult, if not impossible, by factors related to their foreign-born status or, more specifically, to their identification as Jews. Frustrated in their own efforts to achieve significant mobility, many Jews transferred their aspirations to their children. The first generation American Jews recognized the importance of education as a key to occupational mobility and higher income, and made considerable effort to provide their children with a good secular education. Reflecting the great value placed by Jews on education, both as a way of life and as a means of mobility, the Jews of America have compiled an extraordinary record of achievement in this area.

Ben Seligman has noted that very few Jewish community studies

[51] See Gosta Carlsson and Katarina Carlsson, "Age Cohorts and the Generation of Generations," *American Sociological Review*, August 1970, pp. 710–718.

covering the period before and around 1950 yielded usable information on the secular education of Jews.[52] On the basis of the limited data available he concluded that in the period around 1950 the average education of Jews, about twelve years, was higher than that of the general white population, which averaged 9.7 years. He also found that the few studies showing the data by sex revealed "nothing that might be interpreted as a notable difference as between males and females."[53] In recognition of the important effect of education on the social position of the Jew in the larger community, as well as its possible influence on the degree and nature of Jewish identification, most recent surveys have collected information on education. All these clearly document the high educational achievement of the American Jewish population.

On the national level, the 1957 census survey data[54] permit the best comparisons between the educational achievement of the Jewish and the general population. The results of that survey show that for the population 25 years old and over in the United States, the median number of school years completed by Jews was 12.3, compared to 10.6 for the general population. But even this large difference does not fully convey the sharp differentials distinguishing educational patterns of Jews from those of the general population.

As of 1957, 17 percent of adult Jews were college graduates, compared to only 7 percent of the general population. If those who attended college without graduating are included, the percentage of Jews was 30, or exactly twice the 15 percent of the general population. At the other extreme of the educational hierarchy, 29 percent of all adult Jews had received only an elementary school education; this was considerably below the 40 percent of the total population so classified. Since these data refer to the total population, they are considerably affected by differential age composition which, in turn, is correlated with immigrant status. Later examination of community survey data will control for age.

Judging by median years of school completed, Seligman's conclusion that the educational level of men and women did not differ is

---

[52] Ben Seligman, "Some Aspects of Jewish Demography," pp. 83–86.

[53] Ibid., p. 83.

[54] This and the following two sections of this chapter—"Occupation" and "Income"—are based largely on data from unpublished statistics of the 1957 census survey sample and on S. Goldstein, "Socioeconomic Differentials Among Religious Groups in the United States."

confirmed. The median education of Jewish men was 12.5, that of Jewish women 12.3; for both sexes these were above the averages for the total population. However, for Jews in particular, these medians mask some important sex differences in educational achievement. Whereas 22.5 percent of Jewish women had had some college education, this was true of 38.2 percent of all adult Jewish men. Moreover, one out of every four Jewish males had completed four or more years of college, whereas only one out of every ten Jewish females had done so. These data not only show that, as of 1957, more Jewish men than women had gone to college, but that more of the former had completed their college education. For the total population, this sex differential was much less marked. Moreover, for both sexes combined, approximately twice as large a proportion of Jewish adults had had a college education than was true of the population as a whole.

Unfortunately, the census data on education by religion are not cross-tabulated by age, and therefore do not permit determination of the extent to which the differences between Jews and the general population were narrowing among the younger age groups. Since 1957, there has been a considerable increase in education among the younger segments of the American population. For example, the March 1967 Current Population Survey shows a continuous rise in the median school years completed, from 8.5 among males aged 65 and over to 12.6 among men aged 25 to 29, and from 8.7 to 12.5 for females. Jewish community surveys indicate similar increases in education among the younger segments of the Jewish population.

The high proportion of persons aged 25 to 29 who had completed their college education—as indicated in the data from Providence—and the fact that an estimated 80 percent of those in the college age group were enrolled in college, emphasize that a college education is becoming virtually universal for the younger segments of the Jewish population. Within the Jewish population itself the important educational differential will thus be between those with only some college education and those who went on to postgraduate work. At least one caveat should be added to the conclusion concerning virtually universal college education for Jews in the future: If the current emphasis on recruitment of minority group members and underprivileged students persists, especially to the point of meeting certain enrollment quotas, high rates of enrollment by members of other segments of the population may necessarily be reduced. Jews in particular might be affected by such a development because of their very high enrollment rates.

As part of a larger survey of inequality in educational opportunity in the United States, the Bureau of the Census Current Population Survey of October 1965 gathered information about school age children.[55] A 1970 report, limited to white boys and girls aged 14 to 19 who were enrolled in elementary or secondary public or private schools, reviewed the college plans of the sample respondents. Since religion was one of the three key variables for which information was collected (the other two were race and national origin), this analysis provides an opportunity to compare the college intentions of Jewish teen-agers and teen-agers in general.

The religious composition of the student body was based on each principal's estimate of the percentage of Protestants, Catholics, and Jews in his school. Of the estimated 330,000 Jewish students enrolled in public and private elementary and secondary schools, 74,000, or 22.4 percent, were enrolled in schools with half or more of their students Jewish; 118,000, or 35.8 percent, were in schools in which less than half of the students were Jewish; an additional 41.8 percent were in schools for which no religion composition could be obtained.

The study found that 86 percent of the 330,000 Jewish students planned to attend college, compared with only 53 percent of the general student body. Interestingly, the percentages differed strikingly among those teen-agers who were receiving their education in schools with heavy Jewish populations and those in schools with fewer than 50 percent Jewish students. Among the former, 94 percent planned to attend college; among the latter, only 80 percent did.

Other variables obviously affect plans for college. The study attempts to control for the effects of intelligence, mother's education, occupation of household head, and family income. Adjusting for these factors reduced differences among the various religions in the percentage of students with college plans. Yet part of the religious differences persisted; even after controlling for all these variables, 70 percent of all Jewish students, compared to the general average of 53 percent, had college plans. Even within the high IQ subgroup, comparisons between Jews and other segments of the population showed that Jews

[55] A. Lewis Rhodes and Charles B. Nam, "The Religious Context of Educational Expectations," *American Sociological Review*, April 1970, pp. 253–267.

continued to have the highest proportion planning for college education.

The authors conclude:

The high rate of college plans (86 per cent) for pupils with Jewish mothers is particularly noteworthy, especially when the effect of religious context is added to the analysis. If the majority of the student body is Jewish the college plans rate for Jewish students is fourteen percentage points higher than the rate for Jewish students in schools where Jews are in the minority. The rate is fifteen percentage points higher even when the intelligence, mother's aspiration, occupation, and income are included in the analysis. The same results are observed for high-IQ Jews. These results suggest that it would be worthwhile to test the hypothesis that exposure of a Jewish student to the norms and values of a Jewish sub-community is important in formation of educational expectation.[56]

These data have a number of implications for the types of demographic developments considered in this chapter. First, they confirm the projection that college education will be virtually universal among Jewish students, if they can realize their aspirations. Second, because plans for attending college are quite low for a number of other religious groups, ranging in the 40 to 50 percent level, it will be some time before college attendance becomes universal among the non-Jewish population. As a result, some of the differences noted with respect to education can be expected to persist for a number of decades, and continue indirectly to affect occupation and income differentials. Also important is the finding that the proportion planning to go to college differed significantly (14 percentage points) between those receiving their elementary and secondary education in a largely "Jewish environment" and those doing so in more heterogeneous schools. If the Jewish population becomes more generally dispersed, and tendencies toward migration increase, a much higher proportion of Jewish youth may be attending schools that are less densely Jewish. If either residence or school environment is so important for motivating individuals toward higher education, increased population redistribution may lower somewhat the proportion of Jewish youth planning to go to college. This must, however, remain speculative, pending more research on the role of the Jewish subcommunity, as compared to the role of the family, in forming education expectations.

In the meantime, a high level of educational achievement signifi-

[56] Ibid., pp. 263–264.

cantly affects several areas of Jewish life in the United States. To the extent that education is highly correlated with occupation, an increasing proportion of college graduates in the Jewish population will affect its occupational composition. More Jews will be engaged in intellectual pursuits and in occupations requiring a high degree of technical skill. Concomitantly, there also will probably be a reduction in the number of self-employed, both because small, private business will not provide an adequate intellectual challenge and because patterns of discrimination, which have excluded Jews from large corporations, are likely to continue to weaken. However, the impact will go beyond occupation.

In order to obtain a college education, particularly at the postgraduate level, a large proportion of young Jews must leave home to attend colleges in distant places. As a result, their ties to both family and community will weaken. A high proportion of these college-educated youths probably will never return permanently to the communities in which their families live and in which they were raised. Thus education serves as an important catalyst for geographic mobility, and eventually leads many individuals to take up residence in communities with small Jewish populations, to live in highly integrated neighborhoods, and to work and socialize in largely non-Jewish circles. The extent of such a development needs to be closely followed during the decade of the 1970s.

Finally, Jews with higher education may have significantly higher rates of intermarriage and greater alienation from the Jewish community. This involves not only the possible impact of physical separation from home and the weakening of parental control on dating and courtship patterns, but also the general "liberalization" a college education may have on the religious values and Jewish identity of the individual. It would be ironic if the strong positive value that Jews traditionally have placed on education, and that now manifests itself in the high proportion of Jewish youths attending college, eventually becomes an important factor in the general weakening of the individual's ties to the Jewish community.

Occupation

In an analysis of the social characteristics of American Jews prepared in 1954 for the tercentenary celebration of Jewish settlement in the

United States, Nathan Glazer observed that, outside New York City, the homogeneous character of the occupational structure of Jewish communities was beyond dispute.[57] Basing his conclusions on a number of local Jewish community surveys conducted between 1948 and 1953, he noted that the proportion of Jews in the nonmanual occupations ranged from 75 to 96 percent, compared to 38 percent for the American population as a whole. According to Glazer, these studies also suggest that even in New York City, where one would expect to find a substantial proportion of Jewish workers, as many as two-thirds of the gainfully employed Jews were engaged in nonmanual work.

Comparing his finding for the 1948–1953 period with the results of ten surveys conducted during 1935–1945, Glazer found that the proportion of professionals had risen, on the average, from about 11 percent of the Jewish gainfully employed in the earlier period to about 15 percent in the later period, and that this change was accompanied by a decline in the number of Jews engaged in the lower levels of white collar work. Interestingly, this rise in the number of Jews in the professions evidently occurred without any significant change in the proportion of independent Jewish businessmen. Glazer explains:

The American Jew tries to avoid getting into a situation where discrimination may seriously affect him. In a great bureaucracy, he is dependent on the impression he makes on his superiors and, increasingly in recent years, dependent on the degree to which he approximates a certain "type" considered desirable in business. The Jew prefers a situation where his own merit receives objective confirmation, and he is not dependent on the goodwill or personal reaction of a person who may happen not to like Jews.[58]

Whether this point of view is still justified in the 1970s will be considered later.

Another of Glazer's relevant observations is that the extreme rapidity of the rise in social and economic positions is especially characteristic of the Jewish experience in America. Citing a 1947 study of American college graduates, he notes that more Jews than non-Jews became professionals, proprietors, managers, or officials, and fewer Jews than non-Jews became lower white collar or manual workers. Yet this study found that fewer of the parents of these Jews than of the non-Jews had been professionals, proprietors, managers, or officials. In a single

[57] Nathan Glazer, "The American Jew and the Attainment of Middle-Class Rank: Some Trends and Explanations," in Sklare, *The Jews*, p. 138.

[58] Ibid., p. 140.

generation, Jews had increased their proportion of professionals by close to 400 percent, non-Jews by only about 25 percent. Between 1910 and 1950 the proportion of the population engaged in nonmanual work rose from 20 to 38 percent. This development offered Jews great opportunities and, given their strong motivation for social mobility, they proceeded to take full advantage of them. Thus, at a time when the total American population became more markedly middle class in its occupational structure, Jews became even more so.

Glazer further notes a general tendency for the ethnic concentration in a single occupation to suffer dilution as the native-born generation becomes better educated and more familiar with occupational opportunities. But, he points out, for the Jews, "this dilution upward becomes a concentration, for the Jews begin to reach the upper limit of occupation mobility relatively early." For Jews to reflect the general occupational structure of the United States would, in fact, require downward mobility for many. He concludes that since this is not going to happen, "we may expect the Jewish community to become more homogeneous in the future, as the number of first generation workers and the culture they established declines."[59] On the basis of evidence that became available since Glazer's analysis, such a conclusion is warranted, provided the reference is to broad occupational classes, such as professionals and managers. At the same time, this kind of concentration of Jews may be followed, although not to exactly the same degree, by a similar concentration of the general population. In this sense, the marked differentials noted by Glazer and in later studies can only diminish as upward mobility becomes increasingly characteristic of the general population as well. Here again the experience of the Jews may be in the forefront of developments on the larger American scene.

The 1957 census sample survey provides data on the occupational composition of the Jewish population and permits us to compare their patterns with those of the general population. Sharp differentials characterized the occupational composition of the Jewish group, compared to the general population. Three-fourths of all Jewish employed males worked in white collar positions, compared to only 35 percent of the total white male population of the United States. These large differences were to a great extent attributable to the much greater concen-

[59] Ibid., p. 146.

tration of Jewish men in professional and managerial positions. Of the total Jewish male labor force, one in five was a professional, compared to only one in ten in the general population; one out of every three Jews was employed as manager or proprietor, compared to only 13 percent of the total male population. The proportion in clerical work was similar for Jews and the total labor force, but in sales work it was almost three times as high for Jews as for total males. Conversely, the proportion of Jews in manual work was very small: only 22 percent, compared to 57 percent of the total male labor force.

Compared with males, women in the labor force were much more concentrated in white collar positions, but the differentials between Jewish women and all women were less marked than those for the men. Just over four out of every five Jewish women were in white collar jobs, compared to just over half of the total female labor force. A similar pattern emerged from examination of specific occupational categories. Among professionals, for example, the proportion of Jewish women was 15.5 percent, compared to 12.2 percent for the total female labor force. Like men, Jewish women were considerably underrepresented in manual labor categories: only 17 percent, compared to 44 percent for the total female force.

The different occupational composition of Jews compared to the general population has often been attributed to their higher concentration in urban places and their higher educational achievement. Census tabulations enable analysis of the occupational data for the urban population, while controlling for years of school completed by religion. By restricting the data to a more homogeneous social and economic environment, and by holding constant the wide differences in educational achievement, it becomes possible to ascertain more clearly to what extent occupational differences are directly related to religious affiliation and to what degree they may simply be a reflection of differential opportunities available to Jews because of their places of residence and levels of education.

With residence and education controlled, 70 percent of Jewish males were white collar workers, compared to 41 percent of the general male population. Thus, the concentration of Jews in white collar positions remained far above that of the total population, but the difference was no longer in the ratio of two to one, as indicated by the unstandardized data. For selected occupational categories there was an even more dramatic change. For example, with residence and education controlled, only 10 percent of the Jewish males were professionals, compared to 12 percent of the total male population. What originally was a two-to-one differential completely disappeared and was even reversed. On the other hand, differentials in the managerial and the sales categories remained about the same. Similar conclusions held for occupational differentials for females after the data were restricted to urban residence and standardized by education. Overall, therefore, controlling for both education and residence suggests that both these factors explain some, but not all, variations in occupational differentials between Jews and the total population.

In a further attempt to assess the relation between education and occupation, special tabulations of the occupational distribution of employed college graduates in urban areas were examined. Such control again eliminated a considerable part of the differential in occupational distribution between Jews and the total population. Of Jewish college graduates, 97 percent were in white collar occupations, while this was true of 93 percent of the total population. Similarly, 58 percent of all Jewish college graduates were professionals, compared to 63 percent of those in the total population. The only important difference characterizing the college-educated group was the significantly higher proportion of Jewish graduates who earned their living as managers, proprietors, and officials: 22 percent, compared to 16 percent of the total population. But this differential, too, was considerably below that characterizing the population as a whole when education was not controlled.

The 1957 census data obviously are outdated by now. For evidence of the occupational composition of the Jewish population in the 1960s, one must turn to the various community surveys taken during that period. In 1960, 45 percent of the American white urban male population was engaged in white collar work, but in such communities as Providence, Camden, Springfield, Rochester, and Trenton the percentage for Jews ranged from a low of 80 to a high of 92 percent. While percentages in specific occupational categories varied among communities, depending on the character of the community and the nature of occupational opportunities, the proportion of professionals among Jews was from two to three times greater than among the general population, and differentials in the proportion of managers and proprietors were even larger.

Some indication of the changes that may be taking place in the occupational composition of Jews can be gained from statistics on occupation by age for Providence. These point in the direction of a reduced percentage of Jews in the managerial and proprietor group, and an increasing proportion in the professions and in sales work. For example, among males the proportion of professionals increased from 17 percent of those 65 and over to 25 percent of those 25 to 44; conversely, the proportion employed as managers declined from over half of the oldest group to just about one-third of the 25-44 year group. At the same time, the proportion of sales personnel increased from 11 percent of the oldest to almost one-fourth of the 25-44 year group. The concentration of older males in managerial positions must be interpreted within the context of the high percentage of self-employed who tend to remain in the labor force, while those in the white collar and manual labor group must retire. Yet, as many as 17 percent of the aged segment of the employed population still held manual jobs, compared to only 13 percent of those in the 45 to 64 year group and 8 percent of those aged 25 to 44. In general, the same pattern by age characterized the employed females, although the differentials were not always as sharp.

Survey data on the occupation of heads of Jewish families in Detroit covering 1935, 1956, and 1963 provide a unique opportunity to compare changes over 28 years in the occupational composition of the Jewish population. The evidence clearly points to a pattern of occupational concentration. In 1935, 70 percent of the heads of Jewish families were employed as white collar workers. By 1963 their percentage had risen to 90. The most striking changes characterized the professionals, who increased from 7 percent in 1935 to 23 percent in 1963, and the manager-owners, who grew from 31 to 54 percent of the total in that period. At the same time, the proportion of lower white collar workers, that is, sales and clerical workers, declined from 32 to only 13 percent. Using the 1940 and 1960 censuses as bases for comparing changes in the general population, the data also show some upward concentration. In 1940, 31 percent of the population was in white collar occupations; by 1960 this had risen to 38 percent. The proportion of professionals also grew considerably, from 5 to 12 percent, and that of manager-owners increased slightly, from 9 to 10 percent, compensated by a small decline in proportion of lower white collar workers, from 17 to 16 percent. Again the patterns for Jews and the total population were parallel, but the occupational movement of Jews has been much more accentuated. The conclusion seems warranted that, in time, increasing occupational concentration will also take place in the population as a whole, and differentials between Jews and the total population will decline. But in the short run, the discrepancies may be greater as Jews move up more quickly.

The Detroit data by age for 1963 also confirm occupational shifting within the white collar segment of the occupational hierarchy. For example, only 19 percent of the 45 to 64 age group were professionals, compared to 42 percent of the 20 to 34 age group. As in Providence, a lower proportion of younger men were manager-owners: 40 percent, compared to 56 percent. Particularly noteworthy is the decline in the proportion of independent businessmen within the managerial-proprietor group, from 42 percent among those aged 45 to 64, to only 30 percent of the younger group. Even if a considerable portion of those currently engaged as managers or sales and clerical workers should become owners at a later stage of the life cycle, the total percentage is not likely to exceed the proportion of the 45 to 64 year group classified as owners in 1963. Again, the data analyzed here suggest that, in the years ahead, business ownership is likely to decline among the Jewish population.

What do these varied data suggest for future trends in Jewish occupational composition? Although restricted because of their cross-sectional character, they point to a continuing increase in the proportion of Jews engaged in professional work, and to either stability or actual decline for the managerial and proprietor group. A number of younger persons currently classified as sales workers might, at later stages of their life cycle, move into managerial and proprietor positions, but evidence for Providence indicates that half or more of these younger individuals were working for others, outside of family businesses. With the gradual disappearance of small businesses, an increasing proportion of these Jewish men may turn to executive positions in business corporations instead of operating their own firms.

However, the rapid growth in the number of college graduates in the population may give college graduates in general more difficulty in finding jobs in the 1970s than was true earlier. Since such a high proportion of Jews graduate college, Jews in particular would be affected by such a development. Herbert Bienstock, a labor force expert, has suggested the possibility that jobs in nonprofessional technical areas may become more attractive from a pay and security point of view.[60] He has also suggested that, for the same reasons, younger Jews may increasingly return to self-employment, relying upon their professional and technical skills to open firms in the service sector of the economy. Interestingly, he also proposes that the pressure on many college graduates may lead to greater migration on the part of Jews away from the centers of Jewish population concentration, as they are attracted by better employment opportunities available in other parts of the country.

It seems reasonable to assume that, with the general rise in educational level, educational differentials among members of the various religious groups will lessen; as discriminatory restrictions on occupational choice weaken, occupational differentials will also decline. The high proportion of Jews in white collar occupations leading to the "concentration" which Glazer predicted will persist; but within this concentration, there may be more diversity in the future than there was in the past. At the same time, the total population will also concentrate more in higher occupational categories, with a decline in occupational differentials as the net result.

In commenting on educational and occupational changes within the Jewish population, Albert Mayer, the author of the 1968 Columbus, Ohio, study, made a most important observation. He stressed that the organized Jewish community must come to recognize that its constituency is now almost entirely high white collar as well as college educated. Unless the community takes full recognition of this crucial fact in all its activities, it will find much difficulty in gaining the loyalty, interest, and support of its membership. The reaction of the organized community to its membership may very well still be in terms of earlier twentieth century stereotypes, i.e., a largely foreign-born immigrant group in need of welfare and social services. This is a false image in view of generation changes, education, and occupational mobility, and any approach ignoring these changes runs the risk of serious failure. Such an attitude on the part of the community may be compounded by changes in identification patterns within the population itself. More Jews in scientific and executive positions may lead to increased channeling of self-identification through the professional

---

[60] Herbert Bienstock, "Current Economic Developments: Implications for the Jewish Community in the Metropolitan New York Area" (paper presented at the Federation Employment and Guidance Service Second F. W. Greenfield Memorial Inter-Agency Conference, New York, March 29, 1971).

or intellectual subsocieties rather than through the Jewish community. Increased geographic mobility would reinforce such a development and pose still further challenges for the organized Jewish community.

Income

The demographer probably encounters greater difficulty in collecting information on income than on any other standard variable that interests him. Not until 1940 was the first income question included in the federal census. Social surveys focusing on fertility in the United States today often find it harder to obtain accurate information on income than on such intimate matters as birth control practice and sexual activity. Not surprisingly, therefore, few among the large number of Jewish community surveys collected such information; if they did, the data are often either of questionable quality or limited because there are no comparable figures for the general population. Yet, in a consideration of the position of Jews in American society, it is important to look at Jewish income levels, to ascertain whether they differ from those of the general population and, if so, why. For such purposes three sets of national data are available: the findings of the 1957 census surveys, the Lazerwitz study based on survey-research statistics from the University of Michigan,[61] and Bogue's analysis of the National Opinion Research Survey data.[62]

The Lazerwitz material clearly documents that the income level of Jews is above that of the general population. Measured in terms of total 1956 family income, 42 percent of Jewish families had incomes of $7,500 and over, compared to only 19 percent of the general population. At the other extreme of the income hierarchy, only 8 percent of the Jewish families had incomes under $3,000, compared to one-fourth of all families in the United States. Yet if comparison is made with other specific religious groups, the high position of the Jews is surpassed by the Episcopalians, among whom 46 percent of families had incomes of $7,500 and over and only 6 percent were below $3,000. The higher income of the Episcopalians who, like the Jews, are highly urbanized is also consistent with their high educational and occupational achievements.

[61] Lazerwitz, "A Comparison of Major United States Religious Groups," pp. 574–575.
[62] Bogue, *The Population of the United States*, pp. 705–708.

Using National Opinion Research Survey materials compiled in 1953 and 1955, Donald Bogue also investigated the relation between religious preference and family income. His data, like those of Lazerwitz, point to higher income levels for the Jewish population. The median income for heads of Jewish households was $5,954, compared to $4,094 for the total population. Of the Jewish families, 30 percent had incomes $7,500 and over, compared to only 13 percent of the families of the total population. Only 15 percent of the Jewish households had incomes under $3,000, compared to 31 percent of all families.

Bogue also found that Jewish household heads employed as professionals, proprietors, or managers tended to have higher median incomes than did the members of other religious groups belonging to those broad occupations. The same was generally true for Episcopalians. He suggested that this pattern was probably due to internal variations between occupations within each of the broad occupational categories. Thus he concluded that occupation is much more potent than religious preference as a factor determining the income level of household heads.

Similarly, Bogue's comparison of the median income of religious groups by educational attainment suggests that Jewish household heads tended to earn larger incomes than did household heads in the general population with comparable education. He added, however, that these differences may be due to intervening variables, such as age of head, number and type of secondary earners, family structure, and occupation, as well as to cultural factors associated with religious affiliation, and that education, like occupation, was much more important than religious preference in determining the income level of households.

The Lazerwitz and Bogue materials are limited in that they present only gross comparisons. The census data have the advantage of permitting more detailed analysis to document the influence of other factors on differences in income between Jews and the total population. For each person in the 1957 census sample, information was solicited on the amount of money income received in 1956. This included income from such varied sources as wages and salaries, self-employment, pensions, interest, dividends, and rent. Since both high education and high white collar employment are highly correlated with income, the fact that the $4,900 median income of Jewish males was well above the $3,608 median for the male population as a whole comes as no surprise. This sharp differential was also reflected in the more detailed statistics on distribution by income class. Incomes of $10,000 and over were reported by 17 percent of the Jewish males, compared to only 3.6 percent of the males in the total population. On the other hand, just over one-fourth of the Jews, but 41 percent of the total male population, had incomes under $3,000. These differences extended to females as well, as evidenced by the 50 percent higher median income of Jewish women, compared to that of the total female population.

Controlling the census statistics for urban residence and major occupational groups diminished the sharp differentials noted for the unstandardized data. For males, the standardized data showed a median income for Jews of $4,773, just slightly above the $4,472 median for the total population. Narrowing of differentials also extended to the overall distribution by income level. For the standardized data, 18 percent of the Jewish males, compared to 23 percent of the total male population, had incomes under $3,000; the proportion with incomes of $10,000 and over was 8.7 and 5.0 percent, respectively. The same narrowing of differentials appeared for women, as evidenced by the reduction of the difference between the median incomes of Jewish women and all women to less than $100.

Clearly, then, the considerably higher income level characterizing Jews, compared with the general population, is a function of their concentration in urban areas and in high white collar positions. This suggests that, as educational differentials between Jews and the rest of the population narrow, and as increasing proportions of non-Jews enter higher white collar positions, the existing income differentials between Jews and the general population will diminish. Such a conclusion seems justified by additional information showing that for Jews, as for the total population, the median income level consistently rises with increasing education.

For example, for Jews with less than an eighth grade education, the average median income was $2,609, but for those with a college degree it was $8,041. If Jews and the total population with similar levels of education are compared, the differences in median income are generally less than 10 percent for all educational categories below the college level. For the college groups, particularly those with a college degree, the differences increase. In all likelihood, the sharp differential within the college graduate group reflects the higher proportion of Jews who have postgraduate education and are in high income professional and executive positions. As proportionately more persons in the general population obtain a postgraduate education, differences in income level between the Jewish and the total population will probably diminish.

Without further controls, the question of whether religion, occupation, or education is a more important factor in determining income level cannot be clearly ascertained. Control for occupation and place of residence reduced the income differentials in the three major religious groups, but it does not eliminate them completely. Similarly, comparisons of median income level among various educational categories suggest minimal differences for all but the college educated. Moreover, the range of differences by education within both the Jewish and total population is far greater than the differences in median income between the Jewish group and the total population. Whereas the differences between Jews and the total for most educational levels was only several hundred dollars, the range of difference between the lowest and highest educated Jewish group was $5,400. On this basis, the conclusion suggested by Donald Bogue that education is a much more potent factor than religion in determining the income level of households seems justified.[63] This conclusion is further confirmed by a highly sophisticated statistical analysis of the relation between income and religious affiliation undertaken by Galen L. Gockel, which controlled for occupation, education, race, region, and size of place of residence, using 1962 national sample survey data.[64]

In interpreting Gockel's, Bogue's, and this writer's conclusions that nonreligious factors account for a considerable portion of religious differentials in income level, we must acknowledge that the differentials do exist; their statistical elimination merely serves to identify the causes of the differences rather than do away with them. The fact remains that, on the whole, the average income of Jews and the proportion of Jews in high income groups are well above those of most of the population. To the extent that a considerable part of this difference is attributable to factors other than religion, the differences are likely to diminish in the future, both as the occupational composition of the Jewish population changes and as higher proportions of non-Jews achieve higher education and move into better paying occupations.

[63] Ibid., p. 708.
[64] Galen L. Gockel, "Income and Religious Affiliation," *American Journal of Sociology*, May 1969, pp. 632–647.

Overview of Future Demographic Trends

From existing information on the demographic history and structure of the American Jewish community, what patterns of development can be anticipated?

Numbering about 6 million in 1970, after slow growth during all but the first several decades of this century, the Jewish population is likely to continue its slow increase. The low rate of growth results particularly from the low level of Jewish fertility, which is below that of Protestants and Catholics and hovers close to the minimum needed for replacement. Limited data suggest that death rates of Jews are slightly below those of the general population, but the overall death rate of the Jewish population is likely to rise as the average age of the Jewish population increases. This, coupled with possible larger losses from intermarriage, despite some evidence of an increasing tendency toward conversion of the non-Jewish partner, will contribute to maintenance, if not accentuation, of the slow growth rate. As a result, the Jewish population, even while growing slightly, will come to constitute a decreasing proportion of the total American population, having already declined from the peak of 3.7 to less than 3 percent by 1970.

While declining as a percentage of the total population, Jews will also become more dispersed throughout the United States. As a result of continuously higher education and changing occupations, lower levels of self-employment, weakening family ties, and reduced discrimination, Jews are likely to migrate in increasing numbers away from the major centers of Jewish population. This will operate on several levels. Regionally, it will lead to fewer Jews in the Northeast. Jews will continue to be highly concentrated in metropolitan areas, but, within those areas, ever-increasing numbers will move out of the urban centers and former ghettos into the suburbs. In doing so, the Jewish population will become much more geographically dispersed, even while distinct areas of Jewish concentration remain.

At the same time that its overall numbers and distribution change, the Jewish population will also undergo significant changes in selected aspects of socioeconomic composition. In others it will show less change, but, because of changes in the general population, differences between Jews and non-Jews may narrow.

As a result of the significant reduction in Jewish immigration to the

United States since the 1920s and the subsequent aging and death of the immigrants, the most striking compositional change characterizing American Jewry is the reduction in the percent of the foreign-born. Indeed, even the proportion of second generation American Jews will increasingly diminish as third and fourth generation persons become an even larger proportion of the Jewish population, with all this implies for questions of Jewish identification and assimilation. Reflecting their lower fertility, the Jewish population, already six years older on the average than the general population, is likely to undergo further aging. This will mean a considerable increase in the proportion of older persons as well as of the widowed, especially women.

Already unique in their high concentration among the more educated, high white collar, and high income groups, the Jews may undergo still further changes. College education will be an almost universal phenomenon among them, and an increasing proportion will pursue graduate studies. At the same time, continuously rising education levels among non-Jews may narrow educational differentials between Jews and non-Jews. The high proportion of Jews who obtain specialized university training, their tendency to move out of small family businesses and into salaried employment, and their increasing willingness to take positions away from their community of current residence may bring an increase in the number of Jews in technical and executive occupation categories, where they already are heavily concentrated. The general upward shift in the occupational level of the general population will also narrow existing differences in the occupational structure of the Jewish and non-Jewish populations. In turn, this narrowing in both educational and occupational differences will lead to reduction in the income differences currently characterizing Jews and non-Jews. Such a development is strongly suggested by the fact that, with control for education and occupation, income differences between Jews and non-Jews have been shown to be greatly reduced, and sometimes reversed.

These demographic changes point to a number of challenges which the American Jewish community must face. In the last three decades of the twentieth century, increasing Americanization will continue, as judged by greater geographic dispersion, a higher percentage of third and fourth generation Americans, and narrowing of such key socioeconomic differentials as education, occupation, and income. To what extent will the diminution in the distinctive population characteristics of Jews and their greater residential integration lead to behavioral convergence? The risks or opportunities for this to occur, depending on how one views the situation, are increasingly present. Recent research suggests that, while growing similarity on the behavioral level is likely, structural separation and the continuity of Jewish identification will persist.[65] The direction of changes appears to be the adjustment of American Jews to the American way of life, creating a meaningful balance between Jewishness and Americanism.

[65] Goldstein and Goldscheider, *Jewish Americans*, pp. 232–243.

5

American Jewry: Identity and Affiliation

CHARLES S. LIEBMAN

The Strength of Jewish Identity

The problem of Jewish identity has at least two dimensions. First, how strongly do Jews identify with Judaism? Second, how do Jews define their Jewish identity? Superficially, the first dimension refers to the survival of Jewish life and the second to its quality. However, both the question of Jewish survival and the question of the quality of Jewish life may include any number of mutually contradictory programs. Furthermore, both the possibility of survival and the quality of Jewish life are interrelated directly and indirectly through their mutual dependence on the general American environment.

The ultimate test of a Jewish commitment is one of behavior rather than of attitude. Thus, it would be a mistake to underestimate the commitment of most American Jews to a Jewish identity, particularly in light of their response to events surrounding the Six Day War in the spring of 1967. To a large extent, the social scientist cannot measure the depth or strength of Jewish identity, much less uncover its basis. The best that can be done is to judge the behavioral responses of American Jews and to recognize that in a time of communal emergency, when a threat to Jewish survival is perceived, the reaction is likely to be exceptional. Nevertheless, I do not believe that the outpouring of concern and support in the days before and during the Six Day War presages any permanent change in the strength, commitment, or nature of Jewish identity.

One can, however, note some general points about the strength of Jewish identity.

1. American Jews, by and large, feel at ease with their Jewishness, as has been confirmed by a number of studies which report an overwhelmingly affirmative response to the question: "If you were to be born again would you want to be born a Jew?" But whereas most Jews are not ashamed of their Jewishness, they are sensitive to the fact that other Jews may be, and thus most frequently characterize the quality of a "good Jew" as one who "accepts his being a Jew and doesn't try to hide it." What is significant here is that Jews acknowledge the importance of Jewish self-pride and also that they believe the particular quality to be relevant.

2. Judaism occupies a very small place in the American Jew's life space. As Simon Herman has noted, "The American Jew tends to see his Jewishness as relevant only in certain settings and on certain occasions—his being Jewish is related to specific limited regions of the life space."[1]

We might better understand the significance of this fact if we juxtapose it against the theory which gained wide acceptance in the 1950s, namely that religion was the major vehicle through which Americans related to the national society. While this may have been true in the 1950s—which I deem unlikely—it is certainly not true in the 1970s. Jews continue to identify themselves as such because they want to do so or can't escape doing so. But they don't feel that being Jewish makes them better Americans.

3. The American environment is conducive to the maintenance of Jewish identity just as it is corrosive to its traditional content. Here it is worth reviewing some well-known facts whose consequences for Jewish identity are in no way diminished by their obviousness. First, the American Jew is free to identify as a Jew without any legal and, increasingly, even social sanctions being attached to the affiliation. Only someone insensitive to Jewish history would argue that this condition must necessarily continue, but it does remain true today and is, in fact, taken for granted by the overwhelming majority of American Jews.

The second important fact about the American Jewish condition is that Judaism shares enough characteristics in common with other

---

[1] Simon Herman, *American Students in Israel* (Ithaca: Cornell University Press, 1970), p. 36.

legitimate subgroups in the society for there to be nothing peculiar attached to one's self-identification as a Jew. All societies, including the American, tolerate subgroups and depend upon them to perform a variety of social functions. All societies must, therefore, accord these subgroups some degree of freedom and autonomy. But it does not follow that the particular subgroups which society recognizes as legitimate and whose autonomy and freedom it fosters need necessarily be ethnic or religious groups. Indeed, there were signs in the last decade that ethnic and religious differences in America were being replaced by occupational and age-group divisions, such as a youth culture, golden-age culture, college culture, or professional culture—all of which tend to cut across ethnic and religious differences. The cry for "black power" and the demand for racial recognition may retard the expansion of these new subcultures. There is evidence that it has impeded the development of a universalist student culture on college campuses, which has served to invigorate the self-identity of many Jewish students. But black self-consciousness may be moderated to the point where it no longer provides an obstacle to the development of age and professional subgroups. These, in turn, will increasingly preempt the role and function of religious and ethnic groups. In that case, Jewish self-identity will become even less relevant to other aspects of the individual's life space and more idiosyncratic in the American environment.

4. The present condition of American Jews, far from presenting them with an identity crisis, is ideally suited to their identity needs and values. These are the same values which have characterized modern European as well as American Jewry.[2]

When one considers the behavior of Jews in the centuries following their political emancipation, one is struck by two apparently contradictory phenomena. First, there appears to be a constant drive for the Jew to free himself from the condition which Judaism apparently thrusts upon him. For lack of a better term we will call this the "condition of estrangement." The impetus for intellectual and religious reform among Jews, adoption of new ideologies and life styles, but above all else the changing self-perception by the Jew of himself and his condition, was not simply a desire to find amelioration from the physical oppression of the ghetto. It was, rather, a desire for emanci-

[2] The following section reprints in part material from my essay, "Toward a Theory of Jewish Liberalism," in *The Religious Situation, 1969*, ed. Donald Cutler (Boston: Beacon Press, 1969), pp. 1050–1051, 1053–1054.

pation from the very essence of the Jewish condition in which a Jew found himself as a minority different in quality and kind from even other minorities and hence ineligible to participate, as other minorities did, as an equal member of society. This denial of equality was not simply a matter of rights. Even where the Jew was granted full political equality he still sensed his estrangement (indeed, often more acutely). The Jew's problem was his alienation from the roots and traditions of the society. Although the sense of estrangement has been a constant throughout Jewish history, it was felt most sharply in the postemancipation period, when the Gentile society and culture were no longer formally Christian and secularization enveloped the Jewish people, destroying the traditional values which provided religious legitimation to the estrangement and obviating the expectation of its removal in the Messianic period.

Most Jews, however, were not looking to escape from Judaism. Even where such options were open to them, Jews sought to retain their Jewish affiliation. When nothing else remained to give Jews a separate identity, when it appeared as though the promise of a universal society was indeed open to Jews, they still sought a distinct identity, if in no other way than through associations with other Jews. Most Jewish Marxists in Poland were not Communists but Bundists. At least in the early 1920s, all that separated the Jewish Workers' Bund of Poland from the Communists was the former's insistence on retaining their organizational identity. Thus Jews sought the options of the Enlightenment, but rejected its consequences.

Jews were enthusiastic supporters of universal humanism and cosmopolitanism. They embraced democratic nationalism, liberalism, and moderate socialism. To be sure, there were variations among regions and periods, and not all Jews responded in quite the same way. What is striking, however, is the constant search for a universalistic ethic which would cut through the differences that an older tradition had imposed, but which would permit the Jew to retain at least nominal identification as a Jew.

The Jew desperately sought to participate in society and rejected sectarianism as a survival strategy. He wished to be accepted as an equal in society not because he was a Jew, but because his Jewishness was irrelevant. Yet at the same time he refused to make his own Jewishness irrelevant. For that matter, Judaism with its religious particularism and culture and ethnic overtones is indeed not irrelevant to the extent that the developing nation states aspired to a uniform culture and civilization. The Jew wanted the non-Jew to ignore his Jewishness but, paradoxically, the Jew himself was unwilling to do so. At most he was willing to make the effort to redefine the nature of his commitment to Judaism and his perception of the content of Judaism.

5. The foregoing discussion takes no account of differences among American Jews. While it is true that the majority of Jews confront the same stimuli and tend to respond uniformly, not all begin from the same starting point. Moreover, what is true of the majority of Jews is not true of all of them. A good case can be made for an increasing polarization of the American Jewish community as a result of the intensified identity and commitment of a minority. One consequence of defining Judaism as a religion has been that some of the more committed Jews necessarily locate themselves in the more religious, that is, Orthodox, camp, and others of this highly identified minority take their cues from developments and trends within American Orthodoxy. Orthodoxy, in turn, has also been affected by Americanization, so that these tendencies are not without their subtleties. But the trend toward polarization has some very clear expressions. Increasing tolerance toward intermarriage, rather than the intermarriage rates themselves, suggests a diminution of Jewish identity on the part of most Jews. On the other hand, the growth of Jewish day schools, increased emigration of American Jews to Israel, and recent outbursts among impatient Jewish youth (to be discussed below) indicate that one small segment of the community is moving in the direction of heightened identity.

The Nature of Jewish Identity

The way in which the individual relates to Judaism can be examined from several perspectives, but I shall limit myself to two—the American Jew's perception of the values or meaning of Judaism and his relationship to those values, and his relationship to other Jews and the organized Jewish community. These two measures of Jewish identity are related but by no means the same. They are related in two ways. First, Jewish values, both traditionally and in their American transformation, place a high premium on communal affiliation. Second, most behavior which weakens the individual's link to the community (intermarriage is probably the best example) tends to weaken his links to Judaism as well. However, the Jewish community and Jewish values are not identical. Activity in a Jewish organization, rather than serving Jewish purposes, may simply be an instrument for the participant to broaden his contacts with non-Jewish society by virtue of his status as a Jewish leader. Furthermore, institutions which are structurally Jewish may serve the latent function of assimilating the Jew to aspects of American culture. Many commentators have noted that this is precisely the role which the Yiddish press, particularly the *Jewish Daily Forward*, fulfilled for the immigrant Jews at the turn of the century; it was through the medium of the Yiddish press that the immigrants learned about middle-class mores and etiquette, American values of child rearing, romantic love, political participation, and so on. As for Jewish fraternal organizations, these provide an opportunity for Jews to meet socially and, through their adult-education programs, to reinforce values of group survival. By the same token, such social activities as a weekend in Las Vegas, a fishing trip, or a dinner dance conducted under Jewish auspices, legitimize aspects of non-Jewish leisure activity which may in turn suggest a whole new set of values, attitudes, and life styles. On the other hand, many left-wing intellectuals and radicals of the 1930s who denied their Jewish heritage and went so far as to affirm the insignificance of Hitler's anti-Semitism were later led back to a sense of Jewishness through an affirmation of the positive aspects of American life.[3] One writer has noted that the more Americanized the Jewish workers became, "the more enthusiastically they support the fund for Palestine and the Jewish State."[4] Thus, the impact of organizational affiliation or of Americanization and acculturation is complex. Jewish affiliation has served not only as a vehicle for Americanization but even for the internalizing of anti-Jewish values.

JEWISH VALUES

American Jews share a set of characteristic values which relate to the American environment as well as to historical Judaism. I will confine myself to those values which bear more directly on the question of Jewish identity.

1. In one sense, I have already defined the dominant American

---

[3] See Norman Podhoretz, *Making It* (New York: Random House, Inc., 1967), pp. 109–136.

[4] From the Foreword by Joseph Schlossberg to Samuel Kurland, *Cooperative Palestine*, cited in Mordecai M. Kaplan, *A New Zionism* (New York: Herzl Press, 1959), p. 89.

Jewish value—integration into the larger community, a desire which proceeds simultaneously with the wish for Jewish survival. Values of integration and survival are not unique to Jews, but the intensity with which these values are held is probably more pronounced among Jews than among any other group in American society. The Italian immigrants, for example, resisted acculturation more strenuously than did the Jews, but their second and third generations are barely distinguishable as a separate group. Even the Irish, despite their celebration as a proud, defiant, separate subgroup in American society, are not only disappearing rapidly, but seem to take pride in their loss of identity. The Amish, on the other hand, are far more resistant to acculturation than the Jews, but they do not insist that American society close its eyes to their distinctiveness in economic, political, or social considerations. The Jews, however, desire to be treated as more than simply equals. Jews demand that their Jewishness cease to be a factor in any judgments which society exercises over them. For example, Jews do not argue that since they comprise X percentage of New York City's population they are entitled to X percentage of the political offices. On the contrary, they argue that their Jewishness is irrelevant to such considerations. But Jews are quite conscious of their proportion of officeholders, college presidents, or large corporation directors, and where the number of Jews is less than might be anticipated, they suspect that this is a result of discrimination. Jews do not argue that equality means that public support for education should include public support for Jewish schools. Instead they (at least many of them) argue that public support for education should not be extended to any private schools. The incessant demand of Jews is that they be treated as though their Jewishness were not a factor. Nevertheless, Jews still want to be Jews. Very few Jews convert to Christianity, or join the Universalist-Unitarian Church or the Ethical Culture movement. Classical Reform Judaism, as exemplified by New York City's Temple Emanu-El, is the more characteristic affiliation of assimilated Jews.

Jews, in sum, want full acceptance in American society as Americans, not as Jews. However, most Jews are still scandalized by intermarriage and insist that a non-Jewish partner to a marriage convert to Judaism even when, as is usually the case, that partner no longer considers himself (or herself) Christian. They support the State of Israel financially, politically, and emotionally when such support must surely raise the specter of dual national loyalty, and they are outraged, for example, by the discovery that the State Department discriminates against Jews in its personnel policies.

Thus American Jews live in a state of tension between the two values of integration and survival, and, regardless of where they stand on a survival-integration continuum, they find themselves pulled in both directions.

2. It is possible to identify more specific values of American Judaism. Elsewhere I have suggested six such values,[5] and a survey of 1,200 synagogues and local chapter presidents of a national Jewish organization has confirmed their widespread acceptance. Five of these values are of direct relevance to the present discussion.

(a) There is nothing incompatible between being a good Jew and a good American or between Jewish standards of behavior and American standards of behavior. If, however, one must choose between the two, one's first loyalty is to American standards of behavior and to American rather than to Jewish culture.

(b) Separation of church and state is absolutely essential. It protects America from being taken over by religious groups, it protects Judaism from having alien standards forced upon it, and, most importantly, it protects the Jew from being continually reminded of his minority and Jewish status. Only the separation of church and state assures the existence of religiously neutral areas of life where the Jew can function with his Jewish status as a matter of irrelevance.

(c) The Jews constitute one indivisible people. It is their common history and experiences which define them as a people, not any common religious beliefs. What makes one a Jew is identification with the Jewish people, which is not quite the same thing as an identification with the Jewish religion. Religious differences within Judaism are tolerated except when they seem to threaten the basic unity of the Jewish people. Then there emerges an overriding demand for consensus or compromise.

(d) Jewish rituals—up to a point—are to be practiced. Attending the synagogue a few times a year, lighting candles on Friday evening, having the family together for a *seder*, or celebrating a son's *Bar Mitzvah* are proper ways of expressing one's Jewishness and keeping the family integrated. But Jews cannot be expected to observe all the

[5] Charles S. Liebman, "Reconstructionism in American Jewish Life," *American Jewish Year Book*, 1970, vol. 71, pp. 3–99.

rituals of traditional Judaism. These were suitable, perhaps, to different countries or cultures, but not to the American Jew of the twentieth century. Many rituals ought to be changed, and it is up to each person to decide for himself what he should or should not observe.

(e) Among the major tasks that face the Jewish community is insuring the survival of the State of Israel, which is every Jew's obligation. However, support for Israel does not mean that one has to move there or that living outside Israel is wrong, or that one who lives in Israel is a better Jew than one who does not.

3. The question of the definition or classification of Judaism—is it a religion or an ethnic group, a culture, a nationality, or a people?—is not easily resolved. In a nominal sense the American Jew no doubt thinks of Judaism as a religion. This is a largely unconscious accommodation by the East European immigrant or his descendants to the American environment, which proved unreceptive to ethnic, cultural, or national separatism but quite congenial to religious independence. America tolerated ethnic groups as long as they did not use their ethnicity to justify separatism. Jewish or Catholic strictures against intermarriage or programs of supplementary education *were* tolerated.

It took the first generation of East European immigrants some time to learn this, and, having learned what America anticipated of them, it is doubtful if all the Jews really internalized the message. Even when the first generation of immigrants defined Judaism as a religion it is not always clear that they meant it. The religious façade of Jewish life prior to World War II might have been intended to fool the non-Jews at least as much as it was intended to fool the Jews themselves. In addition, institutions and organizations of a nonreligious nature (economic, cultural, ethnic, and national) continued to exist as alternatives rather than supplements to the synagogue.

World War II marks a new period in Jewish self-identification. It inaugurated a period of heightened self-interest and awareness on the part of many Jews, and an increase in the status of Jewishness. It was also a period of tremendous Jewish geographic and social mobility, and of the coming of age of the second generation, which meant increased pressure for Americanization.

This second generation American Jew had lived through the period of the Holocaust and of the creation of Israel, a time of great emotional charge, and it seemed a betrayal of self to deny one's Jewishness, particularly since American values supported Jewish self-identification and economic prosperity released monies and energies for Jewish activity. But this was also a generation of incredible ignorance. Twice removed from the East European Jewish heartland, it had no memory of traditional Jewish life to compensate for its Jewish illiteracy. This Americanized and acculturated generation simply overwhelmed the existing Jewish community and completed the process of "religionizing" or, more correctly, "Protestantizing" American Judaism. Judaism took on the indelible stamp of an American religious denomination whose patterns of religious change showed increasing "secular content and similarity to Protestant-liberal norms."[6]

4. A religious definition of Judaism has a number of consequences, two of the most important of which relate to Jewish ideology and intermarriage. While American Judaism has produced no Jewish ideology of stature, the intellectual creativity it has demonstrated has been in the religious sphere, in contrast to modern East European Jewry, which produced a Jewish historiography, a Jewish literature, and a Jewish national, social, and cultural ideology. But since modern Jewish intellectuals have felt least comfortable with religious and theological categories of thought, the consequences of the religious definition of Judaism has been to increase their disaffection.

Second, if Judaism is defined as a religion, then it follows that someone who is not religious is not to be regarded as Jewish. A religious, as distinct from an ethnic, definition of Judaism makes it easier to enter or leave the Jewish fold. It is significant that it is among suburban residents, who have "the greatest assimilation in almost every aspect of religiosity," the greatest intermarriage rate, and "the weakest affiliation with Jewishness,"[7] that conversions to Judaism are highest. On the other hand, a religious definition reduces the formal pressures on the religiously indifferent Jew to retain any tie to the community when he does not recognize his own ties to that community's sense of purpose.

5. American Jewry has linked itself to the State of Israel through tourism, financial contributions, investments, political support, and immigration. Indeed, it seems as though interest in Israel, particularly in the last few years, has preempted other Jewish concerns. The

[6] Sidney Goldstein and Calvin Goldscheider, *Jewish Americans: Three Generations in a Jewish Community* (Englewood Cliffs, N. J.: Prentice-Hall, Inc., 1968), p. 240.
[7] Ibid., p. 241.

dimensions and intensity of Jewish support for Israel raise questions about the religious definition of American Judaism. For instance, if Judaism is seen as a religion, why should concern for Israel be such an important component of American Jewish identity? One possibility is that American Jews see Israel as the religious and spiritual center of Judaism. But this is not the case. Indeed, in a survey of Jewish synagogue and organizational leaders, a majority, except for the Orthodox, expressed agreement with the following statement: "While there must be a warm fraternal relationship between Jews of the United States and Israel, the center of American Jewish life must be *American* Judaism rather than a Jewish culture which has developed or will develop in Israel."[8] Thus the intensity of American Jewish support for Israel remains paradoxical, given the religious definition of Judaism. Furthermore, support for Israel has reached heretofore inaccessible segments of the Jewish community. This is probably the only major Jewish activity today which involves the "nonreligious" Jew.

It may be that American Jews are shifting to a new stage of Jewish identity in which Israel is replacing religion. Such a change would be totally out of harmony with prevailing American notions of legitimacy. One is inclined, therefore, to explore the possibility that support for Israel is only an extension or evolution of American Jewish identity since World War II, rather than a radical shift.

The first point to note is that the Jewish religion itself emphasizes the importance of the land of Israel. This is not only true in the sense that Zion occupies a central place in Jewish liturgy and ritual. Nor is it true only because the religious establishment, especially the various rabbinical and synagogue organizations, have been unanimous in their declarations in support of Israel. It is especially true because, at the local congregational level, Israel has turned into a focal point of Jewish identity. Nothing illustrates Israel's role in the religious life of American Jewry better than the promotion of Israel Bonds on Yom Kippur. This holiest day of the Jewish calendar stresses the personal relationship of man to God and the idea of repentance. The prayers, devoted to spiritual self-assessment and pleas for forgiveness, are interrupted in hundreds of synagogues by an appeal to the congregants to buy Israel Bonds. Whatever one may think of the practice, most

[8] This and other responses of Jewish synagogue and organizational leaders to Israel are reported in Charles S. Liebman, "The Role of Israel in the Ideology of American Jewry," *Dispersion and Unity*, 10 (Winter 1970): 19–26.

American Jews regard this as a proper synagogue activity, even on Yom Kippur, which says a great deal about their concept of "religious" behavior and the place of Israel in their "religious" outlook.

The foregoing suggests that American Jews continue to define Judaism as a religion, but that Israel increasingly defines the content of that religion. Concomitantly, support of Israel becomes not only support of a state or of its inhabitants; rather, support of Israel is the symbol of one's Jewish identity, like staying home from work on Yom Kippur. It has nothing to do with Zionism, with a national Jewish self-definition, or even with knowing very much about Israel itself or about modern Jewish-Israeli culture. Support of Israel is perfectly compatible with being a good American.[9]

Of course, there are other reasons for the important role which Israel plays in American Jewish life. The stakes involved in Israel's success are obvious, involving the lives of 2 million Jews. Furthermore, unlike the situation vis-à-vis Soviet Jewry, which also involves the lives of many Jews, far more American Jews have relatives in Israel with whom there is regular personal contact. Also, political and financial support of Israel represents an outlet and expression of Jewish activity which is religiously legitimate but entirely secular in content. In a sense, it gives one something importantly "Jewish" to do which, unlike religious practice, demands no specialized knowledge. Finally, the mass media bring Israel to the constant attention of the American Jew, and the agenda of American Jewish life is largely dictated by the concerns of the non-Jewish media. Israel's prominent media coverage thereby reinforces the efforts of Jewish leaders to bring its problems to the attention of the American Jew.

It remains to be seen whether Israel will continue to occupy its present role in Jewish life in the event that the American public becomes less tolerant of Jewish commitment to Israel, or in the happy event that threats to Israel's physical survival diminish.

6. As in the earlier discussion on the strength of Jewish identity, so, too, in considering the nature of Jewish identity, one must not lump all Jews together. Not all of them identify or define Judaism in the same way. The vast majority may define Judaism as a religion while disagreeing among themselves about the content of the religion. Stud-

---

[9] Nathan Rotenstreich makes a similar point in his comments in *Changing Relationships between Israel and the Diaspora* (Jerusalem: The Institute for Contemporary Jewry, Publications of the Study Circle on Diaspora Jewry, Hebrew, 1969), pp. 60–61.

ies of Jewish teen-agers in the 1950s[10] indicated surprising agreement on the ritual requirements of Judaism. The teen-agers accepted traditional, or Orthodox, norms even while deviating from them. One suspects that this is no longer the case. In the portrait which Sklare and Greenblum paint of Lakeville,[11] their pseudonymous name for an American Jewish suburban community, only 12 percent of the respondents thought it essential or desirable for a "good Jew" to observe the dietary laws. There is probably a new level of agreement emerging among Conservative and Reform Jews about the desirable level of traditional observance, but this leaves the Orthodox segment of the community in substantial disagreement.

Furthermore, there are still some Jews who retain a purely cultural, linguistic, or national self-definition. While they represent a small minority and really fall outside the consensus of American Judaism, they may play a prominent public role because of the intensity of their commitment. They are to be found in disproportionate numbers among Jewish professionals in such fields as education, camping, Zionism, and social and communal work.

Finally, there is that assimilationist element which, unwilling to die a quiet natural death, is not satisfied unless it can drag the rest of American Jewry along with it to the grave. This element once thrived within Reform Judaism, but since the 1930s, especially since World War II, assimilationists in the Reform movement have been on the defensive. They are more likely now to be totally outside the religious camp, defining themselves as "Jewish secularists." Their views, which find expression in such works as James Yaffe's *The American Jews*,[12] define Judaism in purely universalist terms. They would abandon all Jewish particularism and, needless to say, they advocate intermarriage.

JEWISH AFFILIATION

We turn now to the second aspect of the nature of Jewish identity, the American Jew's relationship to other Jews and to the organized Jewish community.

1. In a study which has assumed great importance in the literature on American minority groups, Milton Gordon characterized various

---

[10] Bernard Rosen, *Adolescence and Religion* (Cambridge, Mass.: Schenkman Publishing Co., 1965).

[11] Marshall Sklare and Joseph Greenblum, *Jewish Identity on the Suburban Frontier* (New York: The American Jewish Committee and Basic Books, Inc., Publishers, 1967).

[12] James Yaffe, *The American Jews* (New York: Random House, Inc., 1968).

stages of assimilation.[13] The two stages most relevant to our discussion are cultural or behavioral assimilation, in which the minority group adjusts its cultural patterns to those of the dominant society, and structural assimilation, in which there is large-scale entrance of minority group members into the cliques, clubs, and institutions of the host society on the primary group level. In his discussion of American Jews, Gordon suggests that cultural assimilation has taken place, whereas structural assimilation has not. One writer, who relies on Gordon for his theoretical framework, makes the following observation:

The Jews of America associate among themselves . . . they are culturally American, but socially in the ghetto. But, mind you, the ghetto is an American ghetto, not a Jewish ghetto. American Jews in B'nai B'rith . . . do precisely what other Americans do in the Knights of Columbus, the Rotarians . . . and other fraternal organizations. They do not differ in behavior patterns, in ritual, in professed ideals, in activities of all sorts, except for this one very significant thing, that they prefer to associate among themselves.[14]

While there is undoubtedly some truth in this observation, it is exaggerated and misleading. Gordon may be right in a general way, but his categories of cultural and structural assimilation are too gross.

The essence of American Jewish identity, the core meaning of Judaism for many American Jews, may very well be their social ties to one another. We shall call this "associationalism." The distinguishing mark of American Jews is the fact that they increasingly associate primarily with other Jews, rather than what or even how they believe (though, as we shall see, associationalism is related to behavior). As Gerhard Lenski discovered in his Detroit area study, ties binding Jews to their religion are weaker than those of Protestants or Catholics; ties binding them to one another are much stronger. More than other religious groups, "the great majority of Detroit Jews find most of their primary relationships within the Jewish subcommunity."[15] Even among the

---

[13] Milton Gordon, *Assimilation in American Life* (New York: Oxford University Press, 1964). See also the attack on Gordon from a Jewish perspective by Marshall Sklare, "Assimilation and the Sociologists," *Commentary*, 44 (May 1965): 63–67.

[14] Werner J. Cahnman, "Comments on the American Jewish Scene," in *Conference on Acculturation*, ed. Herbert Strauss (New York: American Federation of Jews from Central Europe, 1965), pp. 20–21.

[15] Gerhard Lenski, *The Religious Factor*, rev. ed. (New York: Anchor Books, 1963), p. 37.

third generation, wealthy, acculturated suburban Jews of Lakeville, Jews make their friends almost exclusively among other Jews. By and large this is not a result of anti-Semitism or deliberate exclusion on the part of non-Jews. Rather, as many respondents emphasized:

. . . Jews are predisposed to social contact and intimate association with other Jews because of a common religio-ethnic heritage and a pervasive group identity: "It's because Jews go with Jews and Gentiles go with Gentiles. My background is so Jewish and my life is so Jewish that I'm happier surrounded by Jews," explains a young salesman's wife who is now active in Lilienthal Temple, although as an adolescent she had some close friends who were Gentile. "It's the identity, the background, the religion. It would be hard for a Gentile to be comfortable without those common bonds," elaborates an affluent lawyer and business executive who came to the United States from Russia when he was a youngster. . . . A young businessman who observed almost none of the traditional religious practices to which he was exposed in childhood mentions similar reasons to account for the fact that he lost contact with the non-Jewish friends that he had before marriage. "They went different paths because of differences in economics, education, and a different mode of living."[16]

The first point to be noted is that Jewish associationalism has a behavioral foundation. In other words, Jews seek out other Jews because they apparently find something "different" or "special" which distinguishes Jews from non-Jews. The second point is that Jewish associationalism exists independently of other attributes of Jewish identity. It is a pattern found among all types of Jews and in all types of Jewish communities, urban and suburban, wealthy and poor, first generation and third generation American. Sklare and Greenblum found that those "uninvolved in religion and synagogue life have almost as Jewish a friendship circle as those who possess religious commitments."[17] In his sample of Chicago area Jews, Bernard Lazerwitz constructed nine measures of Jewish identity, one of which was ethnicity. This was defined by the number of close Jewish friends one had or the frequency of visiting Jews as compared to non-Jews.[18] There were no pronounced differences in ethnicity between Jews who scored high or low on other measures of Jewish identification, which

16 Sklare and Greenblum, *Jewish Identity on the Suburban Frontier*, pp. 280–281.
17 Ibid., p. 284.
18 Bernard Lazerwitz, "A First Report on the General Components and Consequences of Jewish Identification," mimeographed (National Jewish Welfare Board Research Program at Brandeis University, 1968).

included religious behavior, Jewish education, Zionism, pietism, traditional beliefs, and Jewish organizational affiliation.

Jewish associationalism, at least among adults, appears to be ubiquitous. This does not mean that it is a permanent phenomenon. Indeed, there is every reason to be pessimistic concerning long-run trends, since many Jewish youth today not only form ties with non-Jews (which was apparently always the case) but explicitly reject the values implicit in Jewish associationalism. Furthermore, many educational, life style, child-rearing patterns that were once characteristically Jewish are now shared by non-Jews. Consequently, the basis of Jewish associationalism among the assimilated, that is, those who associate with Jews rather than non-Jews only because of common life styles, will disappear.

2. While there is no relationship between friendship patterns and other measures of Jewish identity, there is a relationship between organizational affiliation and other identity measures. Those affiliated with Jewish organizations are most likely to identify themselves with the religious community. Lazerwitz found that "the two dominating factors of Jewish identification, which are also strongly associated with one another, are the religio-pietistic and Jewish organizational factors."[19] Sklare and Greenblum, on the other hand, found that among men (although not women) the degree of religious commitment meant little, if any, distinction in the level of organizational affiliation or even in the degree of involvement. However, the religiously uncommitted had "an affinity for social and recreational organizations which avoid any instrumental or Jewish purpose."[20] Thus, their conclusion that Jewish organizational involvement provides a secular alternative for nonreligious Jews seems unwarranted, because Jewish organizations are not of a single mold.

It appears far more useful to distinguish among types of Jewish organizations. Those which are purely recreational or social bring Jews together at the associational level, the lowest level of Jewish identity. They do evidence the pattern of cultural assimilation and structural segregation. But the Jewish organizations which we more

---

[19] Ibid., p. 19. Similar conclusions are to be found in Stanley K. Bigman, *The Jewish Population of Greater Washington in 1956* (Washington, D. C.: The Jewish Community Council of Greater Washington, 1957), p. 68; and Morris Axelrod et al., *A Community Survey for Long Range Planning: A Study of the Jewish Population of Greater Boston* (Boston: The Combined Jewish Philanthropies, 1967), p. 165.

[20] Sklare and Greenblum, *Jewish Identity on the Suburban Frontier*, p. 263.

commonly identify as communal—B'nai B'rith, The American Jewish Committee, American Jewish Congress, Hadassah, Jewish War Veterans, Zionist Organization of America, Organization for Rehabilitation and Training—are not a secular alternative to the synagogue, but a supplement to religious identification. Whatever social, recreational, or purely expressive satisfactions the Jew may derive from such organizations, he also relates to them because they fulfill instrumental Jewish purposes. Contrary to what Gordon suggests, there are types of Jewish structures which still remain culturally independent, and it is precisely those structures which play a crucial role in the network of Jewish communal relationships. This is not to suggest that such organizations have not been Americanized or, as we indicated above, may not even convert their members to anti-Jewish values. But surely we must view an organization as culturally Jewish if its goals are uniquely Jewish. Gordon's description of the Jewish community as structurally segregated but culturally assimilated fits, at least temporarily, Jewish social and recreational organizations. Less clear is the place of Jewish community centers. Do they fulfill purely associational needs, or are they cultural supplements to other forms of Jewish activity? Different centers are probably of varying types, depending on the particular board and executive director.[21]

3. The synagogue is the institution with which Jews are most widely affiliated, comprising approximately 60 percent of American Jews.[22] But estimates of the number of Jews affiliated with communal organizations are subject to greater error. In the absence of organizational figures, we must rely on self-reporting by respondents in various

21 We have been using type of organization as a measure of identity. A far more revealing measure might be contributions to Jewish philanthropy. However, tapping such a measure is fraught with difficulty. We would have to measure relative contributions—but relative to what? To individual income, family income, present income, past income, anticipated income? Would we distinguish types of Jewish philanthropies, rather than lump, say, hospitals and Jewish schools together? How would we hold constant for community and economic pressures to contribute? What would we do about family or corporate contributions? What about contributions to such organizations as the American Israel Public Affairs Committee, which is not philanthropic? Finally, how reliable would self-reporting of such information be? If these technical hurdles could be overcome, we might have a measure of activity which cuts across the entire gamut of Jewish identification and is the best single measure of Jewish commitment.
22 The figure can be misleading, since it includes family members whose affiliation might take place through one parent. On the other hand, it excludes many elderly persons who may disaffiliate in a formal sense while retaining informal ties to the synagogue. Over 90 percent of American Jews express some denominational preference when asked if they identify themselves as Orthodox, Conservative, Reform, or secular Jews.

community surveys. Unfortunately, such data is not always collected or reported uniformly. Based on studies of Washington, D. C.; Camden, New Jersey; Providence, Rhode Island; and Boston, Massachusetts,[23] I would estimate that about 35 percent of the adult Jewish population belongs to at least one Jewish communal organization (this excludes membership in synagogue men's clubs and sisterhoods, the most prevalent type of organizational affiliation, and in Jewish community centers).

There seems to be a tendency for women to affiliate more than men (in two areas more women are affiliated and in one area the same proportion of women are affiliated, but they are members of more organizations), though in one area the tendency is reversed. There are only two Jewish organizations with which at least 10 percent of the Jewish population who are eligible to join are affiliated. The largest Jewish organization is Hadassah, followed by B'nai B'rith. However, in individual communities, a local organization may be much larger. In Providence, for example, 22 percent of the women are affiliated with Zionist organizations (we may assume the overwhelming majority were members of Hadassah), but 26 percent were affiliated with the Jewish community center and 36 percent with synagogue sisterhoods.

As we indicated, membership in Jewish communal organizations does not represent an alternative to membership in the synagogue. We have no knowledge as to whether it represents an alternative for active participation and leadership, though this seems likely.

4. From the preceding discussion, a picture emerges of three types of Jews—the affiliated, the associated, and the nonassociated. The affiliated Jew represents the largest category and includes an estimated 70 percent or more of American Jewry. He is likely to belong to a synagogue and he or his wife probably belong to some other Jewish organization. His closest friends are Jews. While the quality of his Jewish life and the level of his Jewish knowledge leave much to be desired, and he may be gradually assimilating more and more values

---

[23] Studies include surrounding suburbs as well as the city itself. On Washington see Bigman, *The Jewish Population of Greater Washington in 1956*; for Camden see Charles Westoff, *Population and Social Characteristics of the Jewish Community of the Camden Area 1964* (Camden: Jewish Federation of Camden County, n.d.); for Providence see Sidney Goldstein, *The Greater Providence Jewish Community* (Providence: The General Jewish Committee of Providence, 1964); for Boston see Axelrod et al., *A Community Survey for Long Range Planning.*

and life style patterns of the non-Jewish community, he is Jewishly self-conscious and wants Judaism to survive.

The associated Jew is unaffiliated with a synagogue or Jewish communal organization and may even identify himself as a secular Jew, though his closest friends are Jewish. He may be affiliated with a social or recreational group which is nominally Jewish or whose predominant membership is Jewish. While associated Jews comprise a minority of American Jews, they are significant because they are disproportionately third or fourth generation American Jews and disproportionately under forty years of age.

Finally there is the nonassociated Jew, about whom we know the least statistically but, with respect to some individuals, the most anecdotally. He is the Jew least likely to be captured by community studies, most likely to be intermarried, and completely marginal to the Jewish community. He is, I would guess, likely to be of two types. As a member of the working class and a high school dropout, he may drop out of the Jewish community without anyone caring to claim him. Alternately, he may be engaged in a highly professionalized or specialized occupation—university professor, psychoanalyst, artist. His major associates and friends may be Jewish because such occupations are highly attractive to Jews. But from his point of view, however erroneous his conclusion may be, the fact that most of his friends are Jewish is a matter of accident. In fact, most of them may not be Jewish.

Among the many independent and dependent variables associated with these types of Jews, two deserve special mention. Jewish education may be the critical independent variable; that is, Jewish education may be the single best causative explanation for differences among types of Jews and even for differences between the more and less committed of the affiliated Jews. However, even if Jewish education is the single best explanatory factor, it hardly suffices to explain everything.

The second factor is contributions to Jewish philanthropy, which, if we had some accurate way of measurement, might prove to be the most reliable dependent variable. I suspect that this is the case.

5. We have proposed a model of three types of Jews—affiliated, associated, and nonassociated. Even if this model adequately describes the behavior of most American Jews, it misses a qualitatively significant segment. Approximately 8,000 Americans have emigrated

to Israel each year from June 1967–1970; the figure for 1970–1971 was 9,200. About half of these emigrants (*olim*) are Orthodox Jews. My guess is that among the Orthodox, at least 50 percent were not affiliated with any Jewish organization in the United States, and a few, although they may have been active in the day school which their children attended, were not even affiliated with a synagogue. Yet these *olim* were prompted to go to Israel from a strong sense of Jewish identity and despair over the possibility of providing a satisfactory Jewish environment for their children in America. In other words, many of these strongly identified, committed *olim* do not readily fall into the category of affiliated or associated Jews. Among the non-Orthodox *olim*, the proportion of deviates is certainly higher. I would guess that a far smaller percentage were affiliated with a Jewish organization or with a synagogue. The pre-1967 *olim* came out of a much stronger Zionist organizational orientation than the post-1967 *olim*. However, in his study of Americans and Canadians still in Israel who came to the country prior to 1966, Aaron Antanovsky found that 58 percent of those who arrived in the previous decade, and did not settle on kibbutzim, did not even belong to a Zionist organization.[24]

In addition to the *oleh* who does not fit into our classification, there is the phenomenon of the radical Jewish youth. These, too, are not all of a kind. There are radical Jewish youth who are identified with black nationalist and/or anti-Semitic and/or pro-Arab groups—those who mock and pervert the Jewish tradition and the Jewish community. While the destructive capacity of such youth must not be underestimated, and the existence of fellow travelers within the affiliated Jewish community must be appreciated, they do not really constitute an exception to our typology of American Jews. At most, one might be forced to construct a fourth category from them. If we heretofore suggested that nonassociated Jews (non-Jewish Jews) constitute the lowest rung on the ladder of Jewish identity, these youth might, in fact, constitute a fourth level—anti-Jewish Jews.

But our concern is with another type of radical youth who is also disaffected from the synagogue and Jewish communal organizations, but for very different reasons. He is the young person who "sat in" in 1968 at a meeting of the American Conference on Soviet Jewry and charged that organization with being little more than an alibi for

[24] Aaron Antanovsky, "Americans and Canadians in Israel," Report No. 1, mimeographed (Jerusalem: Israeli Institute of Applied Social Research, 1968). The figures are derived from those presented on p. 24 of this report.

inaction on Soviet Jewry. He is the youth who occupied the offices of
the New York Federation of Jewish Philanthropies, or who demonstrated at the 1969 meetings of the Council of Jewish Federations and
Welfare Funds (CJFWF). Here is part of what a spokesman for those
who demonstrated at the CJFWF meetings had to say. It is quoted at
some length to demonstrate that antagonism to the organized Jewish
community is compatible with a high commitment to Judaism:

I am not a part of this convention; neither was I nor any young person
asked to speak at this time. . . . I stand here because of pressure that we
exerted upon the planners of this conference to permit us to address you
directly. Knowing that we were given this opportunity only through threats
of a disruption, you might dismiss us as children of our times, bored with
the battle of the campus and looking for a new stage upon which to play
our childish pranks of doubtful morality. . . .

We were born during and shortly after the war. The Holocaust made a
deep impression on our young minds, as did the new-felt pride in the State
of Israel. We had the best set of blocks, the shiniest bicycles, and piano
lessons. We did well in school. We went to Hebrew school and occasionally
synagogue, but found them dull. There were few exciting models for us in
the Jewish community, little opportunity to give expression to our youthful
ideals. In contrast, the larger world was exciting, a labyrinth of mystery and
challenge. . . . The Jewish publicists spilled seas of ink bemoaning our
alienation. Perhaps it was a sign of our health that we were not attracted to
a Jewish life devoid of intellectual and spiritual energy.

It took us several years to realize our confusion of form and essence and
to recognize that there was more to Judaism than its poor expression in the
American Jewish community. For some it was a trip to Israel, for others it
was the reading of Buber's *I and Thou*, for others an encounter with
Hasidism, for others it was a traditional Jewish education redirected to
confront existential problems, for others the exploration of self could not
overlook the Jewish component. The Six-Day War forced us to reassess our
attachment in deciding to risk our lives if necessary on Israel's behalf. The
black awakening reminded us that the melting pot dream was a fool's
fantasy and that differences were legitimate. We woke up from the American dream and tried to discover who we really were. For many of us this
now means turning our concerns inward into the Jewish community because we were disenchanted with the crass materialism of the larger society.
Yet where can we find inspiration in the multi-million dollar Jewish pres-
ences of suburbia?

. . . As the Jew rose into a secure middle-class niche, he became more of
a social and political being. Organizations multiplied which reflected the
needs of adjustment and defense. . . .

. . . Settlement houses had suburban off-shoots of Jewish community
centers closely modelled after the YMCAs. These Jewish swimming pools
and game rooms were to be instrumental in maintaining Jewish loyalties.

. . . Jewish education was a step-son of organized Jewish philanthropies.
. . . Ironically, constituent organizations have declared a holy war against government support of Jewish education while simultaneously refusing to give any aid themselves.

. . . It is inconceivable for a Jewish community to be guided by Jewish principles and values if its leaders are ignorant of them. Surely some knowledge of Hebrew, of Jewish history and traditions should be a prerequisite. Leaders of Jewish philanthropies should not only solicit funds but educate benefactors to the needs of the community. This requires Jewish knowledge.

Your response to us could be: you pampered kids, if you want things done differently, why don't you do it yourselves and leave us alone? This is the way we want the Jewish community. If that would be your response, then with much pain and disappointment we would indeed be forced to do it ourselves. . . . And then perhaps it will only be the coming of the Messiah that will turn our hearts to yours.[25]

Like the *olim,* Jewish radical youth tend to be unaffiliated and even antagonistic to the organized Jewish community, but hardly indifferent. We leave open the question of whether the affiliational problem relates more to the program of Jewish organizations, their style, their decision-making procedures, some other factor, or to all or some of these.

6. The importance of communal organizations, both in terms of their instrumental goals and as a focus of Jewish identity, means that not only the quality of their programs but their very survival must concern all Jews. It is my impression that though the synagogue fails to attract many Jewish youth and intellectuals, Jewish communal organizations are experiencing even more serious difficulty. The most striking expression of the problem is to be found in a comparison of present-day presidents of Jewish organizations with those of twenty or even ten years ago. Is it only coincidence that there is hardly a president of a national Jewish organization who is a personality of national stature? Apparently Jewish organizations are experiencing difficulty in recruiting prominent figures for lay leadership positions. The shortage of professional staff is another problem. All organizations, public and private, rely increasingly on their professional staffs for program planning as well as for administration. There has always been a shortage of Jewishly knowledgeable professionals, but in the past the organiza-

[25] Hillel Levine, "To Share a Vision" (Speech before the Council of Jewish Federations and Welfare Funds meetings, Boston, November 1969), *Response,* 6 (Winter 1969–1970): 3–10.

tional workers were at least committed to their own organization and its program. Today, Jewish agencies find it more and more difficult to attract skilled personnel, much less a professional staff loyal to the organization.

Finally, the growth and increased role and status of "roof organizations"—such as the Presidents' Conference, the Conference on Soviet Jewry, the National Jewish Community Relations Advisory Council, the CJFWF, the Synagogue Council of America—introduce a desirable measure of unity, but also raise dangers regarding the quality of Jewish communal life. Roof organizations, as the term implies, have individual organizations as their constituents, although some of them go outside their constituencies for funds. But their decisions, which often represent the lowest common denominator of agreement among constituent organizations, are also once removed from accountability to a mass membership. Thus, they are not only ineffective except on those rare occasions where true unanimity exists, but they handicap the constituent organizations from exercising boldness and initiative, since the latter must often clear their programs with the roof organizations. It is no wonder, therefore, that some talented laymen find the national organizations less and less attractive as an arena of activity and power. One national organization complains that it has trained laymen at the local level who then leave it for the larger rewards of the roof organization.

The Future of American Judaism

Marshall Sklare recently noted that "it is a hallmark of the contemporary Jewish community that assimilationists insist upon designating themselves as survivalists."[26] While it would be unfortunate to allow the assimilationists to preempt the survivalist vocabulary, their argument is not without logic in the reality of contemporary Jewish life. When we talk about Jewish survival it is not always clear if the reference is to the survival of a group of people who identify themselves as Jewish or to the survival of Judaism. Of course, there is no

[26] In his response to letters from readers, *Commentary*, 49 (June 1970): 14. By an assimilationist Sklare apparently means someone who persists in calling himself Jewish although he denies the tenets, beliefs, practices, and traditions associated with Judaism.

Judaism without Jews. If our referent of survival is therefore to Judaism, then we also mean the survival of Jews—but in this case not only nominally identified Jews but also those who adhere to some definable essence called Judaism.

Whatever definition of Judaism is adopted, one is sure to despair over the continued adherence to Judaism of large numbers of American Jews. Indeed, the more maximalist a definition one adopts (and highly committed Jews tend to be maximalists), the more pessimistic one is likely to be regarding the prospects for the survival of Judaism in the United States. Assimilationists may therefore argue, with some justice, that Jewish maximalists are reading Jews out of Judaism. It makes more sense, they may contend, to define Jews rather than Judaism, in which case Jews would be people who call themselves Jews and Judaism would be what such people say it is. If the Jewish "Establishment," so the argument proceeds, pushes these self-declared Jews too far, abjuring their nominal identification, they will simply opt out of Judaism. Therefore, Jewish survival, as assimilationists understand the term, requires catering to the lowest level of Jewish identification. A responsible rabbi, according to this argument, will agree to officiate at a wedding between a Jew and a non-Jew, even performing the ceremony jointly with a Christian clergyman, especially if he is convinced that, should he refuse, the wedding will take place in any event. (Not all assimilationists adopt such a broad definition. Certain Jewish militant radicals, for example, taking black radicals as their referent, have begun to think in terms of Jewish identity, although redefining Judaism to suit their own proclivities.)

Maximalists might be more comfortable if assimilationists really assimilated and left them with exclusive control over definitions of Jewish identity, even if this meant the loss of many nominal Jews. But before maximalists gain the moral or intellectual right to persist in their position, they must confront two questions.

The first has to do with the problem of Jewish numbers, a factor not to be dismissed lightly. Jews now represent about 2.6 percent of the American population, and their numbers are declining. To be sure, Jews still enjoy a high status in the larger society. Political leaders woo their votes and they are prominent in the arts and professions, to say nothing of the fact that, despite their small numbers, Jews hold a one-third share in the Protestant-Catholic-Jewish definition of the religious composition of America. But at what point will American society awaken to the fact that the status of the Jews is disproportionate to their numbers in the population? Should the percentage of Jews in the total population continue to decline, inevitably someone is going to wonder why Jews, the Jewish vote, Jewish sensitivity, and so on, have to be taken so seriously. When that point is reached, the cost of Jewish commitment will rise. One may very well say, so be it. In every period of history only a small remnant of Jews has survived. Better to retain only a million or half a million Jews, or even less, as long as these are truly committed Jews. This position has an attraction for many survivalist-maximalist Jews. It should be clear, however, that to accept it means to accept the loss of a far greater number of Jews than was envisioned when I spoke earlier in terms of a dichotomy between the vast majority of American Jews who were affiliated with the community and the minority who were only associational Jews or less. It also means basing one's hope for Jewish survival in America on faith rather than on sociology, on the continued capacity of the Jewish people to defy the normal laws of survival rather than on the normal processes of history. Finally, if Judaism is to survive in America with its ranks so depleted, it will probably exist in a far more sectarian context than is presently the case.

This last point relates to the second question which maximalists must face—the question of how to define Judaism. I offer my own definition, not so much to press my own position as to indicate the problem which I think any meaningful definition of Judaism must confront—namely, the fact that Judaism is not consonant with American, indeed, with Western, currents of thought and behavior.

There are, I believe, three indispensable aspects to a definition of Judaism. One is a sense of peoplehood. A community is not Jewish if its members do not sense a special feeling of unity with and responsibility for the physical and spiritual welfare of all other Jews wherever they may be, for Judaism transcends national, regional, racial, and cultural boundaries. A second aspect is *Torah*. I understand *Torah*, at its least, to mean that a Jew must submit himself to a set of laws and practices which exist objectively or in a reality which is not of his construction. The third aspect is Jewish education—the study of *Torah* as sacred text. This implies the belief that some texts are sacred and that a Jew has special obligations to study them and transmit them to others.

It seems to me that all three aspects in my definition of Judaism are threatened in the United States. Jewish peoplehood is threatened by the growing impulse toward cosmopolitanism and universalism; in a society which increasingly stresses the primacy of conscience and individual freedom against even society's own law, *Torah* and the study of sacred texts become increasingly absurd. The very notion of sacred text is antiquarian, and there is no room for a tradition of study in a culture which affirms the values of sensation and of the individual as the final arbiter of right and wrong. It is, therefore, my strong belief that, at least until we enter a postmodern world, the Jew who wishes to remain in the United States, but who is also committed to the survival of Judaism, has no alternative but to retreat into a far more sectarian posture than has up to this time characterized American Jewish life.

III

Communal Institutions

6

The Synagogue in America

WOLFE KELMAN

I

The formal history of the organized American Jewish community is customarily traced to the establishment in 1654 of Congregation Shearith Israel in New Amsterdam, by twenty-three refugees from Brazil, who were compelled to flee their tropical home when the Dutch were expelled by the Portuguese. However, for several centuries thereafter, the Jewish community of North America remained small and insignificant. Indeed, it was not until the nineteenth century, which witnessed mass migrations to the United States from both Eastern and Western Europe, that the American Jewish community as we know it, with its particular institutions and varied religious life, began to assume shape. Typical of congregations which were established in the nineteenth century was the Central Synagogue in New York City, which recently celebrated its one hundredth anniversary. Central Synagogue, founded in 1870 by a group of middle-class merchants who had emigrated to New York from Bohemia some thirty years earlier, is unusual in that it is still situated in its original location. Few American synagogues of similar vintage can make that claim; most have moved from one location to another, following the migration of their members from the first areas of settlement to areas of greater affluence and, eventually, to the suburbs. In places like Newark, Baltimore, and Cleveland, synagogues have abandoned the inner city altogether.

The featured speaker at the dedication ceremonies of the Central Synagogue, on December 14, 1870, was Rabbi Isaac Mayer Wise. This was the same Isaac Mayer Wise, also a Bohemian immigrant, who shortly thereafter was to found Reform Judaism in this country with the establishment of the Union of American Hebrew Congregations (UAHC) in 1873. The Conservative movement traces its formal beginnings to the establishment of the Jewish Theological Seminary in 1886, a development prompted in large part in reaction to the promulgation the year before of the so-called Pittsburgh platform enunciating the official positions of classical Reform. The United Synagogue of America, the congregational arm of the Conservative movement, was founded in 1913 by Solomon Schechter, the second President of the Jewish Theological Seminary. It was hoped that the United Synagogue would serve to oppose the innovations of Reform, but it soon found itself outflanked by the mass immigration of Eastern European Jews which led to the development of an organized Orthodox community.

In its founding statement, the United Synagogue declared its purposes as follows: "To further the observance of the Sabbath and the dietary laws; to preserve in the service the reference to Israel's past and the hopes of Israel's restoration, and to maintain the traditional centrality of Hebrew as the language of prayer and in the curriculum of the religious school." The concluding section of this statement reflects the tensions which still exist, although in diminishing degree, within the Conservative movement: "It shall be the aim of the United Synagogue of America, while not endorsing the innovations introduced by any of its constituent bodies, to embrace all elements essentially loyal to traditional Judaism and in sympathy with the purposes outlined above." This deliberate ambiguity reflects a not entirely successful attempt to establish a movement which would be hospitable to a wide variety of traditional congregations and yet not exclude those which had introduced some departures from historical Jewish practice. This compromise formula, of course, did not satisfy those synagogue leaders who were opposed to any innovation at all and who had joined in the establishment of the Conservative movement as a counterforce to Reform. Thus it happened that synagogues like Congregation Zichron Ephraim, Kehillat Jeshurun, and the Jewish Center of Manhattan, which were modeled on the Orthodox synagogues of Western Europe, with their large sanctuaries, choirs, and rabbis who preached in a variety of languages, and had originally been served by

alumni of the Jewish Theological Seminary, are now identified with
Orthodox Yeshiva University and led by Yeshiva alumni.

It is revealing to trace the growth in the number of congregations
and their denominational affiliation during recent decades. Volume 31
of the *American Jewish Year Book* (1929) lists 3,118 congregations in
existence as of 1927, without mentioning their denominational affiliation. Volume 39 (1937) lists 290 temples affiliated with the UAHC,
claiming a membership of 50,000 families, and 250 synagogues affiliated with the United Synagogue of America, claiming 75,000 families.
Volume 51 (1950) lists 392 temples affiliated with the UAHC, claiming 150,000 families; 365 synagogues affiliated with the United Synagogue, claiming 100,000 families; and 500 synagogues affiliated with
the Union of Orthodox Jewish Congregations of America (UOJC),
claiming 100,000 families. Volume 62 (1961) finds the United Synagogue with a larger number of affiliates than the UAHC, with 700
congregations as opposed to 605. Volume 64 (1963) contains a statement by the UOJC claiming a membership of 3,900 congregations in
the United States and Canada. In addition to the *American Jewish
Year Book* listings, both the UAHC and the United Synagogue publish lists of all their affiliates. (This practice is not followed by the
UOJC, and it is therefore difficult to verify the accuracy of its stated
number of affiliates.) In 1970 the UAHC listed 698 affiliated congregations; the United Synagogue, 832 affiliates.

As for the rabbis who serve these congregations, the Conservative
group draws its rabbis, the majority of whom are graduates of the
Jewish Theological Seminary, primarily from the ranks of the Rabbinical Assembly, which claims over 1,000 members. About 200 congregations affiliated with the United Synagogue, most of them in
smaller communities, are served by rabbis, graduates of various *yeshivas,* who are not members of the Rabbinical Assembly. To further
confound the observer, a substantial number of members of the Rabbinical Council of America, the largest of the English-speaking Orthodox rabbinical organizations, serve in congregations presently or
formerly affiliated with the United Synagogue. Congregations affiliated with the UAHC are served primarily by members of the Central
Conference of American Rabbis (CCAR) (predominantly graduates
of Hebrew Union College-Jewish Institute of Religion). The Orthodox situation is less clear. It is impossible to determine exactly who are
the rabbis serving the various Orthodox congregations, since there are
numerous Orthodox rabbinical associations as well as many rabbis of

Orthodox synagogues who have chosen not to affiliate with any rabbinical organization.

II

Suburbanization, assimilation, and secularization were the most dramatic developments to mark the American Jewish community in the years following World War II, a period which witnessed the virtual departure of Jews from the inner cities to the suburbs of the major metropolitan areas. Accordingly, the past twenty-five years saw hundreds of synagogues established in new suburban communities. Most of these tended to identify themselves with the Conservative movement and, to a growing extent, with Reform. Orthodox Jews, who depend on a network of religious institutions for their religious needs, including a synagogue within easy walking distance, were less likely to move to suburbs lacking in such basic Jewish institutions as day schools, Sabbath-observing groceries, and *mikvahs* (ritual baths). Even in those urban communities which underwent fundamental demographic changes, the Orthodox synagogues were usually the last to leave. For example, the Hasidic residents of the Crown Heights and Williamsburg sections of Brooklyn (surrounded by black and Puerto Rican ghettos), under the leadership of the Lubavitcher and Satmarer *rebbes,* have insisted on remaining. The *rebbes* have used every moral and political pressure to persuade their followers not to abandon the institutions they had so painfully established.

The postwar period witnessed another development. In the larger cities, numerous synagogues which had not formerly been served by rabbis, or had been served by Orthodox rabbis, switched their affiliation from Orthodox to Conservative. Other synagogues postponed this change until they erected new buildings in more desirable residential areas. In the suburbs themselves there was a mushrooming of hundreds of synagogue-center buildings which soon became the focus of all communal, as well as religious, Jewish activity.

Jewish families who moved to the suburbs made the adjustment to their new surroundings—the ranch houses and lawns and car pools—with relative ease. It was more difficult to perpetuate an attachment to the living reality of historical Jewish tradition and memory. Almost immediately the new suburbanites joined a synagogue, not so much for their own needs as for "the sake of the children," since synagogue membership provided handy Jewish educational facilities. Attendance at Hebrew school or Sunday school, in turn, qualified the children for *Bar Mitzvah, Bat Mitzvah,* and Confirmation (with all the attendant lavish trimmings). These adolescent occasions, however, frequently marked the end of both the children's attendance in religious school and their parents' expensive membership in the temple or synagogue.

This fact leads to a frequent misreading of the statistics regarding synagogue affiliation and membership. The percentages may fluctuate from area to area and year to year, but the statistics often reflect the rotating nature of suburban synagogue membership. Many families join a synagogue only for the period during which their children are required to attend religious school, until *Bar Mitzvah* or Confirmation, after which time they resign their membership and are replaced by other families with children who have reached the age of preparation for *Bar Mitzvah.*

Thus, "child-centeredness" became a feature of postwar American Jewish religious life. Jewish parents, members of a "lost" Jewish generation, became seized with the hope that their children would somehow find in the local synagogue, during the few hours a week allotted for the purpose, enough knowledge and commitment to grow up into members of a secure, rooted, "returning" generation. The hope, unfortunately, was rarely realized.

Aware of the shortcomings of the existing Jewish education, the Conservative movement, shortly after World War II, established a Commission on Jewish Education to devise standards for and to service the growing number of religious schools under congregational auspices. One of the first standards adopted by the Commission was the requirement that a child, beginning at age eight, attend religious school for a minimum of six hours per week (two hours three times a week), and that such attendance be a prerequisite for *Bar Mitzvah* and *Bat Mitzvah.* This standard was enthusiastically supported by Conservative rabbis and educators, for varied reasons. Some welcomed the suggested requirement in order to prevent their synagogues from becoming *Bar Mitzvah* factories for children who had been hastily prepared by professional *Bar Mitzvah* teachers to recite mechanically the requisite *Torah* blessings. Others welcomed this requirement as an incentive for more intensive Jewish education than could be offered in a one-day-a-week, Sunday-morning religious school.

However, the attempt to impose the Commission's standards was not always welcomed by either the lay leadership of the synagogues or by potential members, who regarded this as an unwelcome addition to the suburban child's already overburdened schedule. Some parents were also affronted when their children came home from religious school with information about rituals and demands for observance which were inconsistent with home patterns. Such families often joined the local Reform temple and, in some instances, Orthodox and Conservative synagogues which did not press the particular educational requirements or create unwelcome conflicts.

Although the suburban synagogue boom is a recent phenomenon, occurring only within the last twenty-five years, already it evokes a distant and hollow ring in recollection. As with so many strands of the American dream which inspired so much individual and institutional energy for a generation, the current mood does not seem to find satisfaction in contemplating the achievements, results, and consequences of maturity. As has often been noted, most problems are the result of solutions; pursuing a goal or ambition is often more satisfying than a realized dream. Thus, children raised in permissive affluence envy the struggles and denials of their disadvantaged neighbors. American Jewish children, offspring of parents who sought integration into a society which placed high values on the WASP virtues of dignity and conformity, in many instances now prefer to search for the roots of their Jewishness as well as for other forms of ethnic identity.

An earlier generation abandoned the "old-fashioned" synagogues where the men were segregated from the women and replaced them with modern ranch style, multifunctional buildings decorated with the latest art styles. But apparently this was insufficient to stimulate or retain the religious interest of their children who, along with so many of their peers, became full-fledged participants in the Age of Aquarius. The realization began to dawn that antiseptic buildings, responsive readings in the vernacular, and so on, were not the panaceas that might attract the disinterested back to the synagogue. In this context, one can understand the growing attraction of Hasidism and its romantic appeal to the yearning for the intimacy of a small fellowship and the excitement of the exotic. Similarly, disenchantment with the suburban synagogue helps to explain various recent attempts among Reform and Conservative synagogues at liturgical experimentation, from new High Holiday supplements to rock Sabbath services.

It is difficult, though, to speak with any real authority about the state of the present-day American synagogue. Until recently, there have been relatively few studies in this area, although some communities and synagogues have published histories and a few rabbis have written pertinent memoirs. There have also been scattered attempts at preparing studies of the religious constituency of the American Jewish community (most of them, curiously, under secular sponsorship, like The American Jewish Committee). There are, in addition, the Lakeville studies by Marshall Sklare,[1] which contain considerable information about the religious affiliations and attitudes of the residents of an affluent Chicago suburb. (It is questionable, however, whether "Lakeville," with its high income Jewish residents belonging to four Reform temples and one Conservative congregation, can be considered representative.)

The UAHC-commissioned study on its congregational constituency, by Leonard Fein of Brandeis University, was published in 1972. Not to be outdone by the lay arm, the Reform movement's rabbinic organization has also recently published a study by Theodore Lenn covering a wide "range of rabbinic procedures and thinking, congregational attitudes, personal conceptions of the rabbinate, the behavior of boards and congregants, changes in ideology."

The Conservative rabbinate has also conducted a self-study. At the Seventieth Annual Convention of the Rabbinical Assembly, in March 1970, the members debated the role and function of their calling. A resolution was adopted establishing a representative committee to include the various age ranges and regional distribution of the membership in order to study the status of the Conservative rabbinate. That study by Martin E. Segal was completed in 1971. The congregational arm of the Conservative movement, the United Synagogue, has so far refrained from indulging in such exercises, although individual congregations have commissioned studies for particular purposes.

III

Some light may be shed on the condition of the American synagogue by observing the changing role of the American rabbi, which obviously varies from one end of the religious spectrum to the other, yet

[1]Marshall Sklare and Joseph Greenblum, *Jewish Identity on the Suburban Frontier* (New York: The American Jewish Committee and Basic Books, Inc., Publishers, 1967).

retains certain constant factors reflecting contemporary reality.

The rabbi's traditional role, first as religious authority, then as teacher and communal leader, diminishes in descending order as one moves from the committed Orthodox Jew, who still looks to his rabbi for guidance in ritual questions, to the member of a Reform congregation, who rarely troubles his rabbi about such matters. In ascending order, the contemporary rabbi is expected to conduct religious services which will retain the loyalty of the regular worshipper and attract those who never acquired or have discarded the habit of regular prayer; deliver sermons; be expert in the arts of synagogue and school administration; represent the congregation in the broader community and, increasingly, in efforts on behalf of Israel; and, above all, fulfill a pastoral function.

The changing role of the American rabbi must also be seen in its proper historical perspective. One criterion for measuring the vitality and self-sufficiency of a Jewish community is whether it is dependent on other older or larger Jewish communities for its rabbis and teachers, or has matured sufficiently to establish its own academies of higher Jewish learning. History informs us that the various "Golden Ages" of Jewish life, in Babylon, Spain, and Northern and Eastern Europe, developed only after the scholars and leaders who had migrated to those areas from older Jewish settlements had been persuaded to stay on and establish centers of Jewish learning and train a succession of native cadres of rabbis and other Jewish scholars. Those communities that continued to import rabbis and teachers remained in a sort of satellite state, reflecting the traditions and conditions of the communities to which they looked to supply their needs. Viewed from this perspective, American Jewry is only now beginning to emerge as an independent center of creative Jewish religious life, able to train an increasingly adequate number of rabbis, cantors, and scholars of sufficient stature to assure a continuing supply of professional religious personnel.

Until fairly recently, most of the rabbis of American congregations were either immigrants trained abroad or the children of immigrants. A substantial majority were the sons of rabbis, cantors, and other religious functionaries, whose family circumstances were far from affluent. The American rabbinate recruited few native-born Americans of middle-class background. This led to the unwarranted generalization that anyone who chose the rabbinate had been unable to enter the preferred professions of law, medicine, or education.

Within the past two decades, however, a change has occurred in the manner in which aspirants for the rabbinate see themselves and are seen by others. During this period of unprecedented economic, academic, and social mobility for American Jews, anyone who chose to prepare for a Jewish rabbinical career was more likely to have done so after considering the many other professional opportunities which became open to Jews. The period in question also witnessed the filling of faculty appointments in seminaries and *yeshivas* by their own graduates. American-born and trained Jewish scholars, like Louis Finkelstein and Boaz Cohen (at the Jewish Theological Seminary), or Julian Morgenstern and Nelson Glueck (at Hebrew Union College), were no longer exceptions among faculties dominated by scholars born and trained in Europe. The latter could never fully reconcile themselves to the realities of the American Jewish community, or overcome their suspicion that Jewish life in America was inferior and lacking in real substance and a viable future. It will be interesting to observe the changes in relations between faculty and alumni of seminaries with a growing proportion of faculty trained in the very schools in which they are now instructors.

None of the major Orthodox *yeshivas* are as yet headed by Talmudic scholars born or trained in America. Almost without exception, the present heads are products of the major Lithuanian Talmudical academies, with their emphasis on study by and for an elite and very little concern for the training and calling of the congregational rabbinate. However, it will also be interesting to observe what changes in orientation may be wrought by the graduates of these *yeshivas* who are increasingly assuming positions of leadership in their own schools as well as in those which they are establishing throughout the country. Will these *yeshivas* continue to produce alumni who view their years of study as a necessary prelude to careers, other than the rabbinate, which will allow them to raise families and to establish communities with a maximum Torah atmosphere and the least possible association with any group which might dilute the intensity of their own religious commitments and environment? Or will some alumni of the *yeshivas* follow the model of charismatic leaders like Rabbi J. B. Soloveitchik and the Lubavitcher *rebbe* who encourage their gifted disciples to seek positions of religious and communal activism beyond the perimeters of those already committed to a life guided by Torah as taught and lived in their *yeshivas*?

Turning to another area of advanced Jewish learning, one must take note of the unprecedented rise in the number of chairs and departments of Jewish studies, all staffed by Jewish scholars, in American universities and colleges. Such chairs and departments have multiplied in the past fifteen years until today there are over 200 full-time Jewish scholars teaching a full complement of Jewish studies (Hebrew and Yiddish language and literature, history, Talmud, Jewish philosophy, sociology) in private and state universities, as well as in a growing number of colleges under Catholic and Protestant auspices. In addition, almost 1,000 rabbis now offer part-time instruction on an undergraduate level in their local colleges. This growth of Jewish studies on the campus level will undoubtedly have its effects on the future of American Jewish religious life. Synagogues are bound to feel the positive impact when graduates of Jewish studies programs show up on the membership rolls.

As for the American rabbinate in general, it is reasonable to predict that the proportion of rabbis born and trained in the United States will continue to rise to a point where the fraction born or educated abroad will disappear or become insignificant. History, much of it tragic, provides the reason. There simply are no Jewish communities left with facilities to train rabbis for export to America. Eastern Europe, excluding the Soviet Union, is in the process of becoming virtually empty of Jews; even should a mass Soviet-Jewish emigration come about, there would be no rabbis forthcoming. Western Europe depends for its rabbinical leadership on a diminishing corps of aging graduates of its seminaries and *yeshivas*, on the handful of rabbis who can be lured from America and Israel, and on those North African rabbis who migrated to France from Algeria and Morocco. Israel, for a variety of internal reasons, has ceased being a source of rabbinic supply for America. On the contrary, growing numbers of American-born and trained rabbis, scholars, and educators are settling in Israel and finding a ready market for their special skills. Approximately sixty members of the Rabbinical Assembly are already permanent residents of Israel, and a similar pattern is developing among both the CCAR and the Orthodox rabbinate.

One can therefore assume that the pattern of American rabbinical education and orientation will dominate not only the American Jewish community but, increasingly, the Jewish communities of Europe, Israel, Latin America, and wherever else Jews will be permitted to establish religious institutions of their own choice. Returning to North America, one can even now draw certain conclusions. The next few years will witness some crucial transitions. The generation of rabbis and their leaders and teachers who grew to maturity in the period between 1950 and 1970 will gradually replace the present aging leadership. Venerable leaders of American Jewish religious institutions deserve credit for guiding their organizations and schools during an unprecedented period of expansion and growth. Their successors will assume the leadership of institutions which are in the process of consolidating a more mature and stabilized community. They are also likely to bring a different perspective to their tasks, the result of their having risen to leadership during a more self-confident era of Jewish history.

Whether Orthodox, Conservative, or Reform, the new leaders are more likely to have been trained and recruited from the institutions which they will be heading. (Indeed, this is the case with the Jewish Theological Seminary and Hebrew Union College-Jewish Institute of Religion, which have named their own alumni, Professors Gerson Cohen and Alfred Gottschalk, to head their respective alma maters.) Each group, from the Satmar Hasidim to ultra-Reform, has developed institutions which tend to retain the loyalties of their young, especially those seeking careers in the rabbinate and related pursuits. Thus, *yeshivas* and seminaries find themselves training an increasing proportion of the children of their own alumni, or of families affiliated with congregations ideologically related to these schools. The Reform Hebrew Union College and the Conservative Jewish Theological Seminary now rarely receive applications from *yeshiva* dropouts and no longer depend on Orthodox sources for either faculty or students, since both are adequately supplied from the ranks of their own alumni. All the movements of American Jewish religious life are now almost totally self-contained and self-perpetuating regarding their educational and organizational institutions.

On the other hand, there has been an intensification in the practice of militant separatism among Orthodox groups regarding their organizational and individual relationships with Reform and Conservative Jews. An earlier generation of members of the Union of Orthodox Rabbis would have refrained from public denunciation of Conservative and Reform rabbis, since the majority of the latter were often their own sons or the sons of their congregants and neighbors. However, in 1954, eleven *yeshiva* heads, led by their extremist spokesman and ideologue, the late Rabbi Aaron Kotler, issued an *issur* (prohibition) against Orthodox cooperation with non-Orthodox rabbis and synagogues, especially in such "interdenominational" efforts as the Synagogue Council of America. Subsequently, the situation has deteriorated even further, as exemplified by the picketing by *yeshiva* students of a Synagogue Council of America dinner honoring Rabbis Samuel Belkin, Louis Finkelstein, and Nelson Glueck, then heads respectively, of Yeshiva University, the Jewish Theological Seminary, and Hebrew Union College-Jewish Institute of Religion. However, one should not draw inevitable conclusions about the future of these relationships. As racial segregationists and other fundamentalists have learned, there is no slogan as evanescent as "Never!" Which rational observer of Christian relations would have had the temerity to predict the present ferment and crisis in the Catholic Church even months before the election of Pope John XXIII?

IV

The relative stabilization of American Jewish residential patterns and congregational affiliation has resulted in a marked decline in the building of new synagogue facilities. During the past five years, virtually no new Conservative congregations have been established anywhere in North America, a startling contrast to the activity of the previous decades. The increase in the number of United Synagogue affiliates in recent years reflects more the enrollment or merger of existing synagogues than the establishment of newly organized congregations. The UAHC reports the continuing organization of new affiliates, particularly in the older suburbs. However, it is difficult to determine whether this reflects a rise of interest in the Reform movement or a growing disenchantment with existing Conservative synagogues, whose membership dues are higher and whose religious schools are not only more costly but have more demanding standards. Then again, the rise may be due to the more vigorous activities of national and regional executives of the UAHC in promoting, assisting, and subsidizing groups interested in establishing new Reform congregations.

Although there is less exact data available for the Orthodox wing, it is possible to draw some general conclusions based on informal observation. The number of *shtiblach* (private houses of prayer) in the larger metropolitan Jewish centers has not declined, although such synagogues have moved to more concentrated areas of Jewish settlement and now attract many American-born worshippers. They also tend to draw a more learned and observant type of member than used to be the case. There has also been an increase in the number of synagogues of the Young Israel type, appealing to Orthodox business-men, professionals, and especially scientists, who have revived many a moribund Orthodox synagogue in academic communities like Boston, Washington, and Berkeley. But one rarely hears nowadays of new large Orthodox synagogues, of the kind that used to feature star can-tors, being established in the major cities. The constituency for such synagogues has diminished appreciably. As for the smaller communi-ties which once boasted small Orthodox synagogues reflecting the countries of origin of their founders (for example, the *Russishe* or *Galitzianer shul*), it is rare to find the children or grandchildren of the founders willing to continue to support these "ethnic" congregational efforts.

The declining Jewish population of the smaller communities, the rising cost of maintenance and other professional services, even when available, have led to a growing number of mergers between former fiercely independent and ideologically hostile congregations. First the small Orthodox *shul* might become a Conservative synagogue, with mixed seating, late Friday evening services, and a Seminary-trained rabbi. Recently, more and more of these Conservative synagogues have considered or consummated mergers with Reform temples, which were also suffering from a decline in membership, to say noth-ing of the dwindling of doctrinal difference between the two sets of congregants.

Assuming no drastic reversal in present American trends, no major upheavals in the Middle East, or catastrophic disruptions in other Jewish communities, one may expect no sharp changes in the number, size, and locations of American synagogues. The mass exodus of Jews from the inner cities and the influx of disadvantaged minorities (black, Puerto Rican, or Appalachian) into the large urban centers both appear to have run their course. The suburbs no longer offer guaranteed immunity from overcrowding, pollution, inferior schools, and other urban ills. One even detects a trickle back to the cities of young families as well as older couples who have no further need for their large suburban homes. Many young people of the generation for whom doting fathers endured the discomforts of commuting are not planning to repeat their parents' trials.

It is rare to find a second or third generation of the same family who are still members of suburban congregations to which their fathers and grandfathers belonged. This is due in part to the unprecedented mobility that has come to mark American society. Another factor is the rising proportion of salaried professionals among the Jewish community, who have neither the need nor the opportunity to strike roots in one place for any extended period of time. They move easily among locations as their tastes, circumstances, and employers dictate.

This change in Jewish occupational distribution is likely to have serious consequences in a variety of areas affecting the immediate future of American Jewish institutional life, particularly the synagogue. In earlier decades, synagogues were most often dependent on members of the free professions—doctors, lawyers, and so on as well as on owners and managers of business enterprises. This successful class provided the synagogue with its basic financial support and stability. The enterprising energies of these men, harnessed to a tradition of generosity and communal noblesse oblige, created synagogues which afforded hospitality to those in less fortunate circumstances. The rabbis and lay leaders of these congregations often went to great lengths to attract the less affluent and to imbue them with a sense of communal obligation as the latter's circumstances improved. Now the picture is changing, and one hesitates to predict what effect the rapid turnover in population and the growing ranks of relatively rootless salaried professionals will have on the future stability of the synagogue and on the ability of a particular community to build and maintain its congregations.

National synagogue groups have for some time encouraged their affiliates to adopt uniform patterns of worship and school curricula in order to provide a familiar context for the family moving from one area to another. They are also beginning to urge their affiliates to credit newcomers to the community for membership fees, High Holiday seating, and building assessments which had been paid in former congregations. It is hoped that this trend will lead to greater regional and national responsibility and to coordination of synagogue planning, building, and budgets, and a diminution of local autonomy and responsibility. Already there are signs that this is happening. The New York Metropolitan Region of the United Synagogue has offered help in sponsoring and subsidizing a synagogue for the middle-income residents of the mammoth Co-Op City project in the northeast Bronx. The residents of Co-Op City, mostly "refugees" from other parts of the

Bronx where they had abandoned synagogues and temples built by an earlier generation of escapees from the Lower East Side, were not in a position to establish their new synagogue without outside, regional help. Similarly, Yeshiva University sponsored the synagogue that was recently built in New York's Lincoln Center area. Most of the members of this congregation had already given years of labor and donated substantial resources toward the building of synagogues in their former communities and were not prepared to repeat the process. The Reform movement has had a longer and more varied history of encouraging and subsidizing new temples from a rotating fund, which has enabled the establishment and maintenance of scores of congregations.

As already noted, there has been an increase in mergers between congregations of similar orientation. But mergers have also taken place between congregations of different denominational affiliation. The trend began in the smaller communities and is now apparent in larger centers of Jewish population as well. For instance, the Orthodox, Conservative, and Reform congregations in Duluth, Minnesota, with separate buildings but some overlapping membership, have merged into one congregation with a new rabbi of Conservative background. In San Francisco, an aging Conservative congregation in an older part of the city merged with a struggling new Reform suburban congregation whose rabbi now heads the new congregation. (There has been an intrasynagogue merger development as well. For example, in Philadelphia eight Conservative congregations have merged to form four. The partners in these mergers consisted in most instances of an urban congregation and a younger suburban one, with the former selling its property to join the latter.)

However, as a counter to the trend toward merger, we also find occasional instances of institutional dissent among the synagogue movements. It is perhaps most pronounced among Orthodoxy which, apart from its innate resistance to associating with groups that do not share its outlook, has avoided organizational centralization on the local, national, or international level. (Reform and Conservatism tend to be more accommodating to diversity within their ranks.) Orthodoxy, moreover, remains suspicious of anything that might smack of a *Sanhedrin*, a supreme religious court which might interpret the *halakha* (religious law) on the basis of a vote by a committee and lead to the toleration of ritual innovations. It was for this reason that the attempt of the UOJC to establish a world organization of Ashkenazic and Sephardic congregations (as a counterpart to the Reform-sponsored World Union of Progressive Judaism and the Conservative World Council of Synagogues) did not succeed. The opposition feared that a world organization might encourage the minority of Orthodox modernists in Israel and abroad, who favor a *Sanhedrin*-type of rabbinic authority, to deliver lenient rulings on the unresolved *halakhic* problems which have accumulated in a technological society and a sovereign Jewish state. This may also be the reason why so few (only a small minority) of Orthodox congregations have affiliated with the UOJC. The vast majority of Orthodox congregations remain unaffiliated and restrict their institutional loyalties to their own synagogues, to certain *yeshivas*, and to certain charities.

The Reform and Conservative groups, products of a different history, have a different outlook. Both began their careers with a central seminary for the training of their rabbis, and quickly developed effective centralized rabbinic and congregational organizations. There have always been tensions among the seminaries, their alumni, and the congregational leaders over the distribution of power, prestige, and the allocation of budgets, but these tensions rarely led to splits or the establishment of rival schools or groups. Usually, the hospitable temperaments of both groups have permitted a latitude broad enough to accommodate a wide range of views and practices. Dissent and critical inquiry have not been discouraged, and academic freedom is safeguarded both in the classroom and from the pulpit.

The Reconstructionist movement is a case in point. For many years it considered itself a philosophical fellowship exerting an influence on Conservatism and Reform from within those two movements. Its recent establishment of a rabbinical seminary in Philadelphia and its talk about becoming a fourth denomination in American Jewish life is a departure from the traditional Reconstructionist posture. Professor Mordecai M. Kaplan, the founder of Reconstructionism and a member of the Jewish Theological Seminary faculty for almost fifty years, has enjoyed freedom as a "house" critic within the Conservative structure.

V

It would appear that the current ferment in Christian circles and the emergence, for want of a better term, of the "underground church," with its radical, anti-Establishment clergymen, has encouraged a comparable, although not parallel, Jewish development. Its guiding spirits are drawn primarily from the ranks of Jewish Theological Seminary alumni and dropouts. It is a matter of conjecture as to whether these dissenters develop their ambivalence about Jewish tradition and the organized Jewish community after they enter the Seminary or whether the Seminary, by its very nature, tends to attract a greater proportion of students with unresolved conflicts between their reverence for traditional forms and rebellion against them. In any event, there is a growing vogue for Seminary alumni to establish rabbinical schools, academies, and fellowships known as *havurot*. For some reason, we rarely find Yeshiva University and Hebrew Union College alumni among the leadership of these groups, perhaps because they are afflicted with fewer unresolved conflicts.

The most widely publicized of the radical groups is the *Havurat Shalom*, founded by a group of young Conservative rabbis and a Reform Hillel director in the Boston area and presently located in Somerville, Massachusetts. It has attracted a group of students and teachers, with a high dropout rate, from an odd mixture of pacifists, educational innovators, and dissenters from the institutional synagogue. One should note, however, that the *havurah* members have not lacked for a platform from which to air their views. The organized Jewish community—synagogues, centers, and national organizations, the Jewish "establishment," in short—has vied to provide occasions at which members of the *havurah* might vent their spleen at their elders. I, myself, am inclined to believe that the significance of the *havurot* has been highly exaggerated and it is merely a passing fad, not unconnected with the more egregious manifestations of the so-called "youth culture" that emerged in the late 1960s.

A more serious demonstration of American Judaism's concern with the social issues of the day was evinced by the widespread participation of rabbis and synagogues in the civil rights movement of the early 1960s. Prior to that time, social activism, among Christians as well as Jews, had been restricted to individual clergymen, men like John Haynes Holmes, Reinhold Niebuhr, and Stephen S. Wise, who, in their sermons and writings, inveighed against social evils and thus helped to sensitize the social conscience of their generations. The organized church and synagogue, especially denominations with a tradition of social concern, usually confined themselves to adopting occasional resolutions at conventions to express their views on the problems of war and peace, race relations, and similar issues. Insofar as they allocated material resources and assigned personnel to help the needy and disadvantaged, it was through conventional forms of charity and services.

In the early 1960s, however, organized religion, the clergy in particular, became actively involved in the whole range of social concerns. One may trace this development in part to the general encouragement of religious activism and ecumenism inspired by Pope John XXIII and to the charismatic model of Martin Luther King. This new development was dramatically launched by the Conference on Religion and Race in Chicago in January 1963. Cardinals of the Church and assorted religious establishment figures mingled and shared platforms with emerging religious, social, and political activists like Abraham Joshua Heschel, Martin Luther King, and William Stringfellow. Later that year, scores of rabbis, together with many priests and ministers, joined Dr. King in demonstrations at Birmingham, Albany, Georgia, and Selma, Alabama. Many were arrested. The brutal repressions in the South aroused unprecedented religious engagement. By the winter of 1965, hundreds of rabbis joined thousands of other King sympathizers in Selma to prepare for the historic march to Montgomery.

In the following years these same social activists participated in the peace movement. However, many rabbis, as well as congregants, halted their public involvements in the peace movement when they found it awkward to explain their support of a "hawkish" American role in the Middle East and a "dovish" role in Southeast Asia. They were also forced by internal and external Jewish pressures to mute their selective opposition to militarism. Gradual disengagement by the Jewish religious establishment and by individual rabbis from a program of active social concern was hastened by the racial riots in Watts, Detroit, and Newark, where Jewish shopkeepers were often the first victims. Other events, such as the New York teachers' strike in 1968, added to the disillusion of many Jews with participation in radical causes.

It is difficult to generalize about shifts in Jewish political and social orientation on the basis of religious affiliation. "Conventional" opinion on this matter is often contradicted by personal encounters with Orthodox Jewish radicals and Reform reactionaries. There is in existence an unpublished study by Louis Harris on "Black-Jewish Relations in New York City," sponsored by the Ford Foundation shortly after the explosive New York teachers' strike. The study was based on a total sample of 634 respondents, distributed among 16 percent Orthodox, 32 percent Conservative, 21 percent Reform, and 31 percent non-affiliated Jews, broken down by boroughs. Harris attempted to draw distinctions in attitude based on income, age, and religious affiliation, but I doubt whether such a limited sample, restricted to New York City, excluding the suburbs, and taken immediately after a highly publicized confrontation, can be considered a reliable indication of national trends.

One can also be misled by the greater publicity accorded the radical, militant young Jews of SDS, the Weathermen, and so on. One hears less about the million or so Jewish youths who are not involved in these movements and who probably tend more to emulate the patterns and models of their parents than did an earlier generation. In a recent synagogue bulletin, published by the largest Conservative congregation in Houston, Texas, for distribution to its college students, there are excerpts from four talks prepared by college students for delivery to the congregation at Sabbath services. One of the students, a senior at the University of Texas, commented as follows:

Sociologists today speak of the lack of communication between generations, and it appears to me that with respect to our present lifetime, these words are somewhat exaggerated. If you want to know what a generation gap really was, go back two generations to our parents and grandparents. Most of our grandparents came to these shores not knowing the language or customs. Their children learned a language different from their mothers' and fathers'. They learned customs, traditions, and mores of an American community entirely foreign to their parents. Now, believe me, that was a confrontation of two worlds. Nevertheless, in spite of this social gap between the two generations, their differences were merged in an atmosphere of respect, reverence, and understanding. We see the result of a truly first-generation American Jewry, a foundation laid by the generation we criticize.

I accept this view as far more representative of what Jewish young people think than all the frenzied talk about the existence of a "generation gap."

VI

In conclusion, what can we expect of organized Jewish religious life in the future? It is safe to predict that there will probably be a continuation of the growing cooperation between Reform and Conservative congregational and rabbinical groups, already hinted at by several recent joint study sessions of the Rabbinical Assembly and the CCAR. In addition, education commissions of the Reform and Conservative movements are sponsoring a cooperative pilot textbook publication project.

The differences in Jewish observance and in attitude to Zionism that used to divide Reform and Conservative congregants have narrowed. The number of Hebrew Union College students who observe traditional religious practices is increasing. Jewish Theological Seminary students, reared in decorous Conservative congregations, who, at the moment, cover their heads with prayer shawls at services, Orthodox fashion, may only be indulging a passing yearning to rediscover the life style of their grandparents. Yet both examples point to a more positive probing attitude toward their heritage than was prevalent among their older colleagues when the latter were rabbinical students a generation ago.

Yeshivas for all age levels are likely to multiply and to expand the scope of their activities, although it is possible that they have already attained their potential in reaching their loyal constituency. Reform and Conservative day schools will increase in response to the growing demand for more intensive Jewish education. The assumption that such schools are being filled primarily by "refugees" from racially mixed public schools in the North and South is unsubstantiated. Parents who seek to protect their children from the rigors of an urban public school education either move to the suburbs or send their children to private schools which do not burden their students with a double curriculum of both general and Jewish studies.

It is fashionable to speak about Jewish education in America as a disaster. I disagree. It is my feeling that there has never been a generation of young Jews in the United States who have received a more intensive Jewish education, taught by more qualified teachers employing better educational materials. I believe that greater parental and communal concern, combined with greater financial assistance, will serve to increase the number of young people receiving various forms of Jewish education, from the nursery to the postgraduate level, as well as enhance the quality of the instruction.

Nostalgia has exaggerated both the quality and depth of Jewish knowledge and loyalty of earlier American Jewish generations. Was there really a higher proportion of learned, rooted, or pious Jews in

America thirty years ago than are to be found now? Was knowledge of Hebrew and observance of the Sabbath more widespread then? There are other myths and fallacies which bear little relationship to reality. One is that rabbis are deserting the congregational rabbinate in droves either after a brief period of active pulpit experience or as soon as they are ordained. Actually, most students who enter Hebrew Union College and the Jewish Theological Seminary with the aim of becoming congregational rabbis fulfill their intention after ordination.

It is reported that the Hasidic Master, Rabbi Meir of Premishlan, once discussed the ambiguous merits and definitions of modernity with his disciples. He reminded them of one of the oldest extant *midrashim* which Jews recite in the Passover Haggadah: "In the beginning our fathers were idolators, but now the Omnipresent has drawn us to His service." This is not an unfamiliar mood to a generation eager for service and suspicious of idols which seduced an older, more optimistic generation less certain about both their Jewish and American identity.

The established churches are in crisis and Christian theology is in ferment. Jews are too easily tempted to view their situation in a Christian mirror. Perhaps we should learn to measure Jewish reality in a more authentic Jewish context of qualified optimism and the mature posture of a people who have experienced 4,000 years of recorded history and civilization.

I once concluded an article on the Jewish religious scene in the *American Jewish Year Book* (1961) with the following affirmation: "Each generation somehow manages to surprise its predecessor and foil predictions of doom. Perhaps with a bit of luck, and an enormous amount of anonymous dedication, Jewish religious life will witness the dawn of a genuine renaissance in the years ahead." I see no reason to revise this opinion now.

7

The Jewish School System in the United States

WALTER I. ACKERMAN

Jewish education in the United States, as we know it today, is rooted in the continued attempts of previous generations of Jews to develop forms of Jewish schooling compatible with changing conceptions of Judaism, new styles of Jewish life, and the demands of living in America.[1] The salient features of this process of accommodation, common to most Jewish groups, were an acknowledgement of the primacy of secular studies and a consequent subordination of Jewish education to a secondary and supplementary role. This shift in the focus of education reflects a desire on the part of most Jews to enter the mainstream of American life, even at the price of neglect of the religious imperatives of *Torah l'Shma*, learning for its sake, and *lamdanut*, Jewish erudition.

The present pattern of Jewish education in the United States had taken shape by 1930.[2] Six of the 12 accredited teacher-training schools currently in operation were already in existence then. Bureaus of Jew-

---

[1] This chapter first appeared in the *American Jewish Year Book*, Vol. 70. Reprinted by permission of The American Jewish Committee and The Jewish Publication Society of America.

[2] For a history of Jewish Education in the United States see Alexander M. Dushkin, *Jewish Education in New York City* (New York: The Bureau of Jewish Education, 1918); Abraham P. Gannes, ed., *Selected Writings of Leo L. Honor* (New York: Reconstructionist Press, 1965), pp. 27–143; Hyman B. Grinstein, *Rise of the Jewish Community of New York, 1654–1860* (Philadelphia: Jewish Publication Society of America, 1945); Shmuel Niger, *In Kampf far a Naiyer Derziehung* (New York: Arbeiter-Ring Education Committee, 1940), and S. Yefroikin, "Yiddish Secular Schools in the United States" in *The Jewish People, Past and Present* (New York: Jewish Encyclopedic Handbooks, Central Yiddish Cultural Organization, 1948), vol. 2, pp. 144–150.

ish education had been established in every major city, and the idea of community responsibility was accepted in theory, if not in practice. Curriculum patterns in every type of school had achieved a form and balance which was to change little in subsequent years. A corps of professional educators gained some visibility; a body of literature was in the process of development, and several professional societies had come into being. The essential nature of the Jewish school enterprise was established. A system of supplementary education composed of autonomous one-day-a-week Sunday schools, midweek afternoon schools, and day schools was maintained by the voluntary efforts of their clientele.

Enrollment

Today, more than half a million children receive some form of Jewish education under school auspices. It is estimated that well over 80 percent of the Jewish children in this country receive some Jewish schooling during their elementary school years—the smaller the Jewish community the greater the likelihood that a child will be enrolled in a Jewish school—even though as few as one-third of the children between the age of 3 and 17 may attend a Jewish school at any one time. When the gross statistic is refined by pertinent categorization, some salient features of contemporary Jewish education become clear:[3] (1) Of all Jewish children between the ages of 3 to 5, 11.6 percent are currently enrolled in a Jewish school. For the 6 to 7 age bracket it is 21.4 percent, for the 8 to 12 year olds 69.8 percent, and for the 13 to 17 year olds only 15.8 percent. (2) The distribution of the current Jewish school population is 15.3 percent in the primary grades, 69.1 percent in elementary schools, and 15.3 percent in high school departments. More boys than girls are enrolled (57 percent, as compared with 43 percent); boys receive a more intensive education than girls. (3) Current attendance by type of school shows 13.4 percent in Jewish day schools, 42.2 percent in one-day-a-week schools, and 44.4 percent in midweek afternoon schools that are in session anywhere from two to five times a week. (4) The sponsorship of Jewish schools reflects the dominant patterns of Jewish community organization.

[3] The statistics in this section are taken from the *National Census of Jewish Schools* (New York: American Association for Jewish Education, Information Bulletin No. 28, December 1967).

There are today 2,727 known Jewish schools of all types in the country, serving an estimated 544,468 children. Of these, 35.7 percent are in schools under Reform auspices, 34.3 percent in schools sponsored by Conservative congregations, 21.5 percent in schools under Orthodox auspices, 1.0 percent in Yiddish schools, and 0.6 percent in communal or intercongregational schools.

By way of summary: Jewish education is now primarily a matter of congregational concern; over 90 percent of the children attend religiously oriented schools sponsored by congregations of one of the three major Jewish religious groupings. Despite all the recent clamor concerning the importance of Jewish education, two-thirds of the Jewish school age children in the United States in 1966 were not in any kind of Jewish school. Close to half of those who were attended only one day a week; fewer than 15 percent of the others received more than six hours a week of instruction. Jewish schools by and large are dealing with children of preschool or elementary school age and, despite some encouraging advances, fail to attract or hold high school students in significant number.

The rise of the congregational school at the expense of the more intensive community school and the explosive growth of the day school are perhaps the two most significant developments in Jewish education in the last quarter of a century. Of course, the prominence of the congregational school reflects the rapid growth of synagogue membership after the end of World War II and the suburbanization of the Jewish community. If, as most observers agree, membership in a synagogue is less a matter of religious impulse and belief and more a means of Jewish identification compatible with American mores, the congregational school is faced with the extraordinarily difficult task of attempting to persuade children to adopt a life style which their parents have rejected. The posture permitted the religious school educator in matters of religious imperatives and their implicit concomitants in the Jewish tradition is clearly compromised if the school is regarded as a symbol of Jewishness rather than as a vehicle for the transmission of an embracive code of distinctive behavior.

Sponsorship

The day school is most often associated with the Orthodox, the one-day-a-week school with the Reform congregation, and the weekday afternoon school with Conservative and Orthodox synagogues. But these lines are neither hard nor fast. One-day-a-week schools are found in both Orthodox and Conservative congregations, and many Reform congregations now sponsor midweek afternoon school programs. In recent years the Conservative movement has actively encouraged the establishment of day schools, and its Solomon Schechter Day School Association already has more than 25 affiliates, with a student population of almost 5,000.[4] Reform Jewish educators are also interested in the development of more intensive programs, and have made concerted efforts to add midweek afternoon sessions to the one-day-a-week schools. At the same time they have begun to discuss the feasibility of day schools under Reform auspices.

Day Schools

The growth of the day school is impressive by any standard. Where there were seventy-eight such schools in 1945, today their number exceeds three hundred.[5] The reasons for this remarkable expansion are varied, but the major stimulus is the Orthodox community's deep conviction that the continuity of traditional Jewish life in America is dependent upon perpetuation of the intensive pattern of Jewish education which was the glory of the European *yeshivas*. The circle of interest in the day school was drawn wider and encompassed a broader range than the Orthodox community when the destruction of European Jewry made it clear that American Jewry must henceforth draw upon its own resources for leadership and learning. The quickened identification with things Jewish, aroused by the Holocaust and the establishment of the State of Israel, created a demand in many sectors of the community for a type of Jewish education which promised more than the limited achievement of the afternoon school. Others send their children to day schools for reasons far removed from the essential purpose of the school—as a matter of convenience, to escape the crowded conditions of the public schools, to enjoy the benefits of a private school, and, sad to say, to avoid contact with other racial and

---

[4] Morton Siegel, "In Our School System: United Synagogue Commission on Jewish Education," *Pedagogic Reporter*, March 1969, p. 17.

[5] Alvin I. Schiff, *The Jewish Day School in America* (New York: Jewish Education Committee Press, 1966), p. 67.

ethnic groups. But whatever the background and motivation of its students, the Orthodox day school has consistently maintained its posture as an educational institution dedicated to the inculcation of traditional values and behavior, and it brooks little compromise.

Under ordinary circumstances it would perhaps be proper to assume that the growth of the day schools has reached its highest point. However, events in this country in recent years may serve as a stimulus for yet another spurt. The growing acceptance of cultural pluralism and ethnic independence as legitimate expressions of American life may encourage many Jews to reexamine their conception of themselves and their place in American life, and lead to day school enrollment from quarters heretofore hostile or indifferent to this type of education. Decentralization of the public schools in New York City and the adoption of similar plans in other parts of the country may also affect the day school. Whatever else it may mean, decentralization clearly denotes the passing into history of the public school as the fire under the melting pot. The distance separating ethnically-oriented public schools from private schools with similar purposes is certainly not one of ideological differences. Opposition to the day school grounded in the sanctity of the public school as a "common" school is clearly no longer defensible. The trend toward separatism may well mark the day school as a primary symbol of the Jewish community.

Congregational Control

With few exceptions, each Jewish school, no matter what its type, is a highly autonomous administrative and educational unit. Final authority for the conduct of the congregational school and its affairs is vested in the congregational board, which acts through its appointed school committee. Noncongregational day schools have their own boards and committees responsible for every aspect of the school's activities.

This freedom is not an unmixed blessing. The proliferation of congregations and the attendant increase of schools have taken place without any rational community organization or considered educational policy. There is no question that this development had serious educational consequences—duplication of effort, diffusion of limited financial and personnel resources, and schools too small to be educationally viable are but a few. A desire to avoid these difficulties is now evident in the tendency throughout the country to organize secondary schools on an intercongregational or communitywide basis.

Some observers cavil at the dominance of the congregational school because they conceive the synagogue as a social institution necessarily devoted to its own interests, sometimes encouraging a degree of parochialism potentially inimical to the disinterested efforts of more broadly based agencies to raise educational standards. Division of the community's educational efforts along denominational lines similarly concerns those who accord the idea of peoplehood a central place in their understanding of Judaism. They contend that the congregational school tends to emphasize a particular "brand" of Judaism, thereby encouraging a proclivity toward exclusiveness which vitiates the significance of Jewish peoplehood.

The substance of these arguments—the low level of Jewish learning in the American Jewish community and the indifference of young people to the national and ethnic aspects of Judaism—is no doubt correct. But to lay the fault at the door of the congregational school is to overlook forces in the larger society that are powerful determinants of educational policy, as they are of the policies of other institutions in the community. There is no need here to detail the anti-intellectualism permeating American life; it should suffice merely to note its inevitably disastrous effect on any regimen of study conceived as learning for its own sake. More than a few will concur, however reluctantly, with the observation that

The younger generation views Judaism in strictly religious terms and finds unintelligible the stress on [the] cultural, national and defense oriented Judaism of their parents. . . . the secular culture or nationhood envisaged by many Jews of a previous generation has proved illusory, incapable of fulfillment on the American scene.[6]

Personnel

Whatever its philosophy, a school is only as effective as its personnel. As in all other areas of the Jewish civil service, there is a serious shortage of qualified personnel in Jewish education. While there is a cadre of trained and experienced educators in administrative posi-

[6] B'nai B'rith Messenger, January 14, 1966, p. 6.

tions, these men are largely the products of an earlier period, and replacements are extraordinarily hard to find. The situation is at its most desperate on the classroom level; the idea of a profession of Jewish teacher is either a thing of the past or a hope for the future.

Administration

The administration of congregational schools is in the hands of a principal or educational director who is responsible to the school board and the rabbi of the congregation. The Educators Assembly is the professional organization of educational directors in the Conservative movement. While not all educational directors qualify for membership in the Assembly, it has close to 200 members whose sole occupation is in the congregational school. Prerequisites for membership are a master's degree in education, a commensurate level in Jewish studies, and at least three years of experience as a principal. A recent survey[7] indicates that 36 percent of the members are 50 years of age or older, and 55 percent between the ages of 35 and 49. Fifty-six percent of the sample had served at least five years in their present position and 39 percent reported service of 10 years or more in one post. Close to half of the respondents were earning $12,000 a year or more.

The one-day-a-week structure of many Reform congregational schools makes full-time employment of administrators less common than it is in Conservative afternoon or day schools. Many are public school people who "moonlight" in the Jewish school and lack adequate training in Jewish studies. Despite consistent efforts to raise their level, the activities of the Teacher Education Department of the Union of American Hebrew Congregations (UAHC) show that this remains a problem.

The Orthodox day schools have developed a core of full-time educational administrators drawn from the graduates of rabbinical seminaries who have eschewed careers in the rabbinate in favor of work in schools. Many of them come to their posts without adequate preparation and training in education. But the insistent prodding of Torah Umesorah, the national organization of Orthodox day schools, has noticeably raised the level of qualification.

[7] *Personnel Review and Trends* (New York: Educators Assembly, 1968).

Where a congregational school is too small to warrant a full-time principal or educational director, the rabbi or the cantor, doubling as educator, conducts the school. This sort of arrangement is rarely satisfactory. More often than not, the school is not the major focus of a rabbi's or cantor's professional concern; neither generally has had training specific to the task, and all too often the press of other duties curtails the time and attention given to the school.

As a whole, the professional Jewish educator is at least as well-schooled academically as his public school counterpart. However, it is doubtful that the principal of a Jewish school has had the kind of rigorous practical experience that is demanded of supervisory personnel in the better public school systems. Because of the severe manpower shortage, a person with only a minimum of classroom experience may become principal of a Jewish school. Yet, lacking the supporting services available in the public school, he is almost always dependent on his own resources and imagination, and the degree of his technical expertise is of more than ordinary significance in determining the school's effectiveness.

Within the congregation itself, the position of the school principal is somewhat anomalous. Unless he is a man of strong character, outstanding ability, and not a little *chutzpah*, he generally ranks behind the rabbi and cantor in the synagogue hierarchy. This is yet another index of a symbolic style of Jewish life which ascribes a disproportionate influence to clerical functions. This cannot but seriously impair the educator's potential as a model, and inevitably reduces the significance of his enterprise. Though perhaps incongruous, it nevertheless is true that the man responsible for the congregation's major learning activity is rarely thought of as the exemplar of Jewish learning.

Teaching Staff

If, as our information would seem to indicate, some degree of stability and professionalism has been achieved in the administration of Jewish education, the profession of Jewish teacher, by contrast, has suffered serious retrogression. The elementary Jewish school, which today means almost all Jewish schools, is by and large a feminine preserve. The reason is that the available hours of employment in both the afternoon and one-day-a-week schools, the predominant types of

Jewish schools, are not sufficient to provide a family man with a living wage, even where salary scales are most generous. Indeed, a man can support a family on an income from teaching in a Jewish school only if he holds two jobs—in a day school in the morning, and in an afternoon school.

It would be fatuous to expect to remedy the malaise of the Jewish teacher without giving prompt and effective attention to his economic situation. The Jewish community simply has no right to expect alert, able, intelligent young people—and its schools can suffer no other—to devote themselves to a calling which consigns them to a life fringed by poverty. As necessary as improvement of financial status may be to the creation of a corps of effective classroom personnel, it is not the sole condition for vitalizing a profession. Above and beyond this, Jewish education must provide a sense of purpose and achievement if there is to be any hope of developing a cadre of capable and concerned people who will find their life's work in Jewish schools. Nothing less is required than a modern day counterpart of the Eastern European *maskil*, whose passion for the Hebrew language, unbounded commitment to the Zionist ideal, and deep faith in the moving power of education informed his entire being and transformed his work as teacher into an inspired vocation.

Two types stand out today among the variety of teachers—including part-time and full-time, trained and untrained, religious and agnostic, knowledgeable and Jewishly illiterate, volunteer and salaried —who compose the faculties of Jewish schools of all kinds. One is the *musmach*, a graduate of an Orthodox rabbinical school who has opted for a teaching career, and the other is the Israeli who is in this country for an assortment of reasons. Without the former, the growth of the day school is hardly imaginable; without the latter, the continued functioning of the afternoon school would be severely constrained. However disparate the two may seem at first glance, they share much in their common task as teachers of third and even fourth generation American Jewish children.

All too often both bring an attitude of cynical disdain bordering on arrogance to their work in schools whose approach differs from their own particular conceptions of Jews and Judaism. However, the *yeshiva* graduate at his best is a genuine religious personality, steeped in Talmudic learning and dedicated to a way of life consonant with the Jewish law; the Israeli, at his best, is a fervent nationalist consumed by a love of land and language which would embrace all within its reach. The former is at home only within the small enclave of his immediate community; the latter's perception of himself as a transient permits only the most tenuous ties with the society he serves. Obviously, both are worlds removed from their students, making effective communication difficult.

However, the matter goes beyond the sometimes too simplistic assessment of failure resulting from a teacher's inability to understand his pupils. There certainly are *yeshiva* graduates and Israelis in American schools who are successful teachers by any accepted standard. Indeed, it is the very possibility of their success that may be most troublesome. If they are able to transmit their own belief to their students, they cannot but alienate the youngsters from their own families and backgrounds. It is hard to avoid the feeling that not a little of the criticism directed at both the *yeshiva* graduate and the Israeli by the more "moderate" school people in our midst stems from a fear of their possible success. When the teacher mutes his real beliefs, whether at the suggestion of the administration or because he recognizes their incompatability with the stand of the school, he loses his integrity and, with it, the capability to exert any real influence.

We know too little about the dynamics of career choice to state with certitude what would move American-born and -trained men and women to choose careers in Jewish education. An educated guess would be that the people a youngster encounters in the Jewish school may well play a decisive role. An earlier generation of American Jewish children, anxious to acquire the credentials of Americanism, identified the Hebrew teacher with much of what it desperately wanted to escape. Today's youngster, more secure about his place in America, may see the *yeshiva* graduates or Israelis, who staff the schools in significant percentage, as just the sort of "off-beat" characters who hold a certain romantic attraction in our time. On the other hand, he may not, and their presence in his school may only serve to confirm his worst suspicions about the irrelevance of what takes place there.

The crucial presence of the Israeli teacher, like that of the European-born teacher of an earlier period, underscores the sad fact that the American Jewish community has never been able to produce a sufficient number of native-born teachers and has always been dependent upon outside sources of supply. Current enrollment in American Jewish teacher-training schools offer no promise of early relief. Figures demonstrate that these institutions presently do not attract a significantly larger percentage of potential students than almost a

generation ago. Knowledgeable estimates place enrollment in all accredited and nonaccredited teacher-training institutions at about 2,000
students, a figure which includes a significant percentage of Israelis.[8]
These institutions annually graduate some 200 students. Of this number, only 125 to 150 graduates actually assume teaching positions
upon the completion of their studies. However, a considerable number
of those who do begin to teach have no intention of remaining in
Jewish education, and use teaching in a Jewish school as a temporary
occupation while preparing for careers in other fields. Also, one must
bear in mind that many attend Jewish teacher training schools only
out of a desire to continue their Jewish education on the college level,
and have no interest in education as a career.

While there is much in our teacher-training schools which requires
correction, it is doubtful that internal changes alone will produce an
adequate remedy. The statistics of enrollment in Hebrew teachers
colleges and their high rate of dropouts are indices of the difficulties
inherent in the maintenance of a system of supplementary education
which, among other things, must compete with the demands of general education. The student who enters a Jewish teacher-training
school can look back upon at least nine or ten years of elementary and
secondary Jewish schooling, completed simultaneously with his public
schoolwork; he can look forward to at least four more years of a
similar dual program during his college career. At a time when the
demands of the public high schools are becoming more and more
rigorous and college entrance requirements more stringent, only the
most highly motivated students will continue their Jewish studies
through the secondary level. The pressures of a selective service system keyed to academic standing and the frantic scramble for places in
graduate schools similarly dissuade many Hebrew high school graduates from continuing their Jewish studies on a college level.

However, many students in Jewish elementary and secondary
schools never get to a school of higher Jewish learning for reasons that
have nothing to do with the public schools and their demands. Parental
and communal indifference to Jewish education certainly play a role
and act as powerful negative influences, and Jewish schools themselves must share some responsibility for the continuing, or noncon-
tinuing, education of their students. The programs and policies of the

---

[8] For a full treatment of Jewish teacher-training schools see Oscar I. Janowsky,
ed., *The Education of American Teachers* (Boston: Beacon Press, 1967).

lower Jewish schools all too often discourage even the most interested student, and succeed only in convincing him that continued attendance at a Jewish school would be a waste of time.

Educational Agencies

Each of the denominational groups maintains a national educational commission within the framework of its countrywide synagogue organization. Over the years these commissions have developed characteristic modes of operation, dictated as much by limited funds and personnel as by educational considerations. They generally concern themselves with promulgating statements of broad educational policy, developing curricular materials, conducting regional and national conferences, and, in some cases, planning extensive textbook publication programs.

The impact of the work of these agencies is difficult to assess. Certainly the textbooks they publish represent a direct influence on the schools they serve, but there is no guarantee that these schools will use the books. Since the commissions neither have nor seek powers of enforcement, their programs must stand or fall on the strength of their response to the needs of the schools. Their importance may lie in their inherent authority to develop policy which, even if ignored, becomes the standard by which individual schools and their programs may be judged. The guidelines set by the national agencies can have the power of prodding and stimulating local schools to explore areas of practice that might otherwise be ignored.

Local bureaus of Jewish education have much closer contact with the schools. As the embodiment of the community's stake in Jewish education, the bureau's function is to give disinterested technical assistance and guidance to the schools of the various ideological groupings in the locality it serves. Affiliated schools may avail themselves of the bureau's supervisory personnel, in-service seminars, central audiovisual and pedagogical libraries, testing programs, placement services, publications, and a wide variety of other educational activities. The standards set by an adequately staffed and financed bureau can determine the quality of Jewish education in the community. In some cities the entire structure reflects the strong personality of the bureau head, and is but an extension of his conception of Jewish education.

Despite the claims of its supporters, the bureau is not always as neutral as it claims to be. As the major recipient of communal funds, as inadequate as they may be, it easily can, by its administrative decisions, channel the development of educational activities in directions not always consistent with the felt needs of its constituent schools. Very often the bureau itself becomes an ideological factor promoting its own perceived interests. More subtle is the effect of the private views of bureau personnel, which sometimes are at variance with the stated aims and objectives of the schools they serve. The bureau's admittedly crucial role in the development of Jewish education and the vital function it has yet to serve do not obscure the recurrent friction that results from its position in a community defined by ideological differences.

Nationally, the American Association for Jewish Education (AAJE) assays much the same role as the bureau in its own locality. Through its community surveys, teacher welfare programs, periodic census of Jewish school population, publications, curriculum institute, and training programs, AAJE provides services not readily available through other agencies at the same time as it initiates activities for improving Jewish education. Originally the national organization of the bureaus, AAJE recently was reorganized to represent all agencies involved in Jewish education. The hope is that, as such, it will eliminate unnecessary duplication and serve as a vehicle for a coherent attack on the problems of Jewish education.

Financing

The cost of Jewish education—the services and activities described above—is close to $100 million a year, exclusive of capital investment in facilities and equipment. These funds come from three obvious sources: parents of the students, the sponsoring agency, and the community.

Tuition income hardly covers the cost of operating congregational or day schools. Investment in the congregational school's plant and equipment as well as its operating deficits are covered partly by the synagogue budget and partly by limited fund-raising. Day schools with no specific synagogal connection depend on fund-raising drives directed to the community at large for a major portion of their budget. Bureaus are funded by local federations or welfare funds of which they generally are constituent agencies. In some cities, communal funds, disbursed through the bureau offices in accordance with some established formula, are made available to both congregational and day schools. On the whole, however, the community finances only the bureau and its activities.

Needless to say, there is never enough money—nor will there ever be! However, this should not obscure the equally damaging consequences of the absence of a rational fiscal policy for Jewish education. Current practices hark back to the response of an earlier generation to the needs of its time. If federation funds today are but stintingly allocated in support of Jewish education, it is as much because of commitments made 25 and even 50 years ago as it is because of considered priorities in our time. The total support by the congregation itself of a congregational educational program, which trains a younger generation for responsible membership in the larger community, is dictated by neither logic nor tradition. The distinction in the disbursement of communal funds between nondenominational— read secular—teacher-training schools and religiously oriented institutions of the same purpose is another of the many anomalies of financing Jewish education. The overwhelming majority of the students in the accredited teacher-training schools come from Orthodox and Conservative afternoon and day schools. These alone provide the intensive elementary and secondary education prerequisite to admission to a Hebrew teachers college. Furthermore, most students will find themselves teaching in that kind of school upon graduation, and yet communal funds are available only to schools maintaining a nondenominational posture and withheld from those of clear religious orientation.

A stable financial basis can be established only after a reassessment of the relative responsibility of each of the three sources of support. Jewish federations throughout the country currently provide a total of some $6.4 million annually for Jewish education. Despite the fact that the sum of the allocations has increased markedly over the years— allocations in dollars in 1966 were 58.7 percent higher than in 1957 —the percentage of federation funds earmarked for Jewish education has remained almost the same—11.7 percent of federation allocations for local services in 1957 were for Jewish education as compared to 13.4 percent in 1966, an increase of only 1.7 percent.[9] While it helps

---

[9] S. P. Goldberg, "Jewish Communal Services: Programs and Finances," *American Jewish Year Book*, 1968, vol. 69, pp. 291–343. Published by The American Jewish Committee, New York, and The Jewish Publication Society of America, Philadelphia.

little to demand a greater investment of communal funds in the work of Jewish schools unless that demand is accompanied by some clear rationale for the uses to which such monies will be put, it is clear that many vital services could be provided if federation allocations were raised a mere 2 or 3 percent. Surely the time has come for a thorough evaluation of the allocation patterns of federation and welfare funds.

Congregations must also begin some clarification of their fiscal procedures to determine the obligations that are sensibly within their purview, and to arrive at a reasonable distribution of the financial responsibilities of all who share in the educational enterprise. If tuition is primarily the responsibility of the parent, then there is no question that steps must be taken to bring tuition rates into some realistic proportion to the cost of educating a child. The readiness of Jewish parents to shoulder the burden of high tax rates in support of public education must find its counterpart in Jewish education.

Questions of finance inevitably raise problems of control. Thus, while the principle of community support for day schools has largely been accepted throughout the country, debates leading to recognition of that obligation were not without troublesome overtones. In city after city, as well as at several Council of Jewish Federations and Welfare Funds conferences, the question of the day schools' claim to communal funds was repeatedly connected with judgments concerning their "Americanism," their effectiveness, and their very right to exist—questions rarely or never asked of other kinds of schools receiving communal subsidies. In effect, one sector of the community— federations and welfare funds are rarely representative—was questioning the educational program of another sector and using its financial strength as a lever of educational policy. Surely all sorts of Jewish schools have their place in a democratic society. A community conscious of its obligations to all its members cannot legitimately support a plan of financial aid favoring one type of school at the expense of another.

Curriculum

Personnel and programs for the Jewish school are ultimately as meaningful as the achievements of the institution they are intended to serve. The measure of the effectiveness of any school is how close what it actually does comes to what it wants to do. Where a significant discrepancy exists between the two, both the school's goals and the means used to achieve them require reexamination.

The curricula of most Jewish schools in the United States are based on a religio-national conception of Judaism: the People of Israel, *Torah*, and God. The teaching methods used are grounded in contemporary theories of child development and education. Of course, differences exist in the practices of the schools of each denominational grouping. The abiding division separating the Reform from the Orthodox view of the religious life is clearly manifest in the style and manner of the schools. Yet, a study of the objectives of Jewish education, as formulated in the official statements of each of the three religious groups in American Judaism, discloses elements common to all.[10]

The schools of all three religious orientations would probably agree to the following paraphrase of their educational objectives: (1) to provide knowledge of the classical Jewish texts and the tradition embodied therein; (2) to foster a lifelong commitment to the study of *Torah*; (3) to develop some form of personal observance; (4) to develop a facility in the Hebrew language and a familiarity with its literature; (5) to nurture an identification with the Jewish people through a knowledge of its past and to encourage a concern for its survival and welfare the world over; (6) to stimulate a recognition of the unique place of Israel in the Jewish imagination, both past and present, and to foster acceptance of some sort of personal obligation to participate in its development; (7) to encourage participation in American society, based on a conscious awareness of the relationship between Jewish tradition and democracy; and (8) to inculcate faith in God and trust in His beneficence.

Translation of objectives into curricular content is a complicated process requiring continual evaluation and refinement. That process is usually informed by a series of assumptions regarding the function of the school, the nature of the student, what is to be learned, and how it is to be learned. Though rarely explicit, these assumptions may be inferred from curricular materials and syllabi. A careful examination of the curricula of the various kinds of Jewish schools discloses that all of them share certain assumptions.

No matter what its structure or orientation, the Jewish school con-

[10] Alexander M. Dushkin, "Common Elements in American Jewish Teaching," *Jewish Education*, November 1945, pp. 5–12. For statements of aims and objectives of the various denominations see Alexander M. Dushkin and Uriah Z. Engleman, *Jewish Education in the United States* (New York: American Association for Jewish Education, 1959), pp. 35–38.

ceives its primary function to be transmission of knowledge of the sacred texts. Some schools may study the texts themselves and others may only learn about them, but all center on them. Other subject matters, such as Hebrew, history, prayer, and observance, are merely adumbrations of the basic core. The acquisition of knowledge is thought essential to the attainment of that pattern of pupil behavior which is the objective of the school. This conception of function is at the heart of the dominant instructional method of the Jewish school, text-centered explication and exposition.

It is equally evident that the school, looking upon its pupils as Jewishly illiterate, believes that only it, during the time of their enrollment, will transmit the information or develop the skills which they need for responsible Jewish life. Whatever the validity of this view, it places an impossible burden on the school and eliminates from the curriculum any possibility of building on meaningful Jewish experiences acquired elsewhere. This sense of total responsibility is particularly pronounced in the program of the Jewish elementary school. The proliferation of subjects beyond reason is surely born of the feeling that the child will not continue above that level, and that every effort must be made to cover as much as possible during the few years he attends the school. At all levels, the schools are invariably geared to the proposition that the Jewish child will find his future as a fully integrated member of American society, and that Judaism and the American ethic are essentially compatible.

DAY SCHOOLS

Free of the time limitations of other types of Jewish schools, the day school is best able to provide a thorough grounding in the traditional areas of Jewish study. Its day is generally longer than that of the public school to permit giving equal time to general and Jewish studies. Classes in the latter are usually conducted in Hebrew; some schools use Yiddish or English. Grade eight, the last elementary grade of a typical day school, includes the following Jewish studies: a review of the Pentateuch with Rashi commentary; a regular review of the weekly *Torah* portion; Kings I and II, the early Prophets, Jeremiah; Hebrew grammar, language, and literature; some tractate of the Talmud, which alone takes up almost half of the time allotted to Jewish studies on this grade level; modern history or a survey of the entire range of Jewish history; Jewish law, with special reference to the laws of prayer, Sabbath, and holidays. Since each school day begins with formal prayer, prayer as such is not offered as a separate course of study. The study of Talmud receives even greater emphasis on the high school level and is the dominant feature of a study course including *Torah* with commentaries, law (*Shulhan Aruh*), later Prophets, liturgy, Hebrew language and literature, history, and ethics.[11]

AFTERNOON SCHOOLS

Weekday afternoon schools range from those meeting five times a week, for a total of ten hours of instruction, to those holding two weekly sessions with a total of three or four hours of classwork. The six-hour-a-week school, which is in session two afternoons and a Sunday or Saturday morning, is probably the most common. A suggested curriculum for the sixth, and final, year of such a school provides for: selections from an abridged Hebrew text of Deuteronomy dealing with the law, equality of man, freedom and equality, social justice, administration of justice, humane treatment, God, Israel, and the Lord of Israel; related passages in Hebrew from the later Prophets and narrative selections from the early Prophets together with correlated readings in English; Hebrew grammar, language, and literature; Jewish life and religious practices; a survey of Jewish history.[12] Graduates of this type of school wishing to continue their studies in a secondary school are offered a course of study with major emphasis on Bible and Hebrew, accompanied by courses in history, religion, and rabbinic literature.

The major elements of the curricula of one-day-a-week schools are Bible and history, taught in English. A suggested course of study for the eighth grade of one such network of schools offers modern history, the Prophets and "socioethical living," with the State of Israel and the "Jewish way of life in recent years" as possible alternatives. Course offerings for grades 9 through 12 range over Reform Judaism, the Writings, comparative religion, American Jewish history, early post-biblical literature, modern Jewish problems, later postbiblical literature, Jewish beliefs, Jewish life, a survey of the Bible, and a history survey.[13]

11 For a detailed description of the curricula of the various types of day schools and *yeshivot*, see Schiff, *The Jewish Day School in America*, pp. 106–123.

12 Louis L. Ruffman, *Curriculum Guide for the Congregational School*, rev. ed. (New York: United Synagogue Commission on Jewish Education, 1959).

13 Lawrence Myers, ed., *Teaching in the Jewish Religious School* (New York: Department of Teacher Education, Union of American Hebrew Congregations, 1967), pp. 212–213.

STANDARDS OF ACHIEVEMENT

The similarities in the courses of study cited above should not obscure the differences in approach and achievement that characterize each type of school. For instance, if knowledge of the traditional Jewish texts is to be the criterion of an educated Jew, then only the day school graduate has the background and skills to qualify. Given the inherent limitations of the afternoon and one-day-a-week schools, one might question the wisdom of a scholastic program cast in the mold of the day school. The peculiar circumstances of the former ought to lead to a course of study qualitatively different from the watered-down version of the day school which characterizes their efforts.

Curricula and courses of study, particularly when prepared by agencies having little direct contact with what goes on in the classroom, do not always accurately reflect the actual work of the schools for which they are intended. At best they represent a framework for developing instructional goals and a guide for classroom practice; at worst they are an affectation which obscures more than it reveals and hinders more than it helps. Data about the actual achievement levels of Jewish schools are difficult to obtain, and one is forced to rely on estimates born of inference. The problem is further complicated by the absence of an absolute standard against which academic achievement may be judged.

It is clear that the day school student learns more of the traditional Jewish disciplines than do his fellows in the afternoon and one-day-a-week schools. The real question is whether or not the day school, given the time, effort, and money expended, does all it might do, and really is the instrument for the creation of an "intellectual-spiritual elite," as its supporters claim. We do know that an elementary day school graduate who does not continue his studies quickly forgets much of what he learned and loses many of the skills so laboriously acquired. This is less a comment on the quality of instruction in the day school than a sad fact of the nature of learning. If knowledge is a precondition of behavior, then continued study is essential to the development of the personality, which is the goal of the day school. The statistics of secondary day school enrollment are encouraging, but far from convincing when used as a measure of the effectiveness of the lower school in inspiring its students to continued study.[14]

[14] Schiff, *The Jewish Day School in America*, p. 56.

When judged by even the least demanding standard of what it means to be an educated Jew, it is hard to avoid the feeling that the academic aspirations of the one-day-a-week school are either a joke or an act of cynical pretentiousness. The plethora of subject matter of its curriculum is certainly beyond serious treatment in the available time, and even the most serious and able student cannot hope to acquire more than a smattering of information. The jump from subject to subject from year to year and even within the same year militates against the serious treatment of any one topic. The continuation rate in Reform religious schools, which is higher than in any other Jewish school, is clearly the result of an administrative device: Confirmation, the equivalent of graduation, is postponed until the high school years, and, as a ceremony of completion, it has an attraction independent of the quality of the school.

The three-days-a-week school characteristic of the Conservative movement cannot claim happier results. A recent study[15] shows that even when pupils complete the requirements established by the curriculum, they have no recognizable fluency in Hebrew and cannot understand more than carefully edited texts based on a limited vocabulary. Caught in the crossfire of Bible study as an independent subject and the use of the Biblical text, and an abridged one at that, as a Hebrew language workbook, the pupils learn neither. Although close to 50 percent of the instructional time is devoted to the study of Hebrew and Bible, the pupil graduates from the school with only the most infantile notions of Biblical thought and ideas, and a capability in Hebrew which hardly goes beyond monosyllabic responses to carefully worded questions. The study of history is a pious wish, usually restricted to less than one hour a week. Understanding and generalization fall prey to the hurried accumulation of disconnected fact. The rate of continuation beyond the elementary level in the afternoon school is the lowest of all types of schools and is a significant index of its ineffectiveness. When, in a carefully controlled study recently completed, the 973 graduating students of all the Conservative congregational schools in the Los Angeles area in a given year were asked why they did not continue in a Jewish school, "dissatisfaction with the program of the elementary school" was listed as the primary reason,

---

15 Walter I. Ackerman, *An Analysis of Selected Courses of Study of Conservative Congregational Schools* (New York: Melton Research Center, Jewish Theological Seminary, 1968).

and "insufficient parental interest and support" as the least important.[16]

The reasons for the low level of academic achievement are not hard to determine. First among several external factors beyond the control of the school is the diminished learning capacity of pupils coming to classes late in the afternoon or in the early evening after a full day in public school. But the school itself and its policies are not without blame. Too many courses of study reflect a confusion of means and ends that hinders effective teaching and learning. Hebrew language learning is a case in point. Learning any language is a complicated task and, whatever else may be required, afternoon schools simply cannot hope to develop fluency in Hebrew unless sufficient time is allotted to this subject—a demand which is rarely met. The alternatives are quite clear. If the afternoon school is convinced of the importance of Hebrew, it should give it the priority of time required for significant achievement; if the press of other subject demands prevents the necessary time allotment, then the pretense of teaching Hebrew should be abandoned. Bible study in the elementary school cannot hope to assume a meaningful dimension, so long as it is confused with language instruction and tied to a deadening method of translating the Hebrew text into English. Some selectivity and progression must be introduced into the study of Jewish life and practices; achievement tests on the subject which are prepared and administered by the central office of one large metropolitan Jewish school system ask the same questions for three grades running. In the three days a week Conservative schools, too, the hopeless proliferation of subject matter denies even the most competent and dedicated teacher the possibility of significant achievement in any one area.

Jewish Education and Identification as a Jew

Information on the relationship between Jewish education and the attitudes of the students, their pattern of observance, and the nature and extent of their Jewish identification is not readily available. Some of the difficulty stems from the paucity of rigorous research; most of it

[16] Emil Jacoby, *A Study of School Continuation and Dropout Following Bar Mitzvah* (Los Angeles: Institute for Jewish Research, University of Judaism and Bureau of Jewish Education, Los Angeles Federation Council, 1969).

lies in the evasive nature of the variables in question and the problem of isolating the specific influence of the school. A comprehensive review of the literature leads one investigator to assert that ". . . in no case does there seem to be any dependable relationship between the type of Jewish education received by the child and the nature of his Jewish-American identification."[17] A more recent study reports that

. . . Jewish education has a definite influence on attitudes toward favoring Jewish education and religious practices—what we have called general Jewish identification—and discouraging intermarriage. However, among the adolescents with an extensive religious education, attitudes toward antisemitism, the out-group and Israel are not much different from those adolescents who received limited religious education.[18]

A study designed to determine adolescent attitudes towards Israel[19] notes that

The students' approach to Israel appears to be negatively related to their identity as Americans . . . [and] the over-all cultural climate to which students are exposed both in their home environment and in the formal training of a Jewish school forms the prime influence establishing and reinforcing their outlook as American Jews. . . . The general orientation of the school toward Israel . . . was found to be positively associated with the students' *knowledge* of Israel but was not positively associated with their attitudes toward Israel or their American Jewish environment.

The problem of separating the influence of the home from that of the school is highlighted in an investigation of the religious practices and attitudes of day school graduates.[20] Those participating in the study indicated that they had greater feelings of loyalty toward the Jewish people than the observances of Jewish law. While some of the respondents were active in communal affairs, few retained personal study habits. Indeed, the data indicate rather clearly that religious observance and practice are significantly related to home background and religious background of the spouse. Another study of day school

17 Joshua A. Fishman, "Social Science Research and Jewish Education," *Jewish Education*, Winter 1957–58, p. 55.
18 Victor D. Sanua, "Jewish Education and Attitudes of Jewish Adolescents," in *The Teenager and Jewish Education* (New York: Educators Assembly of the United Synagogue of America, 1968), p. 130.
19 Rina Shapira, *Attitudes Toward Israel Among American Jewish Adolescents* (New York: Center for Urban Education), pp. 5, 9.
20 George Pollak, "The Jewish Day School Graduate," *Jewish Spectator*, February 1962, pp. 11–14.

graduates[21] comments that "where the school succeeded in imparting both knowledge and values it may be assumed that it reinforced other factors in the students' environment, particularly in the home."

These studies represent attempts to measure the influence of the Jewish school. The research findings currently available are clear in their import. The influence of the school is most pronounced in imparting information; it affects basic attitudes toward Jews and Judaism and patterns of religious behavior only slightly, if at all. In this regard Jewish schools are no different from most other schools throughout the world. As comforting as this thought may be, it does not obscure the painful fact that Jewish education in America today falls woefully short of achieving many of its stated goals.

Functions of Jewish Education

Proposals for improvement of the current state of affairs must be preceded by ridding ourselves of the rhetoric of nonsense that permeates most discussions of Jewish education today. Educators must learn to avoid extravagant claims and begin to speak forthrightly about the sensible probabilities of particular circumstances. Critics of Jewish education must come out from behind the shield of exaggerated demands whose fulfillment is beyond the power of any school. Both must acknowledge that the process of formal schooling has inherent limitations and, most important, that it is but one of many possible educative agencies and experiences affecting the developing person both before and after he steps into a school. Such candor would introduce some degree of much-needed realism into the position of both the beleaguered schoolman and his insistent detractors.

When mention is made today of Jewish education, the reference is to schools that serve youngsters of elementary and high school age. It is interesting, and more than discouraging, that the term as commonly used does not include summer camps, youth organizations, adult education programs, work done with college age students, or other educational activities conducted within the Jewish community. The limitations thus implied are not without serious implications, not the least

---

[21] Irving Pinsky, "The Graduates of Rabbi Jacob Joseph School: A Follow-Up Study," *Jewish Education*, Spring 1962, pp. 180–183.

among them the enervating isolation of the Jewish school from the world around it.

This isolation can be overcome only as the school comes to be seen as one point along a continuum of educational experiences and activities involving Jews of all ages. More is implicit here than the truism, which cannot be repeated too often, that everyone, parents and children alike, ought to be engaged in learning. At each age and stage of his life an individual learns in a different way and needs to learn different things. No one age level or life stage is intrinsically more important than any other; an individual can be given the opportunity of an educational experience compatible with his needs and interests at any one given time. At each level educational activity has an integrity of its own, but its full meaning is achieved only when it has an integral relationship to what came before and what will come after.

It is not logical for a synagogue to spend tens of thousands of dollars on a school program for children and only a small fraction of that sum for the education of adults. Nor does it make sense to assume, as most congregations do, that children and adults learn in the same way. The theory and practice of education for adults must be qualitatively different from those of elementary and secondary education. Of course, at some point in life the directed activity of the conventional classroom is the most important and necessary service a community can provide for those who must acquire certain specific skills best taught and learned in such a setting. However, all education is not cognitive, and there are stages in one's life when the affective realm demands primacy of place. It is conceivable that, at a certain age, a camp experience is more decisive in the development of Jewish identity than any number of hours spent weekly in a classroom. For the adolescent concerned not only with himself but also with his relationship to peers and adults, a certain kind of work experience may be crucial to the development of his understanding of Jews and Judaism. A year of study or work in Israel is rarely without impact, but it means many different things to those who have such an opportunity. As a matter of educational policy the investment of institutional funds should be for those age groups whose involvement in Israel promises a maximum return. The point is clear: A comprehensive program for the lifelong education of Jews should consist of differentiated educational activities ordered in a sequential fashion responding to the concerns and requirements of the individual at each stage of his life.

199

Viewed in this perspective, the school assumes a dimension commensurate with its nature and capabilities as one of a wide variety of educational agencies. Quick recognition of the proper role of the school is essential to the development of coherent and effective programs of education.

Aims of the Jewish School

The broad purpose of the Jewish school is to contribute to the continued existence of the Jews as an identifiable group. The authority for this assumption varies, for circumstances of life today deny the imposition of a monolithic approach. There are those who find this authority in a divine command; some derive it from the legitimate will of a group to perpetuate itself; others see it as a historical necessity dictated by the pressure of external events; many are moved by a combination of all these factors. The embracive framework which gives the school its specific direction is rarely the result of its own efforts, and is almost always determined in a wider arena of thought and events.

Whatever the particular rationale, the school has a clear-cut function, and its day-to-day work as well as its long-range goals and objectives are conditioned by its role. The Jewish school must impart knowledge and skills of a particular level, and at the same time it must provide its students with acceptable and meaningful means of identifying themselves as Jews. Beyond this, the school must make available opportunities for its students to engage in activities conjointly with other Jews of all ages. Finally, it must seek to define the terms of interaction between its students and the non-Jewish world around them.

The school cannot and need not operate on all these levels with all its students simultaneously. There is a point in the student's scholastic career when acquisition of skills and ordered information is the first order of business because of his needs and abilities at that point, and because it may be a requisite for moving on to other, more sophisticated levels of learning. Similarly there is a point, probably at adolescence, when a more open-ended and discursive experience is best suited to the student and his sense of himself. Determination of what to teach and, equally important, when to teach it is not a simple task, but there is a growing body of knowledge which provides guidelines. To ignore it, as most Jewish schools at present do, is to undermine the entire educational effort.

Improvement of Teaching Materials and Methods

The curriculum content of the Jewish school must be drawn from the Jewish tradition—an imperative sometimes overlooked by "progressives" and those anxious to fit the work of the school to the demands of the American ethos. That tradition, for all its richness and variety, is essentially literary, and its mastery requires an expertise not easily vouchsafed even the most competent and enterprising teacher. Moreover, it is too vast to be encompassed in its entirety by any kind of school. For that tradition to be readily available for classroom use, several conditions must be met: first, development of some guiding principle of selection; second, assessment of its meaning as understood by the current state of scholarly knowledge; finally, presentation in a form intelligible to a literate classroom teacher.

What is required to produce such curriculum materials is school people working together with scholars, each complementing the other's insights and competency. Some steps in this direction have been taken by the National Curriculum Research Institute of the AAJE and the Melton Research Center of the Jewish Theological Seminary. However, neither of these efforts is sufficient. A model may be found in the joint work of educators and scholars which has resulted in revamping the curricula of public elementary and high schools, first in the physical sciences and more lately in the social sciences and the humanities. Jewish education desperately needs a series of regional centers for the advancement of Jewish education which will develop curricula, instructional material, methodological techniques, and evaluative procedures.

Effective use of the materials of the Jewish tradition in the classroom requires a series of steps. A specific idea must first be understood in its original sense. Like the scholar, the student must be taught to engage in the intellectually demanding task of "reconstruction of meaning." After that, the student must be exposed to the permutations of the idea in its several forms during various periods of Jewish history. He must then know the state and status of that idea in his own time. Finally, he must be given the opportunity to weigh that idea and its contemporary meaning against competing and conflicting ideas. Such an approach admits of a variety of possibilities in curriculum construction. One can study whole books of the Bible, or pertinent sections of several books, in such a fashion. Similarly, one can develop a course of study centered on particular themes selected for their importance and centrality in Jewish thought and existence.

Suggestions for the latter are not difficult. Certainly a course in the idea of God, a subject almost never taught as an entity, is proper and necessary in the scheme of Jewish education. There is something dishonest about limiting the pupils' understanding of the God idea to that drawn from study of a few disconnected chapters of Biblical text. A properly conceived and executed course in this area would help the student discover and examine the various ways in which God was comprehended by Jews from the earliest times to the present, and would provide him with the tools for assessing current theological thought. The relationship of Jews to Israel can be treated in the same way. For the pasteurized pablum characterizing instruction in this area at present one might substitute a review of the role of Israel in the Jewish consciousness throughout the ages, and in this way ultimately force the student into a searching intellectual confrontation with the implications of life in a non-Jewish society. The essential thrust of this technique is use of the standards of the Jewish tradition as the measuring rod of the society in which we live, rather than the other way around.

Development of a curriculum couched in these terms is not an easy task, but neither is it impossible. It requires cultivation of specific skills as well as preparation of sophisticated material, thus making possible the development of a sequential program of study geared to the changing abilities of the maturing student. The elementary school here becomes the locus of skill, where a reasoned allocation of time and a carefully constructed program of language instruction provides the youngster with the Hebrew language skills necessary to continued study. The high school provides the opportunity for broad examination of a wide variety of issues, and the college serves as the center of detailed and intensive examination of specific problems. Under no circumstances should educators or parents be seduced into believing that this complicated task can be completed at one level only, or without a clearly defined investment of time.

Having said all that, it is important to enter a caveat. To guarantee that the intellectual examination of a given set of problems is a warranty for a specific sort of behavior is to stretch the power of the intellect beyond its limits. However, if the Jewish school is to be an agency of moral education—and that is its essential function—its practices and methods must be moral. Specifically, this entails getting the student to arrive at a moral position on issues, justifying that position, and demonstrating consistency in its application to other moral issues. While the school cannot guarantee that its students or graduates will act morally when making decisions, it can provide them with the skills and attitudes without which no truly moral decisions can be made.

At the same time we must avoid the pitfall of assuming that the Jewish tradition provides specific answers to contemporary problems. The search for relevance, aside from its mercurial character which makes long-range planning for schools virtually impossible, can distort the meaning of Judaism and impose connotations never intended. It would be far more honest and efficacious for a teacher to admit that on a specific problem Judaism, in its classic formulation, has nothing to say, rather than attempt to force a position easily recognized as nothing more than an intellectual gymnastic. The Jewish school could do worse than to teach that

What Judaism can do for the individual Jew is to permeate him with the total feel of the tradition and then leave him to make his own personal choices in the realm of man's immediate actions. Many Jews remember . . . a grandmother who said often about such matters, out of the very depths of her being, that a "Jew doesn't do this." As political and social doctrine this may seem imprecise, but one who is not alien to the inherited Jewish experience finds this standard both precise and most exquisitely moral.[22]

Recommendations

FIXING RESPONSIBILITY

Who runs the school is less important than how it is run. The debate over whether the authority for conduct of the Jewish school should be vested in the community or the congregation belongs to another

[22] Arthur Hertzberg, *The Condition of Jewish Belief* (New York: The Macmillan Co., 1966), p. 96. A symposium compiled by the editors of *Commentary*.

age, and has been resolved by the flow of events. There is a common recognition that each has a role to play and the task of the moment is to define the obligations of each.

The responsibility for the day-to-day conduct of its school rests with the congregation. This includes not only supervision of instruction in the limited technical sense, but also development of a philosophy consistent with the views of the synagogue membership. For its part, the community office of education ought to eschew activities which are more properly the province of the individual school, and should concentrate on research and experimentation. Bureau personnel ought to divest themselves of the "inspectorial" role and leave such tasks to the school principal. Community funds should, wherever possible, be diverted from direct support of congregational schools, particularly on the elementary level, and directed for use as seed money which encourages and stimulates innovative practices. Perhaps the most legitimate and vital use for community funds is the establishment of model schools, supervised by a bureau of Jewish education together with a Hebrew teachers college, where one exists. The extension, or perhaps conversion, of the bureau's role obviously requires more liberal financing than in the past. There probably has been no other time in the history of the American Jewish community when federations and welfare funds have evinced as much interest in Jewish education as now, and one senses that additional funds would be allocated if new programs were proposed.

Both bureaus and schools must find more demanding methods of evaluation. There is probably no case on record of a school disaffiliated from a bureau or cut off from funds and services because of failure to meet a mutually agreed upon academic standard. Sporadic efforts at accreditation in cities throughout the country concentrate more on administrative efficiency than on scholastic excellence. This situation probably will fail of satisfactory resolution so long as the process of evaluation is in the hands of the professional educators conducting the schools.

One possibility lies in the creation of community boards of examiners, composed of disinterested but knowledgeable lay people, who would undertake periodic evaluation of the work of each individual school in a given locale. There is no large Jewish community in the United States today which does not have a sizable number of trained, sophisticated specialists willing to give their talent to improve Jewish schools. Such groups, beholden to nothing but a previously determined standard of achievement and free of any obligation to protect a vested interest, are likely to introduce much-needed control. Schools meeting the requirements established by boards of examiners in cooperation with educators should receive public acknowledgement. Schools persistently failing to live up to established standards should be made known to the public. Parents of children attending a congregational school have the right to know whether the school they support meets fair and reasonable requirements of achievement. Synagogues could suffer a more grievous fate than loss of membership resulting from public knowledge of the insufficiency of their schools.

INFORMAL JEWISH EDUCATION

Simultaneous with the school's move to involve lay people in its work should be attempts to work together with other educational agencies. The Jewish school has not fully availed itself of the possibilities inherent in summer camp programs and youth organizations. All too often these various agencies work independently, and fail to use the strengths of one to overcome the weaknesses of the other. We are past the point of regarding a proper summer camp as a luxury available only to those who can afford it; it should be seen as an integral part of the school program, and offered to every child willing to attend, regardless of his family's ability to pay. Coordination of all these activities—school, youth group, summer camp, a trip to Israel —is essential for the maximum effectiveness of our educational efforts.

A summer camp, either day or resident, can offer students an opportunity for both enrichment and remedial work. It can also serve as a place for experimenting with methods and materials, which is not always possible during the regular school year. Most important, school personnel, working closely with camp people, should learn to draw upon the heightened emotional involvement in Judaism developed at camp as a base for continued work in the city. Youth groups may be asked to conduct activities and programs—in the arts, service to the community, prayer services, and holiday celebrations—which otherwise would cut into precious classroom time, and are better suited to the easy informality of self-determined peer groups.

The conception of the school as only one of many possible educational experiences has the additional advantage of offering teaching personnel a broader range of employment possibilities than are currently available in afternoon or one-day-a-week schools. Of course, not all teachers are capable or willing to work with youth groups or in summer camps, but to those who are, the extension of their role beyond the classroom offers an exciting educational challenge as well as a source of additional income. Some Hebrew teachers colleges have responded to this possibility and have begun to develop programs for the training of multiskilled educational personnel.

TRAINING THE TEACHER

As has already been noted, the most sophisticated program of education remains little more than a good idea, unless there is a sufficient number of trained and dedicated people to develop its practice. The personnel problem for Jewish education, as well as for other areas of Jewish life, cannot be solved without a radical revision of both recruitment and training. We also must act on evidence in the field of general education, which indicates that the reform of the lower school begins in the work of institutions of higher learning.

There is little hope for change in our educational system if we continue to rely on teacher-training schools which are inadequately staffed, underfinanced, and limited in scope and influence, and will continue to be so as long as they remain supplementary institutions. We may learn from the example of nations which have created programs and institutions calculated to produce superbly trained personnel for services deemed essential to their survival. The American Jewish community should seriously consider establishment of a Jewish university, national in scope, with the avowed purpose of securing the future of the Jews in this country through the development of a cadre of literate, concerned, and responsible persons who will assume positions of lay and professional leadership in the Jewish community.

The proposed university is not one whose Jewishness is only in the source of its financial support. Neither is it an institution in which Jewish studies are an adjunct to general studies, or vice versa, and separate faculties are responsible for the conduct of its educational program. The proposal is for a school on collegiate and graduate levels in which general and Jewish studies are integrated within a framework suffused by the Jewish ethic. Geared to the highest standards of academic excellence and scholarship, it will seek to establish an atmosphere of free and open inquiry, creating at the same time an environment of Jewish consciousness. The closest model is perhaps the English public school which, in its grandest sense, was training ground for the elite that ultimately was to shoulder the responsibility for Britain's welfare.

That no such institution exists anywhere in the Jewish world should not deter us from the task. The resources of the American Jewish community are equal to the cost of developing such an institution. What is required is the marshaling of the financial, intellectual, and organizational forces, in which our community abounds, for a concerted and imaginative approach to the academic and monetary problems involved in such an undertaking. Hebrew teachers colleges spend an estimated $15,000 for each of their graduates.[23] It is reasonable to assume that a similar expenditure in a different environment will produce happier results.

Until the envisaged Jewish university becomes a reality, and even after, we must strengthen the Hebrew teachers colleges so that they become schools of higher Jewish learning. Salaries, fringe benefits, teaching loads, and opportunities for research must be improved until they are *at least* comparable to conditions in the best colleges and universities in this country. Only as this is done can the Hebrew teachers colleges hope to compete for faculty with the growing number of colleges and universities that are developing programs of Jewish studies.[24] The Hebrew teachers colleges themselves must initiate a serious curriculum review. Most of the schools in existence today are based on the naturalist philosophies of education of their European-trained founders, who also were moved by the ideals and aspirations of nascent Zionism. The passage of time and the changed circumstances of the Jewish people notwithstanding, the present curricula of these schools are essentially the same as they were a quarter of a century ago.

The initial step in curriculum reform should be differentiation between students interested in becoming teachers and those who seek only to deepen their knowledge of Jews and Judaism. Both types of students must be given the opportunity to develop programs of study fitting their individual needs and interests. Fields of concentration, tutorials, independent studies, and small group seminar-type instruction should replace predetermined courses of study which force every student into the same dulling progression of lecture courses. Subject matter priorities must be reexamined with an eye to the development of greater balance and interaction among the various disciplines con-

---

[23] Janowsky, *The Education of American Teachers*, p. 141.
[24] Arnold J. Band, "Jewish Studies in American Liberal Arts Colleges and Universities," *American Jewish Year Book*, 1966, vol. 67, pp. 3–30.

stituting Jewish studies. Above all, disinterested scholarship must be joined with passion and compassion for the Jews of today.

Students in the teacher-training track should be given the opportunity of actually working in a classroom long before graduation. Student teaching can surely begin before the last year of the four or five year sequence. Temporary certification, subject to specific time limits and conditioned by a requirement of continued study, should be granted to able students even before completion of their studies. Many of the subjects of the elementary school curriculum are taught in English, and there is no reason why intelligent, interested college students should not be given the opportunity to begin, while still in school, their careers as teachers of specific subjects for which they qualify. The lessons of team-teaching are certainly applicable here, and it is worth experimenting with instructional programs combining the specific skills of the Israeli teacher with the talents of the American student teacher.

Every student in a Hebrew teachers college should be given the opportunity of a year's study at an Israeli university. The benefits of such a program need no elaboration, so it is difficult to explain why the richest Jewish community in history does not grant enough scholarship and loan assistance to every serious student who needs such help for a year of concentrated Judaica study in Israel. Scholarships and other incentives might similarly be used to encourage college students to take leaves of absence from their schools for a semester or year of full-time study at a Hebrew teachers college.

Function of Jewish School

The young teacher begins his career with the hope and excitement that only the challenges of teaching can provide. All too often that eager enthusiasm is dulled by the sharp reality of the classroom and the deadening hand of an insensitive administration. In the Jewish school his problems are compounded by the impossible hours and the limited time he has for teaching. At times, the school must seem to him as nothing more than a convenient stopping place for an endless succession of car pools. Little wonder that he begins to doubt whether he really can accomplish anything worthwhile. Perhaps only the day school, with its early starting age and sensible school day, can do all that Jewish schools must do. Or perhaps other alternatives might be explored.

The Jewish school is influenced in many ways by the work of the public school. That is inevitable and perhaps even desirable, but it is also somewhat disconcerting. It is not difficult to understand what moves proponents of day schools to point with pride to the fact that their graduates have no academic or social difficulty when they transfer to the public school. One would hope rather that the experience of a day school would make the public school unbearable. In the final analysis the Jewish school ought to be something quite different from the public school.

We reveal no hidden truth in pointing out that American education is job-oriented. The public school and college systems in this country are predicated on the assumption that a major function of the school is to provide an adequate supply of highly trained technicians to meet the demands of an expanding economy. The broader aims of education have been subverted to the narrower goals of developing marketable skills.

If not by choice then by circumstance, Jewish education is both in fact and theory the exact antithesis of general education in our time. With the exception of a few students possibly contemplating careers of professional service in the Jewish community, our pupils are truly engaged in the study of *Torah* for its own sake. The Jewish school serves no pragmatic ends and can have no other real function than to help its students understand and appreciate the "intrinsic value of education." Therefore, when the Jewish school models itself, as it often does, after the public school in organizational patterns, administrative techniques, means of pupil control and discipline, and methods of instruction, it distorts its uniqueness and creates obstacles to the achievement of its goals. To do so is to play a game in which the rules are not related to the results.

It is important to remember that what a child learns in school derives as much from his experiences in that setting as from the specific content of instruction. The structure of the school, the methods of instruction it employs, the sanctions it invokes, and the relationships it fosters are all vital to the development of the norms it seeks to inculcate in its students. A school dedicated to the democratic ideal must perforce mold these variables into experiences quite different from those provided by a school in a totalitarian society. Similarly, a Jewish school, whose ultimate aim is the inculcation of a specific set of behavioral norms, must provide experiences radically different from those available in a non-Jewish school.

Even if successful, plans for the introduction of curricular change and exhortations for increased services and funds must ultimately fall short of real effectiveness, so long as we avoid the broader question of the essential nature of Jewish schools. The belief that the Jewish school must be unique may be chimerical, but the development of this quality surely is worth a try!

IV

Issues

8

Jewish Youth in Dissent: A Psychoanalytic Portrait

MORTIMER OSTOW, M.D.

Psychoanalysis may be described as an exercise in the undoing of self-deception and the reconstruction of past history. However, its ability to project into the future is limited; still more limited is its ability to prescribe preventive measures. From the very beginnings of psychoanalysis, its practitioners have attempted to exploit their knowledge of child development in order to work out some principles for a hygiene of child rearing. This task has proved to be far more difficult than was anticipated, so that recommendations to parents have had to be revised from time to time. Psychoanalysis has also been relatively ineffectual in devising methods for the prevention or deterrence of mental illness.

With respect to the individual's relation to the community, the psychoanalyst's perspective is even more limited. The psychoanalyst himself is usually caught up in responding to community changes, and many changes occur too slowly to be visible during the course of the clinical exposure of any one patient to psychoanalytic examination. In the case of youth problems, however, the changes are somewhat more rapid and therefore more visible. Also, middle-aged and older analysts are not as likely to be as involved in the issues which trouble young people. To be sure, some younger analysts are so involved, and many of these do tend to identify with their young patients and to justify their behavior.

Subject to the above limitations, this chapter is offered in the hope that what the analyst sees of youthful turmoil may be of some assistance in formulating a program of action for the American Jewish community.

Troubled Youth

Some of the behavior of today's youth—I refer here to the radical sector, to participation in what has come to be known as the "counter-culture"—challenges standards and conventions which have prevailed in Western society for generations. The challenges vary from quietly professed attitudes, such as repudiation of the scientific *Weltanschauung*, to serious physical attacks on property and persons. I use the phrase "repudiation of the scientific *Weltanschauung*" to refer to the defiant rejection of science as an arbiter of the real and the credible, a rejection expressed, for instance, in a preoccupation with astrology and the occult. In the field of personal behavior there is a similar rejection of convention and tradition as guides and sources of standards, in preference to feelings and impulses. These challenges often unsettle the adult observer, for they seem to threaten the structure of society as we know it. Description seems scarcely necessary since the behavior stridently calls attention to itself and one cannot fail to see it. Yet a brief account will serve as a point of departure.

The phenomenon prevails most widely among late adolescents, but some of its features have trickled down to pubertal children. I doubt that it is visible earlier than that. The young people in question adopt a striking appearance. Their clothing is shabby, unattractive, often dirty and sexually unappealing, or daring or ambiguous. Their coiffure, too, is ambiguous with respect to sex, and unconventional. They speak with extraordinary freedom about sexual matters and engage in exhibitionistic acts and promiscuous relations. Those who do not themselves indulge in homosexual activities defend homosexuality against the conventional opposition. They criticize their government and all organized society. They engage in political activities which vary from urging people to vote to acts of terrorism. They provoke the police to attack them and then appeal for sympathy. They sabotage university activities and destroy campus property. They defend minorities ardently and violently—minorities other than their own, that is. (This is not true of most blacks, who promote their own cause and

disparage others.) They use drugs socially, or occasionally, or addic-
tively. Some reject conventional living arrangements and retreat to
communes. A number make serious suicide attempts.

How to explain these startling developments? The young people
have their own explanations, usually of an ad hoc nature; that is,
each piece of behavior is afforded its own explanation. The only generalization they offer is that adults are immoral and that no matter
what young people do, the fact that they do it publicly rather than
secretly places them on a higher moral plane than their parents. The
latter are now stigmatized with the additional label of hypocrisy. It is
better to renounce principles and ideals, youth says, than to profess
idealistic beliefs that inevitably fall short. They complain that in view
of what they consider to be imminent world annihilation, and in view
of government immorality, "life has no meaning." Any effort to restore
"meaning" to life, to destroy or circumvent an "immoral" government,
is justified.

These young people offer a variety of arguments to justify their
behavior. With respect to sexual conduct, they assert that the times
have changed, that sexual morals are "irrelevant," and that contracep-
tives have made morality superfluous. Some claim that an obsolete
"traditional morality" has been replaced by a "relevant, revolutionary
morality." (Those who sympathize with the young accept these arguments and ignore the more subtle but essential considerations—for
instance, the fact that morality is, by definition, not a standard which
can be accepted or rejected at one's convenience.)

The shabby dress and indeterminate and messy hairdos are said to
serve several purposes. Boys say that they wear their hair long because they "like it that way." Such a statement, of course, begs the
question. The odd attire is similarly explained. Some say, in addition,
that it avoids the pretentiousness and artificiality of more conventional
dress. A few of those who are less self-conscious about logic and
consistency declare that they will not be made to conform to any
established pattern, ignoring their remarkable conformity to the adolescent stereotype.

Drug use is explained as a matter of personal preference. Some
devotees of hallucinogenic drug experience argue that these experiences open new horizons to them, enabling them to see "the truth" for
the first time. (I might note that I have never found any objective
traces of such revelations.)

Attacks on the university are justified as efforts to rectify the inade-
quacies of the educational system. Political hyperactivism, however
defined, is said to be intended to correct injustices. The democratic
process is alleged to be ineffective or too slow. These arguments are
offered seriously despite the evidence of history that no other system
of government has been consistently freer of injustice. In its most
extreme form, this tendency becomes a revolutionary movement.

Of course, not all of today's troubled youth hold to all of these
positions. A number of fairly easily distinguishable groupings can be
discerned, such as the political activists, the fighters for sexual freedom, the campus rebels, the antiwar protesters, and the drug "freaks."
Yet all these groups overlap to such an extent in membership and
ideology that one must suspect the existence of a substantial common
basis for the various tendencies. Those who are least involved in any
of these groups are also less diffusely involved. The leaders of each of
the groups also tend to specialize. One is most impressed with overlap
among the active followers.

While one tends to associate the problem of black unrest with that
of white youth, I see the two problems as different. I think that the
difference and the relation between the two will become clearer as we
proceed with our analysis, but at this point let me suggest that black
militancy provides a convenient focus for the accusations of white
youth against its own society in the same way that the war in Southeast Asia did. One often sees white youths eager to support black
protesters in the name of universalism and brotherly love. Many
blacks, on the other hand, reject such support in favor of separatism.
This separatism is accepted and "understood" by the same Jewish
young people who reject Jewish identity and Jewish nationalism as
selfish and immoral. The noisy demonstrations common to both the
white and black movements should not obscure the differences between the two.

My observations about present-day youth are derived from my clinical experiences with them. I would estimate that I have dealt with
perhaps fifty young people, mostly in consultation, but a few in more
extensive treatment. One might legitimately question whether those
young people who appear in a psychiatrist's office constitute a representative sample of their generation. In my case, the sample includes
both the sickest and those who are least sick. It also includes some
who have come on their own initiative, and some who came only in
grudging response to parental pressure. From my experience, I infer

that I have probably seen most of the characteristic types of youthful dissent, though the distribution of these types may not conform to the distribution in the general population.

The young people with whom I have come in contact do not form a homogeneous group. Among them one can distinguish at least four subgroups. First are those who commit themselves to the vigorous pursuit of their cause, whatever it may be. Second are those who, while not especially active themselves, sympathize with the first group and, when the latter are challenged, support them more actively. Third are those who do not sympathize with the dissidents. Fourth, there is a small group who actively oppose the dissidents. I know of no actual count of the relative sizes of these groups, but I am told that, in a recent questionnaire addressed to students, 10 percent of those polled identified themselves as active radicals. I would estimate that the proportion of activists of all kinds amounts to slightly more than that number. The followers and those who are indifferent make up the large majority.

From the psychoanalytic point of view, one may say that 10 to 15 percent of the young people we are discussing are so driven by their problematic needs that they cannot engage seriously in the educational, social, and vocational activities that ordinarily occupy young people in Western countries. A much larger proportion of the young people are similarly disturbed, but are able to keep their needs under sufficient control so as to proceed more or less satisfactorily with the adolescent business of maturation. However, these needs can be intensified when the issues which involve them are raised by the activist group. When they are so intensified they may become peremptory and override the inner controls which usually guide the individual's behavior. It follows, therefore, that the behavior of a large proportion of the young people can be determined at times by the uncontrolled needs of a relatively small segment. Of the remainder, most go about their own business, and therefore do little to cancel out the influence of the activists and their supporters. The majority of the "active conservatives," a very small number, are probably no less driven than the majority of their opposite numbers, the "radical activists."

For the purposes of this chapter my analysis will focus on the seriously disturbed radical minority. In the first place, they wield an influence greater than that justified by their numbers. Second, the dynamics of the determination of their behavior are more readily seen and demonstrated than the motivational dynamics of their less disturbed contemporaries. We shall discuss unconscious tendencies. These will be manifest in constant and overt behavior in the "hyper-activists," in occasional disturbance but continuing conflict—sometimes to the point of paralysis—in the marginal segment, and perhaps in nothing more serious than temptation in the stable segment. In assessing the gravity of the problem and in contriving solutions, it is important to keep in mind the relative magnitudes of the various groups.

We come now to a controversial question. If the young people with whom we are concerned contend that they are responding in appropriate manner and measure to a real threat, then the psychoanalyst who finds the motivation for their behavior in unconscious personal needs seems to be denying the validity of the social and political judgment of the young activists. The psychoanalyst is not concerned with assessing the validity of his patient's conclusions. He recognizes that most inferences must be based upon inadequate data, and so relatively normal people may reach any of a large number of conclusions. What does interest him is the quality of the patient's thinking, his contact with reality, the accuracy of his apperception and judgment, his consistency in reasoning, and his appropriateness of response to stimulus and situation. He wishes to know to what extent thought processes are determined by unconscious needs. A psychotic individual may reach a correct conclusion on the basis of delusional thinking, while a normal individual may err though his thought processes are unimpeded by unknown motivations.

The psychoanalyst does not assess the validity of the social and political positions of the young people whom he is treating. Psychoanalytic treatment of their behavior is guided by investigation of their motives and the intrapsychic needs that the behavior serves. One young person who is relatively untroubled but not very perceptive may arrive at a naive view of social problems. Another who is unable to formulate ideas which are relatively independent of his problematic needs, but who is perceptive, may see events clearly but exploit what he sees to justify the positions to which his intrapsychic needs have driven him.

What makes one individual into a revolutionary activist while others stand on the sidelines? The question cannot be answered in terms of social change or social need, but only in terms of the psychology of the individuals involved.

I find in almost all the young people who are participating in the current turmoils two principal complexes: intense ambivalence toward their parents and inhibition in the process of transition from childhood to adult attitudes. Most of these young people will volunteer a long list of their parents' faults. They will assert their own independence and complain that their parents are too possessive, or too indifferent, or both. The hostility to their parents is overt, declaimed, and demonstrated in rebellious, provocative, and offensive behavior. Affection for their parents is largely or completely unconscious, appearing in dreams, fantasies, and symptomatic behavior. The adolescents run off to live in communes, but come home, protesting all the while, to get a good meal and resume the quarreling and bickering with their parents. Those who use hallucinogenic drugs find their parents frequently entering into their drug fantasies and hallucinations. True, the parents usually appear in unpleasant contexts, but if the young people were truly independent, they should appear only seldom. For example, one young man lived in a commune no more than a mile away from his parents' house. He came home once or twice a week to get money for various projects, none of which he ever completed. On each occasion he managed to tease and antagonize his parents. Demanding money from them was testing their love for him. Under the influence of LSD, he would see his parents being destroyed.

Usually it is the hostile side of the ambivalence which is conscious, and the affectionate side which is unconscious. However, in some instances, affection for the parents is conscious and the hostility unconscious. This situation is especially prevalent among young people whose principal concern is revolutionary social activity, and who are supported in their position by similarly minded parents. While they spare their parents from criticism, the hostility they exhibit to the rest of the adult community is easily seen in analysis to arise from their relations with their parents, from whom hostility is displaced onto others of the parents' generation. But even adolescents who are most belligerent and contemptuous of their parents can sometimes be caught in a "weak" moment, that is, at a time when they look for help to contend with threatening depression. Then they are apt to express affection for and appreciation of their parents in earnest terms, and their sentiments may be confirmed by tears of affection.

The maturational process of adolescence involves achieving adult positions in a number of different areas. These include social relations with others, sexuality, assumption of responsibility, obligation, and restriction within the community, and vocational independence and responsibility. The process of maturation may be regarded as a kind of ordeal. While it offers gratifications, giving up old, familiar positions is frequently painful. Yet some adolescents traverse this path with enthusiasm and joy. Many overcome their obstacles with ease. A moderate number encounter serious difficulty but manage to make the transition, at least partially. A small number never accomplish the passage. These show evidences of serious turmoil during adolescence, and in fact seem in many ways never to outgrow the period of adolescence. When they become adults, their behavior shows large gaps which betray the faulty development which is covered over by the appearance and outer symbols of maturity.

When the young person encounters his inability to master the challenges of maturation, whether or not he is consciously aware of this defeat, he becomes subject to a tendency to withdraw from his environment. This withdrawal may take the form of a quiet, solitary misery which has been called *anhedonia,* or of schizophrenic retreat or melancholic depression, any of which may lead to suicide.

If my hypothesis is correct, it can help us to understand the strange and distressing trials of many of our young people. In fact, each of the various forms of adolescent reaction can be seen as a specific method of handling the problems of ambivalence to parents and delayed maturation. In general, the common forms of adolescent behavior will show one or more of the following: anger toward the parents and the society whose demands cannot be met; anger toward the self which cannot meet these demands; and a search for sources of pleasant sensation to obscure unpleasant reality and inner pain. By turning the anger against the self, the young person protects his parents against his conscious or unconscious murderous hostility.

Perhaps the most transparent of the adolescent devices is the commune. Young people leave their parents' home and, in a group, find a domicile in which they live together with a minimum of formal arrangements. They frequently call this group "the family." These youths have found that continuing to live with their parents is inconsistent with their display of independence, and so they move out. Yet by entering into another "family" they betray their continuing dependent need. In these contrived "families," a small number of members usually assume organizing responsibility and function as parents, though the parental role is seldom openly acknowledged. The general lack of discipline and responsibility represents the young child's view of paradise: comfort, food, and care, with no restriction, obligation, or responsibility.

The sexual freedom of the adolescent serves at least three functions. When two or more people live together without formal arrangement, a pseudofamily of the kind we have just mentioned is created, providing companionship with no responsibility. The sensual pleasure of the available sexual experience tends to counteract the tendency to retreat into inner misery. At the same time the demonstration of capacity for sexual performance obscures the real inability to sustain affectionate, interpersonal relations.

The universalist support for other groups, such as the blacks, the poor, the North Vietnamese, the homosexuals, and the Arabs, serves the needs of the troubled youth. It expresses a repudiation of their parents, their families, and their community. The formula is, "I don't love you. I love him, whom you hate and neglect." Put this way, it says that the young person himself feels hated and neglected by his parents, though it is difficult to see, at first glance, what deprivation the young have experienced. The formula also seems to suggest that the young person envies these "disadvantaged" groups and would like to find companionship among them. He supports their cause even when his support is unwelcome. We have noted that militant blacks do not, in general, welcome white support. But the white adolescent supports black causes in the same way that he supports the activities of Arab terrorists, not because the blacks or the Arabs need him, but because he needs them. In essence, the young person joins his parents' enemies and thereby rejects his parents. Certainly the parent feels as if that is what is happening, and that is probably the conscious or unconscious intent of this particular mode of behavior.

Protest against governmental authority and military power gratifies the adolescent in a number of different ways. It expresses the hatred of the young person for his parents, though once removed. When this hatred is deflected against the substitute, its full fury and venom can be voiced more freely. In the unconscious of the adolescent, it is the parent who is being called a "pig," in retaliation for the parent's rebukes to the young child when he would not adopt habits of cleanliness and neatness, or when he used "dirty" language. Since repudiation of cleanliness and neatness and defiant regression to childhood obscenity are part of the adolescent's posture, he can figuratively—and sometimes literally—hear this epithet flung at him once more, and he defends against it by hurling it at the representatives of law and order.

Repudiation of the parent is often accompanied by derogation of the parent. As we have observed, the parent is repudiated overtly because unconsciously the adolescent cannot detach himself, and prefers to see the parent as wholly responsible for his continuing need. But we must take into account another dimension. The crisis created by the conflict between the social demand to detach and the unconscious dependence leads to regression. The adolescent finds himself once more in the frame of mind which prevailed in early childhood, when he was held to his mother by his need for her physical attentions and yet was impelled by a maturational striving and family expectation to "grow up." Mother's attentions then afforded him sensual pleasures related to body care and body function. Regression now recreates the same interest in primitive body pleasures which he had presumably left behind years ago. He is ashamed of these revived primitive needs and attributes the sensuality, dirtiness, and shamefulness to his parents and to the social institutions in which he feels they try to contain him.

Campus and political protests created battle engagements which aroused the young person, distracting him from concern with the areas of his defeat. Students who participated in campus occupations and militant demonstrations reported experiencing an extraordinary sense of elation. The demand that the government disarm unilaterally in the presence of implacable enemies, though enunciated as a program for peace, functions as a program for suicide for the entire society. Indeed, it is not difficult to see that this call to suicide is one tactic in the program for destruction of the society. Another tactic is encouragement of civil disorder and prosecution of terrorism in the hope of alienating the people from their own government, which is forced to become more repressive in order to control the terrorism.

The use of drugs which impair normal mental function is a somewhat different approach to the solution of the adolescent's problem. Here the individual aims not to attack the society which he holds responsible for his problems, but rather to make himself unaware of the problems. This is a kind of partial suicide, a numbing of one's mind. The mode of action of these various drugs and how they bring relief to the anguished adolescent is a complicated subject which cannot be handled within the confines of this chapter. I can summarize by saying that drugs blunt the individual's awareness of his disability and his misery, and substitute pleasant sensations which arise internally and divert the individual from unpleasant outer reality and inner sensation.

Drugs may also be used in ways which provide gratifications other than those afforded by their principal chemical effects. The use of drugs in social groups helps to weaken the barriers that many young people feel in their social relations with each other. The alterations in sensation which the drugs create make sexual activity more pleasurable. Supplying drugs to others and profiting from drug traffic defies government authority and creates the excitement of a small-scale war.

Overt mental illness, sometimes culminating in suicide, may occur in individuals who do not undertake defensive activities such as those we have been discussing, or in individuals undertaking defensive activities whose defenses fail. Eventually most of these disturbed young people are likely to have to face the fact of their disabilities. Projection, denial, provocation, and exciting behavior can go only so far, and when the relief they provide has been exhausted, depressive or psychotic syndromes may become evident.

What is the cause of this epidemic? Since these problems, the behavior turmoil and the pathologic complex behind it, represent difficulties in the process of maturation, one would expect them to be perennial adolescent difficulties rather than peculiar to our times. I believe that they are perennial, but that recurrently the problems become more prominent. I imagine that a good historical study of this phenomenon might help us to understand what is happening today. Was the vagabondage of the thirteenth-century French and German adolescents—called the Children's Crusade—a manifestation of the same kind of adolescent unrest which we see today? The myth of the Pied Piper of Hamelin, which may be based upon these events, reminds us of the attraction of adolescents to alien leaders inimical to their own parents, to bright colors which they now call "psychedelic," and to strange, primitive music.

One way to understand the current problem is to compare the situation in our own country with the situation elsewhere. We are immediately reminded of the youth of present-day Israel, the majority of whom display the traditional virtues of loyalty, obedience, family orientation, and personal ambition. The reasons for the difference are obvious. The Israeli youth are directly and personally responsible for the survival of the nation. Their nation needs them and they are eager to respond to the call. One is tempted to infer that the alienation of American youth from their elders relates in some way to their not being needed. If that inference is correct, and if we may generalize, we arrive at the proposition that challenge and responsibility encourage adolescents to maturity and assumption of an active role within society. Conversely, an adolescence free of challenge lacks a powerful stimulus to maturation. Some commonplace experiences support this view. The eldest of a number of siblings who loses a parent while he is a young adolescent matures rapidly as he assumes the care of his brothers and sisters. The youngest of a family is likely to mature more slowly than his siblings. The overprotected children of wealthy parents tend to mature late and incompletely.

It would follow from these considerations that the adolescent's ability to free himself from dependence on his parents and to advance to the several roles of adult responsibility can be strongly facilitated by challenge and need, and may be deterred by comfort and protection. This proposition should not be too surprising to the psychiatrist. He knows that even psychotic patients, in the face of an emergency, are likely to emerge from their illness long enough to deal appropriately with the threat, and then sink back. I have been told that during the Six Day War in Israel, ambulatory psychotics were not excused from military duty, and that most performed properly. We arrive then at the paradoxical conclusion that the comfort and security which we seek for our children are likely to discourage their psychic development. More generally, we may say that comfort and security exert a noxious influence with respect to the vigor of a population.

Of course, comfort and security cannot be considered the only kinds of stress which retard and deform adolescent maturation. In the presence of excessive comfort and security, the adolescent attempts to grow without the normal resistance of challenge, without a "load," to borrow a metaphor from power engineering. An excessive "load"— that is, unusual stress caused by excessive social pressure or upheaval —can also thwart the adolescent's maturation. History teaches us that at times when existing society is uprooted or violently changed, adolescents exhibit deviant and often destructive behavior. Since it is the adolescent's task to mature from family attachment to membership in society, the success of that transition requires the existence of an organized, vital society which expects and welcomes him. When the society has no need for him, or when it is itself fragmented and ineffectual, adolescent development loses motivation, goals, guidelines, and discipline.

Returning to the problem of today's youth, we can cite as the chief sources of trouble the relative affluence of our society; the absence of a clear and present external danger to our society; the lack of need and even opportunity to assume serious responsibility for any part of our society; and the expectation that young people spend four or more years in higher education. Higher education is desired and can be pursued only by a fraction of the total youth, only those who are so well integrated that they can defer assumption of responsibility and engagement in real work. Others who comply with the expectation to study in universities see this period of higher education as a kind of "holding pattern"—a period of enforced exclusion from adult life— and their attacks against the universities may be interpreted as an expression of anger against what they consider an incarceration.

We have noted above that espousal by the young of the cause of an unfortunate minority is a way of accusing the parent generation of abusing the youth. We can now see what that abuse consists of, namely, overprotection and infantilization which make the young person feel ineffectual and impotent, a member of an inferior minority. How does all this affect our young people? We may assume that a small fraction of adolescents are absolutely unable to make the transition to adulthood in meaningful terms, and I would guess that most of the youthful activists derive from this group. A large minority can make the transition, but only with assistance and encouragement; it is this group who probably comprise the inactive supporters of the activists. Another large segment can find their way into adulthood with little or no external encouragement, and these probably include most of the students who are relatively indifferent to the current malaise.

To avoid misunderstanding, let me emphasize once more that not all protest, not all political action are necessarily the result of mental disturbances. We can imagine a ratio between vigor of response and realistic injustice. We are trying to define segments of the population in which this ratio is very high, high, and moderate. It would be just as much evidence of an unwholesome imbalance of mental forces if an individual failed to respond to the extent that he realistically could, to blatant injustice. In fact, the sympathy that many Jewish young people evince for black rioters but not for their Jewish victims, for Arab guerrillas but not for their Jewish victims, betrays an unhealthy state of affairs.

The influence of noxious social circumstances—affluence, overprotection, security, protracted education—serves to increase the difficulty of the adolescent's task. The ranks of those who fail completely are increased at the expense of those who are just able to get by with encouragement, and the ranks of this marginal group are increased at the expense of those who seemed secure in their development and not excessively responsive to social pressure. To put it another way, what we see today is an *increase* in the number of troubled adolescents and in the intensity of their turmoil, rather than a new phenomenon. What is new is that the number of activists and their sympathizers has increased to the point where they can become a serious nuisance to the rest of society; they can exert an influence upon national policy, and are apt to leave as a residue a generation of adults who will probably show a high frequency of mental illness in the next few decades.

The Jewish Aspects

The above data, inferences, and suppositions are based directly upon my own clinical experience. What I have to say now about the Jewish aspects of the youth question is derived from more casual observation. I venture the following comments primarily to demonstrate how the data and inferences I have presented above *might* be linked to the problem of Jewish continuity.

From the reports that I have seen, there seems to be little doubt that Jews are highly represented among both the activists of the younger generation and their less active sympathizers. What would account for this high representation? We have observed that protracted and poorly tolerated education retards the maturational process of many adolescents. Jewish youth are subjected to greater pressure than others to accept higher education, education always having been one of the Jewish ideals. Education of the young also serves as an indication of the social status of the parents and opens the way for higher social status for the young people themselves. As an especially affluent group, the Jews by and large can afford the costs of advanced education to a greater degree than many non-Jews. Thus, Jewish youth in larger proportion than others will attend colleges and universities; the vulnerable among them will succumb to the prevalent adolescent malaise and find their way into the groups of dissidents. In the days when it was more difficult to gain admittance into the university, only young Jews who were most highly motivated went on from high school to college. Now that university attendance has become almost universal among Jews, a considerably larger proportion of poorly motivated and psychically vulnerable Jewish youth find their way into the university population. Since the proportion of Jewish youths in college still greatly exceeds that of the general college-age population, the proportion of disturbed Jewish young people will greatly exceed that of disturbed non-Jewish young people. (I might note that although education has always been regarded among Jews as a prized goal, in the past relatively few Jews achieved higher education, even in religious studies. The educated were a small elite, membership in which was confined to the most talented students. It is only in the past few decades that higher education has become available to such a very large proportion of Jewish young people.)

The Jewish community in the United States today is for the most part affluent. Many Jewish young people therefore feel less uncertain of their future, economically speaking, than do their non-Jewish contemporaries. Jewish families in the United States are also smaller than non-Jewish families, and in families with fewer children, the ambivalent relation between parents and children tends to become more intense than in families with more children. Since intense ambivalence is one of the chief troublers of youth, it follows that Jewish young people will, in general, be more troubled than their non-Jewish counterparts. This theory can be checked out by comparing the family size of disturbed youth with that of their more stable contemporaries.

Furthermore, Jews probably tend to overprotect their children to a greater extent than non-Jews. This involves discouraging them from adventures which must be met by responsibility and therefore facilitate adolescent development. Overprotection involves excessive indulgence of the adolescents' desires, excessive pressure for education, and a tendency for the older generation to withhold responsibility from the younger. Even after the young man completes his education and goes to work for his father, the father frequently finds it difficult to relinquish responsibility to him. The psychiatrist commonly sees father-son conflict which centers about business relations. From my own experience I cannot say that this situation is more characteristic of Jewish families than others.

The Jewish family is perhaps best known for its unusual closeness. To some extent this may be attributed to the Jews' sense of being strangers and outsiders wherever they have lived, which was countered by a closing of ranks from within. In any event, the intensity of Jewish family life must be expected to generate great hostility. However, this hostility is not permitted to find direct expression within the family or even against others within the same society, so it finds indirect expressions, such as intense vocational ambition or hostility masquerading as love. The parent's ambivalence toward his child may take the form of overprotection noted above. The chief perpetrator of this overprotection is the mother, and today's younger generation of Jews delights in the malicious stereotype of the "Jewish mother." One hazard of the "Jewish mother" is that in some sense she really does seduce the child so that he finds it more difficult to establish his independence from her. The young people complain that their parents are too possessive, and in my experience I have usually found this complaint to be justified. The parents *are* too possessive, and the children too dependent. This is the trap in which the young Jew finds himself and from which he struggles to escape.

We have referred to the fact that when the adolescent is confronted with the challenge of becoming independent of his parents, he tends to regress to the frame of mind characteristic of earliest childhood attempts to increase the distance from his mother. He must contend with revived infantile sensual needs; feeling ashamed of these needs, he attributes them to his parents, to whom they are directed. After his first four or five years, the child enters a period of relative sensual "latency," during which he attempts to overcome sensual needs. At that time he is torn between two opposite tendencies. One is to attribute sensuality to his parents, at whose hands he enjoyed sensuality. The other is to idealize his parents, to imagine them free of sensual urges, in order to suppress memories of the physical contacts, previously enjoyed, and to deny the envy of the currently perceived but ignored intimacy between the parents. One common way of resolving these contradictory tendencies is the creation of a fantasy which Freud called the "family romance." It is true, the child tells himself, that his parents are inferior and despicable, but they are not his real parents. His real parents are fine and noble, but in some way which he cannot understand he has been separated from them and has fallen into the hands of this miserable couple. The reader will recognize here a theme commonly encountered in fairy tales and myths of the child of noble birth who is brought up by peasants but ultimately finds his way back to his royal parents.

Adolescents, too, tend to use the family romance fantasy to resolve their ambivalence toward their parents. They project onto their parents their own sense of degradation and inferiority and pursue associations outside the family which seem to them more admirable. In societies where Jews were considered inferior, the Jewish adolescent who indulged in the family romance accepted the lowly position of the Jew as a confirmation of his own projection. He rejected his parents and the Jewish community in favor of the more respected Gentile society. Once political and social emancipation were accomplished, it became possible for these Jewish adolescents actually to leave the Jewish community, to intermarry, change their names, and seek acceptance by the Gentile majority.

In some instances the substitute parents were indeed of a social status above the Jewish parents. In others, however, the infantile craving for regressive sensual pleasure, together with a masochistic tendency, led Jewish young people to throw in their lot with social, educational, and economic inferiors whom they, in obvious defiance of all realistic criteria, labeled as superior to their parents. While the first tendency, from the point of view of the Jewish community, might be considered as socially undesirable, the second must be considered as frankly pathologic. Today one encounters this second pattern among disturbed Jewish youth perhaps as often as the first.

It is clear that the vicissitudes of intrafamily aggression are not the same among Jews everywhere or at all times. The parent-child relations which I have been discussing do seem to obtain among American Jewish youth and their European-born or first generation American parents. The Jewish male adolescent, therefore, in his maturation, must escape from his father's affection and his mother's overprotectiveness and possessiveness. When he finds this task too difficult, he may be inclined to rebel in one or more of the ways which we have discussed.

Since one prominent form of adolescent protest today consists of the demand for social justice, we must also consider the historic Jewish concern with righting social wrong. This, of course, is an inquiry for the experts and I can claim no special competence, yet what we are learning about historic and social phenomena invites some speculation. One possible explanation for the Jewish preoccupation with social justice may be constitutional. Such a statement will ring so strange in the ears of the liberal, sophisticated, Jewish intellectual that it will probably be attributed to an unanalyzed idiosyncracy on my part. People who subscribe to egalitarian ideals like to believe in the equipotentiality of all human beings. Yet experience has shown that all men have both special gifts and special limitations, some of which are individual, some familial, some ethnic, and some racial. Even if we accept the idea that one group may be more talented musically, and another excel in physical agility, it still seems difficult to accept the idea of an inherited concern with liberty and justice. However, the idea may seem less improbable if we view concern with liberty and justice as derived from the tendency of a population to band together in tightly knit, hierarchical groups, as opposed to a tendency to reject social organization. The former would be regarded as characteristic of an authoritarian population and the latter as characteristic of a freedom-loving population. The Jewish concern with social justice has been strengthened further by the Biblical emphasis on human dignity, the limitation of subjugation, and the restriction of slavery. Three times daily the observant Jew recites, "Blow the great trumpet for our freedom"; once a year, almost every Jew celebrates the Passover festival of freedom, an emancipation alluded to in almost every religious service. Freedom is thus a traditional Jewish theme and this preoccupation has encouraged many rabbis to find religious merit in the political protests of student activists.

It should be pointed out that important as social justice may be in Jewish tradition, it is not the major emphasis. Perhaps the central requirement of Judaism is acceptance of the discipline of religious law. What is specifically and unconditionally prohibited is the dedication of one's life to sensuality, and the cultivation of sensuality is, of course, a major component of adolescent protest, evident in sexual indulgence, drug-induced sensations, and violence for its own sake. Judaism would, therefore, seem to be antithetical to much of the present-day youth culture, and vice versa. Indeed, there seems to be a strong repudiation of the Jewish community by many Jewish adolescents. This takes the form of a desire to date and marry non-Jewish partners, attacks upon Israel, accusations that Jews are mistreating blacks, and rejection of traditional Jewish ideals and morals.

In the repudiation of the community, the troubled Jewish adolescent sees a symbolic emancipation from his parents. Those young people who have difficulty in achieving true instinctual independence from their parents find all kinds of instinctual ties threatening; those ties that represent their parents' sentiments and ideals are especially dangerous. The Jewish community represents the family, and therefore its repudiation symbolizes repudiation of the family. Every Jewish parent whose adolescent child turns away from the Jewish community feels as though he himself had been rejected. That feeling can be taken as an accurate indicator of the young person's intentions.

Jewish young people often attack the Jewish community, under the various banners of universalism, Marxism, rationalism, and progress. I see here a similarity to the current attacks of American youth against American institutions under similar banners. In each case, the young person is, I believe, attacking his own community, because it offers him insufficient challenge, adventure, and responsibility. These he requires for full maturation, and if they are not offered to him he creates them by declaring war on the society which has let him down. (In this connection, I might note that it is the opportunity for adventure and challenge which makes Israel so attractive to some Jewish adolescents.)

The Consequences of Unrest

Let us first consider the general rather than the Jewish population, and individuals rather than the community. Unfortunately, there are no good follow-up studies of today's troubled students. We do not really know how their behavior changes, or how many suffer severe mental disturbance. Observations offer some rough guidelines, however.

We know that there is a high frequency of suicide attempts among these students, as well as a high frequency of accomplished suicide. We can also predict, with some assurance, that since the more disturbed students are unable to establish sound affectionate and working relations, they are likely to have difficulty with marriage and finding a place in society. We should keep in mind, too, that a significant number of troubled young people are frankly mentally ill, and that even those who recover are likely to carry their demonstrated vulnerability along with them.

Turning now to the question of values, I believe that there is a strong tendency for the values of young people to swing back and become similar to those of their parents. It is a commonplace observation that radicalism is to a large extent a phenomenon of youth, and that as the individual ages, his radicalism gives way to a more conservative attitude. Freud has described the phenomenon in psychological terms as *deferred obedience*. Sooner or later the adolescent need to overdo his display of independence subsides, either because he matures sufficiently so that he need no longer make an issue of maturation, or because he fails to mature and comes to terms with his continued dependence. In either case he no longer finds it necessary to reject his parents' values. In fact, he frequently develops a positive need to accept them, which means identifying with the parent, and that is true maturation. It also reestablishes the affectionate link to the parent. Therefore, the phenomenon of deferred obedience is especially likely to occur after the death of the parent, though it usually starts as the adolescent turmoil subsides.

We must keep in mind that the young person's attitude toward his parents is ambivalent throughout. While hostility and rebellion are flaunted, there remains a strong affectionate bond which becomes visible only subsequently. In fact, it is not difficult to find even in the form of the rebellion an identification with some component of the parent's history, personality, or ideals.

Adolescent turmoil is one instance of a general tendency to try to solve psychic problems by action. When problem-solving action is constructive and aids in resolving the difficulty, we call it "sublimation." When the action is destructive, to oneself or to others, and does not effectively dispose of the problem, we call it "acting out." Adolescent turmoil, by and large, can usually be considered a form of acting out. Acting out occurs at any age, but most frequently during the late adolescent and early adult period. This form of adolescent acting out seems generally to subside between the ages of twenty-five and thirty, when impulsive action gives way to thought, appropriate action, or resignation as a way of contending with stress. There is reason to believe that the frequency of suicide attempts peaks in the early twenties. This is true, for example, for most cases of delinquency. The various forms of adolescent turmoil also seem to burn themselves out. I have been told informally that most of the student activists of five to ten years ago have settled quietly down to unexciting and inconspicuous lives, though a small number have become professional revolutionaries.

While the agitation is likely to subside for the individual young person, the country is confronted with a persistent, disturbed, restless population of adolescents and young adults who are unaware of the real cause of their unrest, but who hold their government and the entire society responsible. We have already noted that while the specific accusations which the young level against society are invalid, inappropriate, or irrelevant, we must concede that it is the special conditions of our society which facilitate the adolescent problem. This disruptive minority may be only a nuisance now, but if it grows, it may become a substantial threat to the entire community. The threat can be accentuated if even a very small number turn to terrorism, for terrorism polarizes the population. An agitated younger generation which holds its government and society responsible may weaken the government's defense against attack from without and subversion from within. It does the first by interfering with the nation's military stance and the latter by cooperating with and amplifying the effect of the violence of militant minorities. We must therefore conclude that the phenomenon of youthful turmoil, if it is permitted to grow, can constitute a serious threat to our society.

Before turning to the specific problem of Jewish youth, let us not overlook the fact that radical agitation among the country's youth constitutes a potential threat to America's Jews. While Jews are friends of radicals, radicals are not always friends of Jews. For example, Jews are puzzled by the anti-Semitic and anti-Israel activities of black militants. But few blacks are interested in freedom and equality in the abstract; they are struggling for their own freedom. It is known by all historians of revolutions that once an oppressed group finds that its demands are taken seriously, it becomes more militant, resents the assistance of sympathizers, and literally bites the hands that feed it. Youthful radicals espouse the cause of minorities, lacking an overt and serious cause of their own, and do not hesitate to take over the anti-Semitism of struggling minorities. To the young radical, the Jewish community in the United States is no more free of blame than the non-Jewish majority, and to the extent that it represents the status quo, it becomes an appropriate object for attack. Attacking the Jewish community is his way of disengaging from, and punishing, his parents. The Jews of the United States will certainly not fare well if the population becomes bitterly polarized, and they will not fare better than the rest of the country in the face of war or revolution which may be facilitated by the actions of a large and agitated segment of the nation's youth.

We turn now to the specific problems which appear when Jewish youth turn against the Jewish community. The phenomenon of deferred obedience may give some cause for comfort. As the young people in question grow older, we can expect them to regard themselves once more as members of the Jewish community. To be sure, the problem of intermarriage is serious because the marriage is entered into during the phase of rebellion, and by the time the reverse pull toward Judaism makes itself felt, the marriage is no longer readily reversible. Figures are not yet available, but I would guess that such intermarriages will gradually assume Jewish identification, and that the children they produce are likely to be encouraged to think of themselves as Jews. It is interesting that young Jewish males who intermarry rarely change their names. I take this as an indication that full and enduring repudiation of Jewish identity is not intended. Of course, the strength of the reflex pull back to Judaism can be no greater than the primary conscious or unconscious commitment to it, which in turn was determined by childhood experience, the attitude of the parents, and the prevailing morale of the Jewish community.

Jews self-consciously ask themselves what there is to being Jewish. Religion, it is generally agreed, has the adherence of only a small percentage of Jews; nationalism, perhaps a somewhat greater percentage. Jewish ideals and Jewish morality are frequently listed as reasons for remaining Jewish. I should like to suggest that Jews are loyal to the Jewish community not primarily for any of these reasons, but because the Jewish community, current and historic, is a family, literally a family of families. It encourages family life as a religious value. As a family it acquires the influence of the individual's literal family. By the same token it may come under attack when the individual turns against his own family.

If we were asked why we continue to be members of our own actual, nuclear families, we might point with pride to family achievements or distinctions. However, we would not really be able to discount our loyalty as a primitive psychological, even biological mode of relating to the biosocial group into which we have been born. It makes as little sense to ask why one is attached to one's family as to ask why an infant loves its mother. It is characteristic of infants that they love their mothers; they cannot do otherwise. In the same way it is characteristic of all humans that they cling to their families, overtly or covertly, consciously or unconsciously. The emphasis on family relations and on the family quality of the Jewish entity invokes biological forces to supplement the need to belong to a community. Judaism has, at different times and in different places, taken various forms, meeting the specific psychic and social needs of the occasion. This need to force Judaism to assume different forms—a conservative order, an antinomian revolt, a mystical retreat, an ecstatic fraternity, a philosophic system, an intellectual elite—attests to the strength of the tie to the Jewish family.

It follows that the ambivalence of the troubled Jewish adolescent toward his family is likely to extend to the Jewish community. Therefore, behind the anti-Jewish declarations and behavior one will frequently find a covert and profound loyalty. Radical, drug-using, hippie-mannered young people will occasionally show up in the synagogue. I know of a number who attend fairly regularly. A Jewish young woman who was living with a non-Jewish hippie complained that her mother would not permit her to bring her boyfriend to *Kol Nidre* services. One especially shabby young hippie raged against his father when the latter refused to permit him to accompany him to synagogue on Rosh Hashana because of his disreputable appearance. Analysis disclosed that this young man, who defied, provoked, and tormented his parents, was actually patterning his behavior after their experiences in fleeing the Nazis. Year after year he had heard at the Passover *seder* how various members of the family had fled for their lives from the Nazis, and of their modes of concealment and evasion. As a child he had run away from the *yeshiva* which he attended, and as a young man he engaged in violent campus protests. But in all instances he saw himself repeating the experiences of his parents as they were escaping persecution. I don't know how this young man will turn out, but if he resists mental illness, I suspect that he will be drawn once more to the Jewish community.

An interesting and increasingly common variant of the expression of ambivalence is the turn to religion by adolescents brought up in a nonreligious or marginally observant family. Here the assertion of the religious commitment constitutes both an act of loyalty and an act of defiance. These young people are rebuking their parents by demonstrating greater commitment to the Jewish community than to the parents themselves. An increasing number of students are coming to rabbinical seminaries out of such religiously indifferent families.

What are the consequences for the Jewish community of the unrest of Jewish youth? While the general community may be threatened when the number of agitated young people exceeds a threshold value, the Jewish community is exposed to no special danger by virtue of the disruptive activity of its youth. Some observers feel that the encouragement extended by Jewish young people to anti-Semites and to the enemies of Israel may have grave consequences. To be sure, if a serious polarization of the country occurs, there may be a resurgence of anti-Semitism, and the Jews may be held responsible for the activities of their young people. However, the support of the Jewish community comes from people in their middle years, and we have reason to expect that most of the troubled youth will have made their peace with the Jewish community by the time they arrive at middle life. As parents, they will acquire an interest in family integrity, and in support of that are likely to affirm their Jewish loyalty and cultivate the family-strengthening rituals of the Jewish religion.

It cannot be denied, however, that there are Jewish communities which gradually weaken and die. I suspect that these are usually communities in which the Jews are subjected to no special challenge, and are permitted to respond as equals to the various challenges of the general community. Here the familiarity of the Jewish extended family carries little attraction, while the challenge and novelty of the alien exert a fascination. My clinical experience here relates to third or fourth generation American Jews of German ancestry. Whereas they frequently reject synagogue affiliation and religious observance, they maintain their Jewish identity by actively engaging in philanthropy, especially Jewish philanthropy. One such individual of my acquaintance recalled mysterious religious rituals performed by his grandparents, rituals which were at the time disparaged by his own parents. Aside from his philanthropic activities, which were only partly Jewish, he lived the life of a non-Jew. However, in response to the Nazi persecution of Jews in Europe, which came at a time when he suffered a personal tragedy, he went to Europe and spent several months rescuing Jews, frequently at great expense to himself. One of his children married an Orthodox Jew and is raising an Orthodox family; another married a non-Jew.

We must keep in mind that the Jewish community is not homogeneous. Even when there is least challenge to it, there is a loyal and creative nucleus, and even when it is most challenged, there are defectors. I like to think of an intensely loyal nucleus which continuously produces a community of Jews. A fraction of these Jews drift away at a rate which depends upon external circumstances. When the community comes under attack, the drift is slowed. When it is permitted to prosper, and especially when the general community provides a challenge to youth, the drift accelerates.

The Future

I have tried to show that the most vigorous attacks upon the Jewish community by Jewish young people come from the most unstable elements among them. This anti-Jewish attitude and its manifestations are likely to subside in the most disturbed group, but a positive attitude is not likely to replace it. The marginal group will at first follow the lead of the disturbed cohort, but subsequently is likely to swing back to support of the Jewish community. The stable segment of youth is likely to remain relatively faithful to the Jewish community and to become increasingly responsible with age.

What kind of program can we consider for each of these groups? The members of the most disturbed group are concerned with solving their personal problems, and have little patience with justice, reason, responsibility, and true affectionate concern for others on a personal level. Therefore, during the phase of their activity, they are likely to be unresponsive or possibly negativistic toward any approach by the Jewish community. With the passage of time they are likely to become less active, but they are likely also to withdraw more into preoccupation with their own psychopathology. Thus they will remain relatively insensitive to the needs of the community, Jewish or national, and any investment in them is not likely to pay any dividends.

Turning to the marginally disturbed group, during the period of adolescent turmoil, positive and negative feelings toward the Jewish community are likely to be fairly evenly balanced and to alternate. While under the influence of adolescent turmoil, they are likely to be negative, but when the Jewish community is threatened, they may support it. It would be helpful to keep channels of communication with them open, for example, by providing information, propaganda analysis, and influential leaders, and by attempting to involve them in various Jewish concerns. With the passage of time most of them are likely to become relatively stable and, in accordance with the principle of deferred obedience, accept normal responsibility within the Jewish community.

The group of relatively intact young people is likely to attempt to retain its contact with the Jewish community. However, successful initiative by the community may raise the quality of their involvement from passive support to active service. Different individuals will be receptive to different components of the Jewish experience. Some will respond to the challenge of Jewish historical scholarship, some to Jewish literary scholarship, some to communal responsibility, and others to philanthropy or to Jewish education.

What of the future? One is somewhat hesitant to extrapolate present trends into the future, knowing that we may be overwhelmed by unanticipated events of great magnitude. The events which exert maximum influence are usually those which are unanticipated, so long-range planning becomes a relatively useless exercise. While the Jewish community is usually quick to respond to challenges, the responses are not always well-informed or accurately aimed. What might be useful is a continuing commission to monitor events and report their significance to the Jewish community.

Finally, I should like to note that I see no end to the problems which we are now encountering. The historian may see a dynamic in history which, though not helpful in making specific predictions, can at least warn of increasing instability. The same problem can also be approached by the psychoanalyst, though the psychoanalytic approach to social, as distinct from clinical, problems is difficult and treacherous.

Let me generalize a thesis which I proposed at the beginning of this chapter. While the process of overcoming obstacles and meeting challenges is wholesome and invigorating for society and for its individual members, achievement of a state of comfort and security exerts a noxious effect. Comfort and security weaken the claim of society upon its members and weaken the devotion of individuals to society. They deprive individuals of an important motivational stimulus and source of gratification. Therefore, in their presence, a set of impulses becomes active whose aim it is to restore instability, challenge, and turmoil. The aim of these impulses remains unconscious, and ironically the activities which they motivate are frequently carried out under the banner of freedom, justice, and peace, though in the end the self-designated saviors of society create greater chaos. Our planning for the future cannot afford to ignore the possibility that American society, with the important participation of a sizable proportion of its Jewish community, may have to face a period of increasing social disorganization and individual demoralization.

9

A Radical View of Jewish Culture

JAMES A. SLEEPER

Why Modern Jewish Education
Must Begin Outside the Tradition

In the past, Jewish parents had no more to decide to give their children a sense of Jewish identity or a formal Jewish education than modern American parents have to decide that their children shall speak English; Jewishness was absorbed into the young person's growing identity and self-image as he developed in the midst of a Jewish community. In fact, he had no alternative but to express both his deepest urgings and his most casual preferences through the media of Jewish symbology and language. One did not have to speak of this young person's "commitment" to Jewish values—a term implying attachment to something which one might also ignore or reject; values were absorbed as a natural by-product of immersion in a culture where words like *tzedakah* (which is different from "charity") and *rachmonus* (which is different from "mercy") came to describe complex human relationships which were entered into as second-nature responses to all kinds of situations and predicaments.

I do not mean to romanticize that former community, or even to suggest that modern Americans can possibly recreate the particular ethos. I invoke the past in order to provide some perspective against which to view the dilemma of Jewish educators who today must operate *without* the support of such a community, who must devise programs and curricula for young Jews whose Jewishness is not a matter of natural inheritance.

The problematic situation of the modern Jew, as has often been observed, has its roots in the Emancipation of the eighteenth century. But the present-day problems are possibly unique to our generation, most specifically to its younger members. For these young Jews have not been exposed to the influence of the closed ghetto community, transported from Europe, which in some form still prevailed when their parents and grandparents were growing up. Accordingly, one of the primary components of the socialization and self-image of these parents and grandparents is an ineradicable sense of Jewishness which surfaces at least occasionally to create havoc with carefully calculated loyalties and elaborately reasoned postures on the American scene. However, their children and grandchildren, the current "younger generation," are the first such generation to have had almost no primary Jewish cultural experiences.

It is possible to dismiss the hostility toward the Jewish community that some of these young people exhibit as a function of pathology or adolescent trauma. But the fact remains that many young Jews today simply turn their backs on Jewishness neither in a spirit of spite nor out of personal difficulty. In the wake of the old community's collapse they have almost no memories, no associations with even the glimmer of a viable, organic Jewish community in which Jewish language, symbols, and values were compellingly operative during their early years. Nothing *recognizably Jewish* has shaped their lives. Why, then, should they recognize themselves as Jews?

Thus, in the absence of an organic community, the Jewish classroom is charged with the responsibility of not merely providing education but of supplying an emotional attachment to Jewishness and arranging social opportunities whereby Jewish "values" may be acted out. Somehow the Jewish school is expected to "reach out" to an essentially Jewishly indifferent student, in a language foreign to his tradition, across a widening cultural and philosophical chasm. Given this situation, it is doubtful that even the most extravagantly budgeted and equipped classroom can achieve the task. The best of audio-visual aids, flannel boards, opaque projectors, and the like do not mold Jews, nor, alas, do inquiry and classroom "discussion." The epitome of classroom inquiry was reached in one college Judaica course I attended, in which an assimilated young academic exclaimed over his study of Jewish history: "Amazing! A civilization whose religious values are so well expressed in a cultural matrix, in which every symbol has a divine referent!" He stayed assimilated, rational insight alone not being the stuff of growth, self-authentication, or commitment.

Hence, any discussion of Jewish education must begin with a discussion of the fundamentally *non*-Jewish context in which our students have developed as human beings. The would-be Jewish educator must know the world in which his students move if he is to address them uncompromisingly with the riches of the Jewish tradition, and if he is truly to become a meeting point of student and tradition.

The Search for a Meeting Point

Religious commitment in our time is not a product of academic inquiry alone, whether literary, sociological, or philosophical. It is a complex, organic meeting of a growing, searching individual with the ongoing symbols, values, and language of a religious tradition. The student gravitates toward that tradition, tries on its symbols as a means of personal expression, struggles to reconcile his inclinations with its value judgments, and encounters its moments of holiness and prayer as shimmering and precious arenas of love and trust only if that tradition addresses him in his present state, offers meaningful personal satisfaction, and meets his conscious and unconscious needs for community and self-definition. But what is to be done when his present state, his conscious and unconscious needs, were nurtured in a non-Jewish environment, when his values conflict with those of the tradition, when he speaks, even if only half-heartedly, the non-Jewish language of "charity" and "mercy"?

One option is to emphasize the "relevance" of the tradition to the student's present world, to bend and twist the tradition in such a manner as to render it compatible with his values and whims. I doubt, however, whether this will make the tradition seem very interesting or attractive to him, especially if he is unhappy with his current situation as an American. Indeed, to respond to the pull of Jewish history and tradition is to feel increasingly uncomfortable with much of what is happening in America. Moreover, demonstrations of Judaism's compatibility with American life are pathetically uninteresting, for increasing numbers of Jewish teen-agers have become uneasy with their governmental, cultural, and economic contexts. It is ironic for Jewish educators to despair, as one did at a recent conference, of "ever introducing some American kid off the streets to the meaning of *kedusha* [holiness]," when they have only to go into the streets to find a generation which grants a wider margin of credibility to the craving for this dimension of human experience than did its predecessor. I do not claim that astrology and the occult describe a movement toward Jewish tradition, but they do signify a yearning, an awareness of a vacuum in the religious life of the society into which the young have been initiated.

If such yearning is to be converted into satisfying personal growth and religious movement, if the Jewish experiences of *kedusha,* *tzedakah,* and *rachmonus* are to become compellingly attractive to young people, they will have to encounter a Jewish religious life which operates as a vital force in the lives of people whom they trust, and who are conversant with their "hassles," dilemmas, and often unconscious and unarticulated needs. My own experience is that the Jewish educator who would serve as such an example can hardly afford to be condescending; for all his credentials, he is likely to discover that he has as much to learn from the young about the rejuvenation of the religious dimensions in daily life as they have to learn from him.

The greater the variety of models who radiate enthusiasm about some form of contact with Judaism, the better. As things stand now, it is highly unlikely that the student in the Jewish school will ever meet even one such person in all his years of religious education. The reasons bear repetition: There is no viable, organic, operative Jewish community to nurture such models; there is no setting in which Jewish language, symbols, and values are publicly articulated, shared, celebrated, and employed to embrace the experiences of the young. The controversial *havurot*—the religious Jewish fellowships which have recently come into being—are at least efforts toward the creation of such communities, which may in part explain why *havurah* members who serve as Hebrew school principals and teachers in the greater Boston and New York City areas seem to enter their classrooms with an authenticity and attractiveness which have found an eager response among their students. Because *havurah* members embrace youth culture in order to transform it, they are excellent meeting points between the young and the tradition. The spectacle of critics remote from the scene projecting their own worst demons and fears onto the "promiscuous," "psychedelic," and "underground" activities of groups such as the *havurot* would be cause for amusement were it not so potentially damaging to the first fragile glimmer of Jewish educational success to be seen in some time.

Jewish authenticity on the part of the teacher is indispensable, but authenticity alone is insufficient. It must be coupled with responsiveness to students, with a willingness to approach them in a way that is neither condescending nor therapeutic. That does not involve self-compromise as much as it demands a great deal of openness and energy, as well as the readiness to take seriously the maxim that "from my students I learned most of all."

Truly to know the young Jews of suburbia—which seems to be the locus of the American Jewish community—is to see them in their natural habitat, on their own "turf," so to speak, and only then to see even more in them than they themselves do. It is to see in their often self-defeating experiments intimations of health and strength as well as of sickness; hints of religious growth and awakening as well as of myopic preoccupation with occult escapes; gifts of prophecy as well as of nihilism. Finally, to know the young is to expose oneself to basic and lasting change, for in their questions and life styles lie challenges to the tradition so fundamental as to reflect more than the perspective or the problems of the young alone.

The young people of whom I am speaking, in particular the Jewish young people, are not necessarily representative of the bulk of American youth. Hence they are viewed by some as deviant from an orderly and healthy society whose most serious mistake is to have overindulged them, thereby creating for itself an elitist nuisance. I prefer to view them as a sort of barometer, a group whose alienation and searching bespeak a societal crisis and sickness which they have not caused but are trying with increasing desperation to avert or escape.

A psychoanalytic critique of the young which preferred to remain ignorant of its own rootings in Victorian norms, and which left social irritants largely unexamined, would paint them primarily as negative deviants. On the other hand, a rather severe *social* critique would serve as a backdrop against which these young people would emerge in some cases as strong and healthy resisters to destructive social forces, and in other cases as admittedly sick victims of those forces whose only virtue is that they point their accusing fingers in an uncomfortably accurate direction.

It goes without saying that the truth lies somewhere in between. We have had many examples of the first type of critique, but this is hardly impartial analysis, rooted as it is in a basic acceptance of the society and norms which the young reject. It should be borne in mind that once one accepts the framework of psychoanalysis, *all* views are subject to its scrutiny—not only the protestations and experiments of the young but also the directives and policies of their elders. I am suspicious of critiques which describe one in isolation from the other. That the problems of young radicals should occupy our attention to the complete exclusion of the problems of Richard Nixon and Spiro Agnew is patently incredible. Antinomian behavior is a priori no more deserving of psychoanalytic comment than is the morality the so-called antinomians seem to oppose. Were I to describe the behavior of some of the older generation as "startling" in that they defend their government, speak with reticence about sexual matters, dress fastidiously, cut their hair, and consume conspicuous quantities of barbiturates and alcohol, I believe I could make my point. The views of the young are no more energized by psychic needs than are the views of their academic, professional, and political critics. It may be true that the young radical is playing the part of the son in an Oedipal conflict. Is no one playing the part of the father?

Thus anyone can hold his own values constant, as "given," and proceed to psychoanalyze those who deviate from them. But that would not be good psychoanalysis as I understand it. Since Freud, we have begun to merge psychodynamic and sociological variables, with more fruitful results.

I wish I were able to achieve such a fruitful synthesis. Alas, the preceding paragraphs are not an introduction to an impartial analysis, but merely a notice that I will not pretend to cast what follows in a scientific tone. The values and preferences will be explicit rather than hidden; accordingly, what follows is a description, or perhaps a case example, of youthful social criticism of the kind to which I think Jewish education must respond sensitively and seriously. I hope to present a composite portrait of what some young Jews tend to believe, buttressed, more than occasionally, by the slightly detached observations of sympathetic critics like myself.

A Preliminary Sketch of Youthful Discontent

First, let us hear some of the teen-age students I have known speak for themselves. The reader may do with this material what he wishes;

one option, at least, is to take it at face value and to believe what it says.

Here are some quotes selected from a score of comments I noted in Jewish religious school classes in Great Neck, New York, and West-port, Connecticut:

Everywhere I go I wear masks; at home I'm the dutiful son; at school the performing student; nobody asks for more. The only place I can really be "me" is when I just drop out with a couple of friends. So you might say that my real life is underground.

Jeffrey, age 15

My parents don't love me unconditionally. If I get good grades and behave, I'm a good status symbol; if not, I'm a bad investment.

Daniel, age 17

I feel as if inside of me there's a tender flower which grew, hoped, wanted to be loved, and then wilted and died.

Deborah, age 17

Our friends are the keys to the fun we hope to have whether it's with them or at their expense. Playful stabbing each other in the back and kicking in the teeth are acceptable paths to a false fun with which we hope to replace the genuine excitement and joy we are missing in life.

Martin, age 18, writing in a high-school paper

I always wear shades [dark glasses] to class. Why? Because I have nothing to give to the teachers, and they have nothing to give to me. Besides, half the time I'm stoned.

Kenneth, age 17

I should like to introduce my own comments about this material with some observations by Peter Marin:

The problem is not merely that the "system" is brutal and corrupt, nor that the war has revealed how savage and cynical a people we are. It is, put simply, that "social reality" seems to have vanished altogether. One finds among the young a profound and befuddled sense of loss—as if they had been traumatized and betrayed by an entire world. What is release and space for some is for the others a constant sense of separation and vertigo—a void in which the self can float or soar but in which one can also drift unmoored and fall; and when one falls, it is forever, for there is nothing underneath, no culture, no net of meaning, nobody else.

That is, of course, what we have talked about for a century: the empty existential universe of self-creation. It is a condition of the soul, an absolute loss and yearning for the world. One can become anything—but nothing makes much sense. Adults have managed to evade it, have hesitated on its edges, have clung to one another and to institutions, to beliefs in "the system," to law and order. But now none of that coheres, and the young seem unprotected by it all. . . .

The paradox, of course, is that the dissolution of culture has set us free to create almost anything—but it also deprived us of the abilities to do it. Strength, wholeness, and sanity seem to be functions of *relation*, and relation, I think, is a function of culture, part of its intricate web of approved connection and experience, a network of persons and moments that simultaneously offer us release and bind us to the lives of others. One "belongs" to and in culture in a way that goes beyond mere politics or participation, for belonging is both simpler and more complex than that: an immersion in the substance of community and tradition, which is itself a net beneath us, a kind of element in which men seem to float, protected.

That is, I suppose, what the young have lost. . . . In the midst of it, adrift, the young more than ever seem beautiful but maimed, trying against all odds to salvage something from the mess.[1]

I hope it is not difficult to see, in reading these paragraphs, what kind of task I think is in store for Jewish education, and, at the same time, how ill-equipped our teachers are to approach young people and to help them construct "nets of meaning," the "substance of community and tradition," to suggest to them in their fall that there is something or somebody underneath. Our inability to do this is symptomatic of our own sickness and paralysis. Perhaps we have not experienced what Marin is describing; we may have been fortunate, or perhaps we have simply "managed to evade it, to hesitate on its edges, to cling to one another and to institutions, to beliefs in 'the system,' to law and order." But we have given the young the affluence and perspective of Ecclesiastes, and in their eyes we are certainly not doing anything that strikes them as more significant than evasion and role-playing in the face of the void.

Adolescence and the Crisis in Social Priorities

Clearly I am claiming that there is something more to adolescence than the psychodynamic adjustment associated with a certain stage of psychosexual development. I am suggesting that there are times

[1] Peter Marin, "Children of the Apocalypse," *Saturday Review* (N.Y.: Saturday Review, Inc., Sept. 19, 1970), pp. 71–72. Reprinted by permission of Peter Marin, c/o International Famous Agency. First published in the *Saturday Review*. © 1970 by Peter Marin.

when societal crisis excessively aggravates this stage, times when adolescence exposes the young to questions which society may be failing to answer even for its presumably healthy adults. Adolescent crisis contains referents to societal, existential, and religious crisis, and it should not be examined in isolation from these things.

We can glimpse what kind of social crisis we are talking about by harking back to the *gemeinschaft*, or closed Jewish ghetto community of medieval times. In traditional societies, the individual continues beyond childhood to be socialized into one or two all-encompassing and compatible groups, such as the church and the rulership of the lord of the manor, or the theocracy of the ghetto. Self-definition is about as complicated and as self-conscious as it was in the early family experience. One has little insecurity about status or identity in relation to family, peers, rulers, and cosmos. These things are clearly defined by a ritualized pattern of relationships and symbols which is the common lifeblood of the community. Since the extended family includes grandparents and other relatives in close proximity, and since these figures pass on to the child most of what he will regard as important knowledge, he has a broad range of respected adult models to whom he can relate. The shared symbols of the community permit the individual and society to act out aggressive and other potentially conflict-full impulses in legitimate, safe contexts. It is enough to knock the jouster off his horse in ritualized combat; one need not kill with abandon within the community.

In the modern West, by contrast, the young person's relationship to his society is less apparent. A myriad of *competing* groups (stock exchange, country club, Sunday school), each with its own set of competing values and symbols, plays upon the keyboard of individual needs. To be a member of all these groups is to develop a hyperactive role-playing and rationalizing mechanism. One manages to remain a member in good standing in all of them, though none can provide a sense of "home," with a warm community in which one is accepted *in toto*, aside from one's performance by the group's specialized and limited standards. In the stock exchange, one is primarily an economic animal; in the country club, primarily a genial, social one.

Somewhere along the line, one or two basic needs remain unfulfilled; the need for a sense of personal consistency, for a sense of coherent self with uniform values, may be lost, as the individual tries to be all things to all people. One learns to perform, to "measure up" in various arenas, and it is only a matter of time before the transactional, performance-oriented relationships of the stock exchange and the professional association permeate the schools which are to prepare the young for membership in these groups. Thus is the student-teacher relationship perverted into a trade-off of performance for grades.

Even the family is affected by this behavior, as witness the quote above ("My parents don't love me unconditionally. If I get good grades and behave, I'm a good status symbol; if not, I'm a bad investment"). In the absence of a supportive community, a religious value structure, and an extended family, all emotional, affect-oriented needs are channeled through the only overloaded circuit left to be called "home": the suburban nuclear family, consisting of two parents and a couple of children. That monogamy should be defended in the absence of the supportive contexts of extended family and cultural community is surprising.

Certainly there is virtue in the freedom which the dissolution of cultural and religious norms permits us, and certainly social complexity can be exhilarating. But when presented with a steady diet of conflicts between competing groups, and with a constant lack of arenas for expression of deeper affections and ritualizing of deeper conflicts, most people will experience a certain amount of anxiety, self-consciousness, and strain. When there is no place to come home to, no place where the integrity and wholeness of the individual can be reaffirmed, a desperate search for integrative, all-encompassing communities begins. Thus young people who see in the "Establishment" commuter a man torn among competing loyalties, sacrificing his spontaneity, his body, his moments of joyful integration, the light in his eyes, and the spring in his step, are prone to reject the whole system and the elaborate systems of ethics and ideologies which rationalize it and lead it to war. Indeed, such rejection, depending upon its nature and context, may be a sign of strength and health, not of solipsistic withdrawal.

Thus Mario Savio, a leader of the Free Speech movement in Berkeley in the early 1960s:

The future and careers for which young Americans prepare themselves are for the most part intellectual and moral wastelands; this chrome-plated consumers' paradise would have us grow up to be well-behaved consumer children.[2]

[2] Mario Savio, "An End to History," in M. Cohen and D. Hale, *The New Student Left* (Boston: Beacon Press, 1966), chapter 5, page 252.

Savio goes on to suggest that the forces of "progress" in the great society serve to enervate the sense of autonomy and fragment the sense of selfhood as they isolate and routinize individual lives. Much of the profit system, and the kinds of advertising and consumer self-image which impulse buying creates, take tremendous tolls in human values. One can turn to the acquisition of material goods, and have emotional cathexis upon such objects; but, as Philip Slater[3] points out, material objects cannot return the emotional investment. Yet it is precisely this perversion of erotic energy which is encouraged by an economy based on the myth of scarcity. Other humans become obstacles or facilitators to the acquisition of goods and services; wealth increases, while interpersonal relationships become increasingly delimited and transactional.

It does not matter, for the moment, that youth's rejection of the system is often simplistic and naive. There is enough tension, violence, and fragmentation in our society to suggest that the strain is too great, especially for the young in the process of identity formation. One senses the despair of ever achieving total acceptance, as communication between the young and their elders, and among themselves, is lost in the demand for role-playing in limited groups. The search for meaningful involvements and genuine experience that comprises much of youth culture is predictable.

If the young declare their unwillingness to accept fragmentation at the hands of graders, bureaucrats, and clinical mentalities, it should not be perceived as only a personal problem, but as the root of a serious social critique as well. There are fewer and fewer arenas in which the young are accepted by significant "others"—where they are encountered not on the basis of their performance at limited tasks, but on the basis of more elusive and intangible (and psychodynamically fundamental) criteria. The search for the numinous or loving "other" is not rewarded. During adolescence it is most painfully frustrated and delayed. From the peculiar anguish of the adolescent we learn the general principle that the collective consciousness of the school, peer group, community, or nation can no more remain starved for shared fantasy and myth than can the individual psyche remain starved for love, commitment, faith, and home.

Though the analyst can describe the toll taken by the lack of these things, he cannot himself provide the remedy, and it might be dan-

[3] Philip E. Slater, *Pursuit of Loneliness: American Culture at the Breaking Point* (Boston: Beacon Press, 1971).

gerously wrong for him to urge his patient to "adjust" to a grievous lack of these things brought about by the demands of technology, efficiency, and profit. Perhaps it is better for the victim to rant and rave, point his accusing finger in the right direction, summon his resources, and transcend. Even a healthy person may become crippled; perhaps the healthier he is, the more he will fight, learning gradually to overcome his vulnerability without losing his sensitivity, to shed his naiveté without losing his openness.

In this context one becomes aware of the health and optimism of many early radical experiments such as Vietnam Summer, which gave psychologist Kenneth Keniston much of the material for his study of young radicals.[4] We should be aware of the voluminous literature about activists which suggests that many of the young people who find within themselves the strength to challenge, to experiment, and occasionally to say no are indeed the healthiest of people. One would take seriously Dr. Mortimer Ostow's suggestion in the preceding chapter that "It would be just as much evidence of an unwholesome balance of mental forces if an individual failed to respond to the extent that he realistically could, to blatant injustice." Peaceful adjustment to assembly-line labor or schooling is no automatic sign of health; a desire to disrupt the line, whether principled or capricious, is no automatic sign of sickness. For that matter, the use of such terms as "health" and "sickness" is amoral, particularly when one recalls that the operators of the Nazi gas chambers were good family men, loved classical music, and were declared legally sane to stand trial. This alone should serve to remind us to check our tendency to equate bizarre deviance with sickness and social conformity with health.

It should be noted that I am not claiming that all youthful protest is motivated solely by an explicit, rational concern with the injustice of current social priorities. Perhaps hardly any of it is. But that is not the point. The point is that even the most irrational and self-defeating of radical experiments and negations often reflect the toll taken by a society whose values and priorities have been irrationally perverted by economic and technological factors, not to mention by outright greed and insanity. We should see in the youth revolt an implicit critique and silhouette of our society and the corrupting influence it seems to exercise on human relationships.

It should also be noted that I am not defending the irrationality of

[4] Kenneth Keniston in *New Journal*, vol. 2, no. 6 (New Haven, Conn.: New Journal at Yale, Inc., 1968).

student protest just because I claim that it points to something. Indeed, a fuller commitment to follow the dictates of reason might lead more of us into militant action long after the energizing fires of adolescent trauma have burned themselves out. If there were an adult example of reasoned radicalism, the young might not have to come of age through such agonizing loneliness and bizarre deviance.

Adolescence and Religious Crisis

If adolescent turmoil exposes the young person to a questioning of social structure, it also exposes him to deeper questions about what in life *transcends* the existing order. What resources can he call upon in the face of despair, in the absence of a nurturant environment? The unpleasant discoveries about societal perverseness that I have been describing come to the young at that stage of life in which fidelity, idealism, and the experience of meaningful commitments are most needed. If the Boy Scouts, the army, and the stock exchange will not provide arenas in which these satisfactions can be experienced, youth will look elsewhere, increasingly beyond the pale of what is conventional.

Erik Erikson[5] describes the experience of meaning, the capacity to "mean" something, as the product of an intersection of a growing, need-filled individual with ongoing historical traditions, cultural modes, and vital and viable institutions and communities. Ours is not a time in which such an intersection is easily brought about, for young people see through most of the existing traditions, modes, institutions, and communities. Why shouldn't they? We have taught them to.

We have shaken the sanctity of the conventional meanings and commitments by demonstrating their rootedness in psychic need. We have uncovered the correspondence between the individual's intrapsychic processes and his selective perceptions of outer reality, and suggested that since commitments in the outer world are energized by needs in the inner world, principled assertion is suspect and debate is thinly veiled "ego-tripping" when arguments are not easily verifiable. The ensuing relativism and skepticism with which we teach the young to encounter systems of meaning that once guided our own upbring-

[5] Erik Erikson, *Young Man Luther* (New York: W. W. Norton, 1958).

ing can lead them to a paralysis which gripped the early existential-
ists, but which I believe is being experienced almost en masse in some
suburban communities for the first time today. It is a search for "the
courage to be"—and Paul Tillich, who coined the phrase, would
prefer to see it as at least as much a religious problem as one for the
psychoanalyst.

Unfortunately, the young have been deprived of believable myths,
of arenas and occasions for the engagement of passion, celebration of
fantasy, and expression of eros. This is not only because social scientists' schemata, which should have remained fluid, heuristic, and
tentative, have been abused and prematurely seized upon by experts,
corporations, and government agencies seeking greater social predict-
ability and control. More fundamentally, it is because the very frame
of mind of the social scientists, with which we have all been amateurly
imbued, has a way of becoming idolatrous in untrained hands, of
encroaching upon arenas of experience which ought to retain some
integrity of their own when the moment of living and loving is at
hand.

In the absence of the noted viable arenas, the young people I am
describing grant a wide margin of credibility to spirituality and myth.
Many find themselves living outside available cultural and religious
options. America has exposed them less to baseball than to the bomb,
less to American values than to the void. There is often the feeling
that this society is less a culture than a cosmic stage upon which is
being played out the drama of man's last, best chance. Theirs is an
apocalyptic, not a patriotic, stake in America. Do they exaggerate?

The notion that individuals might be free, *en masse*, to continue their psychological, moral, aesthetic, and spiritual development into their teens and
twenties would have been laughed out of court in any century other than
our own. The new affluence may permit us to examine, as only a few
madmen and artists could in the past, the intactness, zestfulness, and quality
of our lives, as well as the interweaving of fantasy. . . .[6]

So says Kenneth Keniston, who suggests that there is a new revolution which follows the revolution for democracy and material equality; it is the revolution not of quantity but quality. The young are
immersed in it. For them it is not luxury; the stakes are high.

The richer our understanding of the young becomes, the more artis-

---

[6] Keniston, *New Journal*, page 27.

tic, celebrative, and mysterious it ought to be. Erikson's study[7] of the young man Luther is a powerful example of the way in which our talk about homeostasis, need-gratification, and the frank mental illness of the young gives way to talk about procreative behavior, self-transcendence, and mystery. The need is felt anew for a valued affirmation of life which, however much it employs rigor and reason, goes deeper than the scholar's tentativeness and reasoned skepticism. The need is for an existential outreach, a leap of faith which is the nonrational prerequisite of all rational activity. In this dimension the religious educator asks what happens when the young reach the existential moment, when they lose the nerve to make the leap of faith and proclaim themselves unconvinced by ours, or when, having made that leap, they opt not for the centrality of social responsibility and suburban life but for a larger dose of fantasy, celebration, dialogue, and myth in their lives than we have in ours.

I have attempted to remain sympathetic to the Jewish young people I have been describing without glorifying them. To say that their alienation may bear signs of health and be constructive is not, I hope, to deny that when one leaves the social fold one is playing with fire. In the absence of a viable social context in which one can trust, spirals of ecstasy alternate with spirals of despair, and it is the rare individual who can survive indefinitely without a sense of history and communal support. From their forays into the unknown the young bring back considerable wisdom; at times one feels that at seventeen they are at least as sad and as wise as their parents. They are often not happy in their vaunted life styles, though I would suggest on the basis of my own experience that they are deriving more satisfaction from communes than they did from that peculiar living arrangement known as the nuclear family, and at least as much happiness from being carpenters or cabdrivers as they would have derived from being dentists and corporation lawyers.

Any evaluation of youth's turmoil must make us aware of what is legitimate and potentially fruitful in this anguish, what is subtle and beautiful in the search the young pursue in a spiritually and morally barren universe. There is at least as much subtlety and beauty in the secret basements of suburbia's $100,000 homes as there is in the parlors and bedrooms above.

[7] Erikson, *Young Man Luther.*

Will we continue to suggest that those who have departed from traditional answers to the eternal questions are sick when they tell us that our cultural and political arrangements are simply unreal, enshrine no hopes for them, spur no loyalties, engage no passions, provide no personal fulfillment? If we discover (in Dr. Mortimer Ostow's words) that most of the youthful activists derive from the group which is "absolutely unable to make the transition to adulthood in meaningful terms," then we must entertain the proposition that perhaps there is nothing very meaningful in religious and social terms about the transition to the kind of adulthood that is in the offing for suburban children.

Jewish Education

It is not only by the fascination of some young people with Hasidic and Kabbalic aspects of the Jewish experience that Judaism may find itself a crucial contributor to their lives. It has often occurred to me that not only the mystic and prophetic, but even the more rabbinic and normative streams of Jewish tradition would concur with the young in their evaluation of our social priorities and religious decay. It is clear that Jewish tradition would not go with the young all the way on their forays after universal truth; it would suggest that spiritual flight takes communal wings, that the aesthetics of the righteous deed and the soft answer take precedence over the aesthetics of sensual gratification. The point, I believe, is that Jewish tradition would share the young's critique without supporting everything they have done as a result of that critique. It offers examples of constructive alternatives which range as far afield as the mystic and the ecstatic, but which substitute community for conventionality and knowledge for nihilism.

What is equally clear, of course, is that the organized American Jewish community—including most of its rabbis and educators—is offering no real help to many young people struggling along the frontiers of self-fulfillment. This is partly because the young people I am describing are hardly visible to Jewish educators; they sit behind dutiful masks in the classroom, or do not enroll in religious education at all, abandoning what they can see of Judaism with a shrug. What evidence does a young person have to support the contention that Judaism might be activist and communal as well as congregational and middle class? How can he know that the union of Jewish life and suburban life is not inevitable? He may know what the prophets said about people who can enjoy fine food and the pleasantries of parties while others close by shiver and die. But he also knows that on his *Bar Mitzvah* he was made to recite the words of those prophets in exchange for gifts and food and parties. Not even the rabbi will admit to him that the tradition is being raped.

One can only sympathize with the girl in my Westport Confirmation class who said, somewhat wistfully, "My life is too rich and beautiful for Judaism." One can only imagine what kind of experience would induce her to change her mind. For now, she is certainly right, as far as the Judaism as she has known is concerned. What is sad is that the things which do make her life "rich and beautiful" are so meager, so threadbare, yet grasped and held so desperately because they are real.

The Jewish school might be a place where she could feel sufficiently supported and strong enough to examine the limits of her current alternatives, and to encounter the power of Jewishness. But Jewish schools have long been pale copies of public schools. As such they, too, have become what Peter Marin calls

. . . stiff, unyielding microscopic versions of a world that has already disappeared [for the young]. . . . Their corrosive role-playing and demand systems are so extensive, so profound, that nothing really human shows through—and when it does, it appears only as frustration, exhaustion, anger.

That, of course, is the real outrage of the schools: their systematic corruption of the relations among persons.[8]

Where is the Jewish teacher toward whom students could gravitate because he radiates enthusiasm, and acquires through his commitment a natural authority which need not be supported by institutional props? One begins to glimpse what is lacking most sorely in religious education when one rediscovers the Jewish student-teacher relationship, keeping in mind Buber's belief that

The relation in education is one of pure dialogue. . . . Trust, trust in the world, because this human being exists, that is the most inward achievement of the relationship in education. Because this human being exists, meaninglessness, however hard-pressed you are by it, cannot be the real truth. Of

[8] Marin, "Children of the Apocalypse," page 72. Quoted by permission.

course the teacher cannot be continually concerned with the child, nor ought he to be. But if he has really gathered the child into his life, then that subterranean dialogic, the steady potential presence of the one to the other, is established and endures.[9]

It is all very sad, because religious education, or value education, can alone demand this kind of teacher, one whom the young suburban Jew needs most. The school, as a little nexus of community, depends upon this passing-on from teacher to student of the fundamental affirmation that life is worth living. Educators concerned with the public schools and the general society are trying to find solutions while constantly avoiding confrontation with this basic purpose in the educational enterprise. Religious education, on the other hand, is addressed explicitly to this question. It offers the riches of a tradition in which men are not afraid to utter words which make them tremble, in which precious moments and communal settings are cultivated and nurtured, and in which, at least as far as the Jewish people are concerned, there is such rich material, so many colorful associations, such a compelling history of alienated struggle and prophetic anguish. That such a tradition should fail to support and elicit potential parallels among the suburban young would cause outrage if its selling-out to the status quo were not such an old story. To wander through the American Jewish community is to experience the spiritual analogue of Hiroshima after the bomb. There is no religious community, and there are no Jewish teachers to be its spokesmen.

Jewish education for these young people must take place not in modern classrooms but in the context of improvised communities which serve as hints of cultural, spiritual, and interpersonal alternatives to the emptiness of their current pressured daily lives. Given the pattern and orientation of suburban living, Jewishness will be passed on in secret moments, in spite of the surrounding milieu. To engage in Jewish education may be to corrupt the young in the eyes of their parents, for it will most surely support a measure of their alienation from the suburb, as it now exists, and it will not bring them back to the empty temples.

The need for a communal context which serves as an alternative to the youngster's school and home life explains why Jewish education has been moderately successful in the summer camps, to some extent in Israel, and through the *havurot*. It is in the dialogic relationship

[9] Martin Buber, *Between Man & Man* (New York: Macmillan, 1965).

of teacher and student (which cannot often exist in the religious school as it is today) and in the furtive life of minicommunities (which are generally regarded with suspicion by suburban parents) that the search for meaning and for "the courage to be" is pursued, the net of trust and culture repaired. Perhaps, too, meaning is pursued in scientific and academic inquiry, provided that the curriculum is fluid enough to contain referents to mystery as well as challenges to mastery, referents to interpersonal sharing as well as to conquest of text. Education which provides these referents, and which joins them and the internal world of the young to a community with a history of celebrating contact with the mystery and encouraging its permeation in daily life, is religious education.

This is not the place to recount successful attempts at curriculum reform, to tell of Sabbath retreats which released a virtual flood of previously dammed-up emotional and spiritual needs, to describe traditionally authentic uses of evocative Biblical texts to make a classroom into a minicommunity. Suffice it to say that, against the backdrop of what is best in the tradition and what is most needed by the suburban Jewish young, there are three basic ingredients to Jewish education: (1) a knowledge and a powerful personal internalization of Jewishness on the part of the teacher; (2) an openness to dialogue relationship and a willingness to undergo personal change in response to students; (3) the existence, however furtive and primitive, of a Jewish community (like the summer camp, the *havurah*) which the young would like to join. Only in these contexts—knowledge, interpersonal sensitivity, and communal action—can Jewish education take place. In sequential terms, the process of Jewish education will begin with eliciting the students' concerns and with nurturing what is best in them, in an effort to establish trust. Throughout, it must be borne in mind and heart that *knowledge* in this case is more than academic knowledge; *sensitivity* is not technique or therapeutic condescension; *community* is not the school assembly or the synagogue board of trustees.

Education ought to be that arena in which the search for meaningful, human styles of life, both old and new, is pursued by young and old together—by those young who are willing to grant that there may be strength and beauty somewhere in an accessible past, and by elders who are willing to admit that for all their wisdom and perspective they may not be near what they could be. If there *is* strength and beauty in the past, I presume that it will emerge in the personalities, deeds, and messages of those who teach the young, who write papers about them, who make claims upon them. Otherwise it is a dead past, a lost past, and the young will have to survive by themselves. Can that be what has happened in the mindless present of suburbia?

What is demanded of the older generation (although it will be resisted and severely tested by the young before it is believed and joyfully accepted) is that it provides a living spectacle of fulfilled, loving people who radiate a fundamental affirmation, not a series of negative cautions about what will happen if stylized patterns are abandoned.

To me the Jewish community in history has represented an arena which witnessed the joyful passing-on of fundamental affirmations from old to young, and vice versa. I am suggesting that if the Jewish community is to remain such an arena, it may have to alienate itself from, and be increasingly critical of, the general drift of American society. Coincidentally, the young are already there, waiting for something. If the American Jewish community truly rejoined the Jewish people and Jewish history, it might meet its young again. From the Jewish community I would like to envision, we would hear no automatic sigh of relief when, at age twenty-five, the once impatient youth settles peacefully into suburbia and temple membership.

My more hard-headed evaluation is basically that the Jewish community in America is not moving in the desired direction. Too many of its members have too great a stake in the death of all that strikes me as powerful and meaningful in the tradition, all that can meet the crisis of faith and of social priorities which youth experiences and which their elders continue to evade. One hope, of course, is that desperation in the face of complete assimilation will turn the educational resources of the community over to those who share my vision; I suppose that is how members of the *havurot* have practically taken over Jewish education in some communities. But that is not enough, and Judaism at its prophetic and religious best will continue to proceed on the sly and in a state of tension with the operative values of the adult community. This will continue until the adult community begins to take its children's crises more seriously.

Over the past few years increasing numbers of Jewish educators have found that culturally viable Jewish religious communities are not compatible with the life of the urban or suburban nuclear family; in their own lives they feel the weight of American life dissolving cultures and fragmenting identities. The beginning of the great exodus to

Israel is now being monitored across the land. Left behind are the suburban Jewish young, without roots and memories, caught in a limbo of alienation from television and baseball, and of spiritual exile from their people. They are left to join the long line of Jewish intellectuals and artists who tried to overcome homelessness and alienation through creativity, radical activity, and revolution, men who changed the course of Western history through commercialism and Communism, psychoanalysis and relativity, while thrashing unknowingly in the chains of their own Jewish enslavement and estrangement. Unless we would move them to Israel, we will have to face the fact that we cannot create for them a viable Jewish community in America without a severe critique of our current economic and cultural situation.

In this sense, Jewish education is a focus for radical activity, an attempt to restore the moral and prophetic dimension to efforts at social change, to provide a responsible and constructive militancy, not a substitute for militancy. It should aid in the creation of the supportive, healthy communal base from which radicalism emerges not as deviance but as an expression of mainstream prophecy. This kind of radical Jewish community—radical because to preserve its Jewishness it risks economic and political failure—has begun to take feeble root in the thin and shifting soil on the margins of the American Jewish community. It affirms Jewishness and the viability of the resources of the tradition. Its reading of the tradition and of the Jew's potential role in history is becoming increasingly sophisticated, and hopefully will compete with the conventions of the more normative, organization-based community for the minds and hearts of the Jewish young. Its insight is that Jewish commitment is not compatible with what America is becoming. Its hope is that by its meaningful survival, the Jewish community in America may help to heal this incompatibility even as it heals the broken spirits among youth who are the chief and saddest victims of the split.

10

Toward a General Theory of Jewish Education

SEYMOUR FOX

In order to deal effectively with the problems of Jewish education,[1] it is first necessary to locate the particular areas of dissatisfaction. Very often discussions of Jewish educational shortcomings are merely discussions of solutions which are difficult to justify because they have not been related to any specific problems. For instance, we are told that what Jewish education needs most for the alleviation of its ills are large sums of money. Now it is true that Jewish education is woefully underfinanced and that any significant program of improvement would probably require more funds than are currently available, but funding, crucial as this is, should not, I believe, precede decisions concerning ideas or programs. We are also told—and this, too, is indisputable—that Jewish education cannot succeed unless the child attends classes for more than the usual three or six hours a week; but rarely do we consider what might be done with this additional time, and what the nature of any new program should be. Similarly, in the matter of teaching personnel, which some see as the "basic" problem of Jewish education, one can hardly deny that the quality of teaching leaves much to be desired, and that new and different personnel must be recruited; however, any changes that are to be initiated must depend on one's conception of Jewish education.

The above recounting hardly exhausts the list of complaints that

[1] In this chapter Jewish education refers essentially to formal educational programs.

260

have been offered to explain the sad state of Jewish education in the United States. Be that as it may, they all fail to deal with the fundamental problem—the nature of the Jewish education we want to develop or preserve. I stress this point not merely to state the obvious, that means are somehow related to ends in education. Rather, I should like to emphasize that none of the solutions offered can possibly succeed if the nature of Jewish education has not been clarified. We cannot hope to attract talented young teachers—apart from the question of the profession's low status and salaries—unless Jewish education is presented as an honorable cause, worthy of professional devotion. We will not be able to develop new or even different curricula for Jewish schools unless the specialists—scholars, teachers, and educators—are inspired by authentic conceptions. We will not even convince the various funding agencies within the Jewish community to change their priorities and to allocate substantial sums for Jewish education unless we can argue convincingly that the education we want to develop has some chance of substantially affecting the lives of their constituencies.

In short, I maintain that the most urgent problem facing Jewish education today is its lack of purpose and, consequently, its blandness. Therefore, until we engage in serious deliberation aimed at rectifying this state of affairs, we cannot even hope to deal with all the other issues that demand solution. Let me state at once that deliberation alone regarding the ends and content of Jewish education and new conceptions of Jewish education will not solve the problems. Rather, deliberation is both a prior and necessary condition that will make it possible subsequently to tackle such questions as curricula, personnel, structure, and financing.

It is generally assumed that a base for this kind of deliberation already exists, that one has only to study current practice to uncover its implicit philosophy. Of course current practice must be carefully investigated, but it is my feeling that the investigation of most forms of Jewish education, except for the ultra-Orthodox, would reveal that their curricula and methods of teacher training bear little resemblance to what the leadership of the given movement, school, or institution claims to be central in its conception of education.

It is necessary to cite several examples in order to clarify this point. Let us consider first the importance of character development, which all Jewish religious groups in the United States, I believe, regard as one of the main purposes of education. An investigation of the existing programs of Jewish schooling would reveal that character education does not play a significant role. If it can be demonstrated that Jewish education as it is presently constituted barely concerns itself with character education, then I am sure that most Jewish scholars, rabbis, and parents would agree that a serious revision of Jewish educational practice is called for.

Another area of consensus, shared by practically all trends of Jewish religious thought, is the centrality of *halakha* (taken philosophically and psychologically) in Jewish life. An aim of religious education should, therefore, be to find ways to commit the young to the concept of *halakha* and to teach them how to use *halakha* as a guide in their everyday lives. Youngsters, whether attending Orthodox, Conservative, or Reform religious schools, should thus be taught to develop the ability to apply *halakhic* principles to a variety of practical situations. The ability to recall the appropriate principle at the proper time, and to choose properly among different and sometimes conflicting principles, as well as the skill required to apply principles to complex practical situations, are vital if we are interested in developing Jews who want to live by *halakha*. It may be that traditional Jewish education, with its heavy investment of time and energy devoted to mastering the details and method of the Talmudic dialectic, had as its goal the development of precisely such talents. It is questionable whether under present conditions this method remains viable, but we have as yet found no substitute.

There seems to be a good deal of evidence that the State of Israel plays an important part in the lives of American Jews, yet the subject of Israel has been virtually ignored by the American Jewish religious schools. This is not the place to discuss in detail the various aspects of the particular question; indeed, it deserves a separate chapter. Suffice it to note here that Israel is an important issue for the philosophy of Jewish education, and that the study of Israel should be introduced into the curricula of schools and teacher-training institutions. Israel is also a source of teacher personnel and should be utilized for the training of American Jewish educators.

Another subject which has received insufficient attention—as Professor Abraham J. Heschel has noted—is the teaching of Jewish philosophy and theology. Professor Heschel's plea to include these studies in the curriculum of the Jewish school remains unanswered, and his valuable suggestions for the teaching of prayer, while acclaimed in public, are ignored in practice. Finally, the Holocaust is barely mentioned in our classrooms. These are but a few examples of how the Jewish school neglects its responsibilities.

I cannot avoid complicating the discussion by indicating that the means and techniques that have been adopted by Jewish education are often imported indiscriminately from general education. Since the means of education are not neutral, it is quite possible that some of the means employed for Jewish education cancel out whatever there is in Jewish education that is related to "authentic" Judaism.[2] There is, therefore, an urgent need for a serious discussion of what kind of Jewish education would reflect the various conceptions of Judaism. Such a discussion would result in the development of competing philosophies of Jewish education, but this, in turn, would make it possible for creative educators to develop means appropriate to the basic ideas in each of these philosophies.

It may appear frivolous to suggest philosophical discussion when the "house is burning," but I believe that such deliberation is ultimately the quickest, most effective way to extinguish the fire and to rebuild.

Philosophical deliberation would affect educational decisions in several areas, the first of which is curriculum. The current curriculum of the Jewish school is, by and large, based on the models of its predecessors—the *cheder* and the *yeshiva*—but modified in the light of the reduced instruction time in the present-day institutions. This is hardly a sound educational approach. What is possible and appropriate for a fifteen to twenty hour a week program is often impossible and inappropriate for a three to six hour a week program. Moreover, despite the limited time, the modern school attempts to teach subjects that were not deemed necessary in the *cheder* or the *yeshiva*, such as prayer, "synagogue skills," and simple Jewish observances, all of which were formerly handled within the domain of the family and the community. Nowadays, of course, the family and the community are no longer equipped for the task, and the school has been forced to assume the burden. Overburdened by more subjects than it can possibly handle, and lacking a guiding philosophy that would enable it to pick and choose among subjects competing for the limited time available, the Jewish school finds itself virtually paralyzed.

---

[2] I have discussed this matter in detail in "A Prolegomenon to a Philosophy of Jewish Education," in *Kivunin Rabim—Kavana Achat* (Jerusalem: School of Education of the Hebrew University of Jerusalem, 1969), pp. 145–154. This volume was published on the occasion of the seventieth birthday of Professor Ernst Simon.

This lack of clarity, with all its disastrous results, is evident in almost any subject taught in the Jewish school. Let us examine two of these, Hebrew and Bible. Hebrew is taught in most afternoon and day schools and in many one-day-a-week schools. The time allocated to the study of Hebrew in the afternoon school is usually from one-third to one-half of the total available teaching time during the first three years. Results have been most disappointing, and consequently the study of Hebrew is usually a source of tension among parents, rabbis, and educators. When we examine the methods and materials of the various programs developed to teach Hebrew, we discover that almost all of them are geared to the mastery of modern Hebrew speech. The programs devote only token time to the problem of effecting a transition from modern Hebrew to the Hebrew of the Bible and prayer book. There has been even less concern for developing materials and preparing personnel to deal with this transition. Yet it is asserted that the purpose of Hebrew study is to prepare the child to participate in the synagogue service and to understand the prayers, the Bible, and other classic Jewish texts.[3] Some educators, of course, contend that the purpose is to develop spoken language skills. If so, it is difficult to understand how this goal is to be achieved within the limited time available. We have here a striking example of a major school subject whose purpose for inclusion in the curriculum is unclear; the result is a series of inappropriate and dated compromises.

Bible is taught in Jewish schools with almost no concern for the relevance of the subject to the life of the child.[4] By and large, the Bible is not even treated as a religious or ethical text. Often, Biblical verses, commentary, and· *midrash* are used interchangeably, leading to confusion in the mind of the student. The teacher avoids dealing with questions that are of interest to the child, such as the divinity and historicity of the Bible. The teacher cannot help but avoid these issues as he has not been trained to handle them. There are no materials to guide him and there is no effort to provide him with in-service training.

Bible study, therefore, often leaves the child with the impression

[3] Professor Chaim Rabin, the distinguished linguist of the Hebrew University, has asserted that it is extremely difficult to teach spoken Hebrew to children in Jewish schools in the United States as a step toward a mastery of the Hebrew of the Bible and the prayer book.

[4] An important exception is the work of the Melton Research Center, and certain materials prepared by the Reform Movement and by the American Council for Judaism.

that religion deals only in legends. In many cases, it is not until the Hebrew school student reaches college and takes a course in religion that he learns, for the first time, that the Bible is great literature, that it deals with basic ethical issues, and that it expresses a significant world view different from that of other ancient Near Eastern societies. This condition will continue as long as there is no commitment to specific goals for Bible teaching. As soon as such a commitment is made, our educational agencies will be forced to prepare appropriate materials, and to train and retrain teachers so that they can handle or at least grapple with the desired goals.

There is a strong feeling that Jewish educational matters are being dealt with more successfully in the day school than in the afternoon schools. It may be too early to judge, but my impressions are that the day school has only enlarged and intensified the current program of Jewish education. In some cases this has made for "success"; that is, if there are more hours available for the teaching of Hebrew and Bible, the child will certainly "know" more. Also, full-time teachers are likely to be better teachers and remain longer than their part-time colleagues. However, such matters as character education, commitment, and Jewish involvement do not seem to receive novel or consistent treatment in the day school. There have been some attempts to integrate general and Jewish subjects, but there has been little thought given to the preparation of materials that could launch the day school on new paths.

I do not believe that curriculum revision in general is a theoretical undertaking. It is essentially a practical endeavor,[5] requiring an analysis of failures in the educational reality (student boredom, poorly trained teachers, parental dissatisfaction, lack of achievement), a decision on the nature of the problem, and subsequent creation of means to tackle the problem. However, for the Jewish school, a good deal of theoretical discussion will have to precede analysis of the reality, for the latter has been determined in many cases by implicit and explicit commitments that will continue to render Jewish education problematic unless the commitments are disclosed, and criticized. We will have to decide why we want to teach Hebrew, for that will determine

---

[5] For a discussion of curriculum as a practical endeavor see Joseph J. Schwab, *The Practical: A Language for Curriculum* (Washington, D.C.: National Education Association, 1970); and Seymour Fox, "A Practical Image of the Practical," in *Curriculum Theory Network* (Toronto, Ontario: Ontario Institute for Studies in Education, 1973), pp. 60–77.

what kind of Hebrew we teach and how we teach it. We will have to decide whether the Bible must be studied in the original Hebrew, and, if so, how to treat its religious and ethical ideas. We will have to decide whether the majority of children are to leave the Jewish school knowing nothing more about Judaism than the Bible, or whether their course of instruction shall also include Talmud, medieval philosophy and literature, modern Hebrew literature, and modern Jewish theology.[6]

No doubt there will be much discussion as to just how many subjects the Jewish school can reasonably teach and what their content should include. But it is difficult to understand how we will be able to make reasonable or defensible decisions unless we arrive at some kind of consensus as to the basic ideas for the curriculum of the Jewish school.[7] This kind of deliberation will make it possible for us to discover, invent, and import (where appropriate) means that are likely to lead to the goals we have agreed upon. For example, if we identify large portions of Jewish education with character education, we will have to devise means of education, possibly even new educational institutions, to meet this challenge. We will also have to take into account the contribution of informal Jewish education—camping, youth movements, junior congregations, and so on.[8] A clarification of the goals and content of Jewish education will make it possible for us to assign different and complementary tasks to the school, the youth movement, the club, the junior congregation, and the camp. Vacation periods, holidays, and community service would be viewed as integral parts of the curriculum, and thus change the content and form of the formal curriculum. I have been encouraged to believe by the work of the Melton Faculty Seminar—consisting of scholars in Bible history, Jewish and general philosophy, Talmud, Hebrew literature, Jewish and general education—that goals can be agreed upon which will yield content and curriculum materials that would revolutionize the Jewish school.

We will have to invest a good deal of money and energy in social-

[6] These subjects are handled for the most part in the Jewish high school, which no more than 20 percent of Jewish children attend.

[7] Even with consensus, alternative and competing curricula will be developed to attain the same goals.

[8] Though the effectiveness of informal education, e.g., camping, has not been demonstrated "scientifically," there is good reason to assume that it is a very powerful tool for Jewish education. Camps such as Ramah, Massad, and Cejwin appear to have made a great impact.

science research to accompany our investigation of the goals and content of Jewish education. I do not pretend to know whether ample psychological and sociological research has been undertaken concerning the Jewish community. However, almost no information concerning the attitudes, reactions, and commitments of students in Jewish schools is available to the educator. We know even less about parents and the family as related to Jewish education. We do not know the answers to such questions as: What would happen if schools "succeeded"? Would parents then engage in subtle sabotage? What are the expectations of rabbis, teachers, and educational administrators as to the potential of Jewish education? Could young people be induced into the profession of Jewish education if it were viewed as the vehicle by which the Jewish community would be transformed into a subculture struggling to respond to traditional ethical and religious values in the complex world in which we live? How does community leadership feel and think, and how would it react if new, unusual, and expensive programs of Jewish education were presented?

Such problems, and many others, would have to be investigated if the educational reality is to be dealt with seriously, for there is little doubt that, having agreed upon goals and content for Jewish education and even having discovered promising means and methods, logistics and strategy will change means and ends as we are forced to decide about priorities.

Greater clarity as to the goals of Jewish education and sensible curricular suggestions would prepare us for the deliberation concerning personnel and the structure of the Jewish school. It is difficult to justify the current approach to the recruitment, training, and retraining of personnel. No significant recruitment program has been attempted. Teacher training has not been reexamined for years, and the number of students being trained is inadequate. The financing of teacher-training institutions is not treated seriously, and the faculty of these institutions must be supported, enlarged, and supplemented. As to retraining, it is all but nonexistent.

Though we probably ought to defer judgment on how to treat the problem of personnel until we have a clearer notion of the kind of Jewish education we want to develop, there is one aspect of the question that appears to permit discussion even at this early stage of our thinking. It is an astonishing fact that there are practically no scholars or researchers in the field of Jewish education. Obviously, this is a very serious matter, for how can we hope to train proper personnel or look at Jewish education reflexively if there are no experts to undertake these tasks? As long as the leadership of Jewish education is administrative rather than scholarly by training and experience, the problem of personnel will remain insoluble. If Jewish education is discussed only in terms of time, money, and space, or embedded in slogans that ignore complexity and diversity, we can only repel the very people we need most to attract. We should, I believe, learn from experience in the field of Jewish studies at the university level, where a few outstanding scholars have attracted a substantial following and are able to compete successfully for the allegiance of bright and talented Jewish students. This may prove to be the key to many other matters.

It is my contention that the necessary discussion on the goals and curriculum of the Jewish school cannot be undertaken by the present leadership of Jewish education (though it should have a significant role in the deliberation).[9] For this we will need the expertise of scholars in the field of Judaica as well as social scientists, who must somehow be induced to devote their academic talent to the problems of Jewish education. This is by no means a radical suggestion. The pattern already exists in general education, where great benefits are being derived from the partnership of educators, subject-matter specialists, and social scientists. If we can recruit such people to the education faculties of teacher-training schools and rabbinical seminaries, and if we can establish research institutes,[10] we will be well on our way toward the desired restructuring of Jewish education in this country. The challenge to effect needed changes in Jewish education should prove attractive to young Jewish students who are looking for ways to join scholarship with action and commitment. If Jewish education would involve itself in character training, and seek to emphasize the need for roots[11] as well as involvement in the contemporary society, it would undoubtedly attract many talented young people to its professional ranks.

At this stage of our thinking there is little to be gained from consid-

---

[9] This is not to be taken as a negative criticism of the present leadership of Jewish education or their predecessors. They were forced to devote their lives to the building of the institutions we are now looking at reflexively. It is doubtful whether they had any other options open to them.

[10] There are only two institutes in the United States devoted to research in Jewish education.

[11] See Joseph J. Schwab, "The Religiously Oriented School in the United States: A Memorandum on Policy," *Conservative Judaism*, Spring 1964, pp. 1–14.

ering the many other problems of personnel. As I have emphasized, solutions will depend on answers to the prior questions of philosophy, curriculum, and available resources. However, it is important to note that we are currently in the grip of rigid and unimaginative procedures. We train one kind of teacher for all tasks, and training methods are basically the same in all teacher-training institutions. But can one teacher develop language skills as well as conduct an inquiry into the traditional texts? Should this same person also be expected to serve as the model of religious behavior to be emulated by the students? On the other hand, is it necessary to have all tasks in the Jewish school handled only by graduates of teachers institutes? Cannot housewives, for instance, or college students, or even teen-agers be trained to perform certain tasks? It may be that such people can do better at some tasks than the graduate teachers.

The structure of Jewish education—that is, the organization of the schools and the relationship of the schools to each other and to other community organizations—will certainly undergo changes as we begin to ponder the basic issues. We might even conclude that the school, or the school as currently conceived, is not the best place to obtain a Jewish education. At any rate, we must avoid premature and merely administrative suggestions. One such suggestion that has been advanced periodically, and that undoubtedly will resurface, is to combine forces, to merge Conservative and Reform, and even perhaps Orthodox, schools. According to this view, denominationalism is the ogre of Jewish education. But combining confused, tired, and uninspired forces may not prove very useful. More of the same is not always better. Overarching structures or neutral organizational auspices may serve to ease the financial burden, but they cannot provide the requisite inspiration. The issue of the structure of Jewish education is serious and should, therefore, not be viewed in solely administrative terms. Nor would we be acting responsibly if we were to make our suggestions based on extrapolations from past and present experiences, for neither has yielded satisfying results.

In conclusion, we may say that Jewish education can have a significant impact on the future of Jewish life in the United States only if it is prepared to establish, through serious deliberation, philosophies of education to guide the creation of new programs and practices. These programs must be based on a sound analysis of both the reality and the potential of Jewish life. To undertake these tasks, a new kind of personnel will have to be recruited, from the ranks of Jewish scholarship and the social sciences, to assume positions of leadership in Jewish education. Their task will be to develop ideas that will inspire talented Jewish students, in turn, to consider a career in Jewish education. These new sources of energy must inevitably infuse new ideas into the curriculum, teacher training, and the structure of education itself. To accomplish all this will require large allocations of funds— but should the developments I have been advocating come about, the funding agencies will at last be afforded the opportunity to base their decisions on competing futures rather than merely on competing demands.

11

Decision-Making in the American Jewish Community

DANIEL J. ELAZAR

Environmental and Cultural Factors

THE CHARACTER OF AMERICAN JEWRY

American Jewry forms the largest Jewish community in Jewish history and, indeed, is the largest aggregation of Jews ever located under a single government, with the possible exception of Czarist Russia on the eve of the mass migration. Its major local communities are larger than all but a handful of countrywide communities in the past.

The spread of Jews from the East Coast to the West Coast and from the Far North to the Deep South, despite the unevenness of the distribution, has given the American Jewish community major concentrations of population at the farthest reaches of the country. Moreover, the density of Jewish population in the Northeast has been declining, at least since the end of World War II. California now has more Jews than any country in the world other than the United States itself, the Soviet Union, and Israel. Los Angeles, the second largest local Jewish community in the world, has as many Jews as all of France, which ranks as the country with the fourth largest Jewish population. Simple geography serves to reinforce all other tendencies to disperse decision-making in the American Jewish community as in American society as a whole. It has proved difficult for any "central office" to control countrywide operations in the United States regardless of who or what is involved.

The five largest Jewish communities in the United States[1] contain close to 60 percent of the total Jewish population, and the top sixteen communities[2] (all those containing 50,000 Jews or more) contain over 75 percent of the total. At the same time Jews are distributed in over 800 communities, ranging in size from just under 2 million in New York City to a handful of families. Those 800 are organized into 225 local federations or their equivalent, of which only twenty-seven have more than 20,000 Jews, and only ten over 100,000. (Greater New York City, while really a region rather than a local community, is organized under a single limited-purpose federation which includes the five boroughs plus Nassau, Suffolk, and Westchester Counties.)

Local community size contributes directly to the organization of decision-making on the American Jewish scene. New York is not only in a size class by itself but maintains its own—highly fragmented—organizational patterns while holding itself substantially aloof from all other communities. The federation system, which has become the norm throughout the rest of the country, is limited in New York City. There the major Jewish institutions and organizations, beginning with the United Jewish Appeal, conduct their own fund-raising campaigns and operate their own local programs outside of any overall planning or coordinating framework, often from their own national offices.

The major Jewish communities outside of New York are all structured so that the federations play a major, if not dominant, role in communal fund-raising and decision-making. All the significant ones among them are members of the Large City Budgeting Conference (LCBC) of the Council of Jewish Federations and Welfare Funds. While the LCBC itself is essentially an information-gathering body, its members together represent the single most powerful influence on communal fund-raising on the American Jewish scene, and the leaders of its constituent federations are the major source of American Jewry's leadership across the spectrum of functional spheres. The communications network that is generated out of the interaction of those communal leaders may well be the heart of the countrywide Jewish communal decision-making system. Significantly, New York is not a member of the LCBC.

Communities too small or weak to be members of the LCBC stand

---

[1] New York City, Los Angeles, Nassau County (N.Y.), Philadelphia, and Chicago.
[2] The aforementioned communities, plus Boston, Miami, Bergen County (N.J.), Essex County (N.J.), Westchester County (N.Y.), Baltimore, Washington (D.C.), Cleveland, Detroit, San Francisco, and St. Louis.

on the peripheries of the countrywide decision-making processes, no matter how well organized and active they may be locally. Occasionally notable individuals from such communities do attain national prominence, but that is rare. Only in the last few years have the stronger of these communities begun to devise ways to enhance their national visibility in the manner of the LCBC.

Local decision-making has not been systematically studied in more than a handful of these organized communities. What we do know, however, is that there are variations among the cities in each of the categories simply as a result of the differences in scale that change the magnitude of the communications problems. The ways in which patterns of communication are organized vary in communities of different sizes, not to speak of other cultural, historical, social, and economic factors. Size, for example, does much to determine who knows whom and how comprehensive or exclusive are friendship and acquaintanceship nets. These, in turn, determine who speaks to whom on communal matters.

There is also considerable evidence that the percentage of those affiliated with and active in communal life stands in inverse ratio to community size. Since there is always a minimum number of positions to be filled, regardless of community size, smaller communities will, ipso facto, involve a greater proportion of their population than larger ones, not to speak of the greater social pressures for participation often manifested in smaller communities where people know who is and who is not participating.

The size factor works in other ways as well. To some extent, the number and spread of Jewish institutions is dependent upon the size of the community. A community of 10,000 Jews is not likely to have the range of institutions of a community of 100,000. Consequently it will not have the complexity and diversity of decision-making centers or channels or the problems of separated leadership that are likely to prevail in a very large community in which people can be decision-makers in major arenas without knowing or working with their counterparts in others.

The impact of size of place also has a dynamic quality. From the eighteenth century, when Jews first arrived in the American colonies, until the mid-nineteenth century, Jews lived in a number of small communities of approximately the same size, none of which was able to support more than the most rudimentary congregational institutions. All this changed with the subsequent mass immigration of Jews from Eastern Europe, that settled overwhelmingly in the major urban centers. At the same time, Jews in the hinterland communities continued to migrate to the metropolis, because that is where the opportunities lay.

Since the end of World War II there has been another shift in the scale of Jewish settlement that is only now beginning to be fully reflected in the structure of local decision-making. Increasingly, Jews have been moving out of the big cities into suburbs which, while nominally parts of their metropolitan areas, have fully separate governmental structures and substantially distinctive socioeconomic characteristics, both of which they guard jealously. This migration is leading the Jews back to small communities where, unless they are involved with a great metropolitan federation, they are able to maintain only minimal local Jewish institutions. Scattered widely among many small towns, they are tied together at most by a common fund-raising system for overseas needs. From the available data it would seem that 60 percent of American Jews today live in separate suburban communities or in metropolitan communities of less than 20,000 Jews.

New York, with its 31 percent of the total American Jewish population, is the de facto capital of the American Jewish community. Moreover, because New York is really a region, rather than a single community, and is additionally surrounded by perhaps another 15 percent of American Jewry living within the orbit of Manhattan, the Jews of New York tend to believe that all Jewish life in the United States is concentrated in their city and environs. At the same time, what would be considered very large Jewish communities anywhere else are practically buried within the metropolitan area and maintain only those institutions that meet immediate local needs.

The other very large Jewish communities are regional centers of Jewish life as well as major communities in their own right. Los Angeles is clearly the center of Jewish life west of the Rocky Mountains and the second city of American Jewry institutionally as well as in numbers, with branches of all the countrywide Jewish organizations and institutions located within its limits. Because of its distance from the East Coast it has a greater degree of independence from New York than any other regional center in the United States. Chicago is the capital of the Jewries of mid-America in much the same way, although its relative proximity to New York has prevented it from developing the same range of national institutions or local autonomy as Los Angeles. Once the great western anchor of American Jewish life, its overall position has been lost to Los Angeles, along with so much of its Jewish population.

Philadelphia and Boston, although now almost within commuting distance of New York, remain equally important secondary national centers for American Jewry because of historical circumstance. Philadelphia's old, established Jewish community has long played a national role that at one time even rivaled that of the Empire City. It continues to maintain some institutions of national significance. Perhaps more important, as the first major Jewish community outside of the New York metropolitan area, its leaders have easy access to the national offices of Jewish organizations, where they frequently represent the point of view of the rest of American Jewry (insofar as there is any common one) vis-à-vis that of New York. Boston Jewry, though a far younger Jewish community, has capitalized on the city's position as the Athens of America to create major Jewish academic institutions of national scope and to become the home of whatever Jewish academic "brain trust" exists in the United States.

Only in the South is the largest community not the regional center. Greater Miami, still a very new community, the product of post-World War II migration southward and heavily weighted with retirees, has had no significant national impact as a community (as distinct from a location for the conduct of the winter business of American Jewry as a whole). The capital of Jewish life in the South is Atlanta, the region's general capital. Despite its small Jewish population of 16,500, it possesses the panoply of regional offices associated with much larger Jewish communities in other parts of the country. The pattern of Jewish activity in Atlanta is markedly different from that of any of the other regional centers because of the intimacy and proximity within which the regional offices and local institutions must live.

Jewish communities of medium size (here defined as 20,000 to 100,000 population) all play tertiary roles (as communities) in the hierarchy of American Jewish communities. They are generally able to provide the full range of local institutions and organizations found in any American community, although often in rudimentary form, but serve no particular national functions except as a result of historical accident. Among them, national importance is determined by factors other than size. The subsidiary regional centers are all located between the Mississippi and the Pacific coast, where they represent nodes of Jewish population that serve wide areas sparsely settled by

Jews, and thus occupy a more important role in the overall scheme of things than their size or, in most cases, the quality of Jewish life within them would otherwise warrant.

PATTERNS OF PARTICIPATION

Increasingly, American Jews, if they have any Jewish commitment, feel that they are Jews by choice rather than simply by birth. Not that the organic tie does not underlie the fact of choice, but birth alone is no longer sufficient to keep Jews within the fold, and no one is more conscious of this than the Jews themselves. As a result, the Jewish community is no longer a community of fixed boundaries within which all (or virtually all) those born Jews find and organize themselves to meet their communal needs, but rather a series of concentric circles radiating outward from the hard core of committed Jews toward gray areas of semi-Jewishness on the outer fringes.

The hard core of the American Jewish community consists of those whose Jewishness is a full-time matter, the central factor in their lives, whether from a traditionally religious point of view, as ethnic nationalists, or as a result of their intensive and active involvement in Jewish affairs. They and their families tend to be closely linked in their Jewishness internally and to others with similar ties, so that their Jewish existence is an intergenerational affair. Perhaps 5 percent of the Jewish population of the United States falls into this category, with the figure possibly reaching as high as 8 percent.

Surrounding this hard core is a second group—the "participants"—consisting of those involved in Jewish life more than casually and considered active in Jewish affairs, but to whom living Jewishly is not a full-time matter. They may well be officers of Jewish organizations, perhaps take part in adult education programs of various kinds, and make Judaism a major *avocational* interest. Ten percent is a fair estimate of the percentage of such Jews in the United States today.

Surrounding the participants is a third group—the "members"—which consists of those Jews who are affiliated with Jewish institutions or organizations in some concrete way, but are not particularly active in them. These would include synagogue members whose affiliation does not involve them beyond the use of synagogue facilities for the rites of passage or for attendance at High Holiday services, as well as members of some of the mass-based Jewish organizations like Hadassah and B'nai B'rith, or any of the other charitable groups which are identifiably Jewish and whose membership reflects primarily private social interests rather than a concern for the public purposes of Jewish life. This is a large category because it includes all those who instinctively recognize the necessity for some kind of associational commitment to Jewish life, even if only for the sake of maintaining a proper front before the non-Jewish community. One might estimate that it includes approximately 30 percent of the country's Jewish population.

Beyond that circle is a fourth—one might label it "contributors and consumers"—consisting of Jews who occasionally contribute money to Jewish causes and periodically utilize the services of Jewish institutions for marriage, burial, *Bar Mitzvah*, and so on. Perhaps 30 percent of all American Jews fall into this category, many of whom have incomes too limited to develop more formal or lasting attachments with Jewish life in an associational context that makes the payment of money a binding factor.

Beyond the circle of contributors and consumers there is a fifth circle of Jews—the "peripherals"—who are recognizably Jewish in some way but completely uninvolved in Jewish life. While they may be married to Jewish partners and their children are unquestionably of Jewish descent, they have no desire to utilize Jewish institutions for the rites of passage and insufficient interest even in such Jewish causes as Israel to contribute money. Perhaps 15 percent of American Jewry falls into this category.

Finally there is a sixth circle, consisting of an unknown number of "quasi-Jews" who are neither inside the Jewish community nor entirely out of it. These are people who have intermarried but not lost their own personal Jewish "label," or who have otherwise assimilated to a point where Jewish birth is incidental to them in every respect. We have no firm knowledge of how many such people there are in the country and assume that between 5 and 10 percent of the known Jewish population falls into this category, plus a number who are simply not reckoned in the conventional figures.

The boundaries between these circles, as well as their memberships, are quite fluid, and there is considerable movement in and out of all of them, though of course there is more movement along the edges of each than across separated circles. Thus Jews among the participants are more likely to move into the hard core or out into more casual membership than to drop out altogether, while the peripherals may move into the quasi-Jewish category with some ease or, under certain circumstances, be brought into the category of contributors and consumers. Moreover, in times of crisis there will be a general tightening of the circles. Thus, the Six Day War probably increased the extent and intensity of Jewish identification in all the circles, but only in relation to the prior stance of the individuals involved.

This means that the community is built on a fluid, if not eroding, base with a high degree of self-selection involved in determining who is even a *potential* decision-maker. In effect, no more than 20 percent of the Jewish population falls into that category, and by no means all of them define their Jewish concerns as public ones. For many, even in the hard core (Hasidic Jews, for example), the concerns of the Jewish *community* are not their concerns. They are interested in leading private lives that are intensely Jewish but do not seek to channel their Jewishness into the realm of public affairs.

There is some evidence that the "bundle" of circles is getting looser and spreading out further from the hard core. It is likely that a great gap is developing somewhere between circles two and three, a gap paralleled by an even greater one between circles four and five. If this is so, the bases of Jewish communal life in the United States are not only shifting but eroding, making *representative* decision-making an even more difficult problem for American Jewry.

ASSOCIATIONAL FRAMEWORK

Another environmental factor that is vital in shaping decision-making in the American Jewish community is the extraordinary variety of possible forms of Jewish association. Any organized interconnections within the maze of institutions and organizations of American Jewry have had to be forged in the face of many obstacles, including lack of inherent legitimacy attaching to any coordinating institutions, the penchant for individualism inherent in the American Jewish community (derived from both American and Jewish sources), and the difficulties of enforcing any kind of coordinating effort within the context of American society, which treats all Jewish activities as private and voluntary.

Thus the pattern of relationships within the matrix of American Jewish life must be dynamic. There is rarely a fixed division of authority and influence within American Jewry, but rather one that varies from time to time and usually from issue to issue, with different elements of the matrix taking on different "loads," depending on the time and the issue. Moreover, since the community is voluntary, persuasion rather than compulsion, influence rather than power, are the tools available for making decisions and implementing policies. All this works to strengthen the character of the community as a communications network, since the character, quality, and relevance of what is communicated and the way in which it is communicated frequently determine the extent of the authority and influence of the parties to the communication.

THE WORLD JEWISH ENVIRONMENT

Decision-making in the American Jewish community is further shaped by the impact of the world Jewish environment. This is most immediately evident in the role which Israel plays in American Jewish life. Israel has become the major unifying symbol in the community, in effect replacing traditional religious values as the binding tie linking Jews of varying persuasions and interests. Fund-raising for Israel has not only come to dominate all communal activity, but has been the stimulus for the general increase in funds raised for across-the-board Jewish purposes in the United States since the end of World War II.

Until the twentieth century American Jewry was no more than an outpost of the world Jewish community and was treated as such. Major figures in Jewish life did not come to settle in the United States unless forced to do so by external circumstances. Only as a result of World War I and the subsequent disruption of the great European Jewish centers did the American Jewish community begin to come into its own. Finally, the Nazi era established the primacy of American Jewry in every respect. As in the period following World War I, American Jewish relief efforts were in urgent demand and the American Jewish community rose to the highest level of prominence on the world Jewish scene, primarily through its ability to mobilize great economic resources. After World War II, the great organizational talents of American Jewry were placed at the service of shattered European Jewry, and American Jews became the leaders in the monumental task of rehabilitation and resettlement. Fund-raising for overseas needs, through the agency of the local federation, remains a prime American Jewish activity.

TRADITIONAL ELEMENTS AND THEIR MODERN MANIFESTATIONS

While the American Jewish community is, in many respects, cut off from traditional Jewish sources in its outlook and behavior patterns, a number of elements drawn from the traditional political culture of the Jews do persist to help shape decision-making. One of the most important is the use of federal principles to organize Jewish communal life, a system which is as old as the Jewish people itself, having its origins in the federation of the twelve tribes under Moses. The very term "federal" is derived from the Latin *foedus* (which means covenant) and is an expression of the Biblical idea of *brit* (covenant), which defines the basis of political and social relationships among men as well as between man and God. The covenant or federal idea, as translated into concrete principles and institutions, was embedded in Jewish tradition to become part of the political culture of the Jews. Consequently, it persisted as a force shaping Jewish communal life even after external events eliminated the tribal federation as the form of government of the Jewish people.

Federal principles, institutions, and arrangements persist to this day. These federal arrangements are not necessarily the same as those in territorially based political systems, where constituent polities are united under an overarching government in such a way as to preserve the integrity of all the partners. Frequently there are no overarching bodies, or only weak ones, to link the constituent units, but there is the linking of individuals and institutions in contractual partnerships designed to maintain the unity of the whole—especially for operational purposes—while preserving the integrity of all the partners. Moreover, those partnerships take on a character of their own that is more than the sum of their constituent units.

Internally, each Jewish community has always been a partnership, and is so delineated in Jewish law. From earliest times, local communities came into existence as a result of compacts among Jews in a particular locality and functioned according to the terms of such compacts, binding the individual Jews only to the extent that the compacts provided or were allowed to provide within the framework of Jewish religious law. Unlike the idea of the "state" in European political thought, Jewish political thought and Jewish law contain no concept of the community as an organic or reified entity with an existence independent of its members, nor has it ever been considered the property of any particular individual or group of individuals, as was the case with premodern political systems. Rather, every Jewish community was held to be the common property of all of its members, who in effect compacted or federated with one another to create specific communities within the overall framework of the Jewish people.

Beyond the limits of locality, the various Jewish communities have been linked with one another through more or less institutionalized federal arrangements that have varied in extent, duration, and significance in varying periods of Jewish history. At the very least, there were relationships linking the rabbinical authorities of one community to those of others for purposes of interpretation of Jewish law. When and where conditions allowed, the relationships were made even more formal. Today Jewish communities all over the world tend to be organized on some variation of the federal principle, unless the political and cultural framework of the societies in which they are located strongly militate against it. In Central Europe, where Jewish communities have formal status in public law, they are organized on a federal basis by that law. In the English-speaking countries they are so organized either because they are located in countries with federal structures or because of custom. In Latin America, the Jewish communities are federations of *landsmanshaften,* and in the United States they are federations of service agencies. Moreover, all congregations are essentially organized on federal principles to this day.

The thrust toward consensual decision-making which is generated by the federal arrangements among the institutions and their leaders has been raised to new heights in modern Jewish life because of the voluntary nature of the community. In some cases, decisions cannot be made on a public basis because there is insufficient consensus in the community. In others, the general society's commitment to private decisions is so overriding as to prevent consideration of public action. Sometimes there is simply too little communication between the community's leaders and the Jewish population to even indicate that an issue exists or that a decision should be (or has been) made. Obviously it is even more difficult to compel people who are associated voluntarily to accept decisions they regard as unwise or hostile to their interests than it is to deal with people who are somehow bound into the system.

This is not to say that all decisions are arrived at on an open consensual basis in which all parties involved participate in the negotiations until a decision acceptable to all is reached. Not only are there many specialized decisions made in small groups simply because of a lack of widespread interest, but even some very important decisions are taken in that way precisely in order to avoid the difficulties of having to reach a widespread consensus. Of course, the latter situation is possible only when there is some feeling on the part of potential participants in the community that they must accept the decisions reached. It is most noticeable in the case of decisions involving Israel.

The American Jewish community is so closely bound up with Israel and so well perceives the way in which its basic interests are tied to the survival and success of the Jewish state that its members are most reluctant to challenge any decisions made in the name of Israel's best interests. This means that the coterie of leaders who, in effect, set the policies of the American Jewish community in matters affecting Israel have a great deal of leeway, since they know that they are not likely to be challenged. It also means that the same leaders are in a position to extend their power to other arenas by capitalizing on their role in relation to Israel. This ability of leaders-by-consensus to gain authority and influence through their association with the central value symbol of the community is another manifestation of the traditional political culture of the Jews, a transposition of traditional charismatic arrangements that adhered to the rabbinical authorities at a time when the Torah had the same kind of status in the minds of the Jews that Israel has today.

In its own way, then, the American Jewish community relies heavily on charismatic leaders rather than on those chosen by more institutionalized procedures, such as elections or heredity.[3] Indeed, for the most part, Jewish leadership historically has been based on forms of charisma other than personal magnetism. The Biblical judges and prophets were leaders by virtue of a charisma endowed by God according to traditional understanding. Later, charisma derived from special talents of learning and scholarship. More recently, charisma has been associated with wealth. American Jewry has also had leaders with charismatic powers as this is popularly understood, but they were atypical. Today, the ability to achieve great success in the non-Jewish world rivals money as a source of charisma. Most recently, Israelis have acquired a certain charisma in their relationship with American Jewry because of their role in building the Jewish state.

Expansion of the role of professional communal servants in the American Jewish community has clearly diminished the extent to which the community relies upon charismatic leaders. Indeed, there is a constant lament that American Jewry has no great public figures today in the manner of the leaders of earlier generations, that the men

---

[3] It should be understood that the term "charismatic" is used in its original Weberian sense, not in the way in which it has come to be used in popular language, where it refers to men with a particular ability to hypnotize or charm the masses. "Charismatic" in that sense means "compelling" because of qualities attached to the person, rather than to the institutions or the environment.

who run the community are "organization types," essentially colorless and uninspiring to the masses. There is considerable truth in this, but it does not diminish the fact that there is a form of charisma operating to endow certain people with authority (particularly in the fund-raising field, where leadership by example is the norm) in a community in which there are no clear-cut ways to legitimate authority or power.

Leadership in the fund-raising field is often denigrated by critical observers of the American Jewish community, yet in many respects its patterns and methods are closer to the most authentic elements of the Jewish tradition of leadership than those of any other segments of American Jewish leadership, comparable, in this respect, to the much-admired Israeli army. The basic principle of fund-raising leadership is leadership by example, a principle notably absent in other sectors of American Jewish life. "Follow me" is widely recognized as the only successful way to raise funds, just as the Israeli army recognizes it as the only way to lead men.

Israel has become the authority-giving element in Jewish life today in the way that the Torah was in the premodern world. The ascendancy of Israel appears to have ended a period of well over a century in which there was no clear-cut source of authority in Jewish life. The fact that Israel has become the new source of authority is not without problems of its own, but this new situation nevertheless provides a means for uniting a people with very diverse beliefs.

The authoritative role of Israel functions in two ways. First, Israel is itself authoritative. Those who wish to dissent from any particular Israeli policy or demand must be circumspect. Those Jews who reject Israel's claims upon them are more or less written off by the Jewish community; they are certainly excluded from any significant decision-making role. Furthermore, leaders who can claim to speak in the name of Israel or on behalf of Israel gain a degree of authority that places them in advantageous positions when it comes to other areas of communal decision-making. Even the synagogues, which are expected to be bastions of support for the Torah as the primary source of authority, have come increasingly to rely upon Israel and Israel-centered activities to legitimize their own positions.

THE IMPACT OF TECHNOLOGICAL CHANGE

Technological change, as a final environmental factor of crucial importance, is often—and mistakenly—neglected in discussions of decision-making. It is no exaggeration to say that the invention of the jet plane and the telephone have had as much of an impact on the patterns of decision-making in American Jewish life as any more widely hailed social factors. The ability of Jews, wherever they live, to participate in the activities of the world Jewish community, to get to Israel rapidly and to send their children there for brief stays, and to jet around the United States itself to attend meetings in New York, Miami, or Kansas City has had a tremendous effect on the selection of the participants and the conditions of the decision-making process. The equally important influence of advances in telecommunications should be noted. The telephone has radically enlarged the country-wide communications network, expanding the number, range, and geographic distribution of decision-makers. Its international impact is just beginning to be felt.

Institutions and Organizations

INSTITUTIONAL ROLES

The organizations and institutions within which the decisions of the American Jewish community are made group themselves into four categories based on the kinds of roles they play within the community as a whole. They are (1) *government-like institutions;* (2) *localistic institutions and organizations;* (3) *general-purpose, mass-based organizations;* and (4) *special interest institutions and organizations.*

Government-like institutions are those that play roles and provide services on a countrywide, local, or (where they exist) regional basis which, under other conditions, would be played, provided, or controlled, predominantly or exclusively, by governmental authorities. The Jewish federations and their constituent agencies are the most clear-cut examples of government-like institutions in the American Jewish community. Locally, the federations themselves have become something like roof organizations. They are constantly expanding their role in community planning, coordination, and financing. While they are not always comprehensive in the sense of embracing all organizations in the community directly, in most cases they do maintain some formal connections with all significant organizations performing government-like services which are either their constituent agencies, beneficiaries, or affiliates. Thus bureaus of Jewish education, Jewish community centers, Jewish community relations councils, and communitywide welfare institutions are generally linked to the federation.

On the countrywide plane the analogous organizations are not as easily identifiable. The Council of Jewish Federations and Welfare Funds (CJFWF), the Synagogue Council of America, the National Jewish Welfare Board, the National Jewish Community Relations Advisory Council, and the American Association for Jewish Education at least make claims in the direction of performing government-like functions. In fact, however, the Jewish communities of the United States are no more than leagued together; they are not sufficiently federated on a countrywide basis to have generated comprehensive institutions comparable to those on the local scene.

Localistic institutions and organizations, primarily synagogues now that the *landsmanshaften* have virtually disappeared, are those whose foremost task is to meet the primary personal and interpersonal needs of Jews. By their very nature, synagogues are geared to be relatively intimate associations of compatible people. While the growth of the large American synagogue has led to a confusion of functions (which has contributed to the present difficulties of the synagogue as an institution), it still retains primary responsibility for meeting those needs.

General-purpose, mass-based organizations are those that function to (1) articulate community values, attitudes, and policies, (2) provide the energy and motive force for crystallizing the communal consensus that grows out of those values, attitudes and policies, and (3) maintain institutionalized channels of communication between community leaders and actives ("cosmopolitans") and the broad base of the affiliated Jewish population ("locals") to deal with the problems and tasks facing the community in light of the consensus. These mass-based organizations provide the structural parallel to the government-like (cosmopolitan) and localistic institutions, bridging the gaps between them, providing a motivating force to keep them running, and also functioning to determine their respective roles in the community as a whole. In a sense these organizations function as the equivalent of political parties in a full-fledged political system (in some Jewish communities in other countries they are indeed political parties) to aggregate and mobilize community interests.

In the American Jewish community, these organizations are to be found in three varieties. First are the quasi-elite organizations which have begun to reach out to develop a larger membership base, but in such a way that only people with special interests or backgrounds are likely to find their place within them. The American Jewish Committee is perhaps the best example, and in many respects the most important, of these organizations. Beginning as a small, select group, the Committee has developed a larger membership as it has become more democratized, but its base still includes a relatively select group of people (even if they are more self-selected than they used to be). At the same time, it is a very powerful group, since its major principle of inclusion seems to be influential or potentially influential leaders. More than any other organization, it has a membership strategically placed in the ranks of the leadership of the government-like institutions and major synagogues.

The American Jewish Congress is another organization of this type. Its history has followed exactly the reverse pattern of the Committee's. Founded with the intention of becoming a mass-based organization, it has instead become the preserve of a self-selected group interested in a particular kind of civil-libertarian approach to Jewish communal affairs.

The second variety consists of mass-based organizations that remain widely open to all types of Jews, but have not been able to develop the mass base they desire. The Zionist organizations in the United States (with the exception of Hadassah) are the principal examples of this group. They have not only fallen short of their basic aim but have also failed to develop an elite cadre that would place them in the first group.

Finally there are the truly mass-based organizations, of which two stand out: B'nai B'rith and Hadassah. These organizations, whose members number in the hundreds of thousands each, reach out to the lowest common denominator in the American Jewish community, while at the same time speaking for the most sophisticated and complex communal needs.

Special interest institutions and organizations are what their name indicates. They reflect the multitude of special interests in the community, either by maintaining programs of their own or functioning to mobilize concern and support for various programs conducted by the government-like institutions. The number of special interest organizations is myriad, and they cover the gamut of interests which any Jewish community could possibly possess. They concentrate on specific issues and try to raise those issues before both the larger Jewish public and the leaders and decision-makers of the Jewish community. No one of these special interest groups is likely to have a great deal of influence in the community as a whole, though some will be decisive in those specific areas in which they are involved. A whole host of them can wield some influence on communal decision-making, depending on the character of the interest they represent, the degree of sympathy it invokes among community decision-makers, and the caliber of leadership attached to the special interest group.

It should be noted that this description is idealized to the extent that particular organizations and institutions have functions that overlap the categories. For historical reasons that relate to the evolution of the American Jewish community from discrete institutions, functions were assumed in unsystematic ways. Thus B'nai B'rith is responsible for welfare institutions and the Hillel Foundations because, at the time they were founded, no more appropriate organization was available to initiate, finance, or operate them. Today they are slowly being transferred to more appropriate communal bodies.

TERRITORIAL AND NONTERRITORIAL ORGANIZATION

The patterns of decision-making in the American Jewish community must be traced in light of the foregoing fourfold division which contributes so much to the shaping of the community's structural matrix. However, it does so only in combination with the territorial and nonterritorial patterns of organization that inform the community. The territorial organizations are invariably the most comprehensive ones, charged with providing overall direction for the community as a whole or some otherwise fragmented segment of it, while the ideological, functional, and interest organizations (nonterritorial) generally touch the more personal aspects of Jewish life. One consequence of this has been that Jewish reformers seeking to improve the organization of the American Jewish community have constantly emphasized the need to strengthen territorial organization as against other kinds, while partisans of particular interests in the Jewish community have emphasized nonterritorial forms of organization as the most appropriate in a voluntary community.

At the same time, because of the nature of the Jewish community, the territorial organizations rarely have fixed boundaries except by convention. Furthermore, because ideological commitment in American Jewish life tends to be weak, the ideological groupings have little internal strength except insofar as they serve the interests of their members by taking on specific functional roles.

Ideologically based organizations have had more success on a countrywide basis, where until recently the absence of comprehensive territorial institutions has been marked. Such countrywide organizations as developed prior to the 1930s became committed to specific ideological trends, whether they were founded that way or not. However, the impact of American life constantly serves to emphasize the territorial over the nonterritorial elements whenever given half a chance, and to reduce ideologically based organizations to functional specialists responsible for specific tasks. A major result of this has been the limitation of the powers of the countrywide organizations and localization of the primary decision-making responsibilities of the American Jewish community.

With the exception of a few institutions of higher education (and at one time a few specialized hospitals which are now nonsectarian), all Jewish religious, social, welfare, and educational institutions are local both in name and in fact. Some are casually confederated on a supralocal basis, but most are not, and those claiming national status with no local base soon find themselves without a constituency. Indeed, the major institutions of the American Jewish community—the federations and the synagogues—developed their countrywide bodies after their local institutions had become well established. Among organizations which have been built out of a national headquarters, the only ones that have succeeded are those which have been able to develop meaningful local operations under local leadership.

The three great synagogue movements, which are conventionally viewed as the primary custodians of Jewish affiliation in the United States since the end of World War II, are excellent cases in point. All are essentially confederations of highly independent local congregations linked by relatively vague persuasional ties and a need for certain technical services, such as professional placement, the organization of intercongregational youth programs, and the development of educational material. The confederations function to provide the requisite emotional reinforcement of those ties and the desired services for their member units. They have almost no direct influence on congregational policies and behavior except insofar as the congregations themselves choose to look to them as guides. Short of expulsion from the movement, they have no devices they can use to exercise authority, even in those cases in which the congregation was originally established by the parent movement (not the usual pattern, but an occasional occurrence). Once a congregation is established it becomes as independent as all the rest.

The other great countrywide institutions of American Jewry are similarly organized. The CJFWF is an equally loose confederation of hundreds of local Jewish federations which have emerged in the past four decades as the most powerful institutional forces in Jewish life. The role of the CJFWF is definitely tributary to that of its constituents, who do not hesitate to give it direction. As in the case of the synagogue movements, the power of the national organization flows from its ability to provide services to the local affiliates, generate ideas for them, and manage the flow of professionals.

So, too, the National Jewish Welfare Board is the countrywide service agency of the clearly autonomous local community centers; the American Association for Jewish Education is the service agency of the local bureaus of Jewish education plus the countrywide organizations that claim a major interest in Jewish education; and the National Jewish Community Relations Advisory Council is the service agency of the local Jewish community relations councils and the linking agency for the countrywide community relations agencies and organizations. Exercise of these service functions brings with it a certain power which the professionals who staff the national agencies have developed in various ways, but it is a limited power, usually more visible at conferences than in the daily affairs of the local bodies. In recent years the countrywide federations have been supplemented by even more loosely knit confederations of national bodies, such as the Synagogue Council of America, a confederation of the major synagogue movements, and, most recently, the Presidents' Conference, a loose league of the presidents of major Jewish organizations organized for "foreign-relations" purposes.

Whether the federative arrangements involved are of near universal scope and have broad-based, multipurpose goals, or are limited to single functions with rarely more than consultative or accreditative power, it is the consistent use of such arrangements that enables American Jewry to achieve any kind of structured communal unity at all. What emerges is not a single pyramidal structure, or even one in which the "bottom" rules the "top," as in the case of Jewish communities with representative boards in other parts of the world. There is no "bottom" and no "top" except on a functional basis for specific purposes (if then). Thus it is the absence of hierarchy which is the first element to recognize in examining the decision-making process.

The Role of Functional Groupings

The institutions of the American Jewish community can properly be grouped into five spheres based primarily on function: (1) *religious-congregational*; (2) *educational-cultural*; (3) *community relations*; (4) *communal-welfare*; and (5) *Israel-overseas*. Decision-making in the community is organized accordingly.

RELIGIOUS-CONGREGATIONAL SPHERE

Even the synagogues can be seen as a functional grouping, since American Jews' ideological commitment to a particular synagogue movement is very weak except at the extremes of Orthodoxy and Reform. In essence, they provide the immediately personal and interpersonal ritual-cum-social functions demanded by the community, primarily through individual congregations. They have an essential monopoly on those functions locally, while the synagogue confederations, rabbinical associations, seminaries, and *yeshivas* maintain a parallel monopoly over the community's countrywide theological and ritual concerns.

Nationally, the three great synagogue confederations dominate the religious-congregational sphere. Over the years each has expanded its scope and intensified its efforts on the American Jewish scene. In their common quest for an expanded role in American Jewish life, they leagued themselves into the Synagogue Council of America which, for a few years during the height of the "religious revival" of the 1950s, tried to capture the role as spokesman for American Jewry, and which remains the Jewish religious counterpart to the national church bodies.

Each of the synagogue confederations has a seminary of its own which, because of its academic character, projects itself on the American Jewish scene in a quasi-independent way. Even with the growth of Judaic studies programs in academic institutions, these seminaries remain the backbone of organized Jewish scholarship in the United States. Their alumni lead the congregations of American Jewry and, through their rabbinical associations, link seminaries and the confederations. In addition, a growing number of *yeshivas* in New York and many of the other major Jewish communities reflect the proliferation of the new ultra-Orthodox elements in the community. They preserve and extend traditional Jewish scholarship on a scale never before experienced in American Jewish history.

Since World War II there has been an increasing involvement of power centers outside the United States in the religious-congregational sphere. The Israeli rabbinate is a growing force on the American scene by virtue of its role in deciding the personal status of individual Jews. In an age of jet travel between Israel and the Diaspora, such decisions have ramifications which reverberate throughout the Jewish world. In this connection, the Knesset is also acquiring influence in the religious-congregational sphere and, indeed, is the first secular body anywhere to do so, simply because of its central role in defining who is a Jew in a setting where separation of church and state does not prevail.

The controlling power of the synagogue in the religious-congregational sphere means that a large share of Jewish activity—involving perhaps half of the total revenue and expenditure of American Jewry —is managed outside of any communal decision-making system. American synagogues have traditionally considered themselves (and been considered) private institutions, like clubs or fraternal lodges, accountable to no one but their own members. This reflects their status in American law and has simply been carried over unquestioningly into Jewish communal affairs.

EDUCATIONAL-CULTURAL SPHERE

The synagogues also play a major role in educational matters, having acquired that role after a contest of some forty years' duration during which the nonsynagogue schools were defeated in the struggle over who was to assume responsibility for elementary and secondary Jewish education. Today the great majority of Jewish Sunday and afternoon schools at the elementary level, and a large number of those at the secondary level, are housed in and controlled by synagogues. Synagogue control is so complete where it exists that we do not even have decent estimates of how much is spent on Jewish education, since they do not make their budgets public.

Management of elementary and secondary Jewish education carried on outside of the synagogues is vested in three categories of institutions. There are a few surviving secular schools, usually Yiddishist in orientation, managed by secularistic equivalents of congregations, that is, groups of families that carry out the same functions as conventional congregations, but without their overtly religious character. There are also some noncongregational schools, either remnants of earlier days, generally confined to serving the older neighborhoods, or combined high schools created on an intercongregational basis. Finally, there are a handful of communal school systems, the largest of which are in Detroit, Minneapolis, and St. Paul, that function as the comprehensive educational arms of the Jewish community and dominate Jewish educational activity locally.

The only movement in Jewish elementary and secondary education that is growing is the day school movement. Day schools, whether formally attached to some national ideology or not, tend to develop with communal support by default, although, because few communities have any well-defined way to deal with them, they are rarely tied to the central institutions of communal governance but remain nominally private schools that receive some degree of subsidization.

Central agencies of Jewish education in the larger Jewish communities do have some formal responsibility for developing curricula and setting professional standards for the synagogue schools, and in some cases have acquired responsibility for managing secondary afternoon schools and colleges of Jewish studies. Occasionally they even maintain experimental schools which usually provide such intensive supplementary Jewish education as exists in a given community. While their operational role is limited, they usually represent the only links between the synagogue educational programs and the central institutions of the local Jewish community.

Higher Jewish education is also divided into three segments—the colleges of Jewish studies, the seminaries and *yeshivas*, and the emerging Jewish studies programs in general colleges and universities. The latter, whatever their name and format, are beginning to acquire a certain amount of importance within the overall scheme of Jewish education locally, and have even started to affect the character and content of the traditional institutions of Jewish education. However, it would be wrong to overestimate their importance to date, as opposed to the seminaries and *yeshivas*, as sources of Jewish scholars or the colleges of Jewish studies as influences on local communal life.

If anything, Jewish educational activities are even more localized than the religious-congregational activities. The American Association for Jewish Education, the umbrella body for the central agencies and itself a confederation of local and national groups, is limited in the technical services it renders to studies of local needs and problems. The Orthodox day schools are somewhat more clearly linked to their countrywide bodies, particularly the Torah Umesorah schools. The Conservative day schools are linked formally to umbrella bodies which exist in name only, and many such schools have no extracommunity ties at all. The most important ties involving Jewish schools are the professional associations linking Jewish educators. Increasingly, the CJFWF is becoming involved in the educational and cultural sphere in an attempt to develop some countrywide input, but its role must still be considered peripheral.

Worldwide bodies involved in the educational-cultural arena include the Jewish Agency, which represents the Zionist point of view and Israel's interests, and which works most extensively in the realm of adult education and in linking Jewish students with Israel. The Memorial Foundation for Jewish Culture, an international body with headquarters in New York, has become the most potent source of support for Jewish scholarly and cultural activities, since its resources exceed those of any other institution on the scene.

Among the scholarly associations and research institutes, the YIVO Institute for Jewish Research and the American Jewish Historical Society are probably the most potent independent bodies actually engaged in projects, but their activities are distinctly limited, mainly because of monetary insufficiencies. In general, these bodies are small, independent, and outside the mainstream of American Jewish life.

Except for the Jewish Publication Society (JPS) and the small seminary and movement publication programs, publication is a private enterprise in American Jewish life. The JPS is the most significant publishing force on the American Jewish scene, and the only one seriously linked with other institutions in the Jewish community. Only recently has the publication of Jewish books for profit expanded much beyond the textbook business.

What is important about the cultural activities of American Jewry is how peripheral those engaged in them are in the context of American Jewish public affairs. Since the cultural institutions do not even have the advantage of feeling needed by the decision-makers, as is true of Jewish education, they are at a great disadvantage in a community that is not much oriented to scholarly or cultural concerns.

COMMUNITY RELATIONS SPHERE

Most major Jewish communities have a Jewish Community Relations Council which considers itself the central agency for handling community relations problems. In addition, communities often have local offices or chapters of the American Jewish Committee, the Anti-Defamation League of B'nai B'rith, the American Jewish Congress, the Jewish War Veterans, and the Jewish Labor Committee that also engage in community relations work, whether in cooperation with the Jewish Community Relations Council or independently. Indeed, the classic pictures of fragmentation in American Jewish life are usually drawn in regard to the community relations field, and it was in that field that the most publicized countrywide efforts have been made to bring order out of chaos, beginning with the development of the National Community Relations Advisory Council in the 1940s. The latter is a confederation of independent agencies combining both local agencies and countrywide bodies in one league. Of course it is limited in its role precisely because it is a confederation of bodies which are powerful and independent in their own right.

In the educational-cultural and religious-congregational spheres the situation is so structured that the many separate organizations engage in relatively little direct competition. In the community relations sphere, on the other hand, the smaller number of separate organizations overlap because they deal with the same problems, often the same explicit issues. The effects of that competition are potentially great because they are directed toward matters that reach outside of the Jewish community and directly affect its relations with the larger world. Consequently, a considerable amount of self-policing and specialization has developed within the sphere in the past two decades.

The American Jewish Committee, the Anti-Defamation League, and the American Jewish Congress, conventionally recognized as the big three in community relations work, are the most centralized of all countrywide Jewish organizations. Their role in American Jewish life was originally enhanced by their centralized structures at a time when the local Jewish communities were barely organized and the individual institutions within them were too parochial to reach out to the general community. Today their situation is reversed, and they have managed to thrive only through decentralization. The American Jewish Congress, perhaps the most centralized, has not properly taken root on the local plane, and as a result is suffering tremendously as a countrywide organization. The Anti-Defamation League and the American Jewish Committee began earlier to achieve substantial decentralization, though in both cases the national office still plays a major role even in local activities.

More recently, the synagogue movements have attempted to enter the community relations field as part of their drive toward dominance in American Jewish life. Bodies such as the Synagogue Council, the Commission on Social Action of Reform Judaism, and the National Commission on Law and Public Affairs of the Orthodox movement reflect this. However, they still play a relatively limited role in the overall scene.

Increased American Jewish involvement in the concerns of the Jewish people as a whole has sharpened the need for a communal voice that speaks as one, at least in the foreign relations field. This, in turn, has led to the establishment of the Presidents' Conference, consisting of presidents of the major countrywide Jewish organizations who meet together to make policy decisions that the more institutionalized consultative bodies cannot. Since the Presidents' Conference must make all decisions unanimously, it is limited in the degree to which it can play an active role in its prescribed area, but it has brought some order at least in matters pertaining strictly to foreign relations.

Since support and assistance for Israel are now key items on the community relations agenda, the Israeli government has become a prime mover in this sphere. Despite occasional protests to the contrary, official American Jewish action on behalf of Israel in the public relations field is conducted in close consultation with and in response to the initiatives of Israeli authorities. In certain respects, Israel's role in the community relations sphere may well be greater than its role in any other sphere of decision-making in the American Jewish community.

COMMUNAL-WELFARE SPHERE

The communal-welfare sphere has undergone the greatest change in the past generation. As late as the 1950s it was simply another functional grouping among several, albeit considerably better organized internally, since the various Jewish social service and welfare agencies and the Jewish community centers had federated with one another a generation or more earlier. While the local federations had already expanded to include fund-raising for overseas needs, their pretensions to centrality in the community were limited by the fact that, on the domestic scene, they remained concerned primarily with traditional social service functions.

By the end of the 1950s, the federations had been transformed into the major fund-raising bodies in the community, and stood on the threshold of a whole new world of responsibilities. The latter transformation came as federations realized that proper execution of their role as allocating agencies necessitated involvement in community planning of a scope that at least touched all the activities defined as communitywide in any given locality. At the same time, the old leadership in the communal-welfare field, consisting predominantly of Jews of German background, was being broadened to include Jews of Eastern European origin as well, selected from the same income, occupational, and observance levels.

The decade of the 1960s saw the federations undertake community planning on a scale beyond that required for simple allocation of funds. They also acquired greater responsibility for and interest in Jewish education, as well as continuing and deepening their relationships with their constituent social service and welfare agencies. In the process, most made strong efforts to broaden their leadership base so as to include new segments of the community.

All this has served to enhance the central role of the federations locally and to give them the best—if not unrivaled—claim to being the umbrella organizations. There is no question that the key to the growth of the power of the local federations is that they have become the major fund-raising bodies on the American scene. Even though money and influence are not necessarily correlated on a one-to-one basis, there is unquestionably a relationship between the two. Locally, as agencies become more dependent upon the federation for funds, they are more likely to be included in the ambit of federation planning and policy-making.

The same pattern has repeated itself on the countrywide plane, though in a less clear-cut way. The difference is that the CJFWF does not have the fund-raising power of the local federations, and consequently has no such monetary power to exercise over the parallel national associations. The Jewish Welfare Board, for example, is funded the same way as the CJFWF—by direct grants from its local constituents and the local federations, thus limiting the possibilities of CJFWF influence on indirect grants. The national community relations and religious organizations are even more independent.

A new addition to the communal-welfare scene is the Israeli element, the result of the large role played by the federations in raising funds for Israel's needs. The government of Israel has special concerns in American Jewish life which it pursues in many ways, but is finding it increasingly advantageous to pursue within the context of the communal-welfare sphere. The Jewish Agency, particularly since its recent reconstitution, has virtually coopted the federation leadership as its representative non-Zionists, creating an even tighter bond between the institutionalized representatives of the World Zionist movement and the American Jewish community. In both cases, the institutionalization of relationships is still in its incipient stages.

ISRAEL-OVERSEAS SPHERE

This area is both the best organized and the best integrated of all the spheres. Integration dates back to World War I and the founding of the American Jewish Joint Distribution Committee (JDC). In general, the sphere has two interlocking wings, one concerned with fund-raising and the other with political-cum-educational activity. Responsibilities for fund-raising are divided between the federations which handle the United Jewish Appeal (UJA), the Israel Bonds Organization, the Jewish National Fund, and the various friends of Israeli or overseas institutions. Political-cum-educational activities are conducted primarily through the Zionist organizations that are now at least nominally united (except for the Zionist Organization of America [ZOA]) into an American Zionist Federation.

Since the potentiality for competition among these organizations is great, and the need to cooperate for the common good of Israel is universal among them, a system of negotiated sharing has been developed through a network of agreements dividing the funds and/or the campaign arenas. The basic agreements are those reached nationally between representatives of the federations working through the CJFWF and the UJA, dividing the funds raised in the local campaigns. A second agreement, among the UJA, the Israel Bonds Organization, and the various "Friends" groups, more or less spells out their respective jurisdictions and claims to various methods of fundraising. Thus Israel Bonds has a right to make synagogue appeals, while direct solicitation is a province of the UJA through the federations. The problem of cooperation among the Zionist organizations has been more difficult. Since, with the exception of Hadassah, they are tied to the great national (read worldwide Jewish) Zionist parties that participate in the political life of Israel, they have been less than willing to cooperate on the local scene until very recently.

Naturally, the Israel-overseas sphere is substantially influenced by sources outside of the United States. The Israeli government and the Jewish Agency take an active role in the fund-raising process. Similarly, the Jewish National Fund and the Keren Hayesod become active participants, both through the Jewish Agency and to some extent directly on the American scene as well. Aside from these Israel-based bodies, the JDC, the Organization for Rehabilitation and Training (ORT), and the Claims Conference are also involved in the worldwide activities of the Jewish people, both as beneficiaries and constituents of the American Jewish bodies functioning in the field. Their role has been of great significance in the postwar period. The JDC in particular has become the bearer of American Jewish know-how as well as money wherever there are Jewish communities in need of redevelopment.

Basic Divisions in the Decision-Making Arenas

RELIGIOUS AND SECULAR

The division between the religious and the secular developed out of the American milieu and was enhanced in the early days of the twentieth century by the relatively sharp division between those Jews who concerned themselves with their *shuls* and those who, while members of synagogues and temples, were really far more interested in welfare and community relations activities which they saw as divorced from religion per se. This led to the rise of two separate groups of decision-makers. By their very nature, synagogues were localistic institutions, while the secular services became the province of the cosmopolitans.

Despite all the forces making for separation, the division did not remain hard and fast. Indeed, it has been breaking down since the end of World War II. In the first place, there was the great expansion of those educational and cultural functions which could not be neatly divided between the two. Moreover, as the synagogues grew in power in the 1950s and began to see themselves as the true custodians of American Jewish life, they started to claim authoritative roles in areas previously reserved to the secular side. Finally, the whole thrust of Jewish tradition militated against such a separation as artificially enforced. As those concerned with the secular side became more involved in Jewish life, they saw their services as functions that had a specifically Jewish content, and were no less religious in the traditional Jewish sense than the functions of the synagogues. Nevertheless, while ideologically and functionally the lines between the two are weakening, structurally the separation between religious and secular institutions remains as strong as ever.

PUBLIC AND PRIVATE

While there is little conscious perception of the distinction between public and private (partly because there is some notion that, vis-à-vis governmental activities, all Jewish communal activities are private), nevertheless the activities sponsored or funded by the federations and their constituent agencies are implicitly understood to be the public activities of the American Jewish community. The argument for "communal responsibility" essentially has been designed to define them in that manner.

Synagogues, on the other hand, have continued to be regarded as private. Only in the last few years has the notion of the synagogues as private enterprises been questioned within Jewish communal circles, and then only privately, in a belated recognition of the fact that a congregation of 1,000 to 2,000 families, providing a range of services far beyond simple maintenance of the weekly and yearly prayer schedule, is not the same as a collection of twenty or forty men gathered together primarily for a *minyan*. In part, this recognition is a response to the synagogues' encroachment upon the traditionally communal sector. It is also a reflection of the suburbanization of American Jewry, whereby synagogues have become major centers of community activities in their respective suburbs—if not the *only* centers—and movement of a major synagogue from one neighborhood to another affects the whole course of Jewish life within a locale.

COSMOPOLITANS AND LOCALS

The public-private distinction, as it is implicitly recognized in Jewish life today, follows along the lines of the dichotomy between cosmopolitans and locals described by social scientists. Briefly, cosmopolitans are those who see the whole community as a single entity and maintain connections and involvements across all of it. While their cosmopolitanism is first defined in relation to a particular local community, once they develop a cosmopolitan outlook toward the local community they almost invariably take a cosmopolitan view of the larger world of which that community is a part. Locals, on the other hand, are those whose involvement and connections are confined to a small segment of the total community—a neighborhood, a particular social group, or, in Jewish life, a particular synagogue, organization, or club. Their involvement rests overwhelmingly on their commitment to that point of attachment and does not extend to the community as a whole, except indirectly. Moreover, their perceptions of the larger world are quite limited, based as they are on their localistic involvements.

To a very real extent, this is a natural division in society. At the same time, all cosmopolitans have clearly localistic needs—to be tied to something more intimate than the community in the abstract, or even to a set of institutions which must inevitably be depersonalized to some degree. Similarly, locals can be mobilized for essentially cosmopolitan purposes when those purposes strike home at the source of their involvement. Thus every community needs institutions devoted to serving both cosmopolitan and local needs, as well as the local needs of cosmopolitans and the cosmopolitan needs of locals.

In the Jewish community, the organizations and agencies that fall within the federation family generally represent the cosmopolitan interests, and consequently attract cosmopolitans to leadership positions. The synagogues, on the other hand, represent localistic needs and interests, which is actually their primary role (although often neglected in the large contemporary American congregation). Consequently, the leadership they attract consists of a high percentage of locals.

PROFESSIONALS AND VOLUNTEERS

The other major division among decision-makers in the American Jewish community is that between professional and voluntary leaders, with the professionals further subdivided into those whose training is obtained through religious institutions and those whose training is secular. The American Jewish community has the most professionalized leadership of any in the world, probably the most of any in Jewish history. The roots of this undoubtedly lie in the commitment to professionalization which envelops the larger American society.

The day-to-day business of the Jewish community is now almost exclusively in the hands of professionals, or at least people who are paid for their services even if they do not meet professional standards or consider themselves as forever committed to Jewish careers. Because these professionals are involved on a daily basis with the problems of the community, they exercise great influence in its decision-making. On the other hand, there has been no diminution in the number of voluntary leaders. Parallel roles for professionals and volunteers have developed in virtually every Jewish organization and institution, allowing for extensive participation by both. What is not fixed is the way in which they relate to each other.

In some cases the relationship between professionals and volunteers is resolved by separation of functions, and in some by a mixing of functions. As a general rule, wherever the requirements of the profession are most exclusive and demanding, and the need for professional expertise established, separation of functions tends to be the norm. Wherever the line between professional competence and volunteer talent is least distinct, sharing tends to be the norm. Thus, in the rabbinate, Jewish education, and certain of the Jewish social services, operations as well as much policy-making power, are placed in the hands of professionals, who are viewed as trained to bring to their tasks an expertise that endows them with a special role. In such cases, the voluntary leadership often confines itself to endorsing or ratifying policies suggested by professionals, developing and approving very general organizational goals and principles, and finding the necessary monetary and community support for their enterprise, only intervening more actively when the professionals fail to provide the requisite leadership.

In community relations and fund-raising, the lines that divide professionals and volunteers tend to be relatively weak. Professionals are often treated as if they cannot claim very much in the way of expertise (other than the expertise of experience) for handling what are essentially political tasks. In fact, they gain their substantial influence because they are specially trained and, most important, spend all of their working time at what they do, enabling them to know the situation better than the voluntary leadership. Like all professionals, their special power is based on the extent to which they control the amount and kind of information that reaches their volunteer counterparts. In addition, their control of in-house planning, their ability to influence the appointment of voluntary leaders to particular committees, and the fact that they provide continuity in the life of the organization adds to their power. At the same time, some of the volunteers may have special talents, capabilities, or positions, particularly political ones, which place them in strategic positions within the organizations and give them major roles in the decision-making process hardly different from those of the professionals. In fact, the process usually finds volunteers and professionals working in tandem with minimum conflict on common problems.

The sources of professional and volunteer leadership in the community help to mark the division. By and large, the volunteers are recruited from among the wealthier elements associated with any particular function or institution. This is partly because the hierarchy of influence among voluntary leadership is often established in terms of size of contribution, and partly because the costs of playing a leadership role are such that only the well-to-do can afford the time and money. Aside from successful businessmen, professionals, and perhaps young lawyers associated with law firms with a tradition of participation in Jewish communal life, the only people who can contribute the requisite time are academicians, and they are limited by their inability to spend the money required to maintain an active role. Thus, wealth becomes an important factor in determining the voluntary leadership.

This situation is not quite as stark as it seems. Obviously it is far less true in the case of small synagogues and clubs (the most localistic institutions) and most true in the case of the UJA (the most cosmopolitan). Even where wealth is of great importance, it does not function as the only measure of leadership. The wealthiest men are not necessarily the most important leaders. There is apparently some threshold of prosperity past which most men are relatively equal in the pursuit of leadership roles. A man of modest means, from the perspective of the very wealthy, may choose to allocate a high proportion of his resources to the Jewish community and be recognized accordingly, while a man of great means may not be willing to make such a major allocation, and thus will remain unrecognized. Moreover, beyond the willingness to give there must be a willingness to serve.

The Decision-Makers: Their Roles and Functions

There are at least five categories of decision-makers functioning in the Jewish community today. Three of these are dominated by professionals (rabbis, communal workers, and Jewish educators) and two are dominated by lay personnel (congregational boards and volunteers). These categories, in turn, fall into two divisions: congregational decision-makers (rabbis, congregational boards) and communal decision-makers (communal workers, volunteers). (The educators, as we shall see, form a kind of class of their own.)

RABBIS

At the very least, rabbis function as decision-makers within their congregations, while the more talented, important, well-known, or cosmopolitan among them are able to build upon their rabbinical roles to become decision-makers in the larger arena of Jewish communal life as well. Rabbis generally tend to be restricted to their congregations or to their synagogue movements by their reluctance to venture outside of the area in which their authority is rarely questioned.

It is difficult for rabbis to shift roles when they leave the congregational setting, as they would have to do if they were to participate, say, in communal-welfare activities. There they would have to participate as if among equals, but with neither the special competence of professionals nor with any claim to special recognition by virtue of their rabbinical positions. A relationship of equality in such a situation is uncomfortable for both sides, since neither knows how to respond to the other. Thus, it is more convenient for a rabbi simply not to participate.

The field of education and culture, however, is one area in which rabbis can participate fully, although rabbis are not especially eager to become professional leaders in this area for at least two reasons. First, Jewish education tends to enjoy a relatively low status in the eyes of the voluntary leaders who control their destinies as rabbis; second, American rabbis rarely have the training or time to develop excellence in Jewish scholarship to a degree that would give them the kind of status they demand—and receive—in the pulpit.

When the Jewish community was smaller, its leadership concentrated in fewer hands, and its functions (and finances) more limited, a few dynamic rabbis could rise to positions of communal eminence by dint of their virtuosity. None of those conditions prevails today, and the virtuoso rabbi has gone the way of his secular counterpart. Another reason why rabbis are not found in the forefront of American Jewish leadership is that synagogues are essentially localistic institutions, and rabbis, no matter how cosmopolitan in outlook, must adapt themselves to localistic needs and interests.

CONGREGATIONAL BOARDS

Since synagogues account for so much of Jewish activity in the United States today, the men and women who comprise the congregational boards of trustees must be considered important decision-makers, though they are rarely recognized as such. This lack of recognition stems from the fact that there are so many congregations in the United States, each controlling its own budget, hiring its own personnel, establishing its own program, and building its own facilities with barely any reference to an outside body.

The congregations spend no less than $100,000,000 a year, and perhaps as much as $500,000,000. This is an amount of money equal to that contributed to the federations and the UJA in the very best years of their drives.

There are over 4,500 Jewish congregations in the United States, according to the fragmentary figures available. Should the average size of the congregational board be ten members (probably an underestimate), this would mean at least 45,000 congregational board members. In fact, the number is probably larger than that. When we add to the congregational boards the number of men who serve on congregational committees, the number of potential decision-makers increases even further, and our knowledge of what they do and how they do it diminishes even more.

Every form of decision-making is to be found in the government of Jewish congregations in America, ranging from the most autocratic, in which one man decides all congregational policy, hires, fires, and decides as he pleases on all issues, to situations in which the most open forms of town-meeting democracy prevail, and the congregation governs itself without the mediation of any board.

At this stage of our knowledge, it would be difficult to describe the "typical" congregational board member or even the typical congregational board. What unites them all is their essentially localistic commitment to the primary needs of their own congregations. It is rare to find a congregational board that, in its official capacity, will concern itself with the needs of the larger community, even when its members may, in other capacities, be major communal leaders.

This fragmentation of outlook has great consequences for the community as a whole, particularly as regards the largest congregations, with membership of a thousand families or more. The consequences are obviously far less important in connection with congregations of fifty families. What is most important is that even congregations of medium size, whose actions are not likely to jolt the Jewish community as a whole in the manner of the largest ones, have a tremendous impact on the character of the community by virtue of their control over the education of their children.

Relations between rabbis and congregational boards stand at the heart of the congregational decision-making process. While the variety is again great, three general models can be found. The congregational board, or the dominant authority figure in the congregation, may simply dominate the rabbi, confining him to conducting services and carrying out similar ritual chores. In some cases, rabbis are not even allowed to attend congregational board meetings. In other situations, the diametrically opposite condition prevails; the rabbi is so strong that he dominates the congregational board, which exists primarily to mediate between him and the congregation as a whole, or to carry out his wishes in areas where he does not want to be directly or extensively involved. Finally there is the most prevalent situation, in which some kind of division of functions is worked out between the congregational leadership and the rabbi, with decision-making shared in certain relatively clear-cut areas.

COMMUNAL WORKERS

Communal workers gain their power on the basis of either expertise or day-to-day involvement with the problems of the community. Their technical knowledge and perennial availability give them important decision-making roles unless they are directly challenged by voluntary leadership. This rarely happens because, in most cases, the voluntary leadership does not feel interested or competent enough to challenge them.

At present it is likely that the majority of Jewish communal workers have been trained as social workers, with legal training in second place. In relatively few cases are the senior civil servants of the Jewish community trained specifically for Jewish positions; usually they simply fall into such positions as a result of happenstance. This is less true among the younger workers. Jewish agencies, in an effort to overcome the personnel problem, have made some effort to provide their recruits with the resources to attend secular schools for social work training, on condition that they then serve the agencies for a specified period of time.

For the most part, the communal workers are not well grounded in traditional Jewish learning, or even in rudimentary knowledge of Jewish history, law, society, or customs. Consequently, their deficiencies are most glaring when it comes to making decisions involving the Jewishness of their programs. Since their expertise in other respects tends to be among the best available in the country, the contrast is rendered even sharper. This is not to say that many of them have not become seriously interested in fostering the Jewish aspects of their work, but they are in a difficult position when it comes to translating attitudes into concrete programs.

VOLUNTEERS

We have almost no data on the voluntary leaders of the American Jewish community, but one thing that does mark them is their relative wealth, although this is not the only criterion, and energy. They are heavily confined to community relations, communal-welfare, and Israel-overseas activities. Volunteers are a group for whom Jewish activity is a means of expressing Jewishness. In effect, their activity becomes their religion, and their observance is conditioned by the demands of communal life. Some of them are involved in communal leadership primarily for the honor, but many others work as persistently as their professional counterparts for little recognition.

Money and energy are thus key sources of such influence over decision-making as the volunteers have, although neither replaces talent when it comes to the actual decision-making process. Money may buy a man the presidency of an organization or agency, and energy may put a man in a leadership position, but some kind of talent is necessary if a person is actually to have a share in making decisions. This is true if only because of the role of the professionals in screening the advancement of the voluntary leadership.

In at least one area—fund-raising—volunteers are the dominant decision-makers. No matter how much professional help is provided, it is only the voluntary leadership, the men who give the money, who are able to influence others to give money. Moreover, with respect to fund-raising they usually feel that they have as much expertise as anyone else, and therefore are less likely to defer to the ideas or demands of the professionals.

Volunteers are probably representative of the more Jewishly committed elements in the mainstream of the American Jewish community, despite the fact that they are rarely elected to the offices they occupy in any meaningful sense of the term. They are representative because there is a certain sameness in American Jewry; their desires, tastes, attitudes, interests, and educational backgrounds probably depart very little from the norm among the majority of American Jews.

JEWISH EDUCATORS

Jewish educators are considered apart from rabbis and communal workers because they generally pass through different forms of training and pursue different career lines. While some men trained as rabbis become Jewish educators, most educators decided upon Jewish education as a career before entering rabbinical school. It can fairly be said that the educators' decision-making role is confined to the sphere of Jewish education, that is, to schools or camps where they exercise authority as professionals. However, their authority is limited by various external factors. Chief among these are the problems inherent in Jewish education in the United States—the ambivalence of parents regarding the amount of Jewish education they wish their children to acquire, the problems of obtaining qualified teachers and adequate financial support, and the fact that education is lodged in the synagogue, the leadership of which has other priorities.

Still, within this framework there is usually little interest in what the Jewish educators teach except on the part of the rabbi, who may intervene to assure that "loyalty to the institution" is given first priority. Beyond that, even the rabbis tend to pay little attention to the day-to-day operations of "their" schools. A Jewish educator may do more or less what he pleases in his school with little outside interference, provided he does not do anything that violates the Jewish communal consensus.

Decision-Making Tasks

The tasks to which the various categories of decision-makers address themselves are all ultimately geared to the question of Jewish survival. Given this overriding interest, the Jewish community's two most important concerns are defense and education.

DEFENSE

The major defense concerns have changed radically within recent years. From the 1870s through the 1930s, domestic anti-Semitism was the dominant concern of the community. Beginning with the 1930s, this was gradually replaced by efforts to defend Jews in other parts of the world. However, after 1948, Israel became the major focus of Jewish attention; since 1967, insuring the survival of Israel has become the heart of the defense function of the American Jewish community. Even the community relations agencies are now spending a high proportion of their time and resources trying to increase support for Israel in the United States. As a result, the most important decision-makers in the community are those who are related to the defense of Israel, namely, the federation and UJA leadership, voluntary and professional.

EDUCATION

Education is now being recognized as an equally essential concern. Meeting Jewish educational needs is somewhat problematic for the community, since it exposes all the ambivalences of contemporary Jewish life, creating a clash between the desire for survival as a people with the desire for full integration into the general society. Jewish education therefore requires a great measure of commitment to the notion that Jews are different and must educate their children to be different. All agree that Jewish education is important, but the character of the commitment is a different matter. American Jewish education reflects all the ambiguities, and that is one reason why major decision-makers rarely play any real role in the educational field, and why those who are professionally involved in Jewish education are not major decision-makers in the community.

Since these ambivalences are not easily overcome, there is not likely to be any dramatic change in the foreseeable future, although there has been a consistent if gradual increase in support for Jewish schools over the last twenty years. It is now clear that the major decision-makers are willing to provide some kind of minimum base support for Jewish education locally through the federations and their appropriate constituent agencies. This minimum base is progressively being defined upwards, but it remains a base line, not an aggressively advancing one. Moreover, the federations are discouraged from moving beyond the minimum by the unresolved division over control of Jewish education between the community as a whole and the individual synagogues.

SOCIAL SERVICES AND WELFARE

Decision-makers who are most involved in social services and welfare have been losing importance on the communal scene. This is partly because the social services themselves have become progressively less Jewish in appearance, if not in fact, and partly because the rise of the welfare state has reduced their significance in American Jewish life. Jewish hospitals, for example, are now simply institutions sponsored by the Jewish community as one of its contributions to the welfare of American society as a whole. The Jewish community maintains its stake in such institutions partly because it is a customary way of making a contribution to the life of the general community, partly because it provides a bridge to other minority groups with whom the Jewish community wants to maintain good relations, and partly because there is some strong, if unspoken, sentiment in the Jewish community that it is well for Jews to have such institutions under their supervision "just in case."

Pressures are also mounting for the social welfare agencies to give representation on their governing bodies to their non-Jewish clients. While most Jewish communities have resisted those pressures, the fact that the institutions are supported only partially from Jewish funds and heavily by United Fund and government contributions or grants makes it more difficult to hold the line.

Certain of the institutions which are presently considered to be within the social-service sphere are now seeking to broaden their interests, usually by moving into the area of education and culture. This is particularly true of the Jewish community centers, whose social-service functions have been reduced as their educational and cultural functions have increased. Today some Jewish community centers appear to be secular rivals of the synagogues.

FINANCE

Community finance is obviously a central task of the American Jewish community, and the raising of money is a continuing activity. Indeed, such is its importance in determining the organization of Jewish communal life that, from a strictly organizational point of view, it may be considered the most important task of all.

Two major struggles which have developed and been essentially resolved in the area of fund-raising have had significant consequences for the organizational structure and patterns of decision-making in the community. The first was the struggle within each locality as to whether or not to centralize the raising of funds for Jewish communal purposes. By and large, the decision has been to centralize fund-raising for most purposes other than those that fall within the religious-congregational sphere. This struggle led to the creation of the Jewish federations, which, by standing astride of general fund-raising, have acquired the central decision-making role in the community.

The second struggle was between local and national organizations over who should be responsible for the raising of funds. The local organizations won the lion's share of the victory, gaining control over fund-raising even for most national and international purposes. This victory has substantially strengthened the power of the local communities in the overall framework of American Jewish life.

Decision-Making Modes

In the final analysis, what can we say about the decision-making modes of the American Jewish community? A number of modes may be identified. We will consider six of these: (1) the penchant for government by committee; (2) the urge to avoid conflict; (3) the legitimacy of tension between the national office and local affiliates; (4) the patterns of duplication and interorganizational competition; (5) the sources of innovation and the initiation of programs; and (6) the role of personalities in the decision-making process.

GOVERNMENT BY COMMITTEE

The immediate organizational tool of decision-making in the American Jewish community is the committee. Committees—in all shapes, sizes, and forms—carry out the variegated business of the community from the smallest synagogue to the Presidents' Conference (itself simply a high level committee). The multiplicity of committees within organizations and institutions provides for a certain degree of diffusion of power among many decision-makers, and something akin to an intra-institutional "checks and balances" system.

Power and influence accrue to those who can control the committees and their work. Personality conflicts may well be focused more sharply in committees. Consequently, the dynamics of committee behavior are at least a partial factor in any decisions made by the leadership of the American Jewish community.

CONFLICT AVOIDANCE

Despite the existence of conflict as part of life's reality, conflict avoidance is a major principle in American Jewish decision-making. Especially where voluntary leaders are involved, every effort is made to avoid open conflict. When issues are such that they are likely to provoke conflict, there is a tendency to avoid raising them in the first place. When such an issue must be raised, the inclination is to develop a decision in such a way that there is no chance for the conflict to be expressed.

In part, this avoidance of conflict reflects the traditional desire of a minority to avoid risking any weakening of the ties that bind its members together. But it also reflects the fact that the voluntary leaders in the American Jewish community are overwhelmingly recruited from the world of business and commerce, where open conflict is considered bad form and decisions are reached in such a way as to minimize the appearance of conflict, if not its reality.

The desire to avoid open conflict clearly rules out some issues from consideration, no matter how important they might be. It also enhances the role of the professional leadership, since it enables them to administer the community rather than requiring the voluntary leaders to *govern* it. In such situations, the tendency is to rely upon the men trusted with the administration to make what still are, in the end, political decisions. Thus the professionals continue to gain power simply because they can organize decision-making so as to minimize the emergence of conflict, thereby earning the appreciation of the voluntary leadership.

LOCAL AFFILIATES VS. THE "NATIONAL OFFICE"

One perennial conflict which is considered legitimate, provided it is not allowed to spread beyond limited tactical skirmishes, is the tension between the "national office" and the local affiliates. In part, it reflects the simple difference in constituency and interest of the two sectors, and in part it reflects a difference in the situation between Jews in the New York metropolitan area, with its particular set of problems, and

Jews in other, smaller communities with a different scale of operations.

This tension, by its very nature, can never finally be resolved, but shifts which take place in its structure bring about immediate changes in the community's decision-making patterns. What can be said about the present situation, in general terms, is that those organizations which have traditionally been New York-centered are losing power in the community as a whole, while those whose locus of power is in the localities are gaining.

"DUPLICATION" AND INTERORGANIZATIONAL COMPETITION

Interorganizational competition within the same sphere ("duplication") is another perennial feature of the American Jewish scene, stemming from the voluntary and associational character of the community. The attack on duplication is part of the standard rhetoric of American Jewish community life. At the same time, competition itself is not always a negative phenomenon. Moreover, on the local plane, organizations functioning within the same sphere often develop patterns of sharing that effectively divide tasks so as to minimize overlapping. Duplication is not likely to disappear on the American Jewish scene, or even to be substantially reduced in the ways in which reformers usually suggest, because there is no realistic way to curb the proliferation of organizations. When organizational consolidation does take place, it usually reflects a tightening of the belt to cope with decline, a retreat rather than a step forward, such as in the recent formation of the American Zionist Federation.

This is not to say that all efforts to control duplication reflect weakness. Within the sphere of community relations, for example, coordination came about at a time when the individual organizations were all flourishing. Furthermore, even though some of the same organizations are now doing poorly, they are not interested in consolidation, but are rather redoubling their efforts to survive.

Recognition of the realities of interorganizational competition is not the same as condoning the semi-anarchy which prevails in some sectors of American Jewish life, and which is justified in the name of a specious "pluralism" that is no more than a reflection of organizational self-interest. What is needed are better means of enhancing coordination and limiting harmful duplication in ways that are consonant with the American situation.

INNOVATION AND PROGRAM INITIATION

While decision-making in connection with established programs is more or less shared by the professional and voluntary leadership, innovation and program initiation are usually dominated by the professionals, if only because they are involved in organizational and institutional affairs on a day-to-day basis and are recognized as the custodians of programmatic expertise. Their positions, then, make them the initiators of a high proportion of new activities and programs and the prime generators of new ideas. They may not be the only innovators and initiators, but there is no question that they bear a disproportionate share of the responsibility in these areas.

PERSONALITIES

The role of personalities in decision-making is not to be underestimated, even though there have been substantial changes in this regard in recent years. Ironically, personality conflicts are particularly significant at the highest levels in the national organizations. Perhaps because they are so detached from operational responsibilities, the top leaders can indulge in the luxury of personality conflicts. In the local communities, operational necessities lead to greater efforts to control such conflicts.

Problems and Prospects

Despite the limitations of the data, it is not unfair to conclude that the American Jewish community is governed by what may be termed a "trusteeship of doers and givers," in which decision-makers who are generally self-selected on the basis of their willingness to participate hold the reins of communal life in all its facets. They perceive their function as managing the community's affairs in trust for its members, the Jewish people as a whole, just as earlier generations of leaders saw themselves as managing the community's affairs as trustees of God. It is this sense of trusteeship which keeps the communal leadership from being an oligarchy, or a small body that manages the community for its own profit. Every significant Jewish interest has the right to claim a place in the trusteeship, and is accorded that place once it brings its claim to the attention of the appropriate leadership.

Although it is not elected in any systemically competitive manner, the trusteeship is representative of American Jewry in that it reflects the attitudes, values, and interests of the community—except perhaps in one respect. The leaders are probably more positively Jewish than the community's rank and file.

A trusteeship of doers and givers seems to be the system that is fated for American Jewry, and probably for any Jewish community living in a voluntaristic environment like the United States. Those modern Jewish communities which have experimented with communal elections have not found them any better a solution to the problem of representation, because the turnout in these elections tends to be extremely low. Moreover, a voting procedure does not guarantee the election of statesmen to communal leadership. Elections do have one important consequence, however. They raise to the inner circles of leadership men whose qualifications are not simply financial. In most cases these are men who have gained leadership of an important organizational bloc within the community which is able to turn out its members to vote. As such, they are more likely to be attuned to straightforward political considerations than big donors who do not have to conciliate constituencies in any way.

To the extent that it is desirable to broaden the community's leadership base, it may turn out to be necessary to provide support for those potential voluntary leaders who cannot afford to work for the Jewish community under present conditions. Perhaps there should be funds made available for the reimbursement of officers of major Jewish bodies so that they may take a leave of absence from their normal occupations during their tenure of office without suffering financial loss. Such an arrangement would open the doors of leadership to many people who presently cannot entertain the notion of assuming positions in American Jewish life beyond the synagogue level. There is no doubt that this would lead some people to make their careers in the Jewish communal world, not as professional administrators but as communal politicians. This would open up a different set of problems and possibilities, but it might be worth the effort.

The fact that elections are not likely to accomplish the purposes for which they are instituted does not mean that ways cannot be developed to involve a wider segment of the American Jewish community in its crucial decision-making bodies. In any case, efforts in that direction must be founded on the recognition that trusteeship is likely to be the persistent form in American Jewish life. What is called for, then, is an attempt to make the trusteeships properly representative.

This might involve encouragement of a whole host of tendencies already present on the American scene, and the addition of others. The strengthening of the federation movement, for example, might offer the best opportunity for creating a systematic decision-making structure. In this connection, it is vital that the synagogues cease to be considered the private property of their members and be recognized for what they are—public institutions bearing significant communal responsibilities. This is not an argument against congregationalism; indeed, there is every reason to foster true congregational spirit in synagogues of proper scale, provided that it is not a euphemism for communal anarchy.

If this could be accomplished, it might be possible to devise ways in which elections conducted through the congregations would form a major part of the basis of representation in the federations, so that the leadership recruitment process would reach down into every segment of the community. Under such circumstances federations would become more completely and thoroughly communal agencies. Moreover, it would be possible to make better determinations as to who should conduct and finance the different activities of the Jewish community. The advances suggested here should be made on a proper federal basis, in the spirit of Jewish institutions, not through local or national centralization of power.

The greatest organizational problem in American Jewish life is no longer the problem of organization on the local plane, but the linkage between those bodies which purport to speak for the Jewish community countrywide. With some notable exceptions, they are the ones that are least harnessed to any kind of communitywide constituency. Not only do they claim inaccurately to speak for more than their membership, but they often do not speak for those who are affiliated with them.

It is not enough to say that their roles should be reduced, because in fact they do, or at least can, play a necessary role in the community. Rather, efforts must be made to guide them toward the role they can play profitably for all concerned, a role which will add to their own power at a time when so many of them are losing power.

The great community relations and mass-based organizations must become the effective equivalents of political parties and interest groups on the American Jewish scene. That is to say, they should assume the task of raising the difficult questions, suggesting the important innovations, and then taking the appropriate action that will lead to change within bodies that, by their very nature, must be more conservative and conciliatory if they are to maintain the communal consensus necessary for the community to remain united.

INDEX

AAJE. *See* American Association for Jewish Education (AAJE)

Alcalay, Rabbi, 28

Alliance Israélite Universelle, 28

American Association for Jewish Education (AAJE), 188, 201, 285, 289, 292–293

American Conference on Soviet Jewry, 146, 149

American Council for Judaism, 31, 34

American Jewish Committee, 16–17, 30, 34, 143, 161, 286, 294, 295

American Jewish Conference, 31

American Jewish Congress, 17, 30, 143, 286, 294

American Jewish Historical Society, 293

American Jewish Joint Distribution Committee (JDC), 297, 298

American Jewish Year Book, 72, 89, 90, 157, 175

American Jewry: affiliated Jews, 144; age composition, 104–107; and anti-Semitism, 44; assimilationists, 149, 150; associated Jews, 144, 145; associational framework, 278–279; associationalism, 140, 141, 142; basic divisions in decision-making, 298–300; before 1870, 67, 71; at beginning of 1970s, 67, 71, 72; character of, 271–276; and communal organizations, 143–144; communal-welfare sphere, 290, 295–297; communal workers, 302, 303, 305–306; community relations sphere, 290, 294–295; and concept of minorities, 59; congregational boards, 303, 304–305; cosmopolitans and locals, 299–300; decision-making tasks, 307–310; defense concerns, 307–308; demographic analysis, 65–126; dynamics of change, 66; economic participation, 54; education, 107–112, 226, 227; educational concerns, 307, 308; educational-cultural sphere, 290, 291–293; and emancipation, 48; emigration to Israel, 145–146; fertility, 74–78; finance and fundraising, 309–310; generational change, 101–104; growth from 1880 to mid-1920s, 66, 67; ideological issues, 46; and immigration, 67, 71; and impact of technological change, 283–284; income, 120–123; institutional roles, 284–287; institutions and organizations, 284–290; intermarriage, 81–89, 95, 112, 136, 234; Israel-overseas sphere of decision-making, 290, 297–298; Jewish affiliation, 131, 132, 139–148; Jewish educators, 302, 306; Jewish identity, 127–149; and Jewish rituals, 134–135; leadership, 282, 283, 313–316; and liberal universalism, 55; and marriage and the family, 78–81; maximalists, 150, 151; migration, 97–100; modes of decision-making, 310–313; mortality, 73–74; native-born, 67; nonassociated Jews, 144, 145; occupations, 112–120, 168; "other-orientedness," 58; overview of future demographic trends, 124–126; patterns of participation, 276–278; population distribution, 89–92, 271, 272, 274, 275; population growth, 67, 71–72, 76, 77; problems and prospects in decision-making, 313–316; professional leaders, 300–302; public and private divisions, 299; rabbis, 302, 303, 304; and radical agitation, 233; radical youth, 146, 147, 148, 172, 173, 217, 218–226, 244; religious and secular divisions, 298–299; religious-congregational sphere, 290–291; role of functional groupings, 290–298;